Mullā Ṣadrā and Metaphysics

Mullā Ṣadrā is one of the most important Islamic philosophers after Avicenna. In this exploration of his philosophy, the author examines the central doctrine of the modulation of being, and contextualises his work within the intellectual history of philosophical traditions in the Islamic East.

Reading and critiquing the works of Mullā Ṣadrā from an analytical perspective, this book pays particular attention to his text the *Asfar*, a work which, due to its complexity, is often overlooked. Looking at the concept of philosophy as a way of life and a therapeutic practice, the book explores the paradigm of the modulation of being in the philosophical method and metaphysics of Mullā Ṣadrā and considers its different manifestations. The author relates his philosophy to larger trends and provides a review of the field, charting and critiquing the discussion on the topic to date and exploring recent thought in this direction, showing how Sadrian thought was addressed well into the nineteenth and twentieth centuries.

This major contribution to the study of Mullā Ṣadrā and the intellectual life of the Safavid period fills an important gap in the field of Ṣadrā studies and Islamic philosophy, and is indispensable to students of philosophy, religion and Islamic studies, and Islamic philosophy in particular.

Sajjad H. Rizvi is Senior Lecturer in Islamic Studies and Director of the Centre of Islamic Philosophy at the Institute of Arab and Islamic Studies at the University of Exeter, specialising in Islamic philosophical and hermeneutical traditions.

Culture and civilization in the Middle East

General editor: Ian Richard Netton

Professor of Islamic Studies, University of Exeter

This series studies the Middle East through the twin foci of its diverse cultures and civilisations. Comprising original monographs as well as scholarly surveys, it covers topics in the fields of Middle Eastern literature, archaeology, law, history, philosophy, science, folklore, art, architecture and language. While there is a plurality of views, the series presents serious scholarship in a lucid and stimulating fashion.

Previously published by Curzon

The origins of Islamic law
The Qur'an, the Muwatta' and Madinan Amal
Yasin Dutton

A Jewish archive from Old Cairo
The history of Cambridge University's Genizah Collection
Stefan Reif

The formative period of Twelver Shi'ism
Hadith as discourse between Qum and Baghdad
Andrew J. Newman

Qur'an translation
Discourse, texture and exegesis
Hussein Abdul-Raof

Christians in Al-Andalus 711-1000
Ann Rosemary Christys

Nimrod Hurvitz

Arabic literature
An overview
Pierre Cachia

Structure and meaning in medieval Arabic and Persian lyric poetry
Orient pearls
Julie Scott Meisami

Muslims and Christians in Norman Sicily
Arabic-speakers and the end of Islam
Alexander Metcalfe

Modern Arab historiography
Historical discourse and the nation-state
Youssef Choueiri

The philosophical poetics of Alfarabi, Avicenna and Averroes
The Aristotelian reception
Salim Kemal

Published by Routledge

1. The epistemology of Ibn Khaldun
Zaid Ahmad

2. The hanbali School of Law and Ibn Taymiyyah
Conflict or concilation
Abdul Hakim I Al-Matroudi

3. Arabic rhetoric
A pragmatic analysis
Hussein Abdul-Raof

4. Arab representations of the Occident
East-West encounters in Arabic fiction
Rasheed El-Enany

5. God and humans in Islamic thought

7. Al-Ghazali and the Qur'an
One book, many meanings
Martin Whittingham

8. Birth of the Prophet Muhammad
Devotional piety in Sunni Islam
Marion Holmes Katz

9. Space and Muslim urban life
At the limits of the Labyrinth of Fez
Simon O'Meara

10. Islam science
The intellectual career of Nizam al-Din al-Nizaburi
Robert G. Morrison

11. Ibn 'Arabî
Time and cosmology
Mohamed Haj Yousef

12. The status of women in Islamic law and society
Annotated translation of al-Ṭāhir al-Ḥaddād's *Imra'tunā fi 'l-sharīʿa wa 'l-mujtamaʿ*, with an introduction
Ronak Husni and Daniel L. Newman

13. Islam and the Baha'i faith
A comparative study of Muhammad 'Abduh and 'Abdul-Baha 'Abbas
Oliver Scharbrodt

14. Comte de Gobineau and orientalism
Selected Eastern writings
Translated by Daniel O'Donoghue
Edited by Geoffrey Nash

15. Early Islamic Spain
The history of Ibn al-Qutiyyah
David James

16. German orientalism
The study of the Middle East and Islam from 1800 to 1945
Ursula Wokoeck

17. Mullā Ṣadrā and metaphysics
Modulation of being
Sajjad H. Rizvi

Mullā Ṣadrā and Metaphysics

Modulation of being

Sajjad H. Rizvi

Routledge
Taylor & Francis Group
LONDON AND NEW YORK

First published 2009
by Routledge
2 Park Square, Milton Park, Abingdon, Oxon OX14 4RN

Simultaneously published in the USA and Canada
by Routledge
270 Madison Ave, New York, NY 10016

Routledge is an imprint of the Taylor & Francis Group, an Informa business

Typeset in Times New Roman by Swales & Willis Ltd, Exeter, Devon
Printed and bound by MPG Books Group, UK

British Library Cataloguing in Publication Data
A catalogue record for this book is available from the British Library

Library of Congress Cataloging in Publication Data
Rizvi, Sajjad H. (Sajjad Hayder)
Mullā Ṣadrā and metaphysics : modulation of being / Sajjad H. Rizvi.
p. cm.—(Culture and civilization in the Middle East)
Includes bibliographical references and index.
1. Sadr al-Din Shirazi, Muhammad ibn Ibrahim, d. 1641. 2. Philosophy, Islamic. 3. Metaphysics—History—17th century. 4. Ontology. I. Title.
B753.M84R585 2009
181'.5—dc22
2008043527

ISBN 10: 0–415–49073–1 (hbk)
ISBN10: 0–203–87954–6 (ebk)

ISBN 13: 978–0–415–49073–3 (hbk)
ISBN 13: 978–0–203–87954–2 (ebk)

A supplication

O Bestower of munificence and being, O Master of excellence and light, O Healer of the diseases of the heart, O He who saves souls from the baseness of bodies [and elevates them] to the source of bliss,

Place us among the gnostics through the grace of Your sanctity, and among those who hold fast to Your covenant,

Illuminate our intellects with the light of Your gnosis and the perception of Your Lordship,

Make us see by the eye of Your providence and Your mercy,

Purify us from all impurities by the power of Your impeccability, and make us among those who contemplate Your lights and who accompany those close to You,

Make us companions of those who travel through Your heavens,

Indeed, You are the one who bestows every good and sends down blessings, the one who bestows light from darkness.

O Lord, bless the one who guides along the path of salvation and righteousness, who leads your servants to the straight path, and is their leader and director to the Return, Muḥammad, and his pure and glorious progeny.

Mullā Ṣadrā, *Divine Manifestations*

Contents

Preface

The state of research and publication on Mullā Ṣadrā Shīrāzī [d. *c.* 1635], the famous Safavid thinker, is much healthier than it was when I first embarked on my doctoral research at Pembroke College, Cambridge in 1996 under the supervision of the late John (Yahya) Cooper. The conditions for the flourishing of Sadrian studies are in place: proper critical editions of his works, studies in a number of languages on aspects of his thought, a specialised journal dedicated to his philosophy, an organisation promoting his philosophy and recent monographs that analyse his philosophy from the perspectives of both the Anglo-American analytical tradition and the continental, 'Platonic' and sympathetic tradition. This is the context in which I present a central aspect of the metaphysics of Mullā Ṣadrā that tackles the age-old question of the One and the many: how can we reconcile the vision of the unity in existence and the quest for a singular explanation for reality with our everyday, phenomenal experience of plurality and multiplicity?

This book is the result of an inner (almost Platonic) dialogue, questioning one's own intellectual self and one's past philosophical concerns It is a slightly revised version of my dissertation that was submitted to the Faculty of Oriental Studies and awarded a Ph.D. at Cambridge in 2000. It dates from a time when I was convinced that the primary mode of critically presenting and evaluating Islamic philosophy was through the prism, paradigm and terminology of the Anglo-American analytic tradition, a position which I think is still tenable (perhaps at least because of that tradition's increasing willingness to engage once again with metaphysics), although I would be inclined to modify it.

I have not attempted to update systematically references taking into account new critical editions of primary texts. In a few isolated instances, I have updated references if the new edition was vastly clearer and more usable. However, all the references to the *Asfār* are from the standard Qum/Beirut edition found in most libraries and reprinted from the 1950s through to the 1990s (and again most recently in 2007 in post-Saddam Najaf). The new critical edition produced by SIPRIn is quite excellent; but given that it is barely available outside Iran, it makes sense to continue to cite the older, 'standard' edition.

I appreciate the generous funding of the Arts and Humanities Research Board of the British Academy that supported my doctoral research in the late 1990s. While the thesis lay dormant (moving from Cambridge back to London, on to Bristol and finally arriving at Exeter) and the method and concerns within it put aside by my own recent forays into hermeneutics, Sufi metaphysics and the thought of other Safavid philosophers, it was at the encouragement of my colleague Professor Ian Netton, the general editor of this series that it is found in the form of a published book. Ian read the thesis and encouraged me to publish it in his series. I appreciate his encouragement and support.

I follow the standard IJMES transliteration system with the following exceptions: the alif maqṣūra is indicated by á, the yā' is indicated by y, the Persian thā' is rendered s̲, the iḍāfa marker for Persian is -yi after a vowel and -i after a consonant, and the definite article in a phrase is rendered l-. Arabic words in a Persian context are Persianised. I drop the initial al- from names following the Persian convention. Words in common usage such as Imam and Sufi are not transliterated. Finally, I use Shiʿi and Sunni and not Shiʿite and Sunnite (the half-baked Sunni and Shiʿite I find particularly annoying).

The ideas and concerns in the thesis were inspired and nurtured by my late supervisor John Cooper, Ron Nettler, Tony Street, Hossein Ziai, John Walbridge, John Gurney, Parviz Morewedge and Oliver Leaman. Discussions with a number of like-minded friends sustained, questioned and stimulated the research: Toby Mayer, Nader el-Bizri, Sabine Schmidtke, Ahmed al-Rahim, Tariq Jaffer, Lisa Alexandrin, Idris Hamid, Fatima Azzam, Reza Pourjavady, Shaykh ʿArif Ḥusayn, Salim Rossier, Reza Shah-Kazemi, Janis Esots, Annabel Keeler and Paul Hardy.

I would like to thank the following in Iran for their wisdom and good advice as well as help in finding sources and focusing my ideas: Mohammad Amini-Najafi, Christian (Yahya) Bonaud, Gholamhossein Ibrahimi Dinani, Gholamreza Aʿvani, Mehdi Mohaghegh, Nasrollah Pourjavady, Muhammad Legenhausen, and Ayatollahs Ansari-yi Shirazi and Misbah-i Yazdi.

I dedicate this work to the memory of Yahya Cooper. May it be a worthy memorial! Raḥimahullāh!

Sajjad Rizvi
Exeter
ʿĪd al-fiṭr 1429
1 October 2008

Abbreviations

Asfār	Mullā Ṣadrā, *al-Ḥikma al-mutaʿāliya fī-l-asfār al-ʿaqliyya al-arbaʿa*
ASP	*Arabic Sciences and Philosophy* (Paris)
BSOAS	*Bulletin of the School of Oriental and African Studies* (London)
Documenti	*Documenti e Studi sulla Tradizione Filosofica Medievale* (Pisa)
edn	Edition
EI²	*Encyclopaedia of Islam*, New edition (Leiden)
EII	Corbin, *En Islam Iranien*, 4 tomes
Enc. Ir.	*Encyclopaedia Iranica* (New York)
GAL	Brockelmann, *Geschichte der arabischen Literatur*
GAS	Sezgin, *Geschichte des arabischen Schrifttums*
H	Indicates the date given by Hijrī lunar calendar
HI	*Hamdard Islamicus* (Karachi)
IJMES	*International Journal of Middle East Studies*
IPQ	*International Philosophical Quarterly*
IQ	*Islamic Quarterly* (London)
IS	*Islamic Studies* (Islamabad)
IrS	*Iranian Studies*
JAOS	*Journal of the American Oriental Society*
JHP	*Journal of the History of Philosophy*
JIS	*Journal of Islamic Studies* (Oxford)
MIDEO	*Mélanges de l'Institut Dominicain des Études Orientales* (Cairo)
MS	*Mediaeval Studies* (Toronto)
MW	*Muslim World* (Hartford, CN)
OSAP	*Oxford Studies in Ancient Philosophy*
Q	For bibliographical references, indicates lunar Hijrī calendar
repr	reprint
Ṣadrā	*Khiradnāma-yi Ṣadrā* (Tehran)
Sh	For bibliographical references, indicates solar Hijrī calendar used in Iran
SI	*Studia Islamica* (Paris)
SIPRIn	Ṣadrā Islamic Philosophy Research Institute (Bunyād-i Ḥikmat-i Islāmī-yi Ṣadrā, Tehran)
SIr	*Studia Iranica* (Paris)
SUNY	State University of New York.
vol(s)	volume(s)

Introduction

> The truth is that the ignorance of the question of being (*mas'alat al-wujūd*) in humans necessarily leads to ignorance of all the foundations of knowledge and their principles because it is through being that all things are known. It is the most *a priori* of conceptions and most known of all concepts. If one is ignorant of it, one is ignorant of all that follows. But its knowledge is only obtained through inner revelation and direct experience (*bi-l-kashf wa-l-shuhūd*) which is why it is said: 'He who has no inner revelation has no knowledge'.[1]

The problem

Multivocity is an everyday feature of our experiences in this world. Our language is rich with the semantic polysemy of words and terms that we use for a variety of referents. The most immediate and yet abstract of these terms is 'being' which connotes different things for different people. It is this language of homonymy that commits us to an understanding of reality as a layered texture, and permits us to recognise modulation within the scale of being both within and without ourselves. It is this homonymy of the term 'being' and the modulation of the scale of being that, in the later Islamic philosophical tradition, is called *tashkīk al-wujūd*.

The aim of this study is to analyse the central philosophical doctrine of Ṣadr al-Dīn Muḥammad b. Ibrāhīm Qavāmī Shīrāzī, known as Mullā Ṣadrā [d. *c.* 1635], the doctrine of *tashkīk al-wujūd* (modulation of being), and to use this analysis as a key to understanding his philosophical method.[2] I shall focus my textual analysis on his magnum opus *al-Ḥikma al-mutaʿāliya fī-l-asfār al-ʿaqliyya al-arbaʿa* (The Transcendent Philosophy on the Four Journeys of the Intellect), popularly known as the *Asfār*.[3] My contention is that modulation is central to

(*fī-l-ʿibara*) and being in writing (*fī-l-kitaba*)'.[6]

Mullā Sadrā picks up this fourfold scheme of the semantics of being in his logical epitome, *al-Tanqīḥ fī-l-manṭiq* (The Re-examination of Logic): 'The being of a thing is extra-mental (*'aynī*), mental (*dhihnī*), uttered (*lafẓī*) or inscribed (*kutbī*)'.[7]

An analysis of this critical concept of *tashkīk* facilitates our understanding of Ṣadrā's positions on a wide variety of important philosophical issues such as predication, the problem of reconciling unity and plurality in being, and the God–world relationship. It provides an answer to the age-old problem of the One and the many and attempts to forge a new way, a median way (that is often so critical in Islamic thought following the Qur'ānic injunction for Muslims to strike the median path and be the 'middle community') between the ontological monism of the school of Andalusian Sufi Ibn 'Arabī [d. 1240] and the metaphysical pluralism of Avicennism. But *tashkīk* is much more than a philosophical solution or a way out of the aporia of the diverse unity or unified diversity that we encounter; it is the central hermeneutic concept of Sadrian philosophy, and a means for analysing and interpreting texts and ideas. As such, it extends from the *pros hen* homonymy of the term 'being' to the actual structure of reality and the modes in which we experience and interpret it. Significantly, this fourfold scheme of modes of being may be reduced to three upon which I focus: being-in-language (collapsing spoken and written tokens), mental being, and extra-mental being.

This study comprises an introduction and two parts. In the introduction, I present the problem to be addressed and survey some approaches in Sadrian studies in order to take stock of the field as it now exists.

Part I constitutes two chapters. In the first chapter, I outline my methodology, and elucidate some of my assumptions about the cultural history of the period and the context of Ṣadrā. Of particular significance is my contention that a proper understanding of his philosophy requires an appreciation of philosophy in Neoplatonic traditions as 'a way of life' that is often intimately related to spiritual practice and religious commitment.[8] While the analytical core of his ideas will be demonstrated, one should bear in mind that the aim of philosophical inquiry for Ṣadrā is the therapy of the rational soul and its perfecting and development on its path of return to its origins in the One. At the same time, the practice of the history of philosophy encounters the philosophical context of one's time; contemporary concerns in metaphysics and the possibilities of their lexicon thus become the prism through which I present Mullā Ṣadrā's arguments. I consider in this chapter an analysis of his philosophical method and of my focal text, the *Asfār*. The second chapter introduces the concept of modulation (*tashkīk*) of being. I trace its historical development from Aristotelian *pros hen* homonymy to an account of an intensifying scale of being to a hierarchy of being that is singular but with multiple degrees defined by their *intensity* in scales of *intensification* and *debilitation*. I make explicit the Neoplatonic logic of being that it implies and examine how that logic is transformed into a semantic and metaphysics of being once modulation is taken beyond mere discourse. Thus we see the shift from an Avicennan logic of modulation to an explicit metaphysical exposition of the ontological commitment that logic entails.

Part II is an analysis of three case studies of modulated being: the semantics of the term 'being' (taking spoken and written tokens of language together), mental being, and being *in actu*. In the third chapter, I examine the semantics of modulation in Ṣadrā through an analysis of *tashkīk* as applied to the term 'be'. I examine the role of modulation and intensification in the Sadrian theory of meaning, and consider his arguments for the modulated predication of being. The fourth chapter deals with mental being and the concept of being and elucidates aspects of Sadrian epistemology and psychology. First, I present his arguments for the existence of such a realm of being and then examine its relationship with extra-mental reality, the concept of being and with the One. The fifth chapter will examine the ontology of *tashkīk*, the 'circle of being' envisaged by Ṣadrā, an account that begins to engage with the influence of the metaphysics of Ibn ʿArabī. Being descends from the One in a procession and as a process. The processes of descent constitute competing hierarchies of reality defined in various senses of gradation including modulation by intensification. Then I consider the return to the One, the Neoplatonic reversion that is mediated by his Shiʿi notion of *wilāya*, the most intense degree of being and the 'last' degree before the culmination of the return to the One.

I make two major claims in this study, because there are two levels to modulation. First, I argue that *tashkīk* is a hermeneutic concept which describes the threefold division of being and its gradation. Second, gradation and modulation occur in *each* mode of being. In fact, each mode of being refers to a branch of Ṣadrā's philosophy: mental being is a discussion of epistemology and psychology, 'being-in-language' is critical to Sadrian semantic theory, being *in re* focuses on 'traditional metaphysics'.[9] One should also remember, however, that philosophy is not so easily compartmentalised and that the problematic of being cuts across these fields and indeed unites them. Each mode of being as *mushakkak* shares features of intensification. To be sure, I am extending both the normal understanding of *tashkīk* and of being beyond the simple division of the two realms of mental and concrete existence to bring out the importance of the semantics of being, an aspect of Islamic philosophy that is often neglected. I offer a principle of complete ontological correspondence; one can map the constituents of one's linguistic ontology upon mental being and extra-mental being in perfect equivalence.

The *Asfār* is a summation of Islamic philosophy and a useful source for the history of Islamic philosophy especially as understood in the Safavid period. It is the culmination of a 'mystical' trend in philosophical analysis (or philosophical mysticism if one prefers) known in the present century as *ʿirfān* (often translated as 'gnosis').[10] The author himself directs us to this work as the ultimate and perfected expression of his philosophical method. In his *Taʿlīqa ʿalá-l-Ilāhiyyāt min Kitāb al-Shifāʾ* (*Scholia* upon the Metaphysics of the *Cure* of Avicenna), he repeatedly states that he has pursued the same line of inquiry elsewhere and directs readers wishing to examine the complete arguments in greater detail to his 'major work known as the *Asfār*'.[11] This choice of text is significant because it is his most important text, yet the one most neglected by academics. Most other studies on Sadrian thought have focused either upon his treatise on being *Kitāb al-Mashāʿir* (The Book of Ontological Inspirations)[12] or his late work of philosophical theology *al-Ḥikma al-ʿArshiyya* (The Wisdom of the Throne).

The choice of Ṣadrā, a Shiʿi Iranian philosopher in the reign of the Safavid Shāh

'Abbās I [r. 1589–1629], is significant given Seyyed Hossein Nasr's claim that he is a 'household name in Persia, Afghanistan and India'.[13] He was a central player in that flowering of Persianate culture under the Safavids that is a feature of the 'period of the gunpowder empires'.[14] Interest in him in Iran is increasing with the establishment of a Sadra Islamic Philosophy Research Institute (SIPRIn), run by the brother of the *valī-yi faqīh*, Sayyid Muḥammad Khāmanihī, who organised a 'World Congress on Mullā Ṣadrā' in Tehran in May 1999, and again in May 2004 (although the latter was a more modest affair). Mullā Ṣadrā's importance as a creative founder of a new school of Islamic thought is constantly stressed in Iran.[15] The hegemonic nature of Sadrian philosophy in Iranian seminaries and academic philosophy departments is such that it becomes difficult at times to evaluate critically his thought; criticism of his ideas almost borders on heresy. And yet any serious attempt to make sense of Islamic philosophical traditions *qua* philosophy demands a serious *philosophical* engagement, and not merely recourse to established authority and precedent and the rehearsal of ideas, philological analysis and an 'Islamicist's approach'.

I contend that my study will contribute to a more nuanced understanding of the later philosophical or *ḥikmat* tradition[16] in which Ṣadrā participated, a tradition characterised by a mix of intuitive and demonstrative intellectual inquiry.[17] He himself describes his method in the *Asfār*:

> Our argument is based upon intuition and inner revelation (*mukāshafa*) not blindly following the *sharīʿa* without practising demonstrations (*barāhīn*) . . . Mere inner revelation is insufficient on the path [to the Truth] without demonstration, just as mere discourse (*baḥth*) without inner revelation is a great flaw along the path.[18]

The element of direct experience, of 'tasting' (*dhawq*) is critical to his cognitive theory.[19] I locate his discourse within the tradition and attempt to facilitate a dialogue with other philosophical traditions.

Approaches to Ṣadrā

The French chargé d'affaires (1856–8) and later minister (1862–3) to the Qajar court, Arthur, Comte de Gobineau [d. 1882] and the German Orientalist Max Horten [d. 1945][20] initiated the study of Mullā Ṣadrā in European languages at the end of the nineteenth and early twentieth centuries. These early introductions are marred by serious errors of fact and basic miscomprehensions. Gobineau's at times critical yet respectful approach was a function of his own Aryanist racial theories and his

phie en Asie centrale (1865), in which one finds his assessment of Mullā Ṣadrā and the later Iranian philosophical tradition to his day.[21] Gobineau's work derived from his knowledge and acquaintance with Mullā Hādī Sabzawārī [d. 1873], Ṣadrā's most influential commentator and perhaps the individual who contributed most to establishing Sadrian philosophy at the heart of the Shiʿi intellectual tradition, by recognising and using the *Asfār* as a school-text. This makes Gobineau's assessment (for all its racial stereotyping and cultural generalisation) all the more puzzling, since for him, Mullā Ṣadrā was a systematiser and reviver of ancient 'Asiatic' philosophy who lacked originality:

> En réalité, Moulla-Sadra n'est pas un inventeur ni un créateur, c'est un restaurateur seulement, mais restaurateur de la grande philosophie asiatique, et son originalité consiste à l'avoir habillée d'une telle sorte qu'elle fût acceptable et acceptée au temps où il florissait. En Perse, on trouve que le service est grand et vaut la gloire dont il a été payé. Cependant la sympathie qu'il a excitée et excite encore est telle qu'on ne se contente pas pour lui de l'éloge restreint que je viens d'en faire. On assure que l'Akhound a fait plus que de raviver la flamme d'Avicenne et de la faire brûler dans une nouvelle lampe; on prétend que, sur plusieurs points, il a exprimé une opinion indépendante de celle du grand homme et l'a même contredit. Il est difficile, en effet, que dans le long cours d'une existence philosophique très active et très savante, l'Akhound, vivant d'ailleurs dans des temps et dans un milieu fort différents de ceux d'Avicenne, n'ait pas trouvé l'occasion de faire acte de personnalité doctrinale. Je n'ai pourtant rien vu qui impliquât des différences bien sérieuses, et personne n'a jamais pu m'en indiquer qui valussent la peine d'être relevées. Presque tout ce qu'on cite ne consiste que dans des questions de méthode ou porte sur des points secondaires. Non; le vrai, l'incontestable mérite de Moulla-Sadra reste celui que j'ai indiqué plus haut: c'est d'avoir ranimé, rajeuni, pour le temps où il vivait, la philosophie antique, en lui conservant le moins possible de ses formes avicenniques, et de l'avoir rétablie dans de telles conditions que, non seulement elle s'est répandue dans toutes les écoles de Perse, les a fécondées, a fait reculer la théologie dogmatique, a forcé celle-ci, bon gré mal gré, à lui céder une place à côté d'elle, mais a, pour ainsi dire, réparé au bénéfice de la postérité, dont les générations actuelles font partie, toutes les ruines métaphysiques causées par l'invasion mongole.[22]

Nevertheless, Gobineau was the first to recognise the enduring significance of Mullā Ṣadrā for the vitality and continuity of philosophy in Iran, as well as the first to perpetuate the myths of his 'persecution' at the hands of exoteric jurists (a

enthusiasm for Nietzsche.[24] Horten's own career mirrors a chronological charting of the course of Islamic philosophical traditions. Trained in medieval philosophy and the German idealist tradition, he was well placed to examine and understand Mullā Ṣadrā's thought. He began with his doctorate at Bonn University on the *Fuṣūṣ fī-l-Ḥikma* of al-Fārābī [d. 950] in 1904, before moving on to a study of *al-Shifā'* of Avicenna in 1907 and on the Avicennan tradition.[25] Turning to the later Illuminationist (*ishrāqī*) tradition, he published a preliminary selection of translations from the *Asfār*, as well as a study of the philosophy of Suhrawardī [d. 1191] in 1912.[26] The following year saw the appearance of his main assessment of Mullā Ṣadrā: *Das philosophische System von Schirazi* (1913). Despite the flaws in the work, Horten was the first academic to draw attention to the significance of the philosophy of Mullā Ṣadrā, to praise its vitality and rigour, and to examine its 'art':

> Auf diese Weise gewinnt Schīrāzī einen Standpunkt, von dem er die gesamte zu seiner Zeit geltende Philosophie umgestaltet . . .
>
> Als Ganzes betrachtet ist sein Werk eine Leistung allerersten Ranges und ein einzigartiges Kunstwerk der Begriffsbildung und ein Begriffsdichtung. Man wird es nicht ohne Bewunderung aus der Hand legen können.[27]

Horten stressed the originality of the contribution of Mullā Ṣadrā; but his association of his thought with mysticism also signalled a particular tendency within Sadrian studies that remains with us. But, on the whole, such introductions were forgotten and it was not until the voluminous work of Corbin[28] and Nasr[29] in the 1960s and 1970s that Mullā Ṣadrā was truly introduced to western academia. One can discern four different approaches to the study of Ṣadrā, each of which assumes and proposes a particular method for reading and interpreting Islamic philosophical texts.

Esotericism

The first (and in many ways still dominant) approach is Nasr[30] and Corbin's mystical reading of Ṣadrā focusing on the mysterious notion of 'acts of being'. The problem with their approach is their insistence on describing the later philosophical tradition of *ḥikmat* as 'theosophy', and as an essentially esoteric and arcane discipline that expresses the 'interior life'. Corbin's method privileges spiritual intuition over Aristotelian ratiocination and conflates the history of philosophy with spirituality in Islam. He translates '*ḥikmat-i ilāhī*' as '*theosophia*' and remains aware of the problems of the use of the term:

> Le mot théosophie est, lui aussi, frappé de suspicion. Ici encore, que l'on veuille bien penser étymologiquement. Nous rappellerons, à plusieurs reprises, que l'expression arabe *hikmat ilâhîya* est l'équivalent exact du grec *theosophia*; elle désigne cette «sagesse divine» qui n'a point seulement pour objet l'être en tant qu'être, mais l'univers spirituel dont la gnose ouvre l'accès. Son organe, ce ne sont ni les facultés de perception sensible, ni l'intellect ratiocinant, mais une tierce activité de l'âme qui est intuition intime, perception visionnaire intérieure.[31]

He further argues that theosophy is a science that bridges the divide between, and overcomes the limitations of, theology and philosophy; it preserves the prophetic link with the transcendent and acts as an antidote to modern secularisation:

> Précisément, l'on peut dire que la séparation entre théologie et philosophie est le premier symptôme d'une sécularisation de la conscience; elle remonte chez nous à la scolastique latine . . . La théologie reste alors le domaine réservé au «pouvoir spirituel», tandis que le philosophe s'accorde toutes les libertés, sauf celle d'être un théologien, et nous avons ici le premier indice de la sécularisation métaphysique, c'est-à-dire de la désacralisation du monde. La *theo-sophia*, dans sa vérité métaphysique même, en est l'antithèse et l'antidote . . . C'est elle seule qui put faire fructifier toute connaissance et toute initiative de l'homme en une connaissance et conscience de soi-même.[32]

Corbin's 'esotericists' charter' and stress upon the interior does not necessarily render adequately the method of Mullā Ṣadrā. His explanation of the use of the term theosophy remains unsatisfactory because one associates the word 'theosophy' with forms of 'irrationalism' such as the Theosophical movement.[33] It also evinces a retrojection of modern notions of spirituality in the study of what he considers to be the essential 'esotericism' of Islam.[34] While it may be true that Ṣadrā described his philosophy as prophetic without any hint of dissimulation, it retains analytical features and allows for a space for philosophical exchange and dialogue. But a philosopher reading Nasr would not recognise this. Corbin and Nasr are correct to lament the Orientalist assumption that philosophical inquiry ended in Islam after Averroes [d. 1198]. But to re-designate philosophy in Islam post-Averroes as theosophy and mysticism would deter contemporary philosophers.[35]

James Morris's translation of *al-Ḥikma al-ʿArshiyya* (The Wisdom of the Throne) stresses the mystical and mysterious nature of Sadrian philosophy and follows in the Corbin-Nasr tradition; indeed, the work is dedicated to the memory of Corbin. A student of Muhsin Mahdi at Harvard, one of the most important Straussians in the study of Islamic philosophy, he studied with Corbin, Nasr and Āshtiyānī in Iran and imbibed the 'theosophical' approach to Ṣadrā.[36] Sadrian philosophy is a spiritual 'path of enlightenment', and not just a 'metalanguage' that reconcile 'logics of transcendence'.[37] He sees Ṣadrā as an oppositional persecuted intellect in the midst of exoteric jurists opposed to mysticism and philosophy; but in order not to fall into Straussianism, he avoids advocating an esotericist hermeneutical reading of the text that would emphasise the political while insisting that Mullā Ṣadrā had perfected an existing style of expression predicated on double meanings.[38]

Zailan Moris undertook research on the reconciliation of reason (*ʿaql*), revelation (*waḥy*) and mystical insight (*kashf*) under the supervision of Nasr at Temple University. Her 1994 doctoral dissertation was published in 2003. Focusing upon the *ʿArshiyya*, she argues that such a reconciliation was achieved and circumvents, without any explanation, Fazlur Rahman's reservations about the inconsistencies of the Sadrian system.[39] It is significant that her aim is not to 'undertake a philosophical analysis of the truth claims of revelation, discursive philosophy and gnosis respectively but to examine critically whether Mulla Sadra did in fact successfully synthesise the three truth claims in his philosophy'.[40] In many ways, it is a culmination of Nasr's statement on this 'reconciliation' in his pioneering article of the 1960s.[41] The published version is only barely revised and displays the heavy imprint of Nasr in its mystical assumptions about the 'sapiential traditions' of Islam and humans as 'theomorphic beings'. The work on the whole is rather derivative, relying upon Morris's translation, and repetitive. The argument itself is rather tautological: reconciliation is posed and is also concluded. Finally, Moris assumes the extensive influence on the metaphysics of Ibn ʿArabī upon Mullā Ṣadrā; while such an influence is clear at times, she does not explain the relationship between the two thinkers or indeed why there should be such a heavy influence.

What is ironic about this 'esotericist' approach, despite its attempts at presenting Ṣadrā as a serious and important thinker in the Islamic tradition, is that these interpreters share certain 'Orientalist' assumptions about the nature of later Islamic philosophy.[42] They regard the *ḥikmat* tradition as essentially esoteric, mystical, and oppositional with respect to the 'exoteric jurists'. Ṣadrā is thus positioned in opposition to jurists, their authority and their epistemology of *taqlīd* (a term they would translate as 'blind imitation'). Nasr privileges Ṣadrā's mystical writings over his *ḥikmat* writings and defines his division of sciences not from the opening chapter of the *Asfār,* which represents Sadrian philosophy, but from *Iksīr al-ʿārifīn* (Elixir of the Mystics) with its mystical language of the science of the states over and above the noetic and discursive sciences.[43] In his most recent foray into Sadrian studies as part of a wider survey of philosophy in Islam, Nasr has reiterated the esotericist approach.[44]

Comparative philosophy

The second approach is the 'comparativist' in which an attempt is made to map Sadrian philosophy on to paradigms that may be more familiar to contemporary philosophers. One can discern three distinct trends.

The first trend is the phenomenological paradigm. Corbin, in a pioneering introduction to his translation of *al-Mashāʿir* (Ontological Inspirations), made a critical comparative analysis between Sadrian 'existentialism' and continental existentialism.[45] Such a comparison was quite natural given Corbin's own existentialist background and his own project of existential phenomenology and hermeneutics.[46] Devising a common hermeneutics for comparative philosophy remained at the heart of Corbin's work, to discern the realities beyond the phenomena and 'extricate ourselves from historicism'.[47] In his magisterial *History of Islamic Philosophy*, a most un-historical (or rather anti-historicist) history, Corbin explains that phenomenological research is

> based on the rule *sozein ta phainomena*, saving the appearances – that is to say, of taking account of the underlying ground of the phenomena, as these

> phenomena appear to those to whom they appear. The phenomenologist is not interested in material data as such – it is too easy to say of such data that they are 'out of date' . . . What the phenomenologist endeavours to discover is the primordial Image – the *imago mundi a priori* – which is the organ and the form of perception of these phenomena.[48]

The mystic's vision is irreducible and his ontological horizon is the real arena for intellectual investigation. One's saving of the phenomena whilst unveiling the essences is a hermeneutics that locates itself on the horizon of history, indeed beyond it.

Corbin began his career as a phenomenologist inspired by Martin Heidegger [d. 1976]; in fact, his first work was a French translation of Heidegger's *Was ist Metaphysik?* within a decade of its original appearance in German. But in his analysis of Ṣadrā, he did not explicitly discuss the use of Heidegger to make sense of Sadrian thought. The encounter of phenomenology and Mullā Ṣadrā has been the subject of at least two recent works. Alparslan Açikgenç wrote his doctoral dissertation in 1983 at the University of Chicago on comparative ontology juxtaposing Heidegger and Mullā Ṣadrā under the supervision of the eminent Pakistani thinker Fazlur Rahman [d. 1988]. He wished to demonstrate the 'parallelism' between the existentialism of Heidegger (in itself slightly problematic since most commentators do not consider him to be an existentialist) and the 'Islamic existentialism' of Mullā Ṣadrā, parallelism not just of themes and concerns but also of the 'existential analytic' and attention to the '*Seinsfrage*'.[49] While it is arguable to what extent Heidegger's ontological distinction between *Dasein* and *Existenz* parallels the Sadrian distinction between *wujūd* and *mawjūd*, Açikgenç considers both philosophers as indulging in an 'ontological reduction' of restricting philosophy to the question of being.[50] However, comparative philosophy does tend to suffer from a 'commensurability' gap and indeed from a 'credibility' gap of displeasing both sets of specialists. The clearest problem still remains: Heidegger's *Seinsfrage* is designed to explode the complacency of the mediaeval consensus of being as a 'given', a self-evident fact, while Ṣadrā accepts the axiom of this given, although he subverts it by insisting that the reality of being is elusive to the grasp of the human mind.[51]

A further gap between Heidegger and Ṣadrā is that the former is concerned with ontology as anthropology and wishes to investigate the question of being as it is manifest in *Dasein* and in *Existenz* as a human endeavour with human subjects, while the latter's focus upon the reality of being is onto-theological and theocentric. This point is recognised by Muhammad Kamal in his introduction to Mullā Ṣadrā's 'transcendent philosophy'.[52] Kamal considers Mullā Ṣadrā to be engaged in the problem of Platonism and the desire to extricate himself from the mediaeval 'essentialist' consensus; this is consistent with most modern Iranian commentators for whom Ṣadrā is an 'ontological revolutionary' for returning being to the heart of the philosophical enterprise. The core of the book examines three doctrines of the ontological primacy of being, the modulation of being and the reality of knowledge by presence. Throughout the work, Kamal's intention is to elucidate for his peers (he works in a philosophy department) and so he refers to philosophers who constitute the canon of the modern department, not least Hegel and Heidegger, in whom he sees a number of similarities.[53] Kamal is probably correct to stress Ṣadrā's break with Platonism and Illuminationism but he does not explain why it is that key features of these systems such as the theory of knowledge by presence remain central to Sadrian philosophy. The focus on Platonism within this area of comparative inquiry is critical given recent tendencies to re-evaluate Platonism and its impact in the ancient, mediaeval and modern worlds.[54]

The second tendency within the comparative philosophy perspective is the Platonic paradigm. Corbin suggested that Ṣadrā, like the famed Illuminationist (*ishrāqī*) philosopher Shihāb al-Dīn Suhrawardī [d. 1191], was essentially a Platonist and ought to be compared to the well-known circle of Cambridge Platonists, such as Henry More [d. 1687], who were his contemporaries.[55] In particular, he cites the connection between More's notion of the *spissitudo spiritualis* (or spiritual consistency) that connects space and matter (articulated in his *Enchiridion metaphysicum* of 1671) with Ṣadrā's notion of the soul as 'subtle spiritual matter' (*mādda rūḥāniyya laṭīfa*) that plays a role in his explanation of the soul and body's afterlife and resurrection.[56] However, this is an ambivalent endorsement since most Anglo-Saxon historians of philosophy regard More as a second-rate philosopher of merely antiquarian interest. Neither Platonism nor Cartesianism is an attractive philosophical option in contemporary metropolitan academia; Hobbes considered the very notion of spirit and incorporeal substance defended by More to be nonsensical and there are few to defend or even explain it today.[57]

One of Corbin's most faithful students, Christian Jambet, takes Platonism in a more traditional direction, stressing the impact of Neoplatonism mediated by the so-called *Theology of Aristotle* (the famous paraphrase of sections of Plotinus' *Enneads* IV–VI) and the Sufi metaphysics of Ibn ʿArabī.[58] Following Corbin, Jambet has been interested in the Platonism of the Illuminationist tradition.[59] In his most systematic work on Mullā Ṣadrā, Jambet expounds upon Corbin's insight that for Ṣadrā, metaphysics is concerned with 'acts of being', the unfolding and manifesting of being from the One in a series of levels of disclosure with an explicit eschatological goal of returning to the One. Ontology is concerned not only with being but also with the self, self-knowledge and the use of the imagination to envision the future, one's death and the end of time. Philosophy is thus, following both Plato's insight and Heidegger, a 'preparation for death'. In *Phaedo* 66e, the pseudo-Platonic *Definitions* and generally in Neoplatonic Late Antiquity, preparation for and meditation upon death (μελέτηθανάτου) was one of the six classic definitions of philosophy.[60] Attachment to the body distracts one from the pursuit of philosophy; the cathartic 'escape from the body' is essential for proper inquiry. Jambet roots Sadrian philosophy in its religious context, as a 'prophetic Platonic philosophy' in which believers need to make sense of their being and self in the world with a view to their resurrection and future life. Central to Jambet's presentation is the notion that Ṣadrā represents a rejection of Avicennism.[61]

The third mode of comparative analysis is to place Mullā Ṣadrā within the analytical paradigm. Ziai and Morewedge try to present Ṣadrā as a thinker to contemporary analytic philosophers through their use of philosophical terminology and formalisations. Ziai argues that it is critical for Sadrian studies to move beyond the 'theosophical' and reintroduce the logical and semantic bases of Sadrian philosophy, urging problem-based studies.[62] Morewedge clearly states that his translation of *al-Mashāʿir* is intended for analytic philosophers and is an attempt at convincing them of the analytic nature of Sadrian argumentation.[63] He insists that later Islamic philosophy ought to be studied through modern lenses and that one ought to break out of this tendency 'to force every Muslim thought into the artificial Greek-into-Arabic syndrome'.[64] As such, his presentation of Islamic philosophical thinking is designed to foster a cultural dialogue. He further argues for a 'processist' understanding of later Islamic philosophy, which had broken out of the substantivist Aristotelian mould of the earlier tradition.[65] Ziai and Morewedge provide an important corrective to the Nasr/Corbin approach since analytic (and many post-analytic) philosophers take neither mysticism nor Heidegger seriously.

Avicennism

The third approach to Ṣadrā is an Avicennan and mediaevalist reading that closely locates him within the continuities of Islamic philosophy by scholars of philosophical sophistication such as Rahman, Izutsu and Shehadi. Fazlur Rahman remains the best introduction to Sadrian philosophy through a study of the *Asfār*, although it suffers from infelicities and incompleteness at times, no doubt partly resulting from the brevity of the work; critically summarising nine volumes of text in barely 200 pages is quite onerous. Rahman argues that Ṣadrā fits within the Avicennan Peripatetic-Neoplatonic tradition as there is little evidence of an existing Illuminationist or Sufi metaphysical tradition in his time.[66] Recent research on philosophy in Shiraz in the Timurid period has proven Rahman's conjecture to be false. But this does not mean that Rahman considers Ṣadrā to be a purely ratiocinative or discursive philosopher; comparable to Plotinus and Bergson, Ṣadrā is a philosopher (not a theosoph) for whom the content of his experience is the same as his thought and cognitive in character.[67] The Sadrian notion of intuition is not Sufi experience but a non-discursive apprehension of truth that cannot be disproved by a purely logical form of reasoning.[68] Nevertheless, the Avicennan substrate of Ṣadrā's philosophy raises tensions. Where exactly does modulation leave the question of monism and pluralism? Does contingency play a real role in his thought? Do quiddities possess any reference in extra-mental reality?[69] Rahman recognises that the influence of Ibn ʿArabī raised problems but he does not follow through its implications. He also chastises Ṣadrā for being hypercritical (which is broadly speaking a correct assessment). Finally, Rahman provides a good argument for basing any examination of Mullā Ṣadrā on the *Asfār* contending that it is the main locus for Sadrian detailed arguments.[70] Despite the disputes over method, Rahman's survey is the only extensive work on the *Asfār* and has yet to be superseded.

Shehadi focuses on the development of the discussion of 'being' from early grammatical issues through Fārābī [d. 950] and Avicenna to Ṣadrā.[71] But in his focus on Ṣadrā's dialogue with the Suhrawardian tradition, he ignores the importance of the Shiʿi and Akbarian[72] influences. Izutsu provides nuanced and precise studies of Sadrian metaphysics within the wider *ḥikmat* debates and focuses on the Avicennan and Suhrawardian roots of those ideas.[73] Their main contribution is to contextualise Ṣadrā's arguments within the wider discourse of intellectual traditions in Islam. This is critical given Ṣadrā's constant dialogue with the 'ancients' as well as the 'moderns'. The approach also allows us to understand Mullā Ṣadrā's position within the mediaeval and pre-Cartesian traditions of Western philosophy.

Bonmariage's doctoral dissertation at Louvain, written under the supervision of Yahya Michot and later Jules Janssens, is perhaps the best attempt at explicating Sadrian ontology in terms of its Avicennan and Neoplatonic contexts in the mediaeval period.[74] It is the one work that allows specialists of mediaeval philosophy in particular to understand Ṣadrā's contribution to the history of philosophy. This is unsurprising given that it was the result of research conducted at one of the leading departments of mediaeval philosophy in Europe. Bonmariage's study of Sadrian ontology, the texture of being and the ways and modes in which being unfolds is predicated on the twin doctrinal pillars of the primacy and modulation of being, and is thus the one work that in its scope comes closest to this book. The main difference is that we propose two differing methods for reading the text. The Avicennan paradigm remains the dominant method for the study of Islamic philosophy and is exemplified further in the recent work of Megawati Moris on the primacy of being.

Iranian nativism

The fourth approach encompasses various Iranian attempts at appropriating Ṣadrā for their traditionalist, nativist and modernist discourses of authentic culture.[75] All these trends in different ways seek to claim the legacy of Ṣadrā and impose their own preconceptions and *Weltanschauungen* upon the Sadrian text. Philosophy in contemporary Iran is a deeply political practice. Nasr uses Ṣadrā for his own Sufi agenda, while Āshtiyānī places him within the larger philosophical and mystical enterprise in Iran in his extensive study of the doctrine of being in Sadrian thought based upon an analysis of *al-Mashāʿir*.[76] Ziai points out the importance of the work of the *ḥakīm* Mihdī Ḥāʾirī Yazdī in constructing a traditionalist Islamic philosophy that uses Sadrian thought *and* is informed by the Anglo-Saxon analytic tradition.[77]

Ṣadrā's influence upon religious intellectuals and modernising liberals like ʿAbdul Karim Surūsh [b. 1945] has been no less striking.[78] He argues in his first work on Ṣadrā that the principle of 'substantial motion' (*ḥaraka jawhariyya*) permeates everything and hence is a basic tool of scientific analysis that can even be extended to the dynamic development of jurisprudence and religious thought in Islam.[79] As such, Surūsh's early engagement may be seen as the attempts by a trained scientist interested in the philosophy of science to find 'space' for a dialogue with an important intellectual forbear, and to reconcile a religious view of the cosmos with his Popperian training. However, this early enthusiasm has been somewhat doused; more recently, Surūsh has been highly critical of what 'one can learn from Ṣadrā', condemning aspects of the analytically incomplete in his philosophy, the demonstrably false cosmology as well as systematic gender bias, a death blow to the study of any philosopher in the (post-)modern period.[80]

Two important doctoral dissertations submitted to Durham University show how Ṣadrā is used within the modernist discourse in Iran. Khorassani's dissertation reinterprets Ṣadrā as an empiricist with an essentialist epistemology of the objective world in which quiddities constitute the nature of reality.[81] This is a radically dissonant with most interpretations of Mullā Ṣadrā as it draws an odd conclusion from his denial of the ability to grasp truly the reality of existence and the reification of existents as quiddities that one posits in the mind. It shows the need in some Iranian circles familiar with debates within the history of science and influenced by Popper and others to present Ṣadrā as Popperian and to recover him for contemporary analytical philosophy of science.[82] Concerned with the problem of knowledge, Khorassani sees ontological and linguistic issues in Sadrian philosophy as cognitive problems. Most troubling about his thesis is his presentation of Mullā Ṣadrā as an essentialist. As essences (or quiddities) are the essential accidents of existence (and metaphysics studies the essential accidents of existence), therefore metaphysics is concerned with the study of essences: 'To say that the reality of objective entities is nothing but existence is tantamount to saying that existence is nothing but the quiddities that occupy the scope of the objective world'.[83]

But this is not Ṣadrā's point and represents an inversion of his method. Existence presents itself as essences but in themselves, essences are radically 'not-being'. A unified vision of reality and a transcendent intuitive metaphysics does not necessarily render an essentialist and rather sceptical philosophy.

Mahmoud Khatami's thesis proposes Sadrian philosophy as a solution to the 'crisis in modern theories of the self'.[84] Ṣadrā's 'unitary consciousness' and 'ontetic reduction' ellipses the epistemic problem of the knowing self and its stress upon the primacy of being makes knowledge possible.[85] He sees the problem of modern theories of the self to be grounded in subjectivism and argues that Mullā Ṣadrā's metaphysics of the soul allows for a solution. His book reflects an engagement with post-Cartesian theories and the phenomenological self of Husserl and Heidegger. He represents a strong Heideggerian tendency in contemporary Iranian philosophy, and is one of the bright young philosophers in the Department of Philosophy at Tehran University who are much engaged with an attempt to foster an intellectual dialogue between the Anglo-American analytical tradition and Islamic philosophical traditions.

Nader and Fereshteh Ahmadi also use him in their attempt at articulating a peculiarly Iranian form of Islam that draws upon Sufism and mystical philosophy to enunciate a rather modern notion of spiritualised and individualised man, a Perfect Man in a monistic universe who is not alienated from himself and rejects the Cartesian and dualistic nature of modern man.[86] Ṣadrā is thus a 'peculiarly Iranian phenomenon' since Iran is exclusively privileged by the 'ceaseless synthesis of religion, philosophy and mysticism'.[87] Needless to say, the rhetoric is not substantiated with evidence.

Finally, Ṣadrā has been co-opted by a variety of Iranian Islamists and members of the political and hierocratic establishment in Iran. At the World Congress on Mullā

Ṣadrā in 1999, one senior seminarian philosopher proclaimed the political importance of his philosophy: the Islamic revolution was based on Sadrian thought! Mullā Ṣadrā's influence upon Khomeini [d. 1989] is quite clear; but it is quite another thing to link the philosophical account of the soul's path to perfection with a theory of state in modern times.[88] In this way, Ṣadrā has become the official philosopher of the revolution. He, like many other thinkers, has not been spared the spectacular presumption of posterity.

Although these studies focus upon ontology, they fail to work through the implications of Sadrian ontology for his epistemology, logic and semantics. They fail to integrate the insights that Ṣadrā has about the ontology to which one is committed. They all repeat pretty much the same information about his life (very little) and recount the same influences on Ṣadrā: Avicennism, Illuminationist (*ishrāqī*) philosophy,[89] Shiʿi esotericism and theology and the mysticism (*ʿirfān*) of Ibn ʿArabī [d. 1240].[90] Sadrian studies are approaching a critical mass. But for this critical sub-field of Islamic philosophy to develop, we need major studies of particular ideas (still rather noticeable by their absence), a definitive intellectual biography (there are a number of biographies but none which really presents his life and ideas within a context), and good critical editions of his work (SIPRIn has done some excellent work to fill this particular lacuna). It remains a major problem in Sadrian studies that there are no serious translations of his philosophical work in English that would facilitate teaching him in philosophy courses.[91] In the first chapter that follows, I address some of the methodological issues of approaching and analysing the Sadrian text.

Part I

Preliminaries

1 Methodological concerns

> History does not belong to us; we belong to it. Long before we understand ourselves through the process of self-examination, we understand ourselves in a self-evident way in the family, society, and the state in which we live. The focus of subjectivity is a distorting mirror. The self-awareness of the individual is only a flickering in the closed circuits of historical life. *That is why the prejudices of the individual, far more than his judgements, constitute the historical reality of his being.*[1]

Philosophy, mysticism and pedagogy

Before considering issues of method, I should make explicit some of my assumptions, pre-understandings and conceptions of the cultural and intellectual history of the period. We should examine the contexts for Mullā Ṣadrā, not in order to produce a hard contextualist account of his philosophy or even to reduce his method to an impoverished historicist reading of Safavid thought, but to fill in aspects of the key assumptions about the nature of knowledge, philosophy, pedagogy and the practice of mysticism that are essential for a more holistic understanding of his philosophical method.[2]

First, one needs to locate philosophical discourse within the wider pursuit of knowledge as a social good in Safavid society. Its cultural importance within the institutional negotiation of power that was the *madrasa* needs to be recognised.[3] Centres of learning were expressions of courtly patronage, *fora* for the articulation of power and perpetuation of élite ideas, while retaining the possibility for subverting discourses. Knowledge was a social good and practice that facilitated social mobility and for the élites ensured a channel for the retention of power.[4] It also expressed strategies of social positioning for the ʻulema. We know that Ṣadrā was the only son of a prominent court family. His pursuit of knowledge could

was dealt a death blow by the famous refutation *Tahāfut al-falāsifa* of Ghazālī [d. 1111], speculative cosmology and ontology did not come to an end. In the Islamic East in particular, Avicennism was closely merged with systematic theology and even with juristic theory; it was inconceivable for the theologian or jurist to embark on discussions and dialectic with respect to rulings in divine law or statements of doctrine without establishing the principles of discourse provided by logic, epistemology and a descriptive metaphysics that explained the relationship between mind, word and world.[5]

The Timurids, Safavids and Mughals (and their successor dynasties in Iran and North India) patronised the intellectual disciplines (*al-maʿqūlāt*) and certain key texts constituted the core of this curriculum in the gunpowder empires: in logic (*manṭiq*), the short *al-Risāla al-Shamsiyya* of Dabīrān Kātibī Qazwīnī [d. 1276] and *Tahdhīb al-manṭiq* of Saʿd al-Dīn Taftazānī [d. 1389] with the *scholia* and *marginalia* of Mullā ʿAbd Allāh Yazdī [d. 1573] and Mīr Zāhid Harawī [d. 1605]; in systematic theology (*ʿilm al-kalām*), the pithy and dense *Tajrīd al-iʿtiqād* of the Shiʿi polymath Naṣīr al-Dīn Ṭūsī [d. 1274] with the two main commentaries (the 'old'/*qadīm* and the 'new'/*jadīd*) of Shams al-Dīn Iṣfahānī [d. 1349] and ʿAlāʾ al-Dīn Qūshjī [d. 1474] and the myriad of super-commentaries, *scholia* and *marginalia* by Mullā Ṣadrā's predecessors such as Ghiyāth al-Dīn Dashtakī [d. 1542] and Shams al-Dīn Khafrī [d. 1550] and his successors such as his son-in-law ʿAbd al-Razzāq Lāhījī [d. 1661]; and in philosophy (*ḥikma*), *al-Hidāya* of the Avicennan Athīr al-Dīn Abharī [d. 1264] and the commentary of the Timurid court-philosopher Mīr Ḥusayn Maybudī [d. 1504] and of course the later *sharḥ* of Mullā Ṣadrā himself.[6] The existence of multiple copies of manuscripts of these texts in libraries and collection within the Persianate world does not in itself attest to the wide acceptance of the ideas and arguments within them, nor does it necessarily mean that as school-texts they were fully read, digested, debated and critiqued. But the presence of these itinerant manuscripts (many of which are now in the British Library in London, Bibliothèque Nationale in Paris, the Chester Beatty Library in Dublin and Princeton University Library among other places) does signal the patronage and dissemination of the intellectual quest in the Islamic East.

Second, we need to recognise the importance of oral teaching at the heart of the *madrasa*'s pedagogy, what Derrida has pejoratively described as 'the logocentric hegemony of the spoken word over the written' in mediaeval culture originating in the famous Platonic dialogue, *Phaedrus*.[7] In *Protagoras*, Socrates criticises a reliance on books by arguing that books 'have nothing either to reply or the reasons to ask'.[8] It was assumed that dialogue and oral teaching inscribed truth in the soul of the student more efficaciously and in a more lasting manner than the written word.[9] To be sure, the privileging of the oral is also a result of the Islamic culture of transmission of *ḥadīth* and the Qur'ān.

In the Shiʿi tradition, however, written transmission was quite acceptable, even encouraged, in the early period as attested by the survival of the *kitāb* of the first century H controversialist, Sulaym b. Qays Hilālī.[10] The early traditionist Abū Jaʿfar Kulaynī [d. 941] cites a number of narrations extolling the writing of *ḥadīth* in the chapter on 'transmission of books and *ḥadīth* and the excellence of writing and adhering to the written word' of the book on the excellence of knowledge (*faḍl al-ʿilm*) in the *ḥadīth* collection *al-Uṣūl min al-Kāfī* (The Principles of the Sufficient); for example, Abū Baṣīr narrates that Abū ʿAbd Allāh (Imam Jaʿfar al-Ṣādiq) said, 'Write because you will not be able to preserve (knowledge) unless you write (it down)'.[11] In his commentary on this narration, Mullā Ṣadrā states that the import is transparent; narrators are fallible and may forget and so in order to preserve prophetic and Imamic knowledge, they must write it down.[12] In another narration reported from Imam al-Ṣādiq, it was said that 'the heart relies upon writing'; the seat of knowledge and memory is the heart but it requires aid.[13] Ṣadrā further comments that this proves that one may act in accordance with the written word.[14]

Nevertheless, authority of transmission depends upon actual reading (*qirā'a*), audition (*samāʿa*) and repetition to the *shaykh*.[15] This process ensures reliability and credibility of scholarship not only in the scriptural disciplines but also in the intellectual ones. It may even suggest the privileging of the esoteric unwritten doctrines over the exoteric and written ones, since true doctrine is transmitted through oral teaching within a community of shared experience.[16] However, as the debates over the famous passage in Plato's *Seventh Epistle* show, the issue is more complex.[17] Scholars such as Nasr have stressed the importance of oral teaching, of sitting at the feet of a learned *shaykh* and acquiring knowledge 'from heart to heart'.[18] This may help to explain the general trend of writing school-texts that are densely written and require memorisation and exegesis. Moreover, the cost of books before the printing press required that texts be internalised by students with meagre funds. In this context, we can understand the nature of the *Asfār* and Ṣadrā's teaching in the Madrasa-yi Khān in Shiraz. Furthermore, since many texts post-date their authors, one can presume that the oral teaching reflected in the recollections of his students was vital. In fact, only the first *safar* of the *Asfār* is actually Sadrian prose (insofar as we have a holograph attesting to it), the rest being compiled from the notes of his students.[19] Thus, to an extent, we can regard most of the *Asfār* as a series of 'lecture notes'. Such an understanding concurs with our notions of the nature of the Aristotelian corpus and would account for three important features of such a text: incompleteness of argument, textual and conceptual inconsistencies, and stylistic and grammatical infelicities.[20] It is common in the *madrasa* for students to transcribe lecture notes and then publish the transcription in the name of the lecturer. The text is thus authentically the work of the lecturer even though it is not his prose.[21] This is somewhat akin to the process of transmission of *ḥadīth* since *riwāya bi-l-maʿná* is considerably more prevalent that *riwāya bi-l-lafẓ*.

Logocentrism interrogates the status of the book as an aid and preserver of the word. In order to understand the nature and function of the book in Islamic culture, we must pay attention to the role of the text. Carruthers has made a detailed and convincing argument on the role of the book and memory in a mediaeval culture not dissimilar to the Safavid era.[22] While the book is a mnemonic aid, true knowledge resides within the person. Anthropologists have conducted similar studies on Islamic society.[23] The book can be an expression of power, of inscribing the 'truth' and making it 'concrete'; but at the same time the nature of education is more complex and there is no fixed boundary between oral and written reproductions of 'texts'.[24] In this light, arguments made about the fundamentally 'oral' nature of education as opposed to the inferential nature of written texts need to be nuanced.[25] A shifting dynamic between the master and the text as poles of cultural exchange might well be a useful description of the nature of education in this period.[26] The text thus becomes a process of unfolding and educating over a period of time negotiated between a master and a disciple.

Third, this rich textual education might be expressed in the source of influences upon Ṣadrā. It has been noted that four trends of inquiry contributed to the Sadrian 'synthesis': Avicennan philosophy, the visionary metaphysics of Suhrawardī, the tradition of Shi'i theology, and the mysticism of the school of Ibn 'Arabī. These methods were transmitted not only in the inscribed texts and commentaries but also in oral teaching. The production of the *scholia* and *marginalia* of the commentary culture depended upon this oral transmission.[27] In fact, it is possible to retroject '*isnāds*' of learning, those guarantees of authoritative knowledge in Islam, for Ṣadrā back to the epigenous founders of each of these four traditions. This confluence was prefigured in earlier syntheses and intellectual historians have noted the increasingly complex, indeed syncretic, nature of religion in Iran from the Ilkhanid period.[28] The rapprochement between Sufism and Shi'ism was critical in the period preceding the declaration of the Shi'i Safavid state and earlier thinkers such as Ibn Abī Jumhūr Aḥsā'ī [d. 1501] anticipated the Sadrian juxtaposition of mysticism, theology and philosophy.[29] Indeed, given the importance of Ṣadrā's synthesis, one can fruitfully use his texts, especially the *Asfār,* as a source for the history of Islamic philosophies.[30] This Sadrian synthesis is neither derivative nor uncritical. He engages critically with his predecessors. *Tashkīk* is at once a critique of Avicenna for his denial of intensity in being,[31] and of Suhrawardī,[32] who denies it since being has neither reference nor reality and is merely a 'common notion'. In his *Sharḥ Ḥikmat al-ishrāq* (Commentary on the Wisdom of Illumination), Ṣadrā often defends Suhrawardī against Avicenna to suggest his independence from Avicennism.[33] The *Asfār* is replete with quotations from *al-Futūḥāt al-Makkiyya* (Meccan Revelations) and he sees Ibn 'Arabī as his 'complete guide and teacher' (*murshid va mu'allim-i kāmil*).[34] However, we do know that in the *Asfār*, Ṣadrā vehemently attacks those who uphold the doctrine of the 'hypostatic unity of being' (*waḥdat al-wujūd al-shakhṣiyya*), a position associated with Ibn 'Arabī.[35]

What is striking about Ṣadrā's use of previous thought is his intimate and anxious dialogue with it. As one scholar puts it, 'he boldly attacks every school

to him in the *Asfār*.[37] The latter's significance is signalled by his description as 'the seal of the philosophers' (*khātam al-ḥukamā'*) by Ṣadrā's contemporary Quṭb al-Dīn Ashkiwarī.[38] They represented a critical engagement with and confluence of the two main philosophical traditions of Avicennism and Illuminationism.[39] Writing critical commentaries on the works of Suhrawardī such as *Hayākil al-nūr*, they transmitted a critically revised and more extensively Neoplatonised Avicennism. The 'school of Shiraz' as it has been termed influenced Mullā Ṣadrā's understanding of a number of positions in ontology from the nature and reality of existence to the ontological proof (or demonstration) for the existence of God (*burhān al-ṣiddīqīn*).[40]

Fourth, we need to understand the nature of philosophy in Islam. Like its ancient predecessor, it was unlike our contemporary 'speculation' that is confined to academics in their ivory tower with little relevance to practical life, or even any claims to significance beyond their circle.[41] For mediaevals, philosophy was a practice and an art whose goal was wisdom.[42] For Ṣadrā, philosophy pursued the *summum bonum* of enlightened engagement (*maʿrifa*) and goodly action,[43] worthy not only of the Aristotelian but also the pious Muslim scholar. To philosophise was to cultivate piety, since the end of philosophy was the higher pious life, a reflection of a Hermetic ideal.[44] The more truth one knows, the more pious one becomes. In fact, the more intense one's being, the better one is and the more felicitous.[45] Philosophy was a religious commitment that obscures the conceptual boundary between theory and doctrine. The very pursuit of intellectual inquiry and discourse is itself the greatest good and the means through which one knows how to live a good life, and enables one to ascend to the highest heavenly host.[46] The disciplining of the mind cures the soul of incorrect *doxa* and the disease of irrationality. It cures the suffering of the soul insofar as it reduces the alienation of the soul from the truth and ultimately from God through the journey of the intellect back to the One.[47] The Pythagorean tradition as understood in Islam insisted on the medicinal value of philosophy and the philosopher as the doctor of the soul.[48] In fact, a mix of ideas of commitment went into the crucial Sadrian definition of philosophy in the opening chapter of the *Asfār*:[49]

> Know that philosophy is the perfecting of the human soul (*istikmāl al-nafs al-insāniyya*) through cognition of the realities of existents (*maʿrifat ḥaqā'iq al-mawjūdāt*), as they truly are, and through judgements about their being ascertained through demonstrations (*taḥqīqan bi-l-barāhīn*), and not understood through conjecture (*bi-l-ẓann*) or adherence to authority (*bi-l-taqlīd*), to the measure of human capacity (*ḥasab al-ṭāqa al-bashariyya*).

their marginalisation from the discourse of Islamic intellectual history.

One is often left wondering what Ṣadrā means by mysticism and the practice of 'inner revelation' (*kashf*), a problem often discussed with respect to Avicenna.[52] Like the *Asfār*, *al-Masā'il al-qudsiyya* (Sacred Questions) begins with a claim that this philosophical text is not based on the principles of 'common philosophy' or theological dialectic but on the mystical insights of inner revelation (*min al-wāridāt al-kashfiyya*).[53] Yet in the first chapter, Ṣadrā defines metaphysics in precisely an Avicennan way that has resonances of Aristotle as well: 'First philosophy studies the states of being *qua* being and its primary divisions'.[54] He often gives philosophical arguments headings that allude to Sufi terminology but his discourse is quite distinct from that of an Ibn 'Arabī.[55] One should be careful not to accept uncritically mystical claims to ineffability.[56] To avoid this, one ought to be aware of figurative language and its uses, the possibility of using contradictory predicates to characterise the domain of experience and the use of negative dialectics and illocutionary negatives.[57] Mystical claims are propositions of sorts, attempts at articulating philosophical and theological ideas. It is indeed a feature of much mystical writing, both in the Islamic as well as in the Indian context, that it is formulated in syllogistic, logical and technical argument available for rational discussion.[58] The relationship between the symbolic language and the discursive method demands further investigation, and it is clear from Ṣadrā's hermeneutics in his Qur'anic exegesis, for example, that the forms and poetics of the argument retain a literal resonance and sense beyond any second order meaning that they might evince. On the whole, he remains faithful to his broadly Neoplatonic paradigm and his expression is an attempt to rationalise his intuitions and his experiences, the shortcomings revealing the unspoken gaps that must appear on the horizon of discourse.[59]

The final point concerns the nature of pedagogy in Islamic culture. Knowledge was not a personal good to be jealously guarded but a quality and virtue to be disseminated to those worthy of it.[60] Philosophical *paideia* was not only a way of life but also a means of delimiting and marking out a community, the 'philosophers' to whom Ṣadrā refers as the 'people' (*al-qawm*).[61] The philosophical circle was composed of the thought and action of the philosopher.[62] The production of texts, that were easy to memorise, and the development of mnemonic aids and literary genres were external manifestations of this community. However, the philosophy of education was predicated upon both the possibility of knowledge and its acquisition, and the construction of axiomatised sciences and their dissemination in *madrasa*s through a thoroughly hierarchical concept of knowledge. Pedagogy, for the *ḥukamā'*, depended upon a hierarchy of sciences at whose apex stood metaphysics, a discipline that both defined the parameters of syllogistic reasoning and provided the categories, terms and subjects to be studied in all other sciences and humanities. Hence it is not surprising that Ṣadrā's mastery of metaphysics, and his location of it at the heart of his philosophical enterprise, is critical to understanding his method. It is indeed his metaphysics and its connections with other branches of philosophy that concerns my study. Even on this issue one faces the 'paradox of pedagogy' in his thought since he still insists that true enlightenment is somehow ineffable and incommunicable.

A true pedagogy educates souls, leads to contentment of the heart and aims at their salvation.[63] The end of philosophy is thus the formation of character, of virtue; it is both an external examination of one's reality and location, and an internal consideration of one's self. As such this is philosophy not only as hermeneutics but also as soteriology. Arguments are made to have an effect on the student and on the opponent. In this sense is philosophy transformative and therapeutic.[64] Such a method requires a unique approach that is not merely discursive, nor theological, neither legalistic nor purely mystical but oriented as and towards praxis. The curriculum thus becomes important, the order in which texts are studied as a diagnostic for what the student requires at the stage of his ignorance, his intellectual disease.[65]

Like Suhrawardī, Ṣadrā urges the reader to practise philosophy as an art and a method of self-improvement and spiritual enlightenment.[66] The act of meditation is not irrational detachment but rather the exercise of reason.[67] Asceticism is a prerequisite for philosophy following the famous saying of first Shiʿi Imam ʿAlī b. Abī Ṭālib: 'the study of wisdom requires spiritual exercise and forsaking the world'.[68] In the introduction to the *Asfār*, he urges self-purification and the pursuit of perfection to obtain divine grace and knowledge.[69] True pedagogy allied with divine grace leads man to perfection and self-realisation. In his commentary upon *Sūrat al-Wāqiʿa*, Ṣadrā writes,

> The perfection of man lies in the perception of universal realities (*al-ḥaqā'iq al-kulliyya*) and disposition towards divine cognition, and transcendence above material *sensibilia*, and self-purification from the restraints of carnal and passionate appetites. This can only be acquired through guidance, teaching, discipline, and formation of righteous character.[70]

This is the preliminary stage through which everyone must pass, but a philosopher, and a divine philosopher (*ḥakīm muta'allih*) at that, must go beyond this stage in pursuit of the quest for reality. It is this quest that leads the wayfarer to a higher philosophy, a *ḥikma mutaʿāliya* as he describes it in the title of his major work. The term originated in *al-Ishārāt wa-l-tanbīhāt* of Avicenna. In his discussion of separable intellects, Avicenna says of the argument that he has presented that it is 'only understood by those rooted in higher philosophy (*al-rāsikhūn fī-l-ḥikma al-mutaʿāliya*)'.[71] His commentator, Ṭūsī, explains why this method is 'elevated' and transcends mere Peripatetism:

> He calls this an issue of higher philosophy (*al-ḥikma al-mutaʿāliya*) because Peripatetic philosophy is simply discursive (*baḥthiyya*), yet this and similar issues can only be completely understood by discourse, *and* contemplation through inner revelation (*al-kashf*), *and* direct experience (*al-dhawq*). Thus the philosophy that includes them is elevated in relation to the former [Peripatetism].[72]

The Peripatetics had a concept of unmediated cognition that was non-discursive and they referred to it as 'contemplation' (*mushāhada*). For Bahmanyār, certainty is the result of a discursive process in which one grasps the 'middle term' (of the syllogism) through the mediation of 'abstraction by another [cognitive] faculty'; but contemplation is a state of pure, unmediated cognition and as such is higher in rank.[73] However, it was impossible for human intellects to contemplate *intelligibilia* in this sensible and transitory world.

The concept of 'higher' or 'transcendent' modes of cognition is also invoked in the Akbarian school, where it denotes a mystical appreciation of reality that is beyond the discursive, such as the introduction of Qayṣarī's *Sharḥ Fuṣūṣ al-ḥikam* (Commentary upon the Ring-settings of Wisdoms).[74] True knowledge of God can only be obtained through *ḥikma mutaʿāliya*, a methodology of inquiry and self-realisation that is non-discursive. Ṣadrā modifies this claim into one of reconciliation between rational discourse and intuitive mystical vision. Indeed, his success in this endeavour is a recurrent boast.[75] True philosophy is vertically received: the reality of philosophy can only concern 'divine knowledge from on high' (*ʿilm ladunnī*),[76] and he who does not reach this degree, does not become a philosopher.[77] This corresponds strongly with the reports that suggest that the pursuit of knowledge is a sacred and hermeneutic act since the epistemic object is the 'comprehension of the deep or hidden meaning of everything'.[78] This 'divine knowledge' (*al-ʿulūm al-rabbāniyya*) is divinely inspired (*ilhām*) from the 'suprasensible knowledge of God' (*al-ʿilm al-ghaybī al-ladunnī*) and is the strongest and most reliable foundation.[79]

Despite his immense respect for Avicenna, Ṣadrā does not regard him as a sage (*ḥakīm*): 'despite his cleverness, the intensity of his understanding and the subtlety of his nature, the Master could not achieve this rank'.[80] Yet even Avicenna acknowledges the value of non-predicative stations of being that are ineffable and cannot be comprehended in any discourse.[81] A sage who pursues and attains *assimilatio Dei* (*tashabbuh bi-l-bāriʾ*) is elevated above the commonality.[82] His quest for *theosis* (a term popularised by pseudo-Dionysius in the sixth century CE), to become (like) or emulate a god, is a venerable Near Eastern theme and the end of ethical activity, of the practice of philosophy as expounded by Iamblichus of Apamea [d. *c.* 325], but already a key theme in the Platonic tradition.[83] Plato famously discussed the aim of philosophy to be the moral and intellectual inculcation of virtue in imitation of the demiurge as far as is humanly possible (ὁμοίωσις θεῷ κατὰ τὸ δυνατὸν ἀνθρώπῳ) in the *Theaetetus* 176b:

> Of necessity, it is mortal nature and our vicinity that are haunted by evils. And that is why we should also try to escape from here to there as quickly as we can. To escape is to become like god so far as is possible and to become like god is to become just and holy together with wisdom.[84]

It is the rational demiurge that is the true 'measure' and aspiration of the human intellect (after Plato's *Laws* 716c). Similarly, it is the higher, non-physical realm of existence that is the true home of the intellect. *Theosis* involves two elements: the emulation of the virtuous living, perfecting one's practical wisdom and moral insight, and a cathartic 'stripping away' (*khalʿ*) of the body to 'release' the rational soul's pure beatific experience of the higher noetic world as expressed in Plotinus' *Enneads* IV.8.1 and rendered in the first *mīmar* of the *Theology of Aristotle* (*Uthūlūjiyā*).[85] The mainstream Platonic tradition, as expressed in Alcinous' *Didaskalikos*, recognised the link between philosophy and practice in the following prescription:

> We can attain likeness to God, first of all, if we are endowed with a suitable nature, then if we develop proper habits, way of life, and good practice according to the law, and most importantly, if we use reason, and education, and the correct philosophical tradition, in such a way as to distance ourselves from the great majority of human concerns, and always to be in close contact with intelligible reality.
>
> The introductory ceremonies, so to speak, and preliminary purifications of our innate spirit, if one is to be initiated into the greater sciences, will be constituted by music, arithmetic, astronomy and geometry, while at the same time we must care for our body by means of gymnastics, which will prepare the body properly for the demands of both war and peace.[86]

While one strand of Platonism focused upon the cultivation of the intellect and drew up 'lists of virtues' to pursue, another tendency within later Neoplatonism, associated especially with Iamblichus, stressed the inculcation of 'holiness' and separation of the soul from the cage of its body and the realisation of the divine spark in the soul (following *Timaeus* 41c) through *theosis*.[87] It is the latter which introduces the notion of the 'hieratic virtues' that allows for the efficacy of theurgy and assimilation to god.[88] Philosophy is thus more than noesis (discursive and non-discursive) and involves spiritual practice.

For Iamblichus as for Mullā Ṣadrā, spiritual practice (*theurgy, riyāḍa*) is critical to philosophy.[89] Just as Porphyry and others before had delimited lists of virtues, for Ṣadrā, the sage possesses the qualities of generosity, good humour, fine judgement, and a pronounced taste and experience of spiritual disclosure.[90] Truth must derive its legitimacy and foundation from grace and revelation, and can never find fertile soil merely in the rehearsal of the doctrines of previous philosophers. Phenomenological experience is the ground for philosophy. In the *Asfār*, Ṣadrā writes: 'Know that . . . etaphysical doctrines can only be grasped by inner revelation (*mukāshafāt bāṭiniyya*), secret contemplation (*mushāhadāt sirriyya*) and existential investigations (*muʿāyanāt wujūdiyya*) and cannot be really known through rehearsing discursive doctrines'.[91]

But he is no mystical obscurantist nor does he privilege spiritual intuition above demonstration; rather he argues for their complementarity since 'demonstration does not conflict with inner disclosure'.[92] The study of texts moves the seeker to construct a world, to make an intelligible order of the propositions and *aporiai* that he encounters. But the perfected sage also *is* an intelligible world as Ṣadrā tells us in the definition of the *Asfār*, that old Hermetic idea of the macrocosm.[93]

Self-reflection is the key.[94] As Ṣadrā says in his commentary on *al-Uṣūl min al-Kāfī* (The Principles of the Sufficient), 'most remain in the house of their veiling, resting in their primitive state and station'.[95] It is the true seeker who moves beyond and makes the intention of journeying towards the truth. It is that sincerity of intention (*khulūṣ*) and the light of faith (*nūr al-īmān*)[96] that guides the philosopher to truth and closeness to God (indeed of acquiring the 'divine virtues'), which Ṣadrā envisages as his goal.[97] He demands much of his readers and students and sets stringent limits. Not only is not everyone capable of doing philosophy but true faith and self-realisation are goals beyond most people's reach, even proscribed to them: 'It is forbidden for most people to set out to acquire these complex sciences, because those worthy of them are rare and most exceptional. Guidance to them is a grace from God, the Lofty and the Knowing'.[98]

The practice of philosophy, theurgy and living, studying and being the virtuous life are not for everyone but for the select few, initiated into a path and who are truly worthy of these modes of being, guided by divine grace. The continuities from late Neoplatonism and its ethics to Mullā Ṣadrā and philosophy in the Safavid period are striking.

Before the text

Having explained some of my preconceptions about the context, I want to discuss briefly the four methodological approaches that I utilise in this study.

First, I shall approach *tashkīk* as the central hermeneutic of Sadrian metaphilosophy. As such it is no longer regarded as an aspect of his ontology *simpliciter*. As Rahman says, it is 'the pivot of Ṣadrā's philosophy, a pivot around which all problems revolve and are solved'.[99] On the problem to be discussed here, Açikgenç raises an interesting issue relating the Sadrian concept of *tashkīk* to Heidegger's hermeneutics of being which fits my methodology of examining the concept of *tashkīk* as a central defining and organising principle.[100] Therefore, in a sense, one might say that this study examines the 'ambiguity of ambiguity' in Ṣadrā's metaphilosophy. Hence, *tashkīk* is a philosophically significant and influential doctrine. It frames categories of ontological and hermeneutical reference and inquiry for later Islamic philosophy. It pervades his philosophy such that other concepts like that of the intellect (*al-ʿaql*) are conceived as being '*mushakkak'* as well.[101] Further concepts that exhibit 'modulation' include priority,[102] and other *a priori* concepts such as 'contingency' (*al-imkān*).[103] Only a few authors have truly appreciated the centrality of *tashkīk*. Jambet sees it in strictly epistemological terms focusing upon it as a means of conceptualising unity and negating the subjective–objective dichotomy that we take for granted nowadays.[104] Āshtiyānī[105] recognises that later philosophical discourse is dependent upon it as a conglomerate idea and is explained in its own terms – a true reflection of philosophical influence.[106] Indeed, the language of *tashkīk*, of gradation and essential privation (*sterēsis*) of every degree save the One, dominates later philosophical discourses whether in philosophical theological works or in more mainstream exegeses. The Sadrian discourse of *tashkīk* has become the master narrative of the Shiʿi *madrasa* and has influenced comparative works by its proponents. One critical contemporary example is Ḥā'irī Yazdī's defence of the pyramid of being and the logic of being in a comparative framework analysing pure reason.[107] The exception to prove the rule, so to speak, is the work of Ashkivarī, a philosopher of the turn of the century, who, in his discussion of graded reality of being *à la* Ibn 'Arabī, ignores the Sadrian language of *tashkīk*.[108]

Second, I propose to use an aporetic method in analysing Ṣadrā's philosophy. There are two levels to the aporetic method. The first is the Platonic-Aristotelian *aporia* as 'facilitation towards understanding' that results from the intellect hitting 'a lack of passage' (lit. a-poria) to resolving a problem.[109] The *aporia* is the result of the *elenctic* method, the Socratic cross-examination of an opponent's beliefs, disavowing knowledge while ironically debunking the opponent's claims to knowledge.[110] The aim of the *aporia* is to eliminate false belief and is a 'proteptic' that brings 'the student to the first stage of philosophical enlightenment: the recognition of a problem in whose importance and difficulty he had not understood'.[111] In fact, according to Aristotle, philosophy is engendered by this surprise recognition that some things perplex us. He wrote, 'it was because of wonder that men both now and originally began to philosophise'.[112] Booth has argued that ontological paradoxes lie at the heart of mediaeval philosophical systems grappling with the irresolvable *aporia*s of Aristotle.[113] Ṣadrā and philosophers before him structure philosophy as a discourse of *aporia*s, of irresolvable and paradoxical problems. For example, Aristotle lists nineteen *aporia*s in Book β of his *Metaphysics* as the central questions and problems of the science.[114] This allows for the creative process in metaphysics since philosophy arises out of *aporia*[115] and difficulties permit for the 'free play of thought' (and metaphysical speculation).[115] Indeed, Wittgenstein defines philosophy aporetically: a philosophical problem has the form 'I don't know my way about', referring back to the etymology of the aporia.[117]

The second level of the aporetic method concerns the problem of contradictions, paradoxes and antinomies. Rescher has argued that instead of regarding an aporetic method as fundamentally sceptical, we should instead see it as a key to understanding a rich multivocal philosophical discourse through a metaphilosophical appreciation of the aims of the philosophical system.[118] It is at the metaphilosophical level that such an analysis is most appropriate and avoids the attribution of contradictions (*pace* Rahman) in search for dynamic paradoxes. This deals with the problem of the 'apory', which Rescher defines as 'a collection of contentions that are individually plausible but collectively inconsistent'.[119] The metaphilosophical level smoothes out dissonances and obviates the need for excessive multiplication of fine distinctions and levels. I argue that *tashkīk* is a central guiding principle in Ṣadrā's metaphilosophy and permeates all branches of his philosophical system. The aporetic method is not just inferred from the multivocity of discourse or even the polysemous nature of being at various levels and modes that it possesses. *Aporia*s provide puzzles to solve, a method that is rather consonant with the 'language games' of twentieth-century philosophy.[120] Furthermore, some logicians have noted the importance of semantic game analysis especially for the senses of 'be'.[121] However, the question remains: how does *aporia* differ from a contradictory statement? Does contradiction entail the disavowal of knowledge of the subject-matter in question?[122] How is this different from paradox and antinomy? A paradox sounds absurd yet has an argument to sustain it.[123] An antinomy is a self-contradictory compound proposition arrived at through accepted ways of reasoning.[124] The aporetic method does not attempt to circumvent these problems. The aporetic method is also an acknowledgement, and indeed manifestation, of the significance of the Corbinian concept of '*coincidentia oppositorum*', a Romantic dissolution of the Law of Non-Contradiction in which One is both/and many.[125]

Tashkīk is an essentially aporetic idea because it entails concepts of affirmation and scalar gradation, modulation and negation.[126] Indeed, the morphological root of '*shakk*' or doubt was used to translate *aporia* in the early translation movement.[127] It also reveals the important nature of philosophical discourse in *ḥikmat* as a constant negotiation between *apophasis* (*tanzīh, salb*) and *kataphasis* (*tashbīh, ījāb*). Language is thus a constant play between an assumption and affirmation of philosophical analysis and an explanation predicated upon a pure, direct experience of reality that is essentially ineffable ('pure consciousness experiences'),[128] though mystical philosophy affirms the content of that experience. The nexus of 'saying' and 'unsaying' is the critical focus of both religious and philosophical discourse in the traditions that Ṣadrā inherited.[129] Affirmation as well as essential privation is asserted of every level of ontic hierarchy. The negotiation between these poles is graded and ambiguous as well, and in itself a *mushakkak* concept.[130]

Third, I assume that Sadrian philosophy is processual, a tendency noted by Morewedge for most Islamic philosophy after Suhrawardī.[131] His philosophical method continues the shift from substance to process metaphysics in later Islamic philosophy. Traditionally, the dominant metaphysical tradition has seen the world as a collectivity of substances that define and identify things to which accidents occur and in which they inhere. The Aristotelian tradition, that was hegemonic in the ancient and mediaeval worlds, considered substances, particularly primary substances, to be the basic units of ontology and posited a theory of categories in which one could locate anything that one may perceive and conceive as either being 'said-of' or 'present-in', and basic substances and the nine accidental properties that pertain to those substances. The *Categories* and *Metaphysics* Zeta of Aristotle were the key texts proposing this ontology.[132] Substance metaphysics considers reality to be the realm of *being*, constituted by substances that exist independently, do not change but are unchanging subject of change and are the ultimate objects of predication (*ḥaml*). A counter-tradition originating with Heraclitus views things as events and processes determined by the essential principle of constant flux in reality, of *becoming*. Process metaphysics is characterised by the primacy of process over things or substances; it regards processes as the principal category of ontological description and focuses on 'acts of being'.[133] It is a more holistic approach that breaks out of the straitjacket of the Aristotelian categories through the unitive dynamic of process.[134] Whitehead [d. 1947] revived this tradition in the present century in his Gifford Lectures.[135] Sadrian ontology envisages things as structures of events, 'acts of being', and processes.[136] Being possesses processual extension through becoming, and thus, for Ṣadrā, the distinction is blurred since being is becoming, insofar as an essential property of being is to become, to unfold and to overflow. In this sense he is a 'processist'.[137] He is also a process realist, by which I mean that he regards fundamental processes such as the flow of being as having reference and concrete reality, in opposition to some earlier processists such as Suhrawardī for whom processes are merely intentional and mentally posited considerations (*iʿtibārāt*) without reference.[138] Furthermore, this is corroborated by the critical corollary of *tashkīk* in Ṣadrā's thought, the doctrine of 'substantial motion' (*ḥaraka jawhariyya*), that substance is in constant flux.[139] In fact it is this process that ensures that reality remains a universal 'vortex' for the flow of being. Flux underpins reality and is essential to it. Indeed, being 'constantly flows' through events and substances. This does not, it must be stressed, deny the existence of substance. Rather, substance is dethroned as the most basic ontic item and replaced with 'process'. For Ṣadrā, motion is a constant process of 'renewal and lapse' (*al-tajaddud wa-l-inqiḍāʾ*), and the underlying dynamic of things that are 'structures of events'.[140] Such a philosophical approach avoids ousiological reduction, that is the essentialising of the object of metaphysical inquiry as 'substance', and retains the focus upon being as a dynamic of reality that is individuated in its modes yet not reducible to them. This dynamism within the process of being is rather aptly described by Corbin as the 'inquietude of being that makes itself felt from one end of the scale [of being] to the other, among all the degrees of being, and which leads each of the beings in an ascendant motion'.[141]

Finally, I approach Sadrian *ḥikmat* as a metaphilosophical inquiry. Metaphysics is a foundational science for Ṣadrā, instrumental for the possibility of knowledge and the construction of definitions and meaningful discourse. It is also a 'metaphilosophy' which defines '*al-ḥikma al-mutaʿāliya*'.[142] It is not just an ontology, meaning that it is more than a description of the nature of reality; it is a systematic speculation and hermeneutics of the world and the text. Sadrian philosophy has important metaphilosophical concerns because of Ṣadrā's second order conceptual framework for analysing philosophical problems. One of the reasons for my focus on the 'ontology' section of the *Asfār* is that such a study brings out various aspects of the Sadrian system that are integrated in the metaphilosophy of the ontology such as epistemology, logic, semantics and theology. All these elements are discussed within a holistic analysis, which raises it above the carefully scholastic divisions of analyses in Peripatetic and even Illuminationist philosophy. *Ḥikmat* is doubly transcendent: as a higher synthesis of Avicennan, Illuminationist, Sufi and esoteric Shiʿi systematic thought systems, and as a prophetic philosophy that claims to be derived from direct 'revelation'.

The *Asfār*

Since this study is primarily an analysis of the metaphysics of the *Asfār*, it would be useful at this point to present the text. What sort of text are we dealing with?[143] It refuses to follow the standard Peripatetic order for an encyclopaedia: logic, metaphysics, natural philosophy and psychology. Nor does it follow the Stoic/Illuminationist order of logic, physics and ethics. Divisions in the text are related to Ṣadrā's metaphilosophical method. It was commonplace in mediaeval Islam, following the Neoplatonic pattern, to introduce a text by discussing its location within a schema.[144] First, one discussed the aim (*ho skopos, gharaḍ*) of the text. In our case, the answer is a philosophical summa designed to provide a complete training in philosophy. Second, one decided the 'use' of the text: the benefit of this text lies in its clear and comprehensive expositions of arguments. Third, where was it placed in the curriculum? Given the extensive quotation and the fact that it contains neither propadeutics nor the standard introductory section on logic, it is an advanced text at the culmination of a philosophical education. The first section (*al-manhaj al-awwal*) is a 'logic of being' for Ṣadrā. It provides us with the principles for the study of his ontology and gives us the semantic tools we need for analysis. Or the incorporation of logical analysis and method into metaphysics might reflect a faithful adherence to Aristotelianism.[145] A corollary to this is the 'logicisation' of being that results from Suhrawardī's critique of the reality and actuality of 'being'. The text assumes a discursive sophistication on the part of its students (a point he often makes in introducing his arguments). Metaphilosophy requires one first to master the different discourses and arguments and to have mastered the various texts of previous and existing philosophies. Fourth, what are its contents and style? His discursive practice is the key, and that requires the need to 'find' the syllogism and other types of arguments, deductive and non-deductive, syllogistic and allusive, that he marshals. His style is open and argumentative and rarely dogmatic, but rather anti-systematic.[146] Modulation is critical to this.

The text comprises four intellectual journeys. At the culmination of the introduction, Mullā Ṣadrā says:

> Know that wayfarers among the mystics and the saints (*li-l-sullāk min al-ʿurafāʾ wa-l-awliyāʾ*) possess four journeys: the first of them is the journey from creation to God (*al-ḥaqq*); the second of them is the journey in God with God; the third journey is the opposite of the first because it is from God to creation with God; and the fourth is the opposite of the second in a sense because it is with God in creation.
>
> I have arranged my writing to correspond to their [mystics and saints] movement through lights and signs in four journeys and I have named it the 'transcendent philosophy of the four journeys of the intellect'.[147]

The notion that mystics underwent four journeys between unity and diversity, union and separation and intoxication and sobriety was a well-known trope in Sufi metaphysics, especially in the school of Ibn ʿArabī whose own *Risālat al-isfār ʿan natāʾij al-asfār* is probably the foundational text. Perhaps the earliest instance of a discussion of mystics undergoing four journeys described in a form similar to the *Asfār* is the commentary of the Andalusian Sufi ʿAfīf al-Dīn Tilimsānī [d. 1291] on the *Manāzil al-sāʾirīn*, a famous manual of Sufi states and stations penned by the Ḥanbalī Sufi Khwāja ʿAbd Allāh Anṣārī [d. 1088]. He posits the following scheme: first, the mystic wayfarer moves from multiplicity to unity and journeys to God; second, he journeys in God and unity; third, he returns back to multiplicity and the creation but remains with God; and finally, he journeys through existents to the presence of being (*al-safar bi-l-mawjūd ilá-l-wujūd*).[148] But the proximate inspiration for the trope is the short treatise of the Shīrāzī philosopher Shams al-Dīn Khafrī [d. 1550] on the four journeys:

> Know that mystics possess four journeys.
>
> The first journey is from creation to God. When one contemplating contemplates upon creation, he finds himself qualified by the quality of contingency that necessitates reliance upon another. Pure contingents do not possess in themselves anything that has subsistence in itself; rather, all pure contingents participate in not having existence in themselves but being dependent upon a thing external to them that grants them existence, which is God the Necessary in Himself. So the contemplator moves from contingents to the Necessary in Himself . . .
>
> The second journey is the journey in God with God and is the move from the attribute of the essentially Necessary to the other attributes such as knowledge, life, power, will, audition, sight and speech.
>
> The third journey is the journey from God to creation and the move from the attribute of the Merciful to the existentiation of creatures in a perfect form from intellects descending to souls and spheres down to the elements and then progressing to minerals, vegetables, animals, humans and then to angels and the reversion to God.
>
> The fourth journey is the journey in creation to God and is an expression for disclosure and presence of being and attributes of perfection in the Necessary Being and the True Being that subsists in Himself . . . The culmination of this journey is the absolute annihilation of contingents and the manifestation of true subsistence.[149]

Thus already in Khafrī one may discern the structure of the *Asfār* and the mapping of philosophical inquiry on to the mystical path. The actual structure of Mullā Ṣadrā's text is as follows. The first journey from creation to God (*min al-khalq ilá l-ḥaqq*) encompasses Sadrian ontology and metaphysics and comprises volumes I to III. It deals with the logic of being and non-being, the basic divisions of being and its senses, and problems of essence, universals and definition, as well as causation. The main thrust of the argument is to demonstrate that being has sense and reference, and that its referents are modulations within a singular reality. Being is shown to possess modes, concrete, propositional and mental. Causation within the hierarchy of being is explained in terms of degrees of intensity, illuminative relations and the doctrine of 'future contingency'. The dynamics of the system are also discussed: time and substantial motion. At the culmination of this stage, the philosopher-wayfarer acquires a mastery over preliminaries into *divinalia*.

The first journey is divided into ten stages that reveal the principle of modulation and the many senses of being. The first stage focuses on the nature of being *qua* being and its modes within mental being, written and spoken tokens of being and existence (*hyparxis*). The remaining stages examine the secondary divisions of being such as actuality and potentiality, oneness and multiplicity, and the essential accidents of being *qua* being, that is quiddities. Although the theme of *tashkīk* permeates the text, one finds in this part the two explicit discussions of this principle within the three stages of its development. First, the term 'being' and its semantics of modulation are discussed in chapter two of the first stage, where they are distinguished from the notions of synonymy and mere homonymy. Second, modulation is central to the argument for the proof of the reality of mental being, that cognitive mode of being that is critical to the epistemic process, Third, the notion is developed from semantics and epistemology to ontology, a hermeneutic for explaining the nature of concrete existence. At this level, the discussion of *tashkīk* is central to his examination of the process of *jaʿl*, of the making and bringing into being of the cosmos in stage three. It is in this section that one finds the articulation of intensity in the hierarchy of being.

Two other sections of this journey are central to modulation. The first is the denial of modulation in quiddity in his *Isagoge*, the fourth stage that examines the nature of quiddity and the universals. The second is his novel description of the vertical hierarchy of causality in the long sixth stage. At the horizontal level of quidditative multiplicity, causality is a relationship between two things, cause and effect. However, at the unitive vertical level, causality is an effusion and the manifestation of the higher in the lower. The more intense levels of being manifest themselves in lower levels through an illuminative relation (*iḍāfa ishrāqiyya*), an immediate, atemporal relationship.

The eighth and tenth stages of this journey are also salient to a discussion of modulation. The former discusses the nature of time and motion. Here one finds the central exposition of his famous doctrine of motion in the category of substance (*ḥaraka jawhariyya*), that is the corollary of modulation that ties together and relates the different levels and intensities within this account of a dynamic hierarchy of unitive being. The latter is an extensive excursus on the nature of knowledge, its gradation that corresponds to gradation in the reality of being, and the modulated nature and different types of epistemology in his method.

The second journey, by the Truth (God) in the Truth (God) (*bi-l-ḥaqq fī-l-ḥaqq*), is his study of physics, of substance and accidents, hylomorphism and categories. It corresponds to volumes IV and V. It has a broad concept of physics that includes all that exists except for the divine essence and includes Ṣadrā's proof for Platonic forms and the ontological realm of the 'Imaginal' (*ʿālam al-mithāl*). Modulation in this journey is with respect to the Aristotelian mode of being-in-the-categories.

The third journey from God to creation (*min al-ḥaqq ilá l-khalq*) deals with the descent from the divine realm into the realm of *intelligibilia*, and comprises

principle of modulation because it posits a scale of being that is one but modulated in the range of intensities and a scale of perfection. Furthermore this unified vision of being circumvents the famous objection (*shubha*) of the Jewish Illuminationist philosopher Ibn Kammūna [d. 1284] to the proof of the Necessary Being that postulates a hypothesis of two necessary beings.[150] Since being is unified, the question of two necessary beings cannot arise.

The final journey in creation with God (*fī-l-khalq bi-l-ḥaqq*) is a discussion of psychology, soteriology and eschatology and makes up the last two volumes. It includes an initiation into the psychology of the soul, and is an illustration of the maxim that 'he who knows his self, knows his Lord'.[151] It illustrates how the tradition of the *De Anima* in later Islamic philosophy is blended with Sufi accounts of the soul and its return to the One. The soul descends and ascends within the circle of being, traversing its degrees. The major doctrine here apart from the vehement refutation of the possibility of metempsychosis is the 'corporeal incipience' (*jismāniyyat al-ḥudūth*) of the soul. The origins of this doctrine lie in Avicennism. But the text culminates with extensive citations from the work of Ibn ʿArabī to signal the affinity in their soteriology and eschatology.

Ṣadrā's sources

Avicenna, and more generally the Peripatetic tradition, is the ground of Ṣadrā's philosophy.[152] Discussions often begin with a quotation from the Master (*al-shaykh al-ra'īs*) to introduce an issue, support a position or present an argument that he wishes to refute. Bahmanyār's *al-Taḥṣīl*, a summary of his teacher's metaphysics of *al-Shifā'*, is the most cited text in the *Asfār* as a representative of the Peripatetic school. The chapter headings of the *Asfār* closely follow the order and form of those in *al-Taḥṣīl*. His Islamic sources range across the different school traditions extant in the Safavid period: Akbarian, Peripatetic, Illuminationist, esotericist, theological and independents such as Abū-l-Barakāt Baghdādī.[153]

However, there are two pre-Islamic traditions that play an important part in his thought and explain my references to them in this study: Hermeticism and Iamblichean Neoplatonism. Sadrian history of philosophy is profoundly Illuminationist drawing upon a mixed Syrian/Egyptian Hermeticism that informs his Neoplatonism. A good source for gauging what was available to Mullā Ṣadrā is to consult the history of philosophy and philosophers *Maḥbūb al-qulūb* compiled by Quṭb al-Dīn Ashkiwarī [d. *c.* 1684], a co-student with Ṣadrā of Mīr Dāmād. Ashkiwarī rejects a Hellenic origins for philosophy: Thales of Miletus was not the first to philosophise.[154] For him, philosophy began with Adam, the father of humanity and was transmitted until lost in the Flood.[155] After the Flood, it was

Babylonian who instructed Pythagoras in philosophy and medicine, and an

Egyptian, both after the Flood;[156] the other sense signals the threefold divinely bestowed bounties that the first Hermes possessed – wisdom, kingship, and prophecy.[157] Joseph took up the philosophical enterprise and it was passed down the line of prophets to David and his contemporary the Qur'ānic sage Luqmān. Ashkiwarī actually has Empedocles, a 'contemporary of David', study in Syria with Luqmān, 'cousin of Job'.[158] Consequently, philosophy spreads to Egypt through Solomon. Empedocles becomes the father of Greek philosophy.

Like other Illuminationists, Mullā Ṣadrā sees philosophical traditions in genealogical terms, transmitted orally, from Adam to Seth to Hermes/Idrīs from whom both the Hellenic tradition starting with Empedocles, and the Eastern tradition, through the Qur'ānic sage Luqmān, Tat and Asclepius, emerge.[159] Consistent with the Pythagoreanising tendency of late Neoplatonism associated with Iamblichus, the longest entry (longer than that on Plato or Aristotle) devoted to a Greek philosopher in Ashkiwarī concerns Pythagoras, who is considered to be a 'theosist' (*ḥakīm muta'allih*).[160] He studied philosophy from its prophetic source in Egypt (*akhadha-l-ḥikmata min maʿdini-l-nubuwwa bi-miṣr*) and later in Syria. Philosophy retains a strong Oriental provenance. In his treatise on creation (*Risāla fī ḥudūth al-ʿālam*), Mullā Ṣadrā summarises this genealogy of philosophy from Adam and the East to the Greeks:

> Know that philosophy first issued from Adam, the chosen one of God and from his progeny Seth and Hermes – I mean Idrīs – and from Noah because the world can never be free of a person who establishes knowledge of the unity of God and of the return [to God]. The great Hermes disseminated it [philosophy] in the climes and in the countries and explained it and gave benefit of it to the people. He is the father of philosophers and the most learned of the knowledgeable . . .
>
> As for Rome and Greece, philosophy is not ancient in those places as their original sciences were rhetoric, epistolatory and poetry . . . until Abraham became a prophet and he taught them the science of divine unity. It is mentioned in history that the first to philosophise from among them [the Greeks] was Thales of Miletus and he named it philosophy. He first philosophised in Egypt and then proceeded to Miletus when he was an old man and disseminated his philosophy. After him came Anaxagoras and Anaximenes of Miletus. After them emerged Empedocles, Pythagoras, Socrates and Plato.[161]

Doxographical material such as *al-Milal wa-l-niḥal* of Shahrastānī [d. 1153], *Ta'rīkh al-ḥukamā'* of Qifṭī [d. 1248], the Arabic Aëtius and especially *Nuzhat al-arwāḥ* of Shahrazūrī [d. after 1288] provided valuable information on the ancients.[162] Oral teachings, along with partial translations and *pseudo-epigrapha* played a significant part in the transmission of the *Hermetica* and Pythagorean Neoplatonism. On the latter, the teachings of Iamblichus [d. c. 325], author of *On the Pythagorean Life*, and Proclus are significant, complementing their actual works available in Arabic, and the tradition of Ammonius through his disciple, Asclepius (often confused with the Hermetic Asclepius),[163] transmitted through the Syriac into Arabic.[164] Iamblichean ideas were transmitted in Arabic even if he is largely absent from the doxographical literature. Plotinian doctrines play a significant role as attested by the citations of the *Theologia Aristotelis*, a doxastic source of philosophical character of considerable authority for nearly all Islamic thinkers, especially on psychological discussions.[165] The influence of this text can be underestimated and it underwent a revival in the Safavid period as attested to the number of citations and commentaries upon it.

Iamblichus (and later Pythagoreanising Neoplatonism) was a critical influence on the Illuminationists, mediated through translations such as his comments on the *Golden Verses* of Pythagoras, material in doxographical literature and original works that have Iamblichean resonances.[166] Proclus was another significant figure known as a Platonist master and commentator though little of his corpus, mainly the pseudo-epigraphic *Fī Maḥḍ al-khayr* (De Causis), was translated.[167] It was also from the Platonic tradition that Ṣadrā derived his notion of *ḥikma mutaʿāliya*: Ashkiwarī describes all the great Greek philosophers as 'theosists', but he singles out Plato as the one whose teaching involved symbols, allusions and *muthos* and hence it was only those 'possessing *ḥikma mutaʿāliya* and pure minds' who are capable of grasping his intent.[168] Thus *ḥikma mutaʿāliya* is not just the process of philosophy that we encountered in Avicenna and the school of Ibn ʿArabī, it is a higher faculty of wisdom.

Fragments of the *Hermetica* abound in Islamic literature, even if there is little extant evidence of an Arabic *Corpus Hermeticum*.[169] They are found in major doxographical works.[170] Hermes and Agathadaemon (the 'godly spirit'), his teacher who is identified with Seth, are cited as authorities even for the Greeks.[171] Hermes was naturalised into a Muslim context as the prophet Idrīs/Enoch, a law-giver and authority.[172] He was seen along with his master Seth/Agathadaemon to be the founder of philosophy, especially of Illuminationist intuitive philosophy through the mediation of the Syrian Ṣābi'ans.[173] Agathadaemon is quoted in the *Asfār* as an Illuminationist master expounding on doctrines of light, luminosity and the soul.[174] In *Maḥbūb al-qulūb*, he is a prophet sent to the Hellenic Egyptians.[175] Hermes through his disciple Asclepius (or Tat) is seen as the progenitor of this Syrian sect whence Hermeticism enters the Islamic sphere.[176] He plays an important role in Illuminationist visions of the self as the perfect nature, visions that recall the opening of the Poimandrean dialogues of the *Corpus Hermeticum*.[177]

Given the significance of the Illuminationist appeal to the Orient, both the Neoplatonic and Hermetic heritages were seen as unified prophetic 'revelations' from Syria handed down to the Arabs, quite distinct from philo-hellenic Peripatetics who looked to Alexandria and Athens for their 'roots'.[178] It is Syria that is the homeland of the 'theosist philosophers (*al-falāsifa al-muta'allihīn*).[179] It is these philosophers who are involved not only in metaphysics and *divinalia* (*ilāhiyyāt*), but also consider philosophy a spiritual practice that emulates God.[180]

To illustrate the usage of ancient thought both Neoplatonic and Hermetic, one may cite the example of Mullā Ṣadrā's discussion of the precedent of the ancients in support of his postulation that the body and the soul are distinct and that the true abode of the soul is the higher noetic realm in *safar* IV on the soul, *bāb* VI on the immateriality of the soul, *faṣl* II on the transmitted precedents on this point.[181] Ṣadrā begins with a discussion of scriptural sources. First, he cites a number of Qur'anic verses that he adduces to support his case on the origins of the human soul and its reversion to God. Second, he adduces *ḥadīth* material that places in his view the soul in the higher intelligible world and how a meditation upon the nature of the soul and self-knowledge leads to a proper understanding of the nature of God. Third, he turns to the claims of the 'ancients' (*al-awā'il*). Fourth, he cites the sayings of the classical Sufis such as Abū Yazīd Basṭāmī. Fifth, he narrates some *ḥadīth* from the Shi'i Imams. Finally, he reports the positions of the mediaeval Sufi authorities such as Ghazālī. All of these sources are deployed to make his point (which he has proven philosophically in the previous *faṣl*) that there is a spiritual substance (*jawhar rūḥānī*) in humans whose origin is in the higher previous world and that this substance is called the rational soul and it is ontologically and *actually* distinct from the body.[182]

I want to discuss in some detail the third part on the claims of the ancients.[183] Ṣadrā begins with a citation from the *Theologia Aristotelis* of the famous passage of the soul doffing the body adapted from Plotinus' *Enneads* IV.8.1:

> Oftentimes I have been alone with my soul and I have doffed my body aside and become as if I am a substance without a body so that I enter into my essence, separate from everything else. I see beauty and ecstasy in my essence and due to it, I become completely amazed. Then I know that I am a part of the divine and noble world that possesses active life. When I realised that, I ascended with my mind from this world to the divine world and I became as if I were placed in it and attached to it. So I was above the whole of the intelligible world.[184]

This passage also posits the possibility of the soul's union with the One as it involves not only the beatific vision of the noetic realm but an ascension beyond to the very presence of the divine.

After another two short quotations from the *Theologia* to state that the soul is not the same as the body, he cites Empedocles, but this again is adapted through the same chapter in the *Theologia*:

> Indeed the soul was in a lofty, noble place. But when it committed a sin, it fell to this world fleeing from the wrath of God. When it descended, it became a succour for those souls whose intellects had become contaminated [by attachment to the body] . . . So he [Empedocles] called in a loud voice to the people and commanded them to reject this world and return to their

Presocratics and Hellenic philosophers; it deals with *muthos* and not *logos*.

Next, Ṣadrā turns to the Pythagorean *Golden Verses* that were extant at his time, citing an advice to Diogenes: 'If you leave this body, you will become at that time suspended in a higher atmosphere when you will be journeying without returning to humanity [corporeality] and yet you will not be dead'.

Ṣadrā concludes the section with three citations of the *doxa* on the 'divine Plato' on this theme, again taken from the same chapter of the *Theologia*. The first citation alludes to the parable of the cave: the soul is 'imprisoned' in the body as if it were in a cave, and he links this with Empedocles' description of the body as a cage. The second addresses the reasons for the 'fall' of the soul citing the *Phaedrus*: 'The cause of the fall of the soul to this world is the shedding of its wings; if it could re-grow them, it could ascend to its first world'.[187]

Finally, he cites a passage from the *Timaeus* outlining a more positive reason for the descent of the soul:

> The cause of the Creator sending the soul to this world and making it reside in it and then sending our souls and making them reside in our bodies is in order to make this world complete and perfect, for if it were not, this world would not possess perfection or completion, because it is necessary for there to be in the sensible world (*al-ʿālam al-ḥissī*) genera of living things that are in the intelligible world (*al-ʿālam al-ʿaqlī*).[188]

Thus, this last citation relates the reason for the descent of the soul to the Platonic principle of plenitude. What this examination of one passage on the critical concept of the soul demonstrates is Ṣadrā's use upon a variety of texts at the centre of which is the paramount *Theologia Aristotelis*. Since all philosophical authority has a divine origin, it does not matter that he cites scripture alongside Neoplatonic texts, Sufi authors alongside the Shiʿi Imams: truth is a universal good that is manifest in multiple modulated disclosures.

Ṣadrā drew upon this rich variety of sources and often his ideas are elucidated and better understood when juxtaposed with those texts, even if one refers to Greek and other non-Arabic originals.[189] He himself tells us that he had mastered all philosophy that came before him including the doctrines of the ancients that suggests the Pre-Socratics as well as the Hermetists.[190] He engages with them directly. He argues points against the texts attributed to Hermes and Porphyry, Avicenna and Suhrawardī as if they were his contemporaries. Understanding the sources of philosophy in the Safavid and the context of Ṣadrā, and his ways of citing authorities and argument, is critical to a reading of his texts.

The *Asfār* is a rich text woven from these various traditions, Islamic and pre-

2 The modulation of being (*tashkīk al-wujūd*)

> What is called for is not the preference for the One over the Many, an exclusive mystical absorption in the former as the sole ultimate reality, but an awareness of the *coordinate* ontologic status of the realm of the many existents and Existence. The task of elaborating in adequate detail the lineaments of such a coordinative analysis of the two sides or dimensions of existence, of existents and Existence, is the major task of philosophy.[1]

The notion of *tashkīk* lies at the heart of the primitive ontological struggle to reconcile one's phenomenal experience of multiplicity, of many existents, with the notion of unity, of One Being.[2] The apparent conflict between unity and diversity is a major theme in Neoplatonism, especially in the work of Proclus [d. 485].[3] In early Islamic Neoplatonism, Kindī draws upon the discussion in Proclus' *Platonic Theology* to animate his discourse on the relationship between the One and the many in *On First Philosophy*.[4] The common Platonic and Neoplatonic solution to the problem is to pose a scalar hierarchy in reality, a vision of degrees in a singular reality. It is widely accepted, following Vlastos, that Plato regarded reality as graded since there were necessarily gradations within the Forms that constituted 'reality as such'.[5] Modulation thus represents a (Neo)platonic vein in Islamic philosophy and exemplifies the Neoplatonic paradigm that I propose for a study of the Sadrian method.

The Sadrian affirmation of modulation of being by intensity is an attempt to solve the problem of unity and plurality. It offers an holistic account of the structure of reality and its internal relationships and correspondence with other modes and realms of being such as the mental and the propositional. Most significantly, it extends the logical insight of the *pros hen* homonymy of the term 'being' to a descriptive metaphysics of the nature of the 'pyramid of being' in extra-mental reality. The proof of *tashkīk* in each mode lies in the following central characteristics.

First, there must be what I shall term Core Dependent Homonymy (CDH) modifying Shields' definition:

> CDH: a and b are homonymously F in a core dependent way iff: i) they have their name in common, ii) their definitions do not overlap *completely*, and iii) necessarily if a is a core instance of F-ness, then b's being F stands in one of the four causal relations to a's being F.[6]

Second, there must be an ordered hierarchic scale, such as by intensity, or by priority and posteriority that applies to the four senses of being. These four modes of being are discussed in the semantic part [*De Interpretatione*] of Ṣadrā's logical epitome,

> The being of a thing is either actual or mental (*ʿaynī wa dhihnī*), and spoken or written (*lafẓī wa kutubī*). The former two are 'real' (*ḥaqīqī*) and the latter two are conventional (*waḍʿī*).[7]

Finally, each degree should in itself be essentially privative such that it derives its reality from its place in the scale in relation to its principle (*al-mabdaʾ*). These three stages are critical for effecting *tashkīk* in the logic of being proposed by Ṣadrā.

A note on translation

We need to examine how we might translate *tashkīk* or the *tertium quid* of the Late Antiquity. First, let us consider 'systematic ambiguity'. It is a phrase used by Russell to posit a hierarchy of mutually related symbols of different logical types within the same class.[8] Owen uses it to explain '*pros hen* equivocation' in Aristotle.[9] Rahman uses this term to describe the Sadrian theory.[10] Klima uses it within a Thomist context for explaining Aquinas' theory of the analogy of being.[11]

Others use the notion of analogy well known among Thomists, and 'gradation', attested in Neoplatonic explanations of reality.[12] Nasr has 'gradation of being'.[13] Corbin describes this Neoplatonic scale of being as 'degrés de l'échelle de l'être'.[14] Monnot gives us 'intensification et l'ambiguité de l'être'.[15] Similarly, Jambet has 'l'intensification des actes d'être'.[16] Izutsu has 'analogicity' and 'analogical gradation',[17] and describes *mushakkak* reality as 'the existence of degrees in gradual increase of intensity'.[18] *Mushakkak* for him is analogical and graded because all degrees of being have the same ontological principle.[19] Leaman sticks with the term 'equivocity'.[20] Madkur has 'ambiguitas'.[21] However, if being were a mere equivocal, a unified science of metaphysics, of being *qua* being, would be impossible.[22] Our philosopher thinks that the various extensions of being are related and modulated.

Wolfson uses the concept of amphiboly, which he regards as a more accurate description for the predication of the different senses by being in Aristotle and later mediaeval philosophy.[23] His use of amphiboly is in preference to ambiguity, which is far vaguer and less precise. He derives the term from Alexander of Aphrodisias' commentary on Aristotle's *Topics* 110 b 16–7,[24] in which he describes the difference of meanings that are not homonymous but 'in some other way' as ἀμφιβολα.[25] It is Wolfson, who is possibly the source for the vocalisation *mushakkik* [*sic*] used by Bonmariage.[26] This is unusual and not attested in most texts. The correct and predominant form is *mushakkak*. Yahya Bonaud in his book on the philosophical and mystical thought of Ayatollah Khomeini [d. 1989], a thinker heavily influenced by Mullā Ṣadrā, suggests the most interesting translation: modulation.[27] Being is predicated in a modulated manner but it is also a modulated reality, whose scale is analogous to the musical scale with its intensities of tone, volume, form and content. It is the only translation that conveys a sense of unity with gradation and most importantly, intensity. However, one must not be obsessive about consistent translation. It might be better to translate *tashkīk* in four different ways to reflect the four different senses of being. But on the whole, I shall stick with modulation or more precisely modulation by intensity. *Tashkīk al-wujūd* remains an elusive concept.

Being

The problem of being lies at the heart of the metaphysical discourse of both Western and Islamic philosophy, initiated by the discussions of the verb 'be' in Parmenides.[28] Even in the present century, Heidegger privileges this question (*Seinsfrage*), giving it ontological priority.[29] For him, as for Ṣadrā, the study of the meaning of being is critical. While he criticises the mediaevals for their doctrines of the apriority, indefinability and 'unavailability of being, our philosopher takes these as part of a critical paradox that makes scientific inquiry possible.[30] Sadrian foundationalism is predicated upon this concatenation of ontological doctrines.

Al-wujūd (being) is a verbal noun derived from the root W-J-D that denotes 'finding' and 'what is found'.[31] For the mystics, being is a term that is univocally (and hence exclusively) applied to God.[32] If it is applied to contingents, then its usage is metaphorical.[33] ʿAbd al-Razzāq Kāshānī [d. 1337], the famous Shiʿi Sufi and follower of Ibn ʿArabī, described being as the finding of Truth and union as the presence of being.[34] Thus it is a mode of the divine essence that is free of all determination; it is being *qua* being (*al-wujūd al-baḥt*).[35] All relational being (*al-wujūd al-iḍāfī*) is in fact privative (*maʿdūm*) and only has 'reality' attributed to it by virtue of its correlation to 'the face of the Truth' (*wajh al-ḥaqq*).[36] Already here, we may discern three modes of being: divine being that is the only mode worthy of the name 'being', the general concept of being that is akin to Aristotle's being insofar as it is 'being', and being applied to other-than-God is a relational and annexational manner because their sense of being is 'annexed' by the Necessary Being of God.

For Ṣadrā, what is found is not just the divine reality for that would entail a pure monism. The reality of 'being *qua* being' and its concept are *a priori*.[37] But being is not just an immediate concept; it is also a modulated reality. In the Sufi tradition, the concept of being alone is *a priori*, while its reality is ontologically prior but cognitively hidden.[38] Being is a given without which nothing can exist but it is elusive to the attempts of humans to grasp its meaning. The concept of Being is intuited (but not known) *a priori* (*badīhī*) since it has no definition, as it has neither a form nor an essence.[39] Because it has neither a genus nor a differentia,[40] it has no definition since it has no quiddity, the essence that is rendered by the definition.[41] Hence it cannot be a true universal with individuals who participate in its universality.[42] In a chapter in the first *safar* of the *Asfār* on the nature of the Necessary Being,

Ṣadrā deals with the objection that being (and indeed the Necessary) is a universal in which individuals share:

> An objection and its clarification:
>
> You might claim that being is a natural species [i.e. an essence] and argue by stating that it is a singular concept shared by all things. Now a nature does not allow for its concomitants to differ, rather it is necessary for each individual to be the same . . .
>
> The individual [instance]s of the concept of being are not different realities; rather, being is a singular reality and its commonality among beings is not like the commonality of a universal nature, whether essential or accidental, among its individuals. Universality and particularity are the properties of contingent essences, but being as has been explained is neither universal nor particular. Being is self-determining by its very identity and it does not require for its being another because its being is its very essence. We will explain in the discussion on modulation that difference between levels of a singular reality and distinction between their occurrences may be due to that reality itself. So the reality of being is of those things attached essentially to determinations and particularisations, and priority and posteriority, and necessity and contingency, and substantiality and accidentality, and perfection and imperfection, not due to something extrinsic to it that is accidental to it. Conceiving [this point] requires a noble mind and a subtle nature.[43]

Being is not a *summum genera* in which individuals beings participate as 'portions' of being. The apriority of being entails that essences are accidental to it because essences are not intuited *a priori* since they are not *per se* necessary.[44] Any account of being that postulates a form for it *in re* is futile and a falsification of reality since it is merely a mode of that ineffable 'thing' that is being.[45] The self-evidence refers to the reality of being insofar as it is intuited within one's phenomenological experience. Ṣadrā says:

> The reality of being is the most evident of things (*ajlá al-ashyā'*) by its presence and its inner-revelation (*ḥuḍūran wa-kashfan*), and its 'quiddity' is the most hidden (*akhfá*) of things in conception and its inner-reality (*taṣawwuran wa-ktināhan*).[46]

One cannot communicate knowledge of being since it does not have formal, *discursive* content. It requires acquaintance and not acquisition, though a weak and imperfect form of the latter is grasped through the 'traces' of being.[47] True being is apprehended directly by the existential cognising subject through cognitive presential vision (*al-ʿilm al-ḥuḍūrī al-shuhūdī*).[48] Theological definitions of 'being' as what can be predicated are inadequate.[49] Being has three main realms: mental, linguistic and extra-mental. The concept and reality of being are quite distinct; the former is a secondary intelligible posited in the mind whose reference is the reality of being in the extra-mental realm.[50]

Precedents and background

Sadrian modulation has a significant genealogy. Aristotle tells us at the beginning of book Z of the *Metaphysics* that 'there are several senses in what a thing may be said to "be" (*ta onta legetai pollakos*)'.[51] In the *Topics*, he distinguishes between words that have many meanings and singular meanings and Alexander in his commentary tells us that this is the distinction between homonyms (*homōnoma*) and ambiguities (*amphibola*).[52] But it could also be argued, as Alexander does, that the very fact of dividing being into the different senses that are the categories entails a homonymy.[53] Brentano's thoughtful meditation upon this issue discusses the fourfold senses of being as a multivocal homonym: accidental being, truth, predication, and the division between potential and actual being.[54] The first significant philosopher in the Islamic tradition, Abū Naṣr Fārābī [d. 950] follows this with a threefold scheme of the homonymy of being: being across the categories, being as actual and potential and as affirmation and negation.[55] To be sure, the early history of homonymy in the Hellenic tradition was a meditation upon the functions and meaning of the theory of categories. This Aristotelian semantics of being was extended in Neoplatonism and one could try to map *tashkīk* onto it. Within the Neoplatonic hierarchy of being, the existence predicate is a scalar and comparative adjective that corresponds to levels of reality.[56] In fact, Lloyd writes, 'Can we not read the Neoplatonic Being/Existence as a system in which hypostases, processions, and the affairs of men are waves and ripples on, or rather of, a single substrate?'[57]

However, for Porphyry, ambiguity and multivocity refer to words and sentences that are not features of reality. They do not even have reference within our minds and our mental language.[58] This suggests that one must be careful in reading too much back into Neoplatonic antecedents. However, the proposition that reality was composed of grades and modes of being was widely accepted in Neoplatonic circles.[59] Degrees within reality and within *nous* are major themes in Proclus' commentary on Plato's *Parmenides*.[60] So we have the idea of being as a scalar concept as well as a singular reality.

Aristotle has two senses of scales: priority by nature and by relation.[61] Ṣadrā articulates the Aristotelian point by distinguishing between priority by nature and priority by intensity.[62] Being is neither predicated synonymously nor is it purely homonymous but constitutes three types of scales: by being prior or posterior, by precedence and privation (*aphairēsis*), and by intensity.[63] Avicenna allows for five sets of priority–posteriority relationships: by rank (*martaba*), by nature (*ṭabʿ*), by excellence (*sharaf*), by time (*zamān*) and by essential cause (*ʿilla dhātiyya*).[64] Avicenna's disciple, Bahmanyār [d. 1066] argues that such different kinds of priority, related to one other, demonstrate an instance of predication by *tashkīk*.[65] It is clear, therefore, that the Avicennan tradition allowed for a form of *pros hen* homonymy. For Avicenna, however, being cannot be prior or posterior through intensity.[66] There can be no intensity within substance because substances are unchanging subjects of change and the substrates in which changeable properties inhere.[67] But Ṣadrā settles on intensity as the defining principle of *tashkīk*:[68] 'The predication of being by *tashkīk* means 'by precedence and priority' (*al-awlawiyya wa-l-awwaliyya*), and by being more prior and more intense (*al-aqdamiyya wa-l-ashaddiyya*)'.[69]

It is the notion of intensification and debilitation within being where being is both the principle of commonality and differentiation that marks out *tashkīk* from a CDH.[70] The fact that being admits of degrees rules it out as a genus according to Aristotle,[71] and makes it a Porphyrian quasi-genus that is predicated neither synonymously or homonymously but by a *tertium quid* with a focal meaning.[72]

That being admits of degrees was a widely accepted idea among Islamic philosophers. Peripatetic commentators influenced by Suhrawardī held intensity within being through the use of the famous Neoplatonic metaphor of light.[73] Avicenna's primary commentator in the mediaeval period, Naṣīr al-Dīn Ṭūsī [d. 1274] insisted in his commentary on *al-Ishārāt wa-l-tanbīhāt* criticising Rāzī's position that being was not merely a shared word between the divine and the human. Rāzī's mistake was due to his ignorance of the principle of *tashkīk* that had led him to assert the univocity of being with respect to God.[74] He stated quite explicitly that 'being is predicated of things differently by *tashkīk*',[75] arguing that the meaning of being was shared across its referents in a graded scale of intensity.[76] The discussion appears in *faṣl* VI (*ishāra*) of *namaṭ* IV on the causal relationship between being and essence. Ṭūsī writes:

> The respected commentator [Fakhr al-Dīn Rāzī] really did confuse himself on this point. And he assumed that the minds and intellects of philosophers were also confused by it. He inferred that being is applied to all existents by commonality of the term (*bi-l-ishtirāk al-lafẓī*), adducing many proofs to yield this. After that, he judged that being was a singular thing in everything equally such that he asserted that the being of the Necessary was [understood] in the same sense as the being of contingents – God forefend. Then because he considered the being of contingents to be something accidental to their essence, and since he had already judged that the being of the Necessary is taken in the same sense as the being of contingents, he judged that the being of the Necessary was also accidental to his essence. So his essence is not his being – God greatly transcends [such nonsense] – and he conjectured that if he did not make the being of the Necessary accidental to his essence, it would either entail that:
>
> His being was equivalent to caused beings,
>
> Or that being is applied to the being of the Necessary and the being of other-than-him by the commonality of the term.
>
> The source of this fallacy is ignorance of the meaning of predication by *tashkīk*. A term that applies to many different things by *tashkīk* does not apply through the commonality of the term such as the application of the term *ʿayn* to its different meanings, but rather, in one sense in everything but not equally such as the application of 'human' to individuals, but differentiated either:
>
> by priority and posteriority (*bi-l-taqaddum wa-l-ta'akhkhur*) such as the application of continuous to a measure and to a body possessing measure,
>
> or by precedence and its privation (*bi-l-awlawiyya wa-ʿadamihā*) such as

> the application of one to what cannot be divided and to what can be divided in another sense that is not that by which is it one,
>
> or by intensity and debilitation (*bi-l-shidda wa-l-ḍuʿf*) such as the application of white to ice and to ivory. For, being comprises all of these differentiations. It applies to the cause and its effect by priority and posteriority, to substance and accident by precedence and its privation, and to the motive and the motionless by intensity and debilitation. In fact, it applies to the Necessary and the contingent in all three senses. The single sense that is predicated of different things unequally makes it impossible for it to be the essence or part of the essence of these three because essence does not differ and nor does its part; rather, it [essence] is merely accidental and extrinsic, concomitant and separate.[77]

Thus, we can already see in Ṭūsī's formulation two sets of notions about modulation that are critical for Mullā Ṣadrā: first, that modulation occurs in these three sets of scales, and second, that it is being and *not* essence that is modulated.

The notion that there were sets of things that could be predicated by *tashkīk* was fairly common in mediaeval Islamic philosophy. Mītham Baḥrānī [d. 1280] used *tashkīk* for the soul and posited degrees of intellect using intensity.[78] Suhrawardī himself argued that the hierarchy of light is *mushakkak*.[79] Critically, he asserted that 'the totality of light (for which read 'being' in the Sadrian sense) in itself differs by perfection and imperfection'.[80] He also allowed for degrees of intensity within his categories, while retaining a sceptical position on the reality of being.[81] Ṣadrā equates light with being and sees in it the ultimate argument for *tashkīk*, that the principle of differentiation is the principle of commonality.[82] Thus, being admits of degrees of more or less and is itself the principle of distinction.

> Being is a single, simple reality having neither genus nor differentia, nor a definition or a demonstration or a *definiens*. It only admits of degrees by perfection and deficiency (*bi-l-kamāl wa-l-naqṣ*), by priority and posteriority (*al-taqaddum wa-l-ta'akhkhur*) and by independence and dependence (*bi-l-ghiná wa-l-ḥāja*).[83]

The critical feature that ensures the unity in diversity of being, or the 'identity-in-difference' is the principle that being is both that which provides commonality (*mā bihi-l-ishtirāk*) of things as well as that which differentiates things (*mā bihi-l-ikhtilāf*).[84] The Sadrian doctrine borrowed from Suhrawardī's concept of intensity within a scale and replaced 'essence' with being allowing for commonality and difference, for features of univocity and homonymy.[85] The notion of intensity within the scale of being is a critical determinant for Ṣadrā and pervades later discussions.[86] Following Ṭūsī (as we have seen above), Mullā Ṣadrā held that essences are indeterminate and fixed.[87] What is also significant is that this is an Illuminationist departure from the Peripatetic denial of 'intensity' in being.[88] For Avicenna, *tashkīk* of being remains an ontologically innocent concept that does not commit him to the gradation or intensity in being that are so critical to Ṣadrā's account. Merely positing a CDH is insufficient. But the Peripatetic tradition was ambiguous on this issue since Ṭūsī in his commentary on *al-Ishārāt wa-l-tanbīhāt* clearly allows for intensity in being in his critique of Rāzī on the predication of being as we have seen.[89]

The school of Ibn ʿArabī posited grades in reality depending on the intensity of manifestation and emanation (*tashkīk fī-l-marātib wa-l-maẓāhir*) from the Truth.[90] For Ibn ʿArabī, the emanation and unfolding of reality is graded according to a range of intensities.[91] The more one moves away from the One, the less intense and more privative being becomes. The first creation that is the Intellect, or the Muḥammadan reality, is already dependent, privative and limited in relation to the One.[92] Sayyid Ḥaydar Āmulī [d. after 1385], the mediaeval Shiʿi Sufi and follower of Ibn ʿArabī, had a thoroughly graded sense of reality.[93] He also posited three senses of being: *qua* being, *qua* reality and *qua* mental concept.[94] Yet at same time, unlike our philosopher, but like Dāwūd Qayṣarī [d. 1350], he denied any *tashkīk* in the reality of being, because the true referent of being is God and there cannot be gradation in the Godhead.[95] The primary instance of the reference of being is always God; the secondary figurative locus of reference for the term may be man.[96] At that secondary level, one might use the term *tashkīk* to refer to the modulation in the manifestations of divine being but not in the reality of being itself.[97] Thus there is, in a sense, a sharp distinction between the reality of Being and being. The reality of Being (*al-wujūd al-Ḥaqq*) is God, who is hidden, while 'being' is a manifest concept (*al-wujūd al-ʿāmm*) that is intuited by the mind *a priori*.[98] The Sufi tendency towards monism is a constant problematic in the attempts at reconciling unity and multiplicity.

Muḥsin Fayḍ Kāshānī [d. 1680], Ṣadrā's eminent student and son-in-law, bridges the pure mystical vision of *tashkīk* with the Sadrian in his metaphysical work, *Uṣūl al-maʿārif* (Principles of mystical knowledge):

> Being comprehends things like a flow (*sarayān*) and pervades (*inbisāṭ*) the forms of existents through an imperceptible flow. It is particular, and individuated and differentiated in degrees according to the quiddities united [to the individual existents] by modulation (*tashkīk*). Beings are realities individuated essentially, and also differentiated by their very reality [of being]. They share in the common notion of existentiality, which is an intentional factor.[99]

What is clear from this extract is that the scale of being is not a static hierarchy but constantly changing. The unity of semantic content entails a unified sense of reality.[100] But it was only with Ṣadrā that it became associated with *tashkīk*.

Another sense of the gradation of reality in the Akbarian tradition is the doctrine of the divine presences that are levels of reality, and are articulated in the thought of Qūnawī [d. 1274] and Qayṣarī.[101] ʿAbd al-Razzāq Kāshānī[102] provides us with a description of six presences or emanations of the One. The first, most pure and free of determination is *al-dhāt al-aḥadiyya* (the unitive essence). At the second level of the divine essence relating to His attributes we have *al-ḥaḍra al-ilāhiyya* (divine presence) of singularity (*wāḥidiyya*). At the third level lies the realm of incorporeal souls (*al-arwāḥ al-mujarrada*). The fourth level is the isthmus, the intermediary of agent-souls (*al-nufūs al-ʿāmila*), that is the imaginal world (*ʿālam al-mithāl*). The fifth presence is the phenomenal world of our everyday experience (*ʿālam al-mulk*). Finally, the comprehensive being (*kawn*) is the Perfect Man (*al-insān al-kāmil*), who manifests all these presences in a comprehensive form.[103]

A key aspect of the Sufi monorealistic vision of being is the denial of reality of phenomenal being and a sense of dubitability with respect to affirming what one encounters. In this sense, it is worth noting that the *tashkīk* carries within it the root matter of doubt (SH-K-K). The lexical sense of doubt that *tashkīk* connotes is significant. Dictionary definitions yield 'action d'élever des doutes' and 'awakening of doubt', 'skeptical remark'.[104] Dozy has 'ambiguë' for *mushakkak*.[105] Ibn Manẓūr [d. 1312] juxtaposes it with certainty, its opposite.[106] Doubt and negation bring to mind the '*aphairēsis*' (privation) and '*sterēsis*' (negation) of being in Neoplatonism.[107] Different manifestations and degrees of being ultimately are privative and annexed to the being of the One. *Tashkīk* requires us to doubt the ontological independence of each degree and level of being. This sense of being recalls Aristotle's accidental being that is 'obviously akin to non-being'.[108]

Semantics and the 'onymies'

In Avicennan semantics, universals are predicated of their individuals either by univocity (*al-tawāṭu'*) or homonymy *(al-ittifāq, al-ishtirāk*).[109] What is shared in homonymy is not the sense or the intension of the term but the semantic form or the extension of the term. There is also a *tertium quid*, *tashkīk*, which describes terms that are predicated by modulation. Avicenna considers two types of *mushakkak* terms, the first undergoes intensification in sense and the second is the Aristotelian *pros hen* (*bi-ḥasab al-nisba ilá mabda' wāḥid*) homonymy.[110] This draws upon the famous opening chapter of Aristotle's *Categories* on the 'onymies': synonymy, homonymy and paronymy.[111] Category theory is a form of logical 'sorting' with profound ontological implications. The roots of the logic of homonymy arguably lie in the famous attack of Plotinus on the *Categories* because of their problematic ontological commitments.[112]

Synonymous or univocal predication is where the different names are predicated of the same semantic form and of the same concept in all instances.[113] One can use the following definition for synonymy: x and y are synonyms iff (i) both are F and (ii) definitions corresponding to 'F' in 'x is F' and 'y is F' are the same.[114]

For Suhrawardī, being is a prime example of an intentional concept that is predicated univocally (*bi-maʿná wāḥid*) of its instances.[115] It has been argued that one of the results of Avicennan radical contingency that is proved through an affirmation of the distinction between the existence and essence of contingents is that being is fixed as a univocal concept that is added by God to the essence of potentials.[116] This is clearly a mistake since Avicennan metaphysics relies upon the multivocity of 'being' to affirm the unity of the science of metaphysics.[117] Being for Avicenna is indeed *mushtarak* (homonymous) but not merely so.[118]

Bahmanyār, Avicenna's student, defines *mushakkak* predication as the modulation of senses of a name whose name and concepts are one but 'not equally so'.[119]

Mushakkak homonymy is not mere homonymy (*ishtirāk*); in fact Avicenna makes it clear that being is a case of 'special homonymy' and is a *mushakkak* and *not* a *mushtarak* term.[120] Mere homonymy (*al-muttafiqa*), or 'discrete homonymy', occurs when names are shared, and their significations 'resemble' but their definitions do not overlap.[121] The example that Avicenna gives is 'foot', which is applied to a part of a table, and an animal's limb.[122] What is clear is that in Avicennan semantics, what is shared is a 'word' and concept, and not an essence as such, in opposition to Aristotelian denomination where homonymy refers in the first instance to the thing itself, and secondarily to the concept and the word.[123] *Tashkīk* therefore refers to a shared property of words with the same meaning predicated across their 'names'. It describes a relationship between two primary modes of being, mental and extra-mental, a relationship in which the principle of differentiation is identical to the principle of commonality. Being was a term shared across categories (whether interpreted in a realist or nominalist sense), and was said in many ways.[124] Types of homonymy were discussed in late Antiquity. Porphyry commented that apart from discrete homonymy, there were four other types which were mutually related: similarity, analogy, focal and same-goal oriented.[125] It is the focal or *pros hen* type that interests us here. Ṣadrā sums up the controversy over the three types of denomination and makes his preference for focal homonymy or modulation (*tashkīk*):

> People differ over whether the term 'being' is shared [homonymously predicated] among different concepts, or is univocally (*mutawāṭin*) predicated of existents in a singular sense without any distinction, or whether it is modulated (*mushakkak*)[126] across all things in a singular but non-uniform (*lā ʿalá l-sawāʾ*) sense of the 'entity'. This [latter] is the truth.[127]

An important point to note on the denomination of being is that it has reference in extra-mental reality and is not a 'universal' as such, nor is it a name of secondary imposition (*mushtaqq*), that is a class of names that are defined morphologically.[128] Ṣadrā is very keen in the *Asfār* to criticise the argument of Jalāl al-Dīn Davānī [d. 1501] and stress that neither is metaphysics a study of names of second imposition that have no reality, nor is being such a name.[129] If being were such a name, it would be a genus and as such unreal, lacking reference in extra-mental reality while being purely mental and a universal in the soul.[130] Furthermore, such names of second imposition were predicated univocally (*bi-l-tawāṭuʾ*) of their mental referents.[131] They cannot apply to the categories that are the *summa genera* of things.[132] Islamic philosophers were familiar with the theory of the imposition of names and it is in this context that one ought to consider the issue of the *mushtaqq*.[133]

The extension of being and a question of *Theology*

What sort of 'commonality' does being possess? Either the semantic form is shared (*ishtirāk lafẓī*) or the semantic content is shared (*ishtirāk maʿnawī*). Thus being is not regarded as a mere homonym. It is critical to differentiate between the two to avoid the trap of considering the notion of being across its instances to be ambiguous in Ṣadrā as Rahman does.[134] It is misleading to consider *tashkīk* simply as ambiguity in Ṣadrā.

The first position was held by those who interpreted being in a thoroughly intentional and abstracted sense, as a 'super-genus' that cut across the *Categories* that were seen as grouping principles.[135] Even the modalities and predication were interpreted in a non-realist sense. Suhrawardī held that being as a common concept across categories made purely semantic and syntactic sense without reference.[136] Acceptance of modalities is not sufficient to realise modulation.[137] The proponents of this position were keen to safeguard the ontological distinction between Creator and creature, between being and existent.[138] True being was only God and there could be no real shared sense and reality of being across the senses of the term.[139] For others such as the Illuminationist philosopher Shams al-Dīn Shahrazūrī this was strengthened by the fact that being is a meaningful concept but not a predicate and was unreal.[140] The Illuminationist tradition insisted that being lacked reference and was merely a term derived from one's experience of essences that are, a meaning derived (*al-maʿná al-maṣdarī*) from those essences that is a 'being of reason'. Mīr Dāmād [d. 1631], Mullā Ṣadrā's own teacher and the prominent representative of that tradition at the time, asserted both in *al-Qabasāt* and *al-Ufuq al-mubīn* that being was nothing but a term that arises in the mind to describe the fact that an essence exists.[141] Mullā Ṣadrā was keen to refute this position and insist that being had reference and was more than a mere mental consideration of an essence because without the reality of being, the concept of modulation could not be extended beyond homonymy of terms.

Such a position is in fact the 'homonymy' of being, since the same word has different meanings that are not shared. The Neoplatonic tradition in Ismaili philosophy was more radical. God was regarded as a *deus absconditus*, a *hyper-ousion* that was beyond being.[142] The divine reality was utterly ineffable and impossible to articulate.[143] A true believer should avoid ascribing positive attributes to God; rather *via negativa*, the way of Pseudo-Dionysius was preferable.[144] God was beyond being and utterly unknowable, whether by *doxa*, *nous* or *epistēmē*.[145] Being could only (grudgingly) be applied to creatures; in fact in some accounts it was held that being was not a predicate as an adjunct to a denial of an ontological proof for the existence of God in ways similar to Kant's famous refutation. Being could not be ascribed to God because, in true Plotinian style, being was only applicable to the determined and the limited.[146] Or in Aristotelian terms, if God were a being, then he would either be a substance or an accident.[147] For the Ismaili philosopher Ḥamīd al-Dīn Kirmānī [d. *c*. 1021], every *ays* was *mu'ayyas*.[148] Apophasis was upheld and the '*docta ignorantia*' celebrated both in the *Theologia Aristotelis* and Ismaili texts.[149]

also adhered to a thoroughly apophatic theology.[151] The latter rejected any analogy between the One as principle of 'making' (*jaʿl*) and creation; being is univocally applied to the One and homonymously to the many.[152] Therefore, *ishtirāk maʿnawī* and *tashkīk* are categorically ruled out.[153] But even this apophatic tradition is not uniform: some rejected the application of being to God absolutely, while others such as Aḥmad Aḥsā'ī [d. 1826], held to a *deus determinus* as being, but unlike other beings.[154] He argues that being cannot be applied to God and to creatures in the same sense since a concept is derivative and ontologically posterior to the source of derivation. God and humanity cannot be extracted from the same source (*sinkh*). In fact, he argues that such a position renders God as incipient as His creatures.[155] He insists that being only is applied univocally to the True One.[156]

For their opponents who upheld *ishtirāk maʿnawī*,[157] the ontological distinction was retained through the existence–essence distinction in contingents that did not obtain in the Necessary.[158] The process of ontologising the One in Arabic Neoplatonism had begun early in the Kindī circle, or even arguably in Porphyry since he used the term being to apply to God in his commentary on Plato's *Parmenides*.[159] The *Theologia* described the One as an entity or being (*anniyya*), and used the same term to describe existent entities both among *intelligibilia* and entities in the sublunary world.[160] The One was brought into the domain of being further by the attribution of intentionality to it, a far remove from the Plotinian rejection of the simple unintellecting One.[161] The separation of intellect from the One, the first act of boldness (*tolma*) and awareness of existential alterity (*heterotēs*) through desire for the sensible begins the procession of being.[162] If one accepts the hypothesis that the *Theologia* is based upon Porphyry's commentary (*tafsīr*), as the text claims, then *anniyya* is not a translation of the Plotinian '*onta*' or '*on*' but the Porphyryian *ontotēs*.[163] Similarly, Kindī, in his *On First Philosophy*, uses *al-inniyya* for existence, since he argues that it is derived from an inquiry about whether something exists.[164] Frank argues for a Syriac provenance of the term and insists that it translates '*to einai*' or '*ti esti*' and not '*to on*' (following the Arabic translation of *Metaphysics* 1026 b 31) thus allowing for a more processual reading of being as opposed to concrete existing substance.[165] The term once naturalised in Arabic metaphysics becomes a standard way of referring to divine being, a usage in which one finds it in Avicenna's *al-Shifā'*.[166] Of course, ontologising the One immediately raises the problem of the one and the many. Once we have predicated being of the One, we have introduced duality. Even the Hermetic tradition, whilst holding onto God the *hyper-ousion*, as the cause of being but not existent itself, ontologises the 'Pre-existent' as the 'summit of all beings and of all real existents'.[167]

This apophatic tradition, however, remains plunged in equivocation.[168] The problem is that one wishes to ontologise the One to make sense of theology and

iman (Establishment of faith), Mulla Ṣadra's teacher Mir Damad struggles with this problem. God and contingents share a real sense of the term 'being' but God is still set apart as the principle of the chain of being (*mabda' silsilat al-wujūd*).[173]

Tashkīk was used by Ṭūsī to explain Avicenna's position on how there must be a shared concept of being for the term to apply to both *sensibilia* and *intelligibilia*.[174] The position is further proven by the possibility of divisions of being that retain focal sense.[175] His student, the Shi'i theologian Ibn Muṭahhar al-Ḥillī [d. 1325], argued pointedly that it was only with such a position that theology could be meaningful, since theological inquiry depends on the possibility of speaking meaningfully of attributes and concepts that are analogical in relations between the Creator and the created.[176] If one assumes that the only analogy between the Necessary and the contingent is merely the word 'being' suffixed to them, then theology leads to agnosticism.[177] Such a position was a specific critique of the Ash'arite position that denied analogy between divine and human attributes, and assumed that being was a purely homonymous term.[178] Some Sunni theologians with philosophical tastes did insist upon a meaningful analogy between divine and contingent being.[179] But Rāzī has an unusual approach: he suggests that being is univocally applied among contingents and univocally applied for God and the two realms are quite separate.[180] However, already a generation before Ṣadrā, there was a consensus among philosophers and theologians that being was predicated of the Necessary and of contingents by *tashkīk*. In his short treatise *Tajrīd masā'il al-ḥikma* (Summation of the issues in philosophy), Ghiyāth al-Dīn Dashtakī presented a brief exposition of being with which Mullā Ṣadrā would not have disagreed and pivotal within it is an insistence upon the term 'being' as applicable to all its instances in a modulated manner:

> Being is a singular, *a priori* concept that is shared by all existents and added to essences in conception. It is synonymous with affirmation and 'being-a-thing'. It is divisible into mental and extra-mental and predicated of what it covers by *tashkīk*, multiple with many subjects.[181]

A more contemporary Iranian seminarian and philosopher, 'Allāma Ṭabāṭabā'ī [d. 1981], describes how a position of *ishtirāk lafẓī* leads to the destruction of theology and a complete agnosticism.[182] He argues that it negates the meaningful nature of simple propositions such as 'The Necessary exists' or 'The contingent exists', and marks a confusion between the notion of being and its referents.[183] The notion of being is common and the same for both Necessary and contingent but the referents of the two instances of 'being' are different. On the other hand, proofs for the shared semantic content of being rest on the possibility of dividing being into necessary and contingent, and apophatically rest upon the inference that since the contradictory of being – non-being or privation – is predicated in the same sense, then this applies to being as well.[184] Being is a term whose meaning is shared across all its instances, whether mental, extra-mental, individuals or degrees, noumenal or phenomenal.[185] Lawkarī holds several senses of being too, as does Bahmanyār in a rather traditional way of keeping the sense of the word across the Aristotelian categories, and in this sense *tashkīk* only refers to the concept of being and not its reality.[186] Without *tashkīk*, one would not be able to divide being into Necessary and contingent, one and many. Meaningful metaphysical predication demands it. Bahmanyār develops a hierarchy of being based upon a scale of all those predicated of being by 'modulation':

> Know that being is predicated of what is included within it by the predication of modulation (*al-tashkīk*) and not univocity (*al-tawāṭuʾ*). This means that the being that has no cause is prior by nature to that being which has a cause, and hence the being of substance is prior to the being of accident. Furthermore, some being is more potent, and some is less.[187]

Following Avicenna, he had already noted the different types of priority: by nature, by temporal progression, by rank, and by nobility.[188] The first one allows for intensity within being.[189] It is important to reject the univocity of being since it is clear, he argues, from our ordinary language, that the meaning of being is graded across its referents.[190] For a Sufi like Ibn ʿArabī, this 'shared sense' reflects the intimate connection between the Lord and His creatures, where the being of one entails the being of the other and stresses the reciprocity of the relation between the Beloved and His lovers.[191] This is somewhat similar, superficially, to the Thomist idea of the analogy of participation between God and creature. However, true commonality is ruled out in this Sufi metaphysics by a doctrine of *waḥdat al-wujūd* (unity and univocity of being).

We need to be cognisant of the fact that there are two types of *ishtirāk maʿnawī* according to the recent Iranian philosopher Mahdī Ḥāʾirī [d. 1999]. The first is univocally predicated of its referents, and the second is modulated with respect to its referents in degrees.[192] Rather surprisingly, he suggests that being, for Ṣadrā, is predicated univocally of its instances in a graded manner, partly because he regards him as a proponent of a mystical vision of reality which he describes as 'monorealism' (*waḥdat al-wujūd*).[193] This suggests that the predication of being is uniform throughout the scale of being.[194] It has been suggested that the metaphysics of the unity of being entails the univocity of being. This view is based on a reading of *ishtirāk maʿnawī* as univocity.[195] But this reflects a confusion between the two types of *ishtirāk maʿnawī* and is not what I mean by univocity.[196] Nor is it the intent of *tashkīk*, in which the semantic content of the term is 'shared' across its referents. Since there are different modes of being (mental, lexical, extra-mental), the semantic content is not uniform. Ṣadrā's commentator, Ṭabāṭabāʾī, says that being is a modulated singular reality and concept, and that it is a mistake to consider it to be graded and univocal.[197] Ṣadrā himself says that the predication of being is not that of univocity but of *tashkīk*.[198] It is possible that such confusion between univocity and homonymy arises out of some of the later Neoplatonic commentaries upon Aristotle's *Categories* 1 a 1 as denoting a type of synonymy.[199] The roots of the word, SH-K-K, denote homonymy in the Peripatetic tradition. This homonymous sense is required for the Sadrian scale of being. Ṣadrā wants being to be predicated in the same sense across its referents in a graded and core-dependent homonymous way for which he needs the concept of degrees and intensifying 'scale'.[200] It is through core-dependence that he can safeguard the notion of a hierarchy and ordered scale of being.[201] The core sense of being is actual and existential (or in Sufi terms, God), and in relationship to this are other senses of being understood. Indeed, *tashkīk* is the *tertium quid* of ancient philosophy, although one would need to modify CDH by adding the provision that the definitions of a and b need not be uniform but ought to share most of the conditions of identity. In a more Wittgensteinian vein, one might join Rahman in saying that, 'existents are . . . like "family faces" which have something in common yet each is unique'.[202]

One further point needs to be made about the development of the doctrine of *tashkīk* in the thought of Mullā Ṣadrā. I have argued that it is a central doctrine and hermeneutic concept, and this will be borne out by an analysis of his later texts such as the *Asfār*. It is noticeable, however, that his earlier texts such as *al-Mabdaʾ wa-l-maʿād* (The Alpha and the Omega) seem to restrict *tashkīk* to the homonymy of the term 'being'.[203] It is only later in his mature doctrine that we discern an attempt to solve the problem of the One and the many in metaphysics by extrapolating a semantic notion of the *tertium quid* and applying it to the reality of being. The critical doctrine of *tashkīk* for Mullā Ṣadrā entails not only a modulation within the concept of being and its sense but also in the hierarchy of being and the various referents of the term. *Pros hen* homonymy commits Mullā Ṣadrā to an ontology of graded and modulated reality.

Tashkīk revisited

To recap, the history of *tashkīk* begins with the recognition in Greek philosophy of the 'several senses' of being that the term articulates. However, this does not imply a mere homonymy: being does not have radically different meanings across its referents that would suggest the coincidence of semantic form across different uses of sentences with 'be'. Hence the concept of *pros hen* homonymy, that the focal meaning of being that is primary across its four uses is 'substance' and being across the categories. Whether the ontological implications of this doctrine are explicit in Aristotle is unclear. With Porphyry one notices a semantic and linguistic shift in this history that becomes dominant in Islamic philosophy and one begins to find in Ṭūsī an attempt to draw out the ontological commitments resulting from the doctrine of several senses of being possessing a focal sense.[204] Ṣadrā continues this project and describes that ontology. He wishes to hold to the unity of being but accommodate one's phenomenal and speech-actualising experience of multivocity in being through a doctrine of gradation and modulation in being.

It transpires, then, that *tashkīk* has three stages. The first stage is the establishment of the homonymy of being and its core dependence upon 'being' *qua* actual

ontology of gradation. In *al-Shawāhid al-rubūbiyya* (Divine witnesses), Ṣadrā writes that 'being possesses degrees'.[206] These degrees are described in analogy to the relationship between numbers and one, which are related as units in a chain marked by being prior and posterior, more and less.[207] The most important scale of degrees is intensification.

The final stage is the negation of the various levels of being in themselves, affirming their absolute contingence upon the pinnacle of the pyramid of being, the One, and the attribution of the term 'being' to them in a figurative sense. In *Īqāẓ al-nā'imīn* (The Awakening of the Dormant) which is one of Ṣadrā's later texts, the being of contingent degrees within reality is utterly dependent upon the One to existentiate it. Contingents are merely mirror reflections of True Being, (*wujūd al-ḥaqq*) and manifestations of the holy Reality (*al-ḥaqīqa al-muqaddasa*). Their being in itself is privative and 'shadowy' (*ẓillī*). We only attribute being to them in a figurative sense.[208]

Of course, none of these stages are meaningful and can extend the concept of modulation beyond semantics unless one demonstrates that the term 'being' has reference and that being is the foundational reality, expressed in Mullā Ṣadrā's doctrine of the ontological primacy of being (*aṣālat al-wujūd*). This doctrine requires two critical positions: first, that being is not merely a secondary intelligible or a 'being of reason' but is actual and realised (*taḥaqquq*), possessing reference in extra-mental reality;[209] second, that there is a distinction between the concept of being and its reality such that the Illuminationists' critique of the unreality of being entails a conflation between these two modes of being.[210] Only once one accepts that being has reference and is a foundational, can it be meaningful to talk about modulation in the concept and reality of being.

Multiplicity among things *in concreto* is empirically observed, and at one level is due to the difference in their quiddities. Thus we observe that human is different from animal which is different from table and so forth.[211] But *tashkīk* posits a unity that is essential and multiple in its being. It ensures that that being is a principle not only of commonality in reality but also of differentiation. Being is thus a graded reality whose essence differs in degrees and what differentiates each degree is also what is common to each degree, that is, being. Being is and is not what defines each of these degrees and the element of *sterēsis* (negation) is affirmed at every contingent level of being. In the chapters that I follow, I apply this account of modulation to the three case studies of *tashkīk* in their logical order beginning with the concept and logic of being, moving on to the mode of mental being and culminating with the extra-mental reality of being.

Part II

Analysis of Sadrian ontology

3 The semantics of modulation of being

The table was a large one, but the three were all crowded together at one corner of it: 'No room! No room!' they cried out when they saw Alice coming. 'There's *plenty* of room!' said Alice indignantly, and she sat down in a large arm-chair at one end of the table.

'Have some wine', the March Hare said in an encouraging tone.

Alice looked all round the table, but there was nothing on it but tea. 'I don't see any wine', she remarked.

'There isn't any', said the March Hare.

'Then it wasn't very civil of you to offer it', said Alice angrily.

'It wasn't very civil of you to sit down without being invited', said the March Hare.

'I didn't know it was *your* table', said Alice; 'it's laid for a great many more than three'.

'Your hair wants cutting', said the Hatter. He had been looking at Alice for some time with great curiosity, and this was his first speech.

'You should learn not to make personal remarks', Alice said with some severity; 'it's very rude'.

The Hatter opened his eyes very wide on hearing this; but all he *said* was, 'Why is a raven like a writing-desk?'

'Come, we shall have some fun now!' thought Alice. 'I'm glad they've begun asking riddles. – I believe I can guess that', she added aloud.

'Do you mean that you think you can find out the answer to it?' said the March Hare.

'Exactly so', said Alice.

'Then you should say what you mean', the March Hare went on.

'I do', Alice hastily replied; 'at least – at least I mean what I say – that's the same thing, you know'.

'Not the same thing a bit!' said the Hatter. 'You might just as well say that "I see what I eat" is the same thing as "I eat what I see"!'

'You might just as well say', added the March Hare, 'that "I like what I get" is the same thing as "I get what I like"!'

'You might just as well say', added the Dormouse, who seemed to be talking in his sleep, 'that "I breathe when I sleep" is the same thing as "I sleep when I breathe"!'

'It *is* the same thing with you', said the Hatter, and here the conversation dropped, and the party sat silent for a minute, while Alice thought over all she could remember about ravens and writing-desks, which wasn't much.

Lewis Carroll, *Alice in Wonderland*

Ambiguity frustrates the intention of the speaker and is an obstacle to coherent communication. Disambiguation safeguards meaning. But the theory of *tashkīk* demands that this disambiguation retain the multivocity of expression and does not force us into a monistic approach to articulation. In this chapter, I want to analyse the semantics of being, and being-in-language as expressed in the *Asfār* within a broadly Neoplatonic paradigm.[1] If one begins with an interest in the linguistic turn, then naturally its emphasis on meaning and content propels one towards a consideration of semantics.[2]

I discuss Ṣadrā's theory of meaning and reference. One has a direct experience of the world of being and its reality, and then finds a language in which to express and represent that reality in which the terms of being are utilised. Semantics begins with the relationship between words, concepts and entities. Second, we need to decide how they are related and whether the relationship is uniform. In the central discussion of the predication of being, first, I argue that being (or existence) is indeed a predicate and what that entails, and second, I describe how the predication of the term 'being' is by modulation by intensity, a concept that has important Neoplatonic resonances. Third, I consider some co-extensions of being that are its synonyms and which also have properties of the semantics of modulation. These are concepts that have multiple referents and significations with a core sense and are predicated by modulation. I use these examples as a further means of explaining the modulation of being. Finally, I discuss a 'negative theory of meaning' by examining a language of speaking about non-being, the so-called problem of Plato's beard that was popular in some theological discussions in classical Islam before it was rejected as a nonsense by Avicenna. However, for Ṣadrā, meaningful discourse of things that do not exist in some mode of existence is important. Non-being might exemplify a failure of reference since there is no entity 'non-being' that exists, but it does have meaning. That meaning is predicated by modulation and not synonymy. Arguing *via negativa*, thus, further corroborates my position on the semantics of modulation of being in Ṣadrā.

The three modes of being and the *De Interpretatione*

Mediaeval philosophy considers three types of entities that constitute its ontology: things *in concreto*, concepts or mental being, and words or linguistic tokens of being.[3] The resulting interplay of logic and metaphysics dominates the philosophical discourse of that time. Such an analysis originates in the *De Interpretatione* of Aristotle and the late antique commentaries[4] upon the text that filtered into the Muslim world.[5] This threefold structure was expressed in Arabic logical texts. Ibn al-Muqaffaʿ [d. 757] in his famous epitome of the Aristotelian *organon*, one of the earliest examples of the reception of logic in Arabic, wrote that there were four aspects of things: *in re* (*fī-l-aʿyān*), in the mind, in speech (or spoken tokens) and in writing.[6] This fourfold scheme reflected the fourfold scheme of *De Interpretatione* 16 a 1–18: entities, spoken sounds, written marks and affections in the soul.[7] Being-in-language, being in the mind and being in extra-mental reality are the three major modes or extensions of being, components of an ontology to which this language commits one.[8]

How does one relate these three components of ontology? Being-in-language provides declarative sentences whose propositional content is mental being (even mental language). That content is then verified by reality within this metaphysical concept of truth. The final link in this chain of correspondence is critical. One must be self-conscious and have self-knowledge that is a basis for knowing the world. What one knows is metaphysically verified by what there is. If one does not have self-knowledge, one cannot know the world nor have any foundation for action. So to summarise the ontological correspondence between the modes, written tokens refer to utterances that are subordinated to the concept (that is, mental language and being). Those concepts or the content of mental being are then subordinated to things *in re*. The benchmark ultimately of whether something exists is if it exists *in re*.

Truth and a Sadrian theory of meaning

The *De Interpretatione* led to a holistic theory of meaning. The primary signifier was the sentence and not the word, reflecting the metaphysical primacy of the whole over the part.[9] More specifically as a text it was concerned with these sentences as bearers of truth and falsehood.[10] This holistic theory of meaning within the analytic tradition is known as the 'context principle', that is, 'it is only in the context of a sentence that a word has meaning'.[11] The distinction in *ḥikmat* between the concept (*mafhūm*) and its referent (*miṣdāq*) permits a sentence to be true both in terms of its thought or propositional content and its reference (or extension) in reality.[12] This is a critical concomitant of the doctrine of the ontological primacy of being. Thus a theory of meaning is also a theory of truth. It is truth that ties the meaning of language to its use by someone who knows that language.[13] This is a semantic theory of truth.[14] By a theory of meaning, we mean an account of how language works and how we can employ it to construct a theory of understanding and interpretation.[15] At its core it will depend upon a theory of truth.[16] A theory of meaning must deal with four inter-related issues: what is truth, what is meaning, what is reference and what is the relationship between language, mental language and reality?

Truth

Three major theories of truth are prevalent in philosophy.[17] The first approximates to what most people would recognise as truth, that is, the correspondence theory: true beliefs are those that correspond to reality (although there is some debate on what precisely is meant by 'correspondence'). True propositions correctly 'picture' the world.[18] The theory also implies an alethic realism which maintains that the truth-values of propositions are not conditioned by whether someone knows them to be true or not.[19] The second is the verifiability theory: to say that a proposition is true is to say that it would be verified by an appropriate procedure.[20] The third is a pragmatist approach, that is, true beliefs are a good basis for action. But the real issue is not so much what our account of truth is but what we can know about the world, about non-semantic and non-linguistic facts. Truth itself is quite an elusive concept, an elementary, perhaps even an *a priori* concept that evades definition.[21] It is only open to lexical glosses or paraphrases such as 'what corresponds to the facts'.[22] That it is indefinable need not suggest that it is not a useful concept or that it is ambiguous. After all, a number of philosophers hold that the truth is not a property but are content with holding on to the notion and usefulness of 'truthfulness'.

For Mullā Ṣadrā, a true statement is a statement that is true to the concrete facts in existence:

> By the truth one may mean being *in re* (*al-wujūd fī-l-aʿyān*) so that the truth-value (*ḥaqiyya*) of everything is its concrete existence . . . or one may understand from it the value of the statement and connection insofar as it corresponds to what actually is *in re*.[23]

Ṣadrā holds a metaphysical and not formal or naturalistic concept of truth. In Putnam's terms, he is a metaphysical realist and holds to an externalist perspective; the world consists of mind-independent objects that are always true and truth is not what is rationally acceptable within a certain theory of description.[24]

A propositional discussion of being is critical for Ṣadrā because one cannot have access to the reality of 'being', only linguistic analysis (*taʿrīfan lafẓiyyan*) is available.[25] A proposition is 'any sentence in which there is a relation between two things insofar as a judgement of truth or falsehood follows it'.[26] Ṣadrā describes the categorical proposition as one in which there is a judgement of truth or falsehood. What is judged is called the subject and that on the basis of which the judgement is made is called the predicate. Their relation or connection is called the copula whether it is tensed or not.[27] For a sentence to become a proposition, one needs to quantify a combination so that one can consider whether it is true or false.[28] That quantification must be temporal since the metaphysical truth of a proposition depends on its subject being existent at that point in time when the proposition is articulated. Quiddities act as quantifying variables because they limit an existent in reality and limit one's concept of it in our minds where the propositional content resides.

The subject of the proposition is a name in the first instance. On the question of names, Ṣadrā is a conceptualist since he regards names, even divine names as intelligible concepts that do not have literal reference (though their reference is the divine essence). Names thus have no ontological status.[29] In the *ʿArshiyya*, he says that the Divine Names constitute the intelligible 'realities in their primary and most detailed form'. Names as we experience them are sounds and words and not the 'Names' as such.[30] In themselves names are purely intelligible and have no reality but as mental being supported by divine being from which multiplicity ensues.[31] However, Legenhausen goes from this premiss to argue that since everything is a name of God, for Ṣadrā, all creatures, all contingents that are existentially dependent, are merely intelligibles, thus reducing the cosmos to the 'mind of God'.[32] But this is not the case. Ṣadrā is a realist (in the modern sense), affirming the particular existence, albeit qualified, of things 'that are'. His theory of meaning demands that he adhere to a form of alethic realism.

Successful predication (and indeed reference) of a proposition depends upon the existence of the subject.[33] The existence of the subject constitutes the truth of existential propositions.[34] Bahmanyār holds that for the proposition 'x exists' to be true, there must be in existence at least one realisation, one referent for 'x'.[35] That external object, that existent 'x' is for Ṣadrā primary and prior to both our propositional affirmation of it and the propositional content of its meaning that we have in our minds. That is precisely the major implication of his theory of the ontological primacy of being (*aṣālat al-wujūd*) for his theory of truth.[36]

The Sadrian theory has two levels. First, a proposition is true and 'factual' if its elements correspond to things in reality.[37] The importance of his chapter on the concreteness of being is to show that being refers and that it is not merely a logical, intentional or abstract concept that is meaningless. Meaningful inquiry into any thing requires that one presuppose the existence of it.[38] The truth-conditionality of propositions is tied to the issue of the primacy within the existence–essence distinction. Existence must be primary to allow for correct predication. In *al-Mashāʿir*, he says:

> If things existed through their quiddities (*māhiyyātihā*) and not through something else [such as existence], then it would be impossible to predicate one of the other such as our saying 'Zayd is an animal' or 'man walks'. This is because the benefit of the truth [and reference] of predication lies in the union in being between two different concepts.[39]

This follows a realist theory of meaning and predication that was popular in early Muslim grammatical circles.[40] But what if reference fails? What if the sense in which the referent is given to us is wrong? Then surely it has no referent, thus it is not given to us. Hence there is no sense.[41] But it is possible with respect to certain notions and fictionals to consider words that have sense but not reference.[42] 'Sindbad' is a name that has sense since it refers to a character in a fictional context. But it lacks real reference because it does not designate an actual person Sindbad. Ṣadrā's position depends on successful reference in some mode. Words and concepts have correspondence *in concreto* and *in intellectu*.[43]

However, truth conditions are not so restrictive. The second level of the Sadrian theory concerns the mode of the 'thing-itself (*nafs al-amr*)'.[44] A proposition can also be true if it is in conformity with the 'thing itself' in mental being.[45] An established rule in Islamic philosophy is the 'principle of presupposition' (*al-qāʿida al-farʿiyya*) that affirms that the realisation of something, its presupposition and its truth are dependent upon the realisation of its principle.[46] This applies to two major modes of being and none other: the mind and extra-mental reality.[47] The truth of a proposition thus depends upon the being of its content in the mind. For Ṣadrā, both being and truth are real predicates and real properties pertaining to propositions.[48] When one states that 'Zayd exists', its truth is verified by the concept of Zayd's being in the mind and through its reference to Zayd's existing *in concreto*.[49] Thus it is critical to refute the argument of those like Suhrawardī who insist that being is merely a notion that fails to refer.[50] As a common notion and hence a universal, being for Suhrawardī is predicated synonymously (that is, in one sense of many instances).[51] Once we have established what truth is, we need to discover its content and what it is 'true of'.

Meaning

Meaning as I take it here is the sense or concept of a word (that is, an abstract entity from which beliefs, desires and other cognitive states are composed) and not the object referred.[52] The distinction between meaning and referent is related to the epistemological distinction between 'conception' (*taṣawwur*) and 'judgement' (*taṣdīq*), a foundational theory for understanding epistemology in the (Avicennan) Islamic philosophical tradition.[53] Certain knowledge for Mullā Ṣadrā as we shall see later involves things being present to the mind and not acquired through the impressions and images of things that occur in the mind through some form of abstraction. In his *Risāla fī-l-taṣawwur wa-l-taṣdīq*, Mullā Ṣadrā states:

> At times, the cognitive being of things that are coincides with their being *in concreto* as in the case of the knowledge that separable intellects have of themselves or the knowledge that the soul has of itself . . .
>
> At other times, cognitive being and being *in concreto* are distinct as in the case of our knowledge of those things that are extrinsic to us and our perceptive faculties such as the heavens and the earth, human, horse and so forth. This latter is called contingent knowledge or knowledge by occurrence and affection (*al-ʿilm al-ḥuṣūlī al-infiʿālī*). This is divided into conception and judgement.[54]

Meaning thus taken is separated from being ontologically committed to an entity *in re* to which it corresponds.

For Ṣadrā, meaning is analysed in three considerations (*iʿtibārāt*) in terms of intentional background, utterance and its understanding.[55] 'Man' is understood in terms of a sentence that is located in a prior mental language (*maʿrifa*), in terms of the vocalised 'man' and in terms of the knowledge of what man is that the hearer understands again with respect to that prior language. Meaning ultimately relates to the 'fact-itself'.[56] The Sadrian position does not entail static meaning. Language is graded and the sense of meaning shifts. Meaning does not fix reference. As the content of mental language, it is also modulated. In a chapter in the first *safar* of the *Asfār* in which Mullā Ṣadrā takes to task those who deny that being and oneness may be co-extensional, he argues precisely this point:

> [They claim] that different meanings cannot be abstracted from a single referent or a single essence. However, that impossibility is not accepted because a single thing and a singular reality may be an individual and a referent for multiple meanings and different senses such as Zayd's being caused and known and provisioned and associated. For, the difference in these senses does not require that each of them possesses a distinct being; an example is the real

divine attributes that are identical to the singular divine being, as all philosophers agree.[57]

Many senses do not violate the unity of a referent.[58] The Sadrian theory of meaning requires a basic postulation of the distinction between sense and reference of a thing.

Reference

Reference (*al-ṣidq*) is related to meaning and truth, especially in direct reference theories. When one says 'S exists' it only means that S refers.[59] For a name to be a name it must point to a thing or it is not a name.[60] Ṣadrā argues in *al-Mabda'* that 'the referent of the predication of a concept is singular and is true with reference to itself and to the sentence in which it is without any reversion to an external aspect'.[61] The referent and the judgement that we make about that referent must be united in predication. In Abū-l-Barakāt Baghdādī's *al-Kitāb al-mu'tabar*, one finds the following two level theory of signification.[62] Existents have mental forms corresponding to them. At the first level language indicates the meaning, that is, it refers to propositional content in the mind. But at the second level, utterances indicate the existents *in concreto* in themselves.[63] Thus given the concept of mental being (to which we turn in the next chapter), meaning is yielded through two types of referents: in the mind and in extra-mental reality.

There are two concepts of *tashkīk* that have different implications for reference. The first type of *tashkīk* (special *tashkīk*) applies only to the concept of being: the predicate refers (and corresponds) only to a concept.[64] The latter type known as common *tashkīk* applies to the reality of being: the predicate in such propositions refers (and corresponds) to a real entity *in re*.[65] Thus both sense and reference in the Sadrian theory of meaning are modulated. Modulation applies to language, mental language and reality.

Language is interesting as a means of communication precisely because of its semantic polysemy and shared concept of the world that makes our language meaningful and comprehensible.[66] Multivocity of language plays an important role in legal philosophy and the hermeneutics of law in *uṣūl al-fiqh*.[67] After all, if we want to derive rulings from texts, we need to understand the sense of words, especially those that are 'homonymously' used. Some speculate that this results from the fact that 'words and their compositions' are finite but meanings infinite. But it is significant that the semantics of law requires one to recognise the ontological implications of one's language and how predication occurs. Words are not mere words but ontic facts and expressions that ultimately emanate from the source of Being, God.[68] The word 'being' is thus shared by entities and the varied language of being refers and intends these entities with ultimate reference to God. On this Sadrian model if one reduces everything to words, then everything is a word of God.[69] But how does one deal with ambiguity and articulate a language of order and not chaos? The answer lies in the modulated predication of being. But first, we must determine whether being can be predicated.

Is existence a predicate?

Ever since Kant, this has been a central question in European metaphysics and especially in the philosophy of religion. In the *Critique of Pure Reason*, Kant deconstructs the ontological argument for the existence of God as indefensible on rational grounds. While he does not deny that being may be a logical predicate insofar as any statement can involve logical and syntactical predication, being is not a real predicate as the statement 'God exists' does not add anything to understanding of the term 'God'. Similarly, he argues that the statement cannot be a synthetic proposition.

> Being is obviously not a real predicate; that is, it is not a concept of something which could add to the concept of a thing. It is merely the positing of a thing, or of certain determinations, as existing in themselves. Logically, it is merely the copula of a judgement. The proposition, 'God is omnipotent', contains two concepts, each of which has its object: God and omnipotence. The small word 'is' adds no new predicate, but only serves to posit the predicate in its relation to the subject.[70]

However, being is a property for Ṣadrā.[71] It is a real (and not merely a logical or grammatical) predicate because as we have seen above 'x exists' is true for Ṣadrā if and only if 'x' refers. Similarly, if being were not a predicate, we could not speak meaningfully of quiddities that have no direct reference in reality.[72] Being must be a predicate, or else when we say 'black exists', we would be saying 'black is black' which is a basic tautology. But given the Avicennan consensus of the supervenience of being over quiddity (*ziyādat al-wujūd ʿalá l-māhiyya*) and their distinction, this is not the case.[73]

Suhrawardī understands the claim of the predicability (or reality) of being in concrete, almost empirical terms and hence rejects it.[74] He opts for merely copulative status for existence.[75] To say 'Zayd exists' is equivalent to saying 'Zayd is Zayd'.[76] Being as a second order predicate thus applies to concepts and not to objects.[77] Those within the Islamic tradition who deny reference to being and deny that it is an ontic fact seem close to Kant.[78] Mīr Dāmād, Ṣadrā's teacher, holds that being is merely a logical concept and expresses a quantificational approach to the question, saying that to say something exists is merely to say that 'there is at least one x'.[79] Yet elsewhere he uses being as a predicate with reference to the divine essence.[80] This is due to Mīr Dāmād's insistence upon a radical ontological separation between God and other beings such that the term 'being' is applied in a distinct manner to the two cases.

than 'man'. But this does not consider what type of predication is operative here.[83]

For Ṣadrā, existential propositions are not analytic.[84] In *al-Mashāʿir*, he argues that being is not an analytic part of quiddity. If in the proposition 'man exists' we took 'man' and 'exists' to be synonyms, then it would be equivalent to stating that 'man is man', a tautology that does not benefit us.[85] In 'man exists', 'man' refers to a universal 'humanity'.[86] But 'exists' does have reference contrary to those who deny reference to existence, taking it as a purely mental concept.[87] The referent in the predication of the proposition 'Zayd exists' is the very ipseity (*huwiyya*) of Zayd, that is his being (*wujūd*).[88]

For Suhrawardī, being is a copula. For Ṣadrā, the copula is not usually considered a mode of being because it has no reference.[89] Being as the copula is merely a lexical connector between the subject and the predicate in simple propositions,[90] and is distinguished from 'predicative being' and the thing-itself.[91] It is logical predication alone.[92] It has no existence of its own but relies upon correlation with other existential factors.[93] The copula as a 'connective being' is not necessary for the meaning of a simple proposition such as 'Zayd exists' but is for a composite one such as 'Zayd is laughing' where one has three existential components: the being of Zayd, the concept of laughing and the connector.[94]

The copula in Arabic is usually hidden. If it is explicit, it is a linguistic connector between subject and predicate.[95] With the use of nominal sentences it is the hidden connector called the 'nominal copula'.[96] However, Bäck argues that after Avicenna, the copula is increasingly existentiating because to assert 'S is P' requires an existential S and existential connection to the predicate item P.[97] This is another sense of copula that Ṣadrā allows, an actual existential connector. It can be independently intellected. The copula in this sense is

> more general than what is by itself. 1) It is existence by itself, 2) belonging to itself, 3) what it is by virtue of another (such as the existence of accidents and forms) and 4) it is existence in itself not belonging to itself.[98]

There are two types of propositions of 'be', of copulation, that reflect complete and incomplete usages. An example of the former is 'Zayd is writing'[99] and of the latter, 'Zayd is' *simpliciter*.[100] Sabzawārī, Ṣadrā's commentator, discusses this in his magnum opus, *Sharḥ ghurar al-farā'id* (Commentary on the whiteness of pearls [of wisdom]): the former type of 'composite proposition' uses 'be' as 'copulative being' (*al-wujūd al-rābiṭ*), while the latter as the complete form of the verb 'to be' is 'predicative being' (*al-wujūd al-maḥmūlī*).[101] It is critical to keep the two senses of copula separate because correct predication and sensible discourse about privation, for example, depends upon it:

of at least two senses: the copula and existence (*hyparxis*). We now turn to the nature of the predication of being to understand further senses of being and their relationship.

What type of predication does existence possess?

> Being is shared in a single sense for its different instances, a singular sense differentiated by the degrees of perfection and imperfection within it.[103]

Being is not a universal in whose properties individuals participate. Nor is it a universal predicable such as genus since it is not distinguished by differentiae as it has neither genus nor differentia.[104] How is being predicated of its instance? First, we need to establish what we understand by predication.

Predication

Predication (*al-ḥaml*) concerns what is informative (*khabar*) and what is an assent or judgement, that is, related to whether the subject is true/existent or not.[105] Predication can be applied to all three types of entities in one's ontology: expressions, things or concepts. For the Neoplatonists, predication results in primary reference to concepts and only secondarily and incidentally to things.[106] Predication in Porphyry is 'calling something in accordance with something signified'.[107]

There are three senses of predication.[108] The first is syntactic, the linguistic tying together of a subject and a predicate in a sentence. In Avicennan semantics, simple syntactic predication of a subject and predicate is a preconception that is infallibly the case and is not open to truth or falsehood.[109] The second is semantic, relating extra-linguistic and linguistic predicates. The first level of proper predication in Avicennan semantics requires that the subject and predicate be attached to concepts in the mind (but not actual existents).[110] The third is ontologic: the 'tie' (*ʿaqd* in Islamic logic texts) between the subject and predicate is real and extra-linguistic (and indeed extra-mental).

The unity of predication is an important doctrine.[111] Things are predicated either as universals or particulars.[112] A particular concept is true of itself because of the impossibility of negating something from itself, and the same is true of its contrary the universal. A particular is particular and not universal by essential primary predication (*al-dhātī al-awwalī*) and a universal is a universal and not a particular by common artificial predication (*al-shāʿiʿ al-ṣināʿī*).[113] In the first type of predication the subject is the same as the predicate *in re* and in designation (*ʿunwānan*). The subject and predicate are therefore united both in existence and quiddity. It is analytic, tautological and explicative. The second type is a *per accidens* predication where the individuals predicated can either be intrinsic and essential or extrinsic and accidental, the synthetic and ampliative proposition of Kant. This type of (existential) predication considers the subject and predicate to be united in existence.[114] Related to this division are two types of proposition: simple and composite. A simple proposition is a basic answer about the existence of a thing when asked 'what is it?' A composite proposition considers the actualisation of things as well as an abstract account of their being.[115]

Modulation of being depends on being as the principle of commonality and differentiation or, in Carnap's language, of intension and extension. This explains the two facets of being in its predication.[116] The extension of a term and its predicate is its reference and its corresponding class. The intension of a term and its predicate is the individual concept expressed by it and the corresponding intrinsic property. Everything that is called being has a common referent and constitutes a class of 'existents'. But each individual existent has an individual concept that distinguishes it from another.

Ṣadrā's position

Chapter II of the first book of the *Asfār* deals with the predication of being.[117] The title of the chapter announces the intent: 'The concept of existence is a predication shared by what it covers by modulation (*ḥaml al-tashkīk*) and not by synonymy (*ḥaml al-tawāṭu'*)'.[118]

The first point to be made is that being has reference and is a real concept. It is not a universal that remains uninstantiated.[119] 'Bahmanyār said in *[Kitāb] al-Taḥṣīl*: in summary, "the reality of being is that it is *in re* and none other, and how can that which is this reality of it not be *in re*?"'

Universals are mental concepts related to quiddities that may or may not exist in one of the modes of being.[120] A universal is defined as 'being predicated of the many'.[121] Being is not a universal and not predicated of its instances as a universal is of its individuals.[122] In *al-Shawāhid*, Ṣadrā uses the image of being as a flow and an expanse that pervades all things that are to relate a general notion of being, being as such with existence of particular individual things. Being is not a universal property like whiteness that is predicated of individual white bodies but does not itself occur; rather the being of things is identical to their 'existentiality' (*mawjūdiyyatihā*).[123]

Second, being is predicated of the many in a shared common sense.[124] Its instances share extension.

> It is almost axiomatic that its [existence's] being is shared among quiddities, since the intellect finds a relationship and resemblance between [the term] 'existent' (*mawjūd*) and 'existent', whose similitude is not found between 'existent' and 'non-existent'.[125]

But this does not mean that it is synonymous. Being is not a universal and hence cannot be predicated synonymously.[126] Ṣadrā quite categorically denies synonymy to the concept of being: 'It may be clarified that being *qua* concept is a common factor (*amr ʿāmm*) predicated of all existents differently and not by an absolute synonymy'.[127]

Commonality of being is clear from its apriority and its self-awareness:

> One is amazed that someone can claim the absence of its [being's] extension (*ishtirāk*), after having attested to its commonality without being aware of it.

> [This is] because if the existence of each thing is opposed to another existence, how can it be judged against it if it does not have anything in common with it?[128]

This means that if every occurrence of 'existence' was a different concept, there could be no shared sense of being, and the whole point of *tashkīk* is that being is both a principle of commonality and differentiation. That is the nature of its predication.[129] He illustrates the commonality of being with the popular example of *'ayn*:

> The copula in propositions (*al-rābiṭa fī-l-qaḍāyā*) and judgements made from existence have in all their instances, whatever their subjects and predicates, one sense (*maʿná wāḥid*). It is attested that when a man utters a poem and makes the verses rhyme with the word 'being' (*al-wujūd*), no one needs to know that the rhyme is repeated, as opposed to what [happens] if the rhyme of all the verses was made with the word 'eye/spring' (*al-ʿayn*), for example, so it [rhyme] is not judged to be repeated in it [the word *ʿayn*].[130] Were it that everyone would necessarily recognise that the concept of the word 'being' was one in all [the verses], then they would not judge there to be a repetition in this context, just as they did not judge it to be in the other case [i.e. that of *ʿayn*].[131]

The third point is that being is graded by priority and intensity. The concept of being is a syntactically monadic scalar predicate and a property of comparative degrees[132]

> Being in some existents is necessitated by itself, as will come [to be explained], above others, and in some it is more prior (*aqdam*) by its nature (*al-ṭabʿ*) from others. In some it is more complete (*atamm*) and more potent (*aqwá*), so that that being which has no cause is primary in its existentiality to others, and is prior to all other existents by nature. Similarly the existence of all the Active Intellects (*al-ʿuqūl al-faʿʿāla*) is prior to all consequent existence (*wujūd tālīhi*), and the existence of a substance is prior to the existence of an accident.[133]

This is the logic of intensity. Sadrā makes it clear that quiddities cannot undergo intensification nor can accidental categories such as 'quantity'. *Genera* are also ruled out as structures for intensification. A number series is not one in which one number is differentiated by degree, nor does intensification and debilitation occur in accidents such as abstractions of colour or temperature.[134] But it must be understood that he does not mean that we do not perceive such grades of intensity or that

to quiddities and quiddities do not undergo modulation.[137] However, whether we are aware of it or not and whether our modular concept of being falsifies being as such is not the point. Being is modulated in its reality. Thus the modular semantics of being ought to be retained.

Signification and the *Categories*

Signification is a process of establishing understanding by representing an object. The one who articulates it 'arrests his mind on it', and the hearer finds it sufficient to understand.[138] Signification depends on the thing itself being signified and unlike supposition does not rely merely on using the substantive term alone.[139] The smallest unit of signification in legal hermeneutics in Islam is the word, insofar as it is the smallest unit of 'meaning'.[140] 'Atomic' meaning (*al-maʿná al-ḥarfī*), that is meaning pertaining to consonants within a word, is not distinguished from 'nominal' meaning (*al-maʿná al-ismī*).[141] The former is meaningless in itself.

Avicenna has two approaches to categories: a logical one of types of predicates and an ontological classification of entities.[142] He often follows the Plotinian tradition of regarding the categories as *summa genera*.[143] Within the Islamic traditions from an early point on, categories were read as ontological entities, and categoriology was an enumeration of types of entities that could be predicated.[144] In the Arabic Aristotle, categories are described as 'existents'.[145] If we understand the categories of Aristotle to be about meanings and not the things themselves, then we can see a shift of semantics ontologised already in the Arabic translations of the *Categories* where the famous 'onymies' are how one talks about things.[146] However, it is arguably the case that Aristotle did not intend to use the *Categories* as ontological tools but as highest principles through which one could discourse about logic, metaphysics and other sciences that require categoriology.[147]

In the *Categories*, Aristotle provides us with an enumerative ontology of 'what there is' in terms of predication and how it is 'said'.[148] First, things are said of but not in a subject, that is, as a universal, for example, man. Second, things are said in a subject but not of it, that is, individual accidents. Third, things are said of and in a subject, that is, universal accidents like blackness. Fourth, there are things that are neither said of nor in a subject, that is, individual substances such as Zayd. Thus what we have are types or *genera* of being divided into substances and accidents. Being across the categories is still predicated homonymously.[149] Thus it was Plotinus in his criticism of the *Categories* who recast these genera of being into a hierarchically arranged scale of being that was no longer purely homonymous.[150] The doctrine of diversity-in-unity required surrendering pure homonymy.[151]

Ṣadrā draws on this tradition for his notion of modulation (*tashkīk*) of being.

our assumptions and the possibility of illocutionary speech acts. Is this a problem of our confusing word meanings with different sentence types?[154] This is inadmissible for Ṣadrā. Signification for him is graded according to the cognitive and hermeneutic capability of the one experiencing it. In commenting upon the Qur'ān, he says that words and sounds are forms of 'food' for the listeners and reciters whose intellects are like birds that fly to feed upon them, specific to each one.[155] Thus each type of food/word has a specific level of signification appropriate to the person, whilst being focally related to its divine source whence it issued. Discussing the universal and particular terms, he states that the multivocal or *mushakkak* is differentiated by perfection and imperfection, that being *qua* the term is a scalar predicate, while a pure homonymous term is merely *mushtarak* or shared among its uses.[156]

The co-extensions of being

We have concerned ourselves thus far with the meaning of being and its predication considered in itself. We should examine some of the co-extensions of being that are very much part of any theory of meaning and of the semantics of being in Ṣadrā. Thus in this section we are concerned with synonymy, with uses of being that are equivalent. These terms pick out the same class of phenomena as 'being' and are notions convertible to it since they are partial identities that also undergo modulation. These following concepts have the same extension, meaning that the extension of the class of beings is, for example, the same as the class of 'things'. They do not possess, however, 'L-equivalence', meaning that their intensions are distinct as they have individual and class properties intrinsic to each.[157] An important feature of their synonymy with being is that they are often defined in the same terms and are also *a priori* anapodeictics (*lā burhāna lahā*).[158] The consideration of modulation, in these cognate terms that exhibit it, will elucidate for us the concept of modulation in being.

The first is most salient to any discussion of existential propositions: affirmation (*thubūt*). Ibn ʿArabī, in common with most Islamic thinkers interested in the metaphysical implications of logic, held in *Inshā' al-dawā'ir* (The composition of circles) that 'being and non-being are expressions for the affirmation of the thing or its negation'.[159] However, for our philosopher, the issue is broader. Affirmation can be propositional and non-propositional.[160] Affirmation can be a mere relational concept tying together a subject and a predicate without entailing, or depending upon concrete existence *in re*. Again we return to his point about the truth condition of a proposition, in opposition to Ṭūsī. Attached to this synonymy is that of being and *per se* identity (*huhuwiyya*). If one says that something exists then the very identity and essence of that thing is tied up in its existence. To have existence is to have identity, critical for the possibilities of predication.[161]

The second is 'being-a-thing' and as such draws upon the Avicennan equation of *wujūd* and *shay'iyya*.[162] To say that something exists is the same as saying that it is a thing. Suhrawardī had earlier denied that the two concepts are co-extensive partly within the context of his denial of reference to being.[163] However, for our philosopher, affirmation of 'thing-ness' is an affirmation of being in some mode whether *in concreto* or not. On this issue, he draws upon an old Shiʿi doctrine of calling God a thing. Being and 'being-a-thing' are not just concepts but realities that are co-extensive, whose focal referent and sense is God himself.[164] A denial of this equation leads to agnosticism, as the report from the Sixth Imam itself suggests. To say that God is not a thing implies that He is no-thing and thus a denial of God.[165] The doctrine has inclusive and exclusive intentions. Exclusively, it denies the application of 'thingness' to non-existents as some theologians allow by equating being and 'being-a-thing'.[166] On this point he quotes the Illuminationists to illustrate some of the pitfalls of naïve Hellenism in philosophy that led to a denial of the agency of God in creation.[167] It is inclusive because it is ranged against the Peripatetic denial of this found in Avicenna and Bahmanyār.[168] The Peripatetic position regards 'being-a-thing' as a secondary intelligible that is 'neither synonymous with being nor with affirmation'. Again this position is dangerous with respect to the possibility of theology. To speak of God meaningfully one must be able to call Him a being and a thing.[169]

The third co-extension of being is 'oneness' (*al-waḥda*) following Neopythagorean, Aristotelian and Neoplatonic doctrines of how an existent thing must be one.[170] Being and unity are identical in an existent.[171] 'Unity is a close companion of being and is found where being is since they are both co-extensive in reference to things'.[172] Both concepts are *a priori*.[173] One precedes all numbers in the chain of numbers just as the Necessary precedes all beings and they 'exist' in reference to it.[174] Numbers manifest the 'one' just as beings manifest the True Being.[175] One is also used in a modulated sense following Peripatetic precedent.[176] Divisions of oneness are also like the divisions of being, and they both undergo intensification and debilitation.[177] Like being, unity has two main senses: an abstracted concept when one says 'the thing is one', and a singular reality that is the reality of unity.[178] Like being, unity has no definition.[179] However, intensionally being and unity are different: 'the two are the same in their essence but not in concept'.[180]

One of the most significant co-extensions of being that is so very close to it is light (*al-nūr*). Both terms are 'defined' in the same way:

> Know that what is meant by light is that which is manifest in itself and manifested in others (*al-ẓāhir bi-dhātihi wa-l-muẓhir bi-ghayrihi*) and is co-extensive (*musāwiq*) and synonymous with being. Rather it is itself a simple reality (*ḥaqīqa basīṭa*) like being with divisions, such as Necessary and all else, intelligible, psychic and corporeal lights. The Necessary is the light of lights of infinite intensity (*nūr al-anwār ghayr mutanāhī-l-shidda*), while everything else is of finite intensity, meaning that there is something above them in intensity.[181]

Light and being are synonymous because they are defined in the same way and they both undergo intensification and are modulated in the same way.[182] Like being, light can be considered in terms of its concept that is abstracted and is intentional such as the luminosity of a thing or in terms of its reality as such.[183] He claims that this position was that of the ancient Persian philosophers and explains the hierarchy and the privative levels within it thus:

> The reality of being is uncontaminated by debility (*ḍuʿf*) and incompleteness (*quṣūr*). It does not [ontologically] follow quiddity. Incompleteness and debility are descending degrees of contingency (*marātib al-imkānāt al-tanazzulāt*), just as the shadow is a descending degree of light, since what is meant by shadow is not an existential fact, but rather a degree of absence of light, since absence is privative. Similarly the descending degrees of being, which is the reality of light, and their absence only issue from their specific ipseities that are not supervenient over their common [shared] reality in the base of being and luminosity.[184]

Being and light are synonyms but their intensions differ since they posses different concepts and are different in name or semantic form.[185]

The final co-extension of being that I shall consider here is individuation (*tashakhkhuṣ*).[186] Ṣadrā's teacher Mīr Dāmād says: 'What is not individuated does not exist and what does not exist is not individuated because the two are co-extensive [and equivalent in meaning] neither of which is prior to the other'.[187]

For Ṣadrā, being is what determines a thing, and in this sense is it a real predicate.[188] The individuation of a thing is its being, its specific existence. However, the intension of individuation and being differ since individuation is not a principle of commonality nor is it 'shared'.[189] The identity of being and individuation both in mental and extra-mental reality is a central doctrine of Sadrian philosophy.[190] Sabzawārī says that 'individuation is the same as being *in re* (*fī-l-aʿyān*) and coincides with being in the mind as a concept'.[191] The equation of being and individuation is one of the eleven principles that Ṣadrā says are critical to his philosophy: 'The individuation of everything and their principle of distinction is the same as particular being (*al-wujūd al-khāṣṣ*). Being and individuation are the same in essence (*dhātan*) but different notionally and nominally (*mafhūman wa-isman*)'.[192]

The 'bound' of the individual may well be the quiddity of the thing but what individuates it and the individual itself is identified with the act of being.[193] The individual itself and individuation are regarded as the same just as he makes no distinction between the act or flow of being (*wujūd*) and a specific existent (*mawjūd*). These two terms are synonyms in Sadrian logic of being but paronyms in Aristotelian[194] and Porphyrian logic.[195]

All these co-extensions of being undergo modulation and are scalar predicates in the same way as being. Light is especially significant and commonly used in the Sadrian tradition to explain modulation of being. We now move to the final element in the argument: the modulation of non-being that implies the modulation of being.

Plato's beard

Arguing from opposites is a popular form of proof in Islamic philosophy. Ontology draws on disontology and the concept and reality of being is analysed and explained in terms of its lack and negation; hence my discussion here of non-being. In this final section I want to show that, first, Ṣadrā permits the predication of non-being and, second, this predication of non-being is also modulated. Thus by implication it strengthens my contention about the modulation of being. In this, I follow the method of the *ḥukamā'* who analyse the concept of non-being to elucidate their doctrine of being.[196]

Ṣadrā addresses the problem of Plato's beard, the term that Quine used to describe the predication of non-existents.[197] How can a non-entity be the subject of a proposition?[198] When we say that Pegasus is, then we commit ourselves to an ontology of Pegasus. But when we say it is not, no such ontological commitment takes place.[199] The problem of Plato's beard is one of the failure of reference.[200] It poses a basic paradox: that which does not exist cannot be said or thought and yet our very affirmation of the negation of its existence is itself an application of being to not-being. The root of the problem lies in the discussion in Plato's *Sophist* 256 d–257 e between Theaetetus and the Visitor. In the Islamic tradition, the pure unconditioned non-existent or privative cannot be predicated as it does not have a 'thing-itself' by which it can be true.[201] The non-existent *qua* non-existent has no occurrence, not even conceptually as an intelligible.[202] Ṣadrā says:

> The non-existent cannot be predicated except as the word [non-existent]. So quiddity which does not exist cannot be a thing, not even itself because its entity which is its essence is derived from its realisation (*taḥaqquq*) and existence.[203]

On the question of whether one can say that a non-existent is a thing (as some of the Mu'tazila hold), Ṣadrā is opposed to the possibility because there is no mediate position between non-existence and existence, of affirmation and negation.[204] *Kalām* ontology, particularly among the Mu'tazila tended to consider the *summum genera* to be 'thing' which was divided into an existent and a non-existent. Hence it was feasible to describe a non-existent as a 'thing' that could be predicated and considered.[205] The problem arose in the late ninth century with Abū Ya'qūb al-Shaḥḥām, a teacher of Abū 'Alī al-Jubbā'ī. The Mu'tazilī argument concerned the mode in which God creates. He takes prime matter and essences and bestows upon them existence. The non-existent thing is ultimately the essence prior to its existentiation. The Ash'arī response focused on their difference reading of the process of creation, defending what they considered to be a more Qur'ānic account. A thing must be actual and existent *in concreto*; however, it may have a referent in the mind without being *in concreto* allowing for one to speak meaningfully of possibles. It is thus possible to say of a non-existent that it is known (*ma'lūm*), referred to (*madlūl 'alayhi*), mentioned (*madhkūr*) or even predicated (*mukhbar 'anhu*).[206]

Mullā Ṣadrā makes arguments against the four well-known theological positions on this.[207] First, Ṣāliḥī argued that a non-existent was neither an object of knowledge nor a meaning nor a thing nor any such entity whatsoever. It was 'non-existent' *simpliciter*. Second, Abū-l-Qāsim al-Ka'bī al-Balkhī [d. 931] argued that it was a thing and an object of knowledge but not a substance.[208] Third, the Jubbā'īs stated that it was a substance and accident but not a body since it did not pertain to the world of generation and corruption as a sensible. Finally, Abū-l-Ḥusayn Khayyāṭ [*c*. 940] argued that it was a body as well but not a motive one, and an object of knowledge but not qualified by affirmation or existence. All such positions are roundly condemned. As a later commentator puts it, 'what does not exist is non-existent' since being-a-thing is synonymous with being.[209] Ṣadrā considers their argument with three counter-arguments.

> If they claim that the being of the non-existent contingent is negated and everything negated is impossible according to them, then contingent being becomes impossible. This is impossible (*muḥāl*).
>
> If they claim that being has something affirmed and for every attribute affirmed for a thing, it is permissible for the thing to be qualified by it [attribute], then it is valid for the non-existent to be qualified in the state of privation by being. Thus it is both existent and non-existent. This is impossible.
>
> If they deny the qualification (*ittiṣāf*) of the thing by an attribute affirmed for it, then it must not be correct for it to be said of the non-existent quiddity that it is a thing. So 'being a thing' is affirmed for it, and if someone maintains against this argument that it is not correct to qualify the thing by a thing affirmed for it, then it is not a thing. It has already been said that it is a thing. Such is contingency.[210]

Existence remains the ground of actuality. Contraries in reality are defined as things that share a genus and a single substrate or subject.[211]

However, the concept of the non-existent has reference in mental language and can be predicated by accidental predication that does not depend on the existence of the subject.[212] Naṣīr al-Dīn Ṭūsī says in *Sharḥ al-Muḥaṣṣal*:[213]

> Removal of affirmation that includes both external and mental reality can be conceived in what is not a thing and what is not conceived at all. The judgement of it is valid insofar as it is that [which is] conceived, and is not valid insofar as it is not a thing. It cannot be contradictory by the distinction of the two subjects and there is no prohibition that a thing be a division of thing in a sense and a division of it in another sense. For example, if we say the existent is either a thing (*al-thābit*) in the mind or not a thing in the mind, then the non-existent (*lā-wujūd*) in the mind is a division of existent insofar as it is a concept in which the prefix 'non' has been adjoined to 'existent', and insofar as it is a concept, it is a division of the thing in the mind.[214]

This is an Avicennan doctrine.[215] Affirmative predication of the absolute non-existent is not possible because affirmation is the proof of something else and what itself is not proven cannot be the basis for the proof of another (by the presupposition rule).[216] Negation is only possible if one can conceive of it in the mind.[217] Everything that exists and is predicable is so because one reverts to the concept of being and its reality to make it meaningful and intelligible. Ṣadrā says:

> It is permissible for the thing to be existent in the intellect (*thābitan fī-l-ʿaql*) and non-existent in extra-mental reality (*maʿdūman fī-l-khārij*). If they mean something else, then it is invalid and it can not be predicated nor can it be another predicated by it.[218]

If what one is considering does not revert and refer thus, then it cannot be predicated. A specific conceptual non-existent is one whose concept refers and is meaningful through the concept of being.[219] Thus the concept of non-being is related and opposed to the concept of being as its absence.[220] Our concepts depend on universals and quiddities and non-being is such a concept that is non-occurring and hence is quiddity privative (*maʿdūm*) in itself.[221]

The problem is related to the laws of Non-Contradiction and the Excluded Middle as they are discussed in Aristotelian science. With respect to things *in re*, it is not possible for them to both exist and be privative at the same locus and time and in the same mode and modality. Similarly, concepts such as whiteness and blackness, or motion and rest, as opposites cannot be predicated of the same thing at the same space-time (*fī ān wāḥid wa-mawḍūʿ fārid*).[222] An existential affirmation of a non-existent *in re* is impossible partly because of the law of Non-Contradiction and that two contraries (*ḍiddān*) cannot be present in the same space and time, whether ontologically or predicably.[223] Since it is not a genus, being itself cannot permit contradiction and opposition within its 'genus', even if one takes opposing 'concepts' for it.[224] Nor is being divided into species, since that would entail a violation of the definition of metaphysics.[225] Being *qua* being cannot allow for such opposition within itself.[226] But the law holds if one reads it as referring to properties and not purely in propositional terms. Thus certain objects cannot both have and not have the same property in the same time and place, *ceteris paribus*. The law does not hold that one cannot posit a proposition and its contradiction at the same time since of course the mind is capable of such a conception.[227] Contradictory propositions can be posited in the mind at the same time but ontological contradictories cannot exist in the same locus and time.

Absence is quite distinct from negation.[228] Ṣadrā permits a relative sense of privation that is absence. The incomplete sense of 'be' as a copula allows for such usage. Thus one can say 'Zayd is (*mawjūd*) at home and not (*maʿdūm*) in the market' and it would be a correct proposition.[229] One cannot negate a non-entity since a negation must have an entity as its negation.[230] Judgemental cognition of a thing depends upon its property and location. Fictionals, however, have neither existence nor presence to own perception, thus their range is unlocatable.[231]

Negative propositions entail non-being of the subject.[232] Avicenna distinguishes between these two modes of non-being, between privation *per se* that is negation, and a privation *in potentia* that may have been actualised in existence in the past or will be in the future.[233] Ṣadrā discusses negatives in the following manner:

> There is no relation in negations apart from the affirmative relation (*al-nisba al-ījābiyya*) that is in affirmatives. What is signified (*al-madlūl*) by the negative proposition and its provision is only the elimination of that affirmative

> relation, and there is not in it a predication or a connection (copula), but rather a negation of a predication and cutting of a connection (*qaṭʿ rabṭ*).[234]

In the following the former is a proposition but the latter is not since it has neither reference nor can it be true or false (nor is it quantified):[235] 'Zayd is not white' (*laysa Zaydun bi-abyaḍ*)' and 'Zayd is non-white' (*Zayd lā abyaḍ*).[236] This is due to the position in logic expounded in the *al-Risāla al-Shamsiyya* of Dabīrān Kātibī [d. 1276] that positive predication of non-existents cannot be true but negative predication of them can.[237] There is a similar distinction between 'Zayd is a non-existent', an affirmative proposition, and 'Zayd does not exist' and even 'Zayd is non-being'.[238]

Is privation (non-being) multivocal? Ṣadrā says: 'There is no distinction or multiplicity in privation. Multiplicity can only be ascribed to it through adjunction. There is no such distinction in the mind or *in re*'.[239] This refers to pure privation that has no reference. But:

> Distinction of privations only occurs with respect to modes. The intellect can conceive of things distinguished in themselves and their accidents, such as cause and effect . . . and then attach to them the concept of privation. Thus the concept of the privation of the cause is distinct from the privation of the effect.[240]

Privation is scalar in keeping to the lexical sense of *tashkīk*, and fitting into a hierarchical worldview in which lower levels of being are essentially non-existent, only exhibiting being by virtue of their Principle. In the Neoplatonic scale lower levels are thus privative with respect to higher ones: 's is not-p if and only if object s falls into a class lower in the ontological order than that occupied by those things in extension of p'.[241] Since being is equated to light, then non-being is related to its absence, to darkness and is similarly graded in a *mushakkak* manner.[242] The mode of thing-itself permits predication of non-being in a purely syntactic predication. Non-being, thus, is not ontologically actualised either *in re* or *in intellectu*.[243] Being and non-being are opposing (contradictory) concepts and similarly graded. Thus if one asserts the existence of a particular degree of being, one denies privation of it, and the converse is true if one is considering particular specific 'portions' of non-being.[244] Thus, not only can we predicate non-being but that concept of non-being is itself modulated in its predication mirroring the modulated predication of being.

4 Mental being

> Once when mind had become intent on the things which are, and my understanding was raised to a great height, while my bodily senses were withdrawn as in sleep, when men are weighed down by too much food or by the fatigue of the body, it seemed that someone immensely great of infinite dimensions happened to call my name and said to me:
>
> 'What do you wish to hear and behold, and having beheld what do you wish to learn and know?'
>
> 'Who are you?' said I.
>
> He said, 'I am Poimandres the *nous* of the supreme. I know what you wish and I am with you everywhere'.
>
> 'I wish to learn', said I, 'the things that are and understand their nature and to know God. O how I wish to hear these things!'
>
> He spoke to me again. 'Hold in your *nous* all that you wish to learn and I will teach you'.[1]

Mental being is one of the three Sadrian modes of being and in its origins seems to invoke the famous Platonic notion of mental language. In this chapter, I examine his proofs for the existence of mental reality and mental language, and discuss its relationship with three other aspects of mental being that relate to the other modes of being. The first of these is the being of the mind that is extra-mental and distinct from mental being. How does it relate to mental being and to other extra-mental beings such as other minds, souls and intellects? It is at this point that the question of panpsychism and the intensification in the psychic mode of being is considered. The second aspect is epistemological. The relationship between mental being and the extra-mental realm concerns knowledge. I discuss the homonymous nature of knowledge and focus on his theory of knowledge by presence, an intensifying method of knowing that reflects a cognition of an intensifying scale of being. The third aspect is the concept of being that is a secondary intelligible and distinct both from mental being and the being of the mind and yet it acts as a crucial mediator between the two.

Proofs of mental being

For Ṣadrā, the mind possesses an ontological realm that one calls mental being, a concept that is equivalent to being-knowledge.[2] He is a realist in the sense that every thought must correspond to a real object even if it is a Meinong object, that is, an unreal object of cognition.[3] By positing a realm of mental reality, he is a dualist.[4] But the being of the mind and mental being are not the same since the being of the mind is itself an extra-mental reality, while mental being is what refers to extra-mental being.[5] This is a subtle but significant distinction. He clarifies this in response to an objection that the existence of a thing cannot be analytically dissolved into the mental and extra-mental (i.e. concrete) being of a thing. Consequently, for Ṣadrā, the 'hard problem' of mind-body does not occur since the existence of the mind is extra-mental existence.[6] There are two primary modes of being each distinct and radically non-interchangeable: being *in re* and mental being.[7]

> The philosophers have agreed, in opposition to most of the speculative theologians (*al-mutakallimīn*) that apart from this mode of being, things have another mode of being (*naḥw al-wujūd*) and manifestation (*al-ẓuhūr*) that is similarly arranged and undergoes similar causation. [That mode] is called mental being.[8]

Mental being shares the same qualities, features and description as extra-mental being because it is merely another mode of being, a certain sense of the term. Just as extra-mental being is not ambiguous, neither is mental being.[9] It is *mushakkak*.[10] Similarly mental being is not a universal; we have seen above the argument denying that the concept of being is a universal.[11] The distinction between mental and extra-mental is rooted in the Platonic distinction between sensible and intelligible being, and in the Avicennan distinction between existence and essence in contingents.[12] The concept of mental being has a history in which both Abū-l-Barakāt al-Baghdādī and Fakhr al-Dīn Rāzī play important roles, being the first Islamic philosophers to devote sections of their philosophical works to the discussion of the problem.[13] In fact two of the major Sadrian arguments affirming mental being are derived from the latter.[14] In the generations before Ṣadrā, philosophers such as Jalāl al-Dīn Davānī [d. 1501] and Mīr Ghiyāth al-Dīn Manṣūr Dashtakī [d. 1542] affirmed the mode of mental being as critical for the possibility of knowledge even if they argued that being did not refer in extra-mental reality. Dashtakī has an extended discussion of the problem of mental being in his commentary on Suhrawardī's *Hayākil al-nūr*: there must be a mental mode of being for us to make valid judgements about non-existent entities and about fictionals because knowledge is an ontic, non-dualistic relation between subject and object and not about the acquisition of images in the brain.[15]

Mullā Ṣadrā states that one needs to consider two preliminary issues before tackling the philosophical proofs for the existence of mental being. The first relates to the Avicennan distinction in contingent beings between existence and essence.[16] Going back to Plotinus, these two analytic components of a contingent represent links in two parallel chains of causality. But for Mullā Ṣadrā, it is being that is the active causal principle. It is being that is the immediate effect emanating from the One and a process that undergoes perfection and intensification and debilitation. Essence by contrast is indeterminate. The clear implication is that knowledge involves the presence and production of forms in mental being and not in the essences of things in the mind that correspond to their forms in extra-mental reality.

The second preliminary point relates to the productive power of the mind and especially the imaginative faculty that is capable of producing existential forms of things that have no correspondence in extra-mental reality.[17] This imaginative and creative power of the human mind is a direct result of God creating it in his image; it is a similitude for the essence, attributes and actions of the divine. The human mind's capacity for forging and creating anew forms of things that may exist is related to the role of the imagination in Sufi metaphysics. It is therefore significant that at this point Mullā Ṣadrā quotes a long passage from the chapter on Isaac in the *Fuṣūṣ al-ḥikam* (Ring-settings of wisdom) of Ibn ʿArabī on the nature of imagination:

> Through imagination (*al-wahm*), every human may create in the faculty of his imagination (*quwwa khayālihi*) what has no being except in it [the faculty]. This is common to all humans. The mystic (*al-ʿārif*) creates through his spiritual concentration (*himma*) what has being in extra-mental reality to act as a locus for his concentration; indeed, his concentration continues to sustain it and support the perpetuation of what it created. When oblivion from preserving what he created overcomes the mystic, that created thing becomes non-existent, unless the mystic commands all planes of existence (*ḥaḍarāt*) in which case such oblivion does not arise since at all times he is present on some plane or another. When the mystic who has such a command creates something through his spiritual concentration, it is manifest in his form on every plane. In this case, the forms maintain each other so that if the mystic is absent on a certain plane or planes which present on another, all the forms are maintained by the form on the plane to which he is not oblivious. Neither the commonality of people nor the elite are ever completely oblivious. So I have explained here a secret the like of which the people of God have been reluctant to expose . . .
>
> This issue as I have been informed has never been committed to writing by anyone previously, either me or another except in this book. It is unique and exclusive. You must not forget it for that plane of being in which you remain present with the form may be compared to the Scripture in which God said: 'We have missed nothing out of the Scripture' [Q 6:38], for it comprises all that has occurred and all that will occur. Only he whose soul is a comprehensive reality (*qur'ānan*) truly knows what we have said. For one who fears God, 'He will make a distinction (*furqānan*) for him' [Q 8:29].[18]

Ṣadrā says that he will explain this issue further in his discussion of the nature of the soul; suffice it to say that the question of mental being is directly related to the creative power of the human soul-intellect.

After these preliminaries, Ṣadrā provides six proofs (or 'ways') for proving the existence of mental being. On the whole they depend on his twin doctrines of the modulation of being and the primacy of being. First, one can conceive of entities that do not exist in extra-mental reality and even those that are impossible such as a partner to God, and the coincidence of two contradictories in violation of the famous logical law of Non-Contradiction.[19] This argument has four premisses and a conclusion.[20]

1 We can conceive of things that do not exist in extra-mental reality.
2 Each of these concepts is differentiated since,
3 Absolute non-existents have no existential distinction and so to conceive of them, they must be a mode of being, as conception depends on being.
4 These entities have no extra-mental existence.
5 Therefore, they must have a mode of being that is mental.

This is a weak argument. An objection could be made in the following way. If knowledge is the acquisition of a form in the mind, then that which has no external corresponding reality has no form that can be grasped in the mind. Hence there is no form in the mind and consequently no mental being. Ṣadrā counters by saying that the form is not an abstraction but a manifestation and being that is mental. His commentator Sabzawārī acknowledges this objection and says that the real issue with non-existents is the ability to predicate affirmative judgements of them and not the comparison with mental forms.[21]

> The proper answer to the objection is that the correspondence of everything is with respect to itself . . . So the realisation of what corresponds to the non-existent (*taḥaqquq muṭābiq al-maʿdūm*) and its extra-mental essence is not through the realisation of an extra-mental existential essence (*bi-taḥaqquq dhāt khārijiyya wujūdiyya*). Similarly the mental concept . . . negates the thing and is unlike another mental form.

This is the second proof, the possibility of affirmative predication of absolute non-existents, especially fictionals.[22] This argument can be analysed into four premisses and a conclusion.[23]

1 We can make positive judgements about entities that have no extra-mental reality ever.
2 The rule of presupposition (*qāʿida farʿiyya*) applies: the affirmation of a thing

Dashtakī proposes a similar argument invoking the rule of presupposition in his

Ishrāq hayākil al-nūr li-kashf ẓulumāt shawākil al-ghurūr commenting upon the text of Suhrawardī:

> One repeats the famous proof that we can conceive of things that have no being in extra-mental reality and we can make affirmative judgements about them and what is judged to possess the property of being-existent (*al-mawjūdiyya*) must be existent because the affirmation of a property of a thing presupposes its affirmation (i.e. the affirmation of the thing). Since it is not (existent) *in re* then it exists in the mind. Thus is proved the doctrine of mental being.[25]

An objection could be made that 'every gryphon flies' is a hypothetical and not a proper categorical proposition. But for Ṣadrā, definite descriptions apply and Meinong objects are posited.[26] It only has to be true of one mental instance and not a universal. The positing of fictional entities is an important proof for mental being. 'Intellectual fictions' are things posited in the mind that have no extra-mental reality and are pure intelligibles.[27] They are 'beings of reason' that have sense and being in the mind alone.[28] To speak meaningfully of non-existents *in re*, one must have thingness of them in the mind at least.[29] The fact that one can conceive of actual non-existents such as the Gryphon (*ʿAnqāʾ mughrib*) is a proof for mental being, that one can predicate an affirmative judgement of it as a logical concept.[30]

> We can make true affirmative judgements (*aḥkām thubūtiyya ṣādiqa*) about things that have no existence in extra-mental reality (*fī-l-khārij*) at all. Similarly, we can judge what possesses being . . . We judge it comprehensively for all its quantitative realised particulars. For example, we say 'every Gryphon flies' (*kullu ʿanqāʾ ṭāʾir*) and 'every triangle has three sides'. Now we know the reference [truth] of every affirmative judgement (*ṣidq al-ḥukm al-ījābī*) requires the existence of its subject. Since we know that the subject of the judgement has no concrete existence (*al-wujūd al-ʿaynī*), we know that it must have another existence. That is mental being (*al-wujūd al-dhihnī*).

Fictionals are products of the imagination in the mind and not derived from the Active Intellect.[31] They are products of the mind acting *like* the Active Intellect, such that in the imaginal realm, these forms are *like* universals, whereas for Avicenna it is a universal insofar as one can conceive of instances, which would be true referents of it in the mind.[32] One can differentiate particulars in the imagination just as one would distinguish individuals of a species.[33] The Gryphon is not a possible that is unrealised in this world, but an impossible as much as a square circle.[34] It is rather

The realm of conceivable entities is thus wider than that of possible entities.

The third argument is that realities in their pure simplicity can be conceived such as blackness.[39] We can abstract universal concepts such as species and genera from their individuals, by stripping them of their particular characteristics.[40] Since universals do not exist *in re* they must do so *in intellectu*.[41] This is an issue of the mental universal. Thus on the question of universals, Ṣadrā reveals his nominalism.[42] One can express this argument in the syllogism:

1 All existents occur as specific particulars that are essentially and accidentally differentiated.
2 Yet for all of these one can abstract a single sense that relates to each particular in turn.
3 This single sense exists but as a universal.
4 Universals exist only in the mind.
5 Therefore, the single sense of being exists in the mind.

Universal concepts such as quiddity thus have an essential occurrence in the mind that relates to its existential manifestation (not existence of itself) *in re*.[43] Ṣadrā provides two further proofs for why this single universal sense must exist in the mind alone. The first takes the form of an exceptive syllogism (*qiyās istithnā'ī*). If forms existed in a single sense in extra-mental reality, then to be differentiated they would need specific and different concomitants by contradictory properties. Now since the consequent is invalid, the antecedent must be too. Hence that single sense cannot exist *in re*, but in the mind. The second argument concerns predication. If the single sense abstracted existed in extra-mental reality, then the particular must too since every existent in extra-mental reality is individuated (*mutashakhkhiṣ*). Particulars cannot be predicates, since in categorical (*ḥamliyya*) propositions, the predicate must be an unconditioned concept while the particular is conditioned. Yet the single sense in categorical propositions is a predicate. Therefore, that single sense must only exist in the mind.[44]

One can posit two objections to this argument. The first is that natural universals (drawing on the authority of Avicenna) do exist in extra-mental reality. Second, every existent is a particular species and does not have a shared quality that is predicated in the mind of many.[45] Ṣadrā responds with the following. As for the first objection, if natural universals existed then the secondary intelligibles that are its accidents would also have to exist. Thus the universal 'humanity' would be instantiated as would its specific accidents as Zayd and Zaynab and so on. But this is invalid. The universal considered in itself has no existence *in re*.[46] The second objection is also refuted in the following manner:

> One does not mean by 'human' that exists in the mind (*fī-l-dhihn*), for example, a specific particular person . . . Rather, one means that we can conceive of the notion of man that corresponds to the many and it is present in the mind. We know with certainty that 'human', known . . . in this sense, does not exist in extra-mental reality nor is he an individual individuated in extra-mental reality (*fī-l-khārij*).[47]

The fourth argument is called an insight (*istibṣār*).

> We can conceive of abstracted entities (*al-umūr al-intizāʿiyya*) and privative attributes (*al-ṣifāt al-maʿdūmiyya*) in extra-mental reality and we can predicate them of things. It follows that they have some affirmation, which is either in extra-mental reality and that is impossible because they are 'beings of reason' (*umūr iʿtibāriyya*), or they exist in the mind.[48]

We can analyse this into three premisses and a conclusion.

1 Beings of reason, that is secondary intelligibles, have no reality but are predicable.
2 But predicates in categorical propositions must exist.
3 Insofar as a predicate is an abstracted thing, it does not exist *in re*.
4 Therefore it must exist in the mind.

This proof is not complete and as Sabzawārī says the second premiss is problematic given the rule of presupposition. These beings possess 'inexistence' (to use Brentano's term) and are intentional, existing *only* in the mind.[49]

Ṣadrā claims that his fifth argument is divinely inspired (*ilhām*) directly experienced from the divine throne (that is by his heart, the seat of such experience). Every intentional agent acts with a goal in mind. However, it cannot realise that act if there is no form of the goal of the action in the mind. That goal has no extra-mental reality. Therefore it must have mental being. This argument depends on a distinction between the final cause and the *telos*, as well as an unarticulated fourth premiss that the quiddity of the *telos* of the action that is in the mind and that will be realised *in re* be the same.[50]

The final argument concerns non-actual and imaginary entities.[51] Non-actual things, that is estimative (*al-wahmiyya al-ghayr al-wāqiʿa*) entities that do not occur *in re* (*fī-l-aʿyān*), can be causes for effects *in re*.[52] But non-being cannot be a cause for being.[53] So these estimative entities must have mental being. Mental being does have causal relations with the actual world since pain and its recognition does make us react physically. But the effects of mental are quite distinct.[54] This does not mean that mental being has effects within itself that are real. That would entail one's concept of fire in mental being literally burning up one's brain.[55] He bolsters the argument with two supporting arguments. First, physicians agree that disease can have psychosomatic causes and their healing can also be psychosomatic. Second, given that souls are graded in a psychic hierarchy, some souls are so potent and elevated in nobility that their conceptions can create and manifest being *in re*. This is also true of spiritual and psychic healing.[56]

The discussion of mental being has its weaknesses. For Ṣadrā, it applies to all levels of perception and of perceived consciousness, but he also demonstrates it for the imagination (and estimation) and for intellection (though not for sense perception).[57] But there are two problems. First, mental being as a philosophical concept seems to depend upon and work if one accepts the logical priority of quiddity over being, a thesis unacceptable to Ṣadrā. Because mental being considers entities that are never actualised, it is known as 'shadowy manifestation' and non-principal in contrast to actual being *in re*.[58] As such, an affirmation of mental being seems to smack of idealism, despite the psychic realm's complementarity with extra-mental being.[59] Idealism is also more consonant with an ontological priority of essences and an epistemological theory of eidetic vision, each of which underlie his concerns and yet in their explicit form are rejected.[60] Second, the Sadrian theory is open to the criticism of 'perspective realism'. Take a table that exists *in re*. The form that corresponds to it is not a singular one but perspectival depending on the perspective of one's perception of it. Therefore, how can one verify the concept of table? This is in fact an objection to most of his proofs, at the very least to the first three. However, for Ṣadrā, perception is complete and unhindered by 'clinical dysfunctions' of the senses. The concept of table is grasped as a whole.

Consciousness and panpsychism

Mental being is the realm of experience or consciousness.[61] A conscious person is aware of the existence of the content and intentional objects of his conscious states as well as of his own existence.[62] Consciousness thus consists in the existence of a world and what it is to be something.[63] Being is thus prior to or at least a prerequisite for consciousness.[64] The world is a 'field of objects of awareness'.[65] At this point, one raises the objection that if you are conscious that a chair exists in this room, what prevents it being the case that that chair exists merely for you and no one else?[66] But the existence of the chair is actually quite independent and separate from one's consciousness of its existence, a bit like the Sadrian separation of mental being from actual being.[67] It is a grave category mistake to confuse mental being for extra-mental being.

Consciousness for the Illuminationists is that experience that underlies metaphysics and is foundational for epistemology.[68] Consciousness is not considered in terms of specific minds, but in terms of a source of experience that transcends individual subjects. Conscious experience is of something since it is characterised by intentionality and not immanent subjective states.[69] One experiences the world and oneself. Consciousness like knowledge and reality admits of degrees.[70] Ṣadrā defines consciousness (*shuʿūr*) as perception without affirmation or judgement, a pure first stage in attaining knowledge in the intellecting faculty.[71] It is identical to being: 'If one does not have cognition (*maʿrifa*) of oneself, his self has no being, because being is the same as light, presence (*ḥuḍūr*) and consciousness (*shuʿūr*)'.[72]

Like being, it is immediate and intimate, yet quite mysterious and hidden.[73] It is characterised by the considerations of intentionality as it can conceive of objects

more generally and participates in its causality. The further distinction between the concept of being and mental being allows for our definition of consciousness in terms of intentionality.

Ṣadrā is a panpsychist. The equation of being and consciousness demand it. All beings are conscious for two reasons, one by proof and the other by faith. The first is connected to the proof of the union of intellect: all *intelligibilia* are beings that are conscious. One can only know like, hence one can only know conscious beings, and since one can know all beings, all beings must be conscious.[76] For the second he quotes Qur'ān 44:17: 'everything sings His praise but you do not understand it', and 49:16: 'all things in the heavens and the earth worship God'. The whole discussion stems from the notion of the erotic motion at the heart of the cosmos that one finds in the Neoplatonic tradition, mediated by the famous *Treatise on Eros* (*Risālat al-ʿishq*) of Avicenna. In the *scholia*, the commentator Sabzawārī argues that everything possessing life possesses consciousness and every conscious being has an erotic desire that attracts it to beauty and seeks out its beloved. This process begins the emanation of the cosmos from the One who sees the beauty of himself and the process of reversion whereby entities in the cosmos desire to return to the beloved One whence they issued. The continuity with late antique thought is stark.

Neoplatonism upholds panpsychism in a psychic series of procession with differing levels of intensity because of the difference of potency between the cause and the effect.[77] It posits a hierarchy of experience or consciousness that is not defined in physical terms.[78] The *nous* that is God constitutes a psychic realm and all extra-mental beings are thus grades of His knowledge in the sense of being by His knowing them.[79] Knowledge as a process seeks processes not static things.[80] This psychic chain is related through the rule of 'noble contingency', a view of reality important in post-Avicennan philosophy that draws upon Avicenna's observation that 'the reality of being begins from the higher principle down to the next until the hierarchy of nobility ends in [base] matter'.[81] Ṣadrā discusses the same process in his psychology with respect to causality:

> The being of souls in their intelligible origin (*al-mabda' al-ʿaqlī*) is the being of a thing in a thing *in potentia*, such as the being of infinite forms in their receptive origin (*wujūd al-ṣuwar al-ghayr al-mutanāhiya fī-l-mabda' al-qābilī*), that is, prime matter (*al-hayūlá al-ūlá*). This is because the being of a thing in the agent is not like its being in the recipient [effect, that which receives the agency], since its being in the agent is more intense in its occurrence and more complete in its activity than its being in the effect. Its being in the recipient may be less complete and inferior to its being
>
> separated.[83]

The soul is unitary and *mushakkak* with respect to its faculties:

> The soul is all [its] faculties (*al-nafs kullu l-quwá*). It is a unitary comprehension of them and their principle and *telos* (*mabda'uhā wa-ghāyatuhā*). Every higher faculty has a faculty below it that serves it, whether its service is by priority or posteriority (*bi-l-taqdīm wa-l-ta'khīr*). Some of these faculties are prior to others and whatever is temporally prior is last in rank and nobility (*bi-l-rutba wa-l-sharaf*).[84]

This follows from the rule of the simple reality, which is all things that are predicated of it.[85] This is a soul that is a unity-in-plurality.[86] This is a response to Peripatetic faculty-based psychology that divided the soul into parts that perceive *sensibilia* and that perceive *intelligibilia*. For our philosopher, such division is unacceptable. It is the united self that is the agent of intellection.

The intellect itself is graded in levels of intensity that account for its unity-in-diversity or its identity-in-difference.[87] A simple expression of this is the threefold levels of the intellect (or perhaps the tripartite intellect) and intellection acceptable to most philosophers.[88] The first level is that of the intellect *in potentia* in which none of the *intelligibilia* exist *in actu*.[89] The second level is that of psychic intelligible forms that occur in imaginal potentiality. The third level is that of the simple intellect in which the *intelligibilia* exist stripped of their multiplicity and detailed discursive content.[90]

Panpsychism is problematic. That all matter has conscious states is a direct opposite to idealism but for many philosophers equally fallacious.[91] First, the idea that rocks and elementary particles have an inner conscious life is 'outrageous'. Mere matter gives no signs of such states and nor do we know what sorts of mental states they might have.[92] Second, panpsychism holds that mental states are supervenient on physical properties. How does this come about? Third, we are asked to believe that, at the very least, such inanimate matter has proto-consciousness and not quite full-fledged sensations and dispositions.[93] But even this is an extravagant claim.[94] The outrage against panpsychism thus seems to boil down to the problem of inanimate matter based on a static concept of mind and matter. This is clearly an impoverished concept and Ṣadrā's processual and developmental model of the intensification of the mind and soul from its material origins provides a credible alternative view.

The soul as a substance permits intensification and motion within its being.[95] This intensification is an act of purification and a Neoplatonic theurgic reversion to the One drawing upon Iamblichus' metaphysics.[96] The soul itself develops and grows from its quasi-material beginnings towards union with the simple intellect.[97] It is bodily in its inception and spiritual in its sempiternity (*jismāniyyat al-ḥudūth wa-rūḥāniyyat al-baqā'*).[98] This draws upon the Neoplatonic idea that the soul requires a physical vehicle (*ḥammālat al-badan*) to drive it forth, though it itself is not corporeal nor does it possess extension as a body, clearly a dualist notion.[99] The soul begins materially united with the body (thus qualifying dualism) and becomes immaterial.[100] Knowledge is a self-perfection of the soul from potency to act.[101] This process of growth is explained with recourse to modulation.[102]

The soul-intellect comes from God and given the precedence of man in the chain of being, is a strong cosmological proof for God, a book to be read and a sign of Him.[103] The Neoplatonic arguments about its pre-existence and fall are discussed and considered before being rejected.[104] The texts that Ṣadrā considers include the Avicennan 'visionary recital' of *Salamān and Absāl* as well as the views of Empedocles and Plato from the *Phaedo* and *Timaeus* as quoted in the *Enneads/ Theologia*.[105] The account of the being of souls in the previous world is, however, reconciled by the modulation of the concept. Separable being is not the same as 'attached' being, and the being of souls in the intelligible world is not the same as their being in this world where sensible being is multiple temporally, by position and so on.[106] The process of intellection is one of the substantial change of the soul-intellect through the three ontic domains of *sensibilia*, *imaginalia* and *intelligibilia*:

> The soul perceives universal intelligibles as intelligible incorporeal essences (*dhawāt ʿaqliyya mujarrada*) and not through abstracting from *sensibilia* their intelligible [form] . . . Rather, [it intellects] by transferring from the sensible to the imaginal to the intelligible (*al-maḥsūs ilá l-mutakhayyal ilá l-maʿqūl*), and its own transferral from this world to another and then beyond the two. It journeys from the world of bodies (*ʿālam al-ajrām*) to the [mediate] world of archetypes (*ʿālam al-mithāl*) and then to the world of intellects (*ʿālam al-ʿuqūl*).[107]

Since the soul supervenes over the body and has no extension, it is not confined by it.[108] How does one retain individuality in a panpsychist world? Most ancient theories held that the individuals through a lifetime of change have a bundle of qualities that keeps their identity distinct and intact.[109] For Ṣadrā being is the source of identity and undergoes constant process. Things and identities are structure of these events or processes. Strawson posits two materialist objections to the processist problem of identity.[110] First, for objective and identifiable particulars to be known, they must be distinguishable from others and re-identifiable over time. Second, only material objects meet these conditions.[111] But processual entities do retain identity through their being that is a vortex and structure of events. Identity lies in the connection between those events over time.[112] Besides, Strawson's critique begs the questions because the principles of distinction and identification that he posits are themselves material.[113] For Ṣadrā, the principle of differentiation is identical to the principle of commonality, that is, being. Personal identity resides in being, in the rational soul whose extension is not the same as that of the body. It is the rational soul that, despite its material beginnings in its body, defines the person. The extension of the brain is not the same as the mind.[114] Also we need to take care in ascribing a notion of a personal self that grew out of Cartesian scepticism and doubt to our philosopher.[115] Identity does not reside in this self that is uniquely personal and essentialist.

What is knowledge?

So how does this self know? Mullā Ṣadrā inherited a variety of theories ranging from Platonic recollection (*anamnesis*) and division to Peripatetic syllogistics, definitions and axiomatic science. Broadly speaking, our author recognises three different epistemological methods. The first is a co-relational (*iḍāfī*) model of knowledge.[116] In this model, knowledge is a relation between a subject and an object that is devoid of cognitive content in itself and is not intrinsically intelligible. It is a property of the knower and devoid of actual process. Knowledge is dispositional; 'know' in this model is a 'capacity verb' to use Ryle's formulation.[117] As such, this theory is marked by radical internalism. This is a view associated with later mediaeval theologians (especially Fakhr al-Dīn Rāzī) and rejected.[118] It is unacceptable to Ṣadrā precisely because it is predicated upon a denial of mental being.[119] According to this model, knowledge is negative insofar as it is solipsistic.[120]

The second model is the correspondence or representation theory of knowledge by apprehension (*al-ʿilm al-ḥuṣūlī al-irtisāmī*).[121] 'I know that P' means that there is an external object P that corresponds to an internal concept P. The mind is thus the 'mirror of nature'.[122] It judges a relationship between the extra-mental object and the mental picture of it as described in Wittgenstein's picture theory.[123] The inadequacies of this model are clear. It fails to account for conceivables that do not exist. Knowledge is the correspondence between the object and the subject, and mediated. It presupposes the existence of independent extra-mental entities 'out there' and is strongly dualistic. The mind abstracts the form from the matter of the thing and represents it. As such it is a negative fact (*amr salbī*).[124] One can only grasp the form in the mind since the essences of things are not available to us. But Ṣadrā argues that the consequent is clearly false, so the antecedent is as well.[125] They are available to us insofar as they exist and are present to us. Knowledge is not an abstraction.[126] The accidental material forms of intelligibles thus grasped are not the true objects of knowledge; those are the pure intelligibles experienced directly.[127] This Peripatetic doctrine is rejected. It is quite wrong to assume in this model that perception is so mediated that it requires an interface between the mind and external objects (often called qualia).[128] This model does not actually yield the reality of the thing, though it does seek the quiddity of things. Ṣadrā quotes Avicenna's *al-Taʿlīqāt* on this.

> The realities of things are not available to man; we only know the specific attributes (*al-khawāṣṣ*), the concomitant attributes (*al-lawāzim*) and the accidents (*al-aʿrāḍ*) of things, and we do not know the differentiae that are constituents of everything, one of which indicates its reality. Rather, we know that there are things that have specific attributes and accidents.[129]

It remains the case that Ṣadrā accepts a correspondence theory of knowledge though it is not his preferred option for arriving at indubitable knowledge.[130] However, these models are insufficient and do not yield certainty, which is only available through the third model of knowledge by presence.[131]

> Being can only be known by visionary presential knowledge (*al-ʿilm al-ḥuḍūrī al-shuhūdī*), and the inner-reality of light can only be perceived by an immediate illuminative correlation (*al-iḍāfa al-ishrāqiyya*) and actual presence (*al-ḥuḍūr al-ʿaynī*). If something is known by formal knowledge (*al-ʿilm al-ṣūrī*), it changes the reality (*inqilāb al-ḥaqīqa*) of it.[132]

Knowledge by presence

Knowledge by presence is defined as the 'priority of an immediate, durationless, intuitive mode of cognition over the temporally extended essentialist definitions used as predicative propositions'.[133] All *intelligibilia* are part of the same class of entities related in a set-theoretical model of metaphysics. There is neither duality nor a strong 'me-world' distinction. This is Platonic epistemology, whose roots lie in the famous parable of the cave.[134] True knowledge resides in the direct experience of objects of knowledge.[135] The true philosopher seeks his own self and reality that lies in uniting with the intelligible realm such that he becomes knowledge.[136] The *nous*, the intellecting subject and intelligible object are united: that is how one defines intellection.[137] This union is existential and not quidditative.

In this model, knowledge is a flow of acts of being that are mental acts, with each knowledge-episode corresponding to a degree of actual being.[138]

> Knowledge is neither a negative affair (*amran salbiyyan*) like an abstraction from matter (*al-tajarrud ʿan al-mādda*) nor is it correlative (*iḍāfiyyan*) but a being, not just any being but being *in actu* (*bi-l-fiʿl*) and not being *in potentia* (*bi-l-quwwa*). It is not even every being *in actu* but a pure being uncontaminated by privation (*wujūdan khāliṣan ghayr mashūb bi-l-ʿadam*). To the extent that it is pure from any contamination by privation, its intensity as knowledge increases.[139]

It is only presential knowledge that discloses the reality of being,[140] since being is presence.[141] Experience justifies belief (and hence leads to knowledge).[142] 'The process of perception is itself a section of the ascending scale of knowledge', which is itself the ascending scale of being reverting to the One.[143] The top of the scale, or the most simple being is also the level of the *nous*, of pure intellect and of pure unmediated, non-propositional knowledge.[144] Any discussion of knowledge, the unity of knowledge, the knowing subject and the known is part of metaphysics proper since it is an essential accident of being *qua* being.[145] One does not fall into the problem of God's knowledge of particulars since all knowledge is of particulars, a strikingly nominalist (and empiricist) position.[146] Furthermore it allows for greater possibilities of knowledge. The mind can grasp a limited number of forms given the theory available to Ṣadrā, but the presence of forms and *intelligibilia* to the mind is infinite. He adduces this from the famous saying of the Prophet that 'the heart of the believer is more vast than the Throne of God', that the heavens and the earth can be present to the mind of a believer.[147] The soul itself is the creator of the images that are pure extension identical with the soul and not in the soul.[148] These things are immediately present one to the other within the class of being as variables within the same set, and related to each other by an 'illuminative relation' (*iḍāfa ishrāqiyya*) defined by Ziai as a 'non-predicative relation between subject and predicate',[149] that is also atemporal.[150] 'I-ness' is thus nothing but dependence on the other and as such indicates a class of entities.[151] In this process the nature of the soul is thus:

> The state of the soul with respect to intelligible forms (*al-ṣuwar al-ʿaqliyya*) of foundational species (*al-anwā' al-muta'aṣṣila*) is that a purely illuminative correlation exists between it and luminous intelligible essences (*dhawāt nūriyya ʿaqliyya*) occurring in the world of creation (*ʿālam al-ibdā'*) [that is, of archetypal forms] relating them to the bodily manifestations of their species.[152]

This argument draws upon the theory of Platonic forms as the converse of the Aristotelian concept of abstracting forms from individuals. Pure perception of the universal *intelligibilia* by the soul is not an abstraction from *sensibilia* as most philosophers think, but a direct experience of intelligible incorporeal essences (*dhawāt ʿaqliyya mujarrada*).[153]

Presential knowledge begins with self-knowledge (articulated in the doffing metaphor from Plotinus through the *Theologia*).[154] Self-knowledge is part of the proof of the incorporeality of the soul and one's immediate awareness of oneself devoid of one's body and of the transcendent 'I'.[155] Ṣadrā quotes Suhrawardī's famous dream vision of Aristotle in which the Stagirite tells him to 'start with yourself' to understand knowledge.[156] Self-knowledge is immediate, primitive and presential. If it were not, it would entail an infinite regress.[157] There is no pre-epistemic doubt since it is indubitable that the knowing subject and the 'I' are identical.[158] Hence there is no distinction between knowledge claims and their objects.[159] The knowing 'I' of pure knowledge is shared at the level of union with the Active Intellect; such knowledge is a perfection of existence.[160] A knowing subject that is incorporeal must be conscious of himself, or else perception would not be available to him.[161] One cannot separate the fact that one knows from being known [by oneself].[162]

> No particular sense-perception or phenomenal state of mind, even though in the form 'I', can ever bear witness to the truth value of the existence of myself. This is because any phenomenal event which I attribute to myself, such as my feeling cold or warm and so on, must be and is presupposed by an underlying awareness of myself.[163]

For Ṣadrā, 'I know that I know' has two senses.[164] First, self-knowledge as a non-propositional fact is the same as being and is not an affirmation of some universal knowledge that instantiates itself in 'I know'. It is merely predicative and not verifiable.[165] Second, the propositional form of 'I know that I know' is not being, since any representation of being is a falsification because no mode of being has a cognitive form corresponding to it.[166] It identifies the 'I' and represents it to oneself.[167] Ṣadrā puts it thus:

> It is said that our knowledge of our self is the same as our being and our knowledge of our knowledge is not the same as our existence. Rather, it is a mental form that supervenes upon us (*ṣūra dhihniyya zā'ida ʿalaynā*) which is not the same as our individual ipseity (*huwiyyatunā al-shakhṣiyya*) and is a separate ipseity. Thus our knowledge of our knowledge is a form supervening upon the ipseity of the first two acts of cognition.[168]

Experience of the reality of being is non-conceptual and an intuitive 'tasting' (*dhawq*).[169] Yet the paradox of this experience lies in the dependence of a non-linguistic phenomenon on language to express its existence.[170]

Union of the intellecting subject and object

Critical to presential knowledge is the Porphyrian doctrine of the unity of the intellect, the intellecting subject and its intelligible object.[171] Proclus similarly posits a unity between being and knowing that expresses this epistemic union: there is no difference between having a thought about a thing and being that thing.[172] In Plotinus, one finds the following description of intellection using light symbolism:

> In the intelligible world, seeing is not through another but through itself, because it is not divested outside. Intellect therefore sees one light with another, not through another. Light then sees another light; it therefore itself sees light.[173]

Pure self-knowledge for Plotinus depends on union with the divine intellect that self-intellects.[174] Such a noetic experience is non-discursive.[175]

Avicenna (on this point followed by Suhrawardī)[176] strongly criticises this doctrine. One thing cannot become another substantially, nor can a rational soul unite with the Active Intellect which is indivisible. The human intellect cannot be united with *intelligibilia*.[177] Rather one knows things by conjunction (*ittiṣāl*) not union (*ittiḥād*) with the Active Intellect from whence one grasps the universals of things immanent in it.[178] The soul receives the forms from the Active Intellect but remains unchanged itself. The forms inhere in the soul-intellect through the material intellect. Avicenna criticises Porphyry for popularising the fallacy of union and change.[179] But in doing so Avicenna marks a sharp distinction between God's knowledge and human knowledge, for which he is criticised by some philosophers,[180] especially Ṭūsī.[181] One cannot hold such a view about God's knowledge because it violates both His unity and the fact of His knowledge of particulars.[182] Yet in his *al-Mabda'*, Avicenna actually proposes knowledge by presence for God because the nature of the divine intellect is radically different from human intellect and indeed needs to be if one wishes to avoid violating the unity of the godhead.[183]

Ṣadrā's criticism of Avicenna is predicated upon two central doctrines of his that are intimately linked to the hermeneutic of modulation.[184] First, the primacy (and modulation) of being proves this union.

> Being in everything is foundational (*al-aṣl fī-l-mawjūdiyya*) . . . It is the principle of individuality (*mabda' al-shakhṣiyya*) and the source of the

> quiddity of the thing (*manshāʾ māhiyyatihi*). Being can become more intense and become weaker, it can become more perfect and it can become imperfect, yet the individual remains who he is (*al-shakhṣ huwa huwa*). Do you not see that man from his beginning as a foetus to the end of his being intellects and is intellected while his contexts and situations change yet the mode of his being and his individuality remain constant.[185]

Second, the doctrine of (trans-)substantial motion defends union.[186] The soul is in motion as 'pure act' (*fiʿliyya, energeia*).[187] Further, union is not a substantial or even conceptual one but an epistemic and referential union in which the components 'become one existent insofar as a single intelligible notion refers to it'.[188] Ṣadrā even argues that Avicenna himself allows for such a reading of union in his *al-Shifāʾ*.[189] Presential knowledge is intuitive for him and he claims to have realised its truth in an inner-revelation (*kashf*) when on pilgrimage to Qum.[190] The ultimate nature of knowledge, like being, does not distinguish strictly between the divine and human. Multiplicity in the intellect does not entail multiplicity in God because these *intelligibilia* are correlated as 'illuminative relations'.[191] Being-intellecting (*ʿāqiliyya*) and being-intellected (*maʿqūliyya*) are correlatives that cannot exist independently.[192]

The simple intellect (that is God) knows all things since all things are present in it and it is the ultimate referent for all concepts.[193] This is the 'internality thesis', that all *intelligibilia* are internal to intellect and the objects of sense perception are external.[194] Our philosopher strongly criticises Avicenna for holding the concept of the simple intellect (which for Avicenna is simple cognition that is non-discursive and without recourse to forms) whilst denying the union of the intellecting subject and its object.[195] Furthermore, for the Peripatetic tradition, the human intellect in this life cannot attain the level of the pure simple intellect.[196] Ṣadrā refutes this:

> If the simple intellect (*al-ʿaql al-basīṭ*) (which he believes exists in the human species and in separable substances) is not [all] *intelligibilia*, then how can souls benefit from what does not occur in them? How can souls move from potentiality to actuality from what is not in them?[197]

The mode of the being of things in this simple intellect is known as 'the thing (or fact) itself' (*nafs al-amr*) or the immanent object.[198] This simple and higher intellect is not abstracted but contains all lower and complex forms and degrees of being.[199] It is in this sense that this *nous* is a 'unity-in-plurality'.[200] It is also the Aristotelian Active Intellect of *De Anima* III.5.[201] In Hermetic terms it is this *logos* that guides human intellects through their lives.[202]

But how does one safeguard individuality and the ontological distinction of man and God?[203] The solution is through the concept of intelligibility and forms. All *intelligibilia* and forms exist in the Simple/Active Intellect *in potentia*, but their actualisations are individual existents extrinsic to the intellect.[204] The Active Intellect is thus the referent for the predication of *intelligibilia*.[205] This union does not dissolve the individual being of intellects.[206]

> The intellect is all things intelligible (*al-ʿaql kullu l-ashyāʾ al-maʿqūla*) . . . This does not mean that it is all those things in their extra-mental individual modes of being collected together as this is impossible . . . Rather it means that all quiddities that exist in extra-mental reality through many different beings exist in the intellect through multiple intelligible beings in a singular intelligible being that in its unity and simplicity is all those meanings.[207]

True knowledge resides therefore in uniting with the Active Intellect, a doctrine rejected by the Peripatetics.[208] Union does not entail multiplicity in the divine essence in any sense.[209]

Ṣadrā claims to follow (pseudo-)Aristotle on union quoting from the *Theologia*. First, he insists on the unity of the intelligible realm:

> The higher [intelligible] realm that is complete and living contains in it all things because all things are created by one creator. In it are all souls and intellects, and there is neither dependence nor need in it.[210]

Distinction within this realm is by modulation, by varying motion and lights upon lights in order of nobility.[211] Second, drawing on Plotinus, he holds that: 'All things are in intellect and from intellect, and intellect is all things'.[212]

In this model of knowledge, there is pure self-reflexivity, no *doxa* about forms and no *epistēmē* about *sensibilia*.[213] It is a form of infallibilism.[214] One cannot mistake state A for state B since one must first cognise state A.[215] But is this form of knowledge useful and does it communicate? Or it is merely ineffable like so many beliefs and feelings that are important to the way we live our lives? In the simple intellect one knows things at once. Thus for a proposition A, we do not know S first and then P but both *dafʿatan wāḥidatan*, that is simultaneously.[216] But the content of the simple intellect unlike Avicenna's account is not different to the discursive dianoic intellect. S and P are contents of A whether one knows A simply or discursively.[217] This deals with one of the famous objections to non-propositional thought in Plotinus, that of entailing non-complexity.[218] What is required is an adequate metalanguage of such experience since one can and does talk about such knowledge.[219] One can forge a linguistic discipline to discuss it but the presential knowledge involved is not informational and cannot be grounds for public knowledge but indicators for initiates.[220] The immediacy, infallibility and successful cognition of presential knowledge privileges it over other epistemological models.

The 'private language fallacy'

Does this theory lay itself open to the private language fallacy? Wittgenstein defines a private language as one whose '[W]ords . . . refer to what can be known only to the speaker; to his immediate, private sensations. So another cannot understand the language'.[221]

For it to work, one would need to establish a language for those sensations and establish connections between one's signs for those sensations as rules that apply over time. These connections would not verify in terms of truth but of meaning. One understands expressions by grasping the patterns of their application.[222] Wittgenstein established that such rule-forming was impossible because it was circular. Language as a means of communication is defined by agreement in human behaviour and in this sense is not atomic.[223] Meaning only occurs in the context of a linguistic community and is formed contractually in communal practice.[224] Mental phenomena are not characterised by introspection but mediated through language into which they are woven, an expression of constructivism.[225] Thus one's pains although immediate are described as pains not because they are self-intimating but because of a shared concept of 'pain'. The whole possibility of epistemic privacy is laid bare. Internalism is rejected in line with the Kantian refutation of idealism and with a critique of a Platonic mental language.[226]

But this objection is based on three assumptions. First, one assumes a dichotomous relationship between subject and object, and as a corollary, a distinction between the subjective and objective in the knowledge process. But the idea that everything 'out there' is objective and 'given' and that one is utterly different is untenable.[227] Objective and subjective are more relative terms and co-dependent for their intelligibility. Second, one assumes that language mediates thought whereas being-in-language for Ṣadrā is quite independent of mental being (and indeed of being *in actu* as well). Third, one assumes a post-Cartesian concept of a private self that is utterly separate from its others raising the epistemic problem of other minds.[228] Experience and language is public and shared. Is a private language really impossible? Can one not allow for a language that is seemingly public, using public concepts and terms, but has a personal code and signature that is incomprehensible to others? Common language is thus a set of linguistic propensities but not common notions of use of meaning.[229] I would contend that such a language is indeed possible. One can write notes to oneself that are indecipherable to others even if ostensibly in a common language.

For Ṣadrā, knowledge and experience cannot be merely subjective and cannot fall victim to the private language fallacy since his whole philosophical method is predicated upon presential knowledge. Rather, experience, the intellect and consciousness are not properly limited to individual selves *qua* bodies or minds. They participate in an intelligible world that is beyond the bounds of the quiddities 'Zayd' or 'Zaynab' precisely because knowledge and the intellect are identical to being. It is indeed possible for one to track mental being on to instantiated being, the private language fallacy notwithstanding. He holds a certain form of panpsychism whereby the psychic realm or the domain of mental being is *mushakkak*, a unity-in-plurality. Just as particular beings are certain degrees of a wider reality of being, so too are those particular intellects associated with them degrees of a wider intellect-*psuchē*. A further defence is mystical experience, a form of non-discursive experience that is presential knowledge.[230] The attestation of pure consciousness experiences expressed and analysed in a metalanguage of mystical experience indicates the possibility of presential non-discursive language.[231]

Propositional content and secondary intelligibles

The content of mental being is mental language. Hence, does knowledge depend on language, or on being-in-language? Davidson holds that one 'cannot have thoughts unless it is an interpreter of the speech of another'.[232] That is, thought is dependent upon mental language and thus self-referential. But to have a belief surely does not entail having a second order concept of belief, *pace* Davidson? However, for Ṣadrā, knowledge is not dependent upon concepts and beliefs, not even the concept of being. One might even say that language and speech presuppose the existence of a mind.[233] At the level of the concept of being where there is no propositional representation,

> No being of an intelligible character occurs or does not occur by virtue of the perception of axioms (*al-awwaliyyāt*) and general notions (*al-mafhūmāt al-ʿāmma*) insofar as a thing does not actually occur by virtue of some obscure, general state of affairs as long as it determines no state that is actually real.[234]

Language is, as mental being, a shadow of actuality. But the content of thought is often linguistic insofar as it is a reflection and not simple sensations.[235] Most mediaeval theories of mental language following Plato posit synonymy that explains homonymy in conventional languages. More recent philosophers consider this to be a non-natural language known as 'mentalese'.[236] But for Ṣadrā, this mental being and language is natural and also *mushakkak,* not synonymous but graded as both sense and reference are.[237] Natural and conventional languages are sharply distinct and types of homonymy characterise this natural language.[238] Indeed, successful hermeneutics depend upon it. Thus language depends on mental being that provides the propositional content of discourse.[239]

However, this mental being is quite distinct from another use of being, that is, its concept.[240] The concept of being is distinct from its reality as it possesses no reality in itself.[241] 'It is clear that the common notion of being is mental, derivative and abstracted (*dhihniyyan maṣdariyyan intizāʿiyyan*). But its 'individuals' [to which it refers] and its concomitants [that is, beings] are concrete actualisations'.[242]

The senses of the concept of being are what logic considers.[243] These are Ṣadrā's 'secondary intelligibles', whose ontic status is indeterminate insofar as they neither exist purely mentally or extra-mentally.[244] These are the logical universals that Avicenna discusses in the *Isagoge* of *al-Shifāʾ*, universals as such that are not related to natural kinds or quiddities, nor to the instantiation of the universal itself.[245]

The concept of being *qua* being mediates between the sense of being, the propositional content of being that is mental being, being-in-language that expresses it and its reference that is the reality of being.[246] As such it is a connector.[247] In itself it is not an ontic fact because it is distinct from both being *in re* and *in intellectu*.[248] The very definition of concept expresses this three-way relationship. A concept 'is an expression for the predicative judgement that follows the specificity of the meaning intended by the term'.[249] It mediates between what is expressed (*al-manṭūq*), mental language, and the referent (*al-miṣdāq*).[250] The concept of being is a secondary intelligible that has no reality but this does not mean that being has no reference.[251] It is a secondary intelligible [second order predicate] and a common abstracted notion.[252] Just because it is unreal does not mean that it is identical to quiddity.[253] Mental concepts are those whose 'qualification and occurrence' are solely in the mind.[254] They yield only mental propositions.[255]

How is the concept of being a secondary intelligible? First, we need to consider what a secondary intelligible is.[256] Secondary intelligibles as objects of pure logic are intentional, have no reference and are characterised by being content-less.[257]

> 'Secondary intelligible' is applied to intelligible predicables and their intentional and mental principles (*mabādīhā-l-intizāʿiyya al-dhihniyya*) such as . . . concomitants of quiddities, relations and correlations. It may also be applied to logical meanings and concepts (*al-maʿānī al-manṭiqiyya wa-l-mafhūmāt al-mīzāniyya*) . . . They are predicables (*al-maḥmūlāt*) and intelligible accidents that correspond to judgement and what is accounted in their predication upon concepts and their abstraction from attributes.[258]

Being as a secondary intelligible is distinct from its reality and reliant on mental being for its occurrence:

> Being in the derivative sense, and not what is its reality and its essence and such . . . is a secondary intelligible (*al-maʿqūl al-thānī*) . . . Secondary intelligibles correspond to the predicate (*al-ḥukm bihā*), which is a mode of the being of primary intelligibles in the mind, provided that it is considered as a limitation that it has and not as a condition in the subject (*al-maḥkūm ʿalayhi*). This is what is meant by the statement that secondary intelligibles rely upon primary intelligibles.[259]

This concept acts as a link to mental being and real being because it is capable of being understood in mental propositions and propositions with real subjects because it in itself is neither.

> Some attributes have no concrete being (*al-wujūd al-ʿaynī*) in any sense . . . They are the mental states of a mental being such as 'being-a-species' for humans and particularity for individuals. We do not mean by 'Zayd is particular in actuality' that the particularity belonging to it is an external form subsistent in Zayd. Similarly, we do not mean that there is a 'Zayd' in extra-mental [reality], insofar as he is in extra-mental [reality], a particular in the observa-

between two concepts, that is, the concepts of being and quiddity.

> The meaning of being in extra-mental [reality] and in the mind is a vessel for the qualification (*ẓarf al-ittiṣāf*), that is, the existence of the thing attributed in one of the two as a source for the validity of the abstraction by the intellect of that qualification from it.[261]

It is because of this ability that the concept of secondary intelligibles ought to be considered in metaphysics as well as logic. Thus he is critical of those who restrict it to logic.[262]

The concept of being is modulated by intensity.[263] There are two types of *tashkīk*: common and specific. One applies to the graded concept whose reference is a notion, and the other applies to the reality of being whose referents exist *in re*.[264] The concept ranges over a variety of instances of the reality of being from the Necessary down, each unique in itself.

> Indeed things differ in their existentiality. Every attribute possesses a degree of being against which their effects specified are arranged, even adjunctions, privations, possessions, faculties and predispositions. They possess weak portions of being and actuality and cannot be qualified by them except in their subsistence through their qualities (*mawṣūfātihā*).[265]
>
> The most Glorious and Transcendent is Rich, Subsistent and Necessary essentially . . . He is, *qua* He, pure activity (*fiʿliyya*), transcending above any contamination of potentiality and contingency and imperfection and weakness. Essential weakness and contingency accompany everything else in differing degrees and distinct levels. The weakness of everything that succeeds the source of being and necessity is more intense and its contingency is greater, until being culminates [at the bottom end] in the most base and vulgar. That is substantial being whose subsistence is through a form disposed in it, and whose activity is pure potentiality and predisposition . . . Then you know this mode of weakness in the substance with respect to the descent.[266]

The final point to make about the secondary intelligible as a mental concept is that it provides an imitative account of reality.[267] The concept of being and conceptualisation of reality falsify it according to Ṣadrā. It is how the mind represents reality to itself and mediates between our three modes of being.[268]

Beings of reason and the existence–essence distinction

There are two levels to the content of mental being: corresponding entities and

issues are directly relevant: the modes of quiddity, quiddity as a universal and its relationship with existence expressed in the famous medieval existence–essence distinction.

First, we need to define quiddity, the answer to 'what is it' when asked of a thing.[271]

> Quiddity (*māhiyya*) is used in two different senses: the first sense is identical to existence (*inniyya*),[272] that is, it is neither universal nor particular in the sense of its being individuated by an individuation additional to its essence, rather it is identical to individuation [as Aristotle and others hold]. The other sense is not the essence and is commonly shared and universal. The concomitant properties of the first sense are actual and individual essences while those of the latter are purely universal and abstract/intentional, and have no referent.[273]

These are two senses of quiddity: what a thing is *qua* its essence, that is as a universal such as 'animal', and what a thing is in its identity as an individuated thing.[274] We are concerned here with the former concept. Quiddity is contrasted with being in that it does not undergo modulation because it is a common notion.[275] Ṣadrā quotes the view of Avicenna that blackness cannot be more or less with respect to itself. The shared nature of a quiddity cannot undergo intensification and debilitation. An essence cannot thus be differentiated in itself with respect to its essence and properties.[276]

Quiddity has three modes: unconditioned, *in re* and in the soul.[277] Purely unconditioned quiddity *qua* quiddity has no mode of being.[278] It is indifferent to both being and privation.[279] It is neither one nor many nor universal nor particular.[280] This mode actually has two sub-sections: complete non-conditionality (*lā bi-sharṭ qismī*) and non-conditionality related to the parts of the essence abstracted (*lā bi-sharṭ muqsimī*).[281] In this mode, if one is asked whether a human *qua* humanity exists, then the proper reply is to say that it neither exists nor does it not exist.[282] It is not quite a universal but a natural universal that shares one-to-one relationship with its particulars.[283] The very fact that one can talk about quiddity *qua* quiddity and predicate it suggests this latter mode in which quiddity possesses at the least a copulative mode of being (discussed in the previous chapter).[284] Quiddity in the soul is a universal: that is, it is shared without occurring in extra-mental reality. It is 'representative and cognitive, not existing independently in the world and is a kind of shadow'.[285] Quiddities in this mode, are very much like qualia (or sense data as they were called earlier in the century) functioning within what is now known as a Cartesian-cum-materialist concept of perception.[286]

Universals are of three types in Porphyry: transcendents (like Platonic forms), products of the transcendent that exist in each individual, and genuine universals, that is those which are posterior and only exist in conception.[287] What is important to note is that Neoplatonists are not nominalists, that is, they do not identify universals with expressions.[288] But our philosopher is more of a conceptualist as we have seen. Quiddity *in re* is what is qualified by being insofar as its concept is attached to an entity.[289] It is what picks out and distinguishes an entity.[290] As such one ought to be careful to differentiate the concept of quiddity from universality since any identification must exclude quiddity's predication of an individual.[291]

Having considered what quiddity is, we need to examine its relation to being. The distinction between the existence and quiddity of contingents is famously associated with Avicenna, though arguably a more ancient concept.[292] In *al-Ishārāt*, he says:

> Know that one can understand the meaning (*maʿná*) of triangle while doubting whether it is qualified by existence *in re* or not, after the conception of an image that is composed of shape and surface was impressed within one, but it was not impressed whether it existed or not.[293]

For Ṣadrā, the distinction has a diminished role given his position on quiddity and being respectively. But it is still articulated:

> Quiddity is united with extra-mental existence *in re*, and with mental being in the mind. However, the mind, insofar as it can conceive the quiddity without regard to anything pertaining to being, judges a difference between the two.[294]

The ontological priority of being is critical to this distinction.[295] In *al-Mashāʿir*, Ṣadrā provides six proofs for the reality of being, to affirm that being has extra-mental reference and reality.[296] It is not a real distinction because quiddity is unreal.[297] Being is fundamental and the reality of everything.[298]

Being is logically supervenient upon quiddity since they are identical in reference and reality but distinct in the mind.[299] Their union in extra-mental reality is why their combination is called a 'composite dyad' (*zawj tarkībī*).[300] The distinction between the two is therefore mental.[301] A thing considered without any condition (*lā bi-sharṭ*) yields the quiddity, while considered negatively conditioned (*bi-sharṭ lā*), it yields its being.[302] It is being that is essential and quiddity that is accidental.[303] In fact it seems that quiddity is quite unreal since it cannot manifest itself.[304] It is 'virtual'.[305] For Ṣadrā, being defines the reality of something separate from its quiddity.

> This does not mean that there is a correspondence between the two in any reality, and the reality of everything is a mode of being specific to it. It is not an accident established in it like the establishment of accidents in their substrates that would require that quiddity had apart from being another existence. Rather [it is an accident] in the sense that the entity of contingent being due to its poverty and baseness includes a meaning apart from that of the reality of being, abstracted from it and predicated of it and established due to its imperfection and contingency, like the windows/networks that you see in degrees of imperfections of light and shadow occurrent from the conceptions of light.[306]

Being is the identity of the thing while its identification is its quiddity.[307] 'That which is experienced is being but that which is understood is quiddity'.[308]

This latter is through the action of the mental differentia that picks out the item in the mind.[309] Quiddity is thus mentally prior though ontologically posterior to being.[310] All things are beings and quiddities merely intentional. Khorassani draws from this the startling conclusion that our philosopher is an essentialist since quiddities are what one seeks and ultimately quiddities are all that there is.[311] But this is untenable especially if one considers that he is not withdrawn into solipsism or a hierarchical idealism in which nothing exists beyond the mind.[312] Identification is a process of conceptualisation and of the use of language to ascertain individuals.[313] On this, he quotes Ṭūsī's *Muṣāriʿ al-muṣāriʿ* that first the mind intuits being and then the mind attaches accidents and quiddities to the specific being intuited.[314] Here we have the distinction between two types of realisation or becoming, nomological and metaphysical.[315] Nomological realisation refers to the essences of things, follows rules and is subject to the relationships between universals and particulars and the definition of the thing. As such, this is complex and 'accidental making' (*al-jaʿl al-murakkab bi-l-ʿaraḍ*). In fact, 'making' is only applied to quiddity figuratively since it is not in any real sense.[316] But true metaphysical realisation refers to beings and is both real and simple 'essential making' (*al-jaʿl al-basīṭ bi-l-dhāt*) that is not subject to what a thing is *qua* its definition.[317] Being is thus logically prior, fundamental in reality and has reference, an argument mainly directed against Illuminationist essentialists.[318]

> Being in everything is the ground of existentiality (*al-wujūd fī kull shay' huwa-l-aṣl fī-l-mawjūdiyya*), and quiddity follows it. The reality of everything is a mode of the being that is particular to it devoid of its quiddity and its thingness. [The reality of] Being is not, as many of the recent philosophers have claimed, a secondary intelligible and an intentional thing that does not imply something in extra-mental [reality]. In fact the truth is that it is said that it is a concrete ipseity (*min al-huwiyyāt al-ʿayniyya*) that does not imply a mental thing.[319]

It is also being that is the principle of instantiation and not quiddity.[320] The qualification of quiddity by being is such that 'The being (*kawn*) of quiddities *in re* is an expression for its union with a mode of the reality of being, not in the sense that those who deny the natural universal conclude'.[321]

The existence–essence distinction is critical to Avicennan metaphysics of radical contingency.[322] But Ṣadrā, whilst paying lip-service to it, is more faithful to the Illuminationist tradition whose metaphysics of necessity regards even contingents as ultimately necessary by another. The mental distinction explains the role of quiddity in Ṣadrā's thought but in themselves quiddities are purely privative fictions.

not arise from quidditative differentiation. As we have seen above, Mulla Ṣadra does not hold that there is any distinction or scalar modulation within quiddity. Essences remain indeterminate and indeed must be for definitions of things to be meaningful and communicable. These beings are fashioned by the concept of being that mediates between actual entities *in re* and abstracted mental entities in the mind. The correspondence between these three modes is defined in terms of modulation of being.

5 Reality and the circle of being

> The reality of being, insofar as it is so unconfined by absoluteness or limitation (*ghayr muqayyad bi-l-iṭlāq wa-l-taqyīd*), is essential activity and manifestation (*al-fiʿliyya wa-l- ẓuhūr*). Contingent meanings and mental qualities only attach to it [being] with respect to its degrees . . . So being becomes absolute and limited, universal and particular, one and many with the occurrence of distinction in its essence and its reality.
>
> The reality of being (*al-ḥaqīqa al-wujūdiyya*) is the most common of things with respect to its inclusivity and its deployment among quiddities . . . Through the light of being are some privations differentiated from others in the mind since it can judge the impossibility of some of them and contingency of others.
>
> Being encompasses everything in its essence and through it do things subsist. If being did not exist, nothing would exist either in the mind or in external reality. In fact being is the same as these [modes], and what is disclosed in its degrees and manifest by its forms and its realities in knowledge and *in re*.[1]

For Ṣadrā, being is a process, a modulated reality that corresponds to the modulated semantics of the term 'being' and modulated nature of mental being.[2] Because reality is primary, being as a modulated reality entails a mental language that is modulated and semantics of modulation.[3] This final chapter describes the Sadrian 'circle of being'. First, we need to show that being has reality, that there is a mode of being that is actualised. Being must have reference for *tashkīk* since what is shared in this modulated way is an actual ipseity (*huwiyya ʿayniyya*).[4] Ṣadrā must espouse realism and reject the Illuminationist contention that being has neither reference nor actuality. The reality of being is ontologically primary and singular with many occurrences that are connected at differing levels of intensity.[5]

> Being is fundamental in what exists and is differentiated by [scales of] perfection and imperfection, intensification and debilitation (*kamālan wa-nuqṣan wa-shiddatan wa ḍuʿfan*). More perfect and more intense being has many referents and senses, and this amelioration entails greater simplicity and singularity. And vice versa . . .[6]

This is a description of the Sadrian circle of being. Second, we describe the One,

God, in His simple relationship with the cosmos in terms of modulation and as the most intense being from which the being of the cosmos proceeds. Third, being descends from the One in a series of differing hierarchical processes including the Avicennan discourse of the modalities and a Sufi/Shiʿi discussion of the 'togetherness' of the One with the many. The relationship of God and the world is complex and fluctuates between the poles of monism and pluralism. Modulation posits two hierarchical axes. The vertical (*ṭūlī*) hierarchy orders reality from the One through the intelligible realm and down to this sensible world, while the horizontal (*ʿaraḍī*) hierarchy pertains to this world of generation and corruption and arranges an order within this phenomenal world of *sensibilia*. It is the former order of being that delivers to us the Sadrian ontological proof for the existence of God called the 'Proof of the truthful' (*burhān al-ṣiddīqīn*). Intensity remains the key determinant of these hierarchies and of the reality of modulation. Finally, the circle of being is completed by the reversion to the One that is mediated by *wilāya* and the Perfect Man, who is the most intense degree of being and hence closest to the One. *Wilāya* is the proximate rank to the One and the most intense level of being, while in its comprehension of all degrees of being, it is the intimate mediator between the cosmos and the One.

Process and the reality of being

Being is a flow, a procession that runs through the fabric and structure of reality.[7] Being-process (*al-sarayān al-wujūdī*) pervades contingents like the spirit in a body.[8] It is thus a flow from the One through reality.[9] The unity of graded reality means that there is a continuum that does not suffer any gaps in being or knowledge.[10]

Ṣadrā suggests that reality comprises monadic vortices. Each reality in its manifestation intensifies to the point of revealing infinite monads.[11] Vortices as complexes of processes replace substances as units of reality and account for phenomenal change, contradiction and opposition that we experience.[12] An existent is a vortex, a structure of events that is an act of being.[13] An event may be defined as a 'change in substance'.[14] According to Ṣadrā, entities are in constant flux, in constant substantial motion.[15] Their identity is retained through the 'structure of these events'. The 'world process' is eternal and nothing is constant.[16] The key principle in determining the identity of the event is not so much that it occupies that same location and place, but the same stretch of time, significant since Ṣadrā regards time as a co-ordinate of being.[17] These vortices are essentially in motion at grades of becoming.[18]

This procession has degrees and levels within the series from the One in layers of intensity.[19] In the Proclean scheme, two series of monads proceed from the One: *per se* causation and p-series, defined in degrees of priority. One is imparticipable and the other is participable. The chain of being is a p-series in Proclean Neoplatonism in which each link is an appropriate degree of reality with a degree of participation in the One.[20] This is true of Sadrian process: each degree of reality is part of the chain of being insofar as it participates in being. That being, which is pure and simple, is thus all things *qua* their existence.

'The simple reality is all things'

Critical to the relationship of the One and the many is the doctrine of the 'simple reality'. This is central to Sadrian philosophy, drawing upon the simplicity of the prior One in *Enneads* V.4[7].1.5–15,

> For there must be something prior to all things which is simple, and this must be different from all that comes after it, being by itself, not mixed with those that come after it; yet being able to be present in the others in a different way, being truly one, and not something else which is then one.[21]

In his Treatise on the union of the intellecting subject and object, Ṣadrā draws on the *Plotiniana* and states that the Active Intellect is all things (*al-ʿaql al-faʿʿāl kull al-mawjūdāt*).[22] This follows from his doctrine of the primacy and logical priority of being.[23] In the *Asfār*, he quotes the following text from the tenth *mīmar* of the *Theologia*, an extract that exemplifies how the doctrine of the simple reality reconciles monism and pluralism by advocating neither.

> The Pure One (*al-wāḥid al-maḥḍ*) is the cause of all things and not of all things. Rather it is the beginning (*bada'*) of everything and not all things. All things are in it and not in it. All things flow from it and subsist and are sustained by it and return to it. So if someone says: how is it possible that things are from a simple one that has no duality or multiplicity in it in any sense? I say: because a pure simple one has nothing in it, but because it is a pure one, all things flow from it. Thus when there was no existence (*huwiyya*), being flowed from it.[24]

In his commentary, Ṣadrā espouses a form of Neoplatonic procession and doctrine of the intellect-*psuchē* that is at odds with most of his philosophical discourse in the *Asfār*. First, he accepts the standard account of the *Theologia*. *Nous* as the first existent flows immediately from the One and from it, existents proceed through the mediation of the intelligible realm. Second, the One is itself above perfection and plenitude. The first existent and the first perfect being is *nous*.[25] This Neoplatonic background is significant because it seems to cause a problem for modulation. Can this simple reality be modulated and if that is the case does it not entail multiplicity in the godhead? The second part of the objection is answered in the quoted objection in the passage above. But for the first, following *Enneads* VI.2.20 it is clear that being is a quasi-genus in which the whole is prior to its parts but, because of its 'potency', remains unaffected by any procession.[26] This refers to the One, *nous* and all beings.

The doctrine of the simple reality is difficult but central to Sadrian philosophy.[27] The argument presented in *al-Ḥikma al-ʿArshiyya* concerns the nature of God as that simple being and illustrates His knowledge of things through it.[28] The concept is central to resolving many theological problems relating to the nature of God. Indeed, it is an important ontological proof for the existence of God through an analysis of simplicity. 'Every simple reality is, by virtue of its unity, all things. It is not deprived of any of these things except by way of imperfections, privations and contingencies'.[29]

God is simple being because He is described by being, and being is a unique, simple reality.[30] It is simplicity devoid of quiddity.[31] That simplicity is uncontaminated by multiplicity, privation, imperfection or any such negative property.[32] God's being is pure and unencumbered by complexity such as a quiddity that might raise questions of genera, division, composition and definition.[33]

This is God without multiplicity, at the level of singularity (*aḥadiyya*) that encompasses the attributes considered intrinsically and not manifested towards and manifesting the cosmos.[34] The concept of a thing does not entail or include either its privation or its imperfection as there is 'no alterity in being since alterity is privation'.[35] Thus the simple reality that is God does not include or entail imperfections or privations. An objection to this could be that negative attributes are affirmed in theology, especially in the Shiʿi tradition in which one emphasises those concepts and properties that cannot be predicated of Him such as 'He is not a body', nor 'confined in a space' and so on.[36] The answer is that since these properties are negative, privative and imperfect, one can affirm them because 'the negation of negation is being and the negation of imperfection is perfection in being'.[37]
Ṣadrā then proceeds to an analysis of language and signification:

> Thus [taking the example] you say C is not B. In this context, if that with respect to which C is C is exactly the same as that with respect to which C is not B, so that C in itself would in its very essence be the referent for the negation, then [if this were so] the essence of C would be privative fact since everyone who intellects C would also intellect not B. But the consequent is invalid so the antecedent must be too. Thus it is established that [for every C] the subject of C-ness is a composite essence. Thus the mind distinguishes an existential meaning by which C is and a privative meaning by which C is not B or anything else negated of it.[38]

The point being made concerns the existence–essence distinction. Everything that is not simple but complex is a composite pair of being and quiddity.[39] But it also illustrates how the simple reality is a being and encompasses things *qua* their being and *not* their quiddity. Even more so, the simple being has nothing to be negated because simplicity cannot be analysed into parts or components.

> If anything can be negated of an existential factor, then it is not a simple reality. Every simple reality is all things with respect to their being and completeness and not with respect to their privation and incompleteness.

A simple reality cannot be predicated of anything since it is simple and unconditioned. This affirms diversity-in-unity since if nothing can be predicated of God, then it follows that the cosmos cannot be predicated of Him. Thus, it denies existential monism.

The final part of the argument then relates this to the nature of God's knowledge and His immediate presence to things such that the 'claim of the unjust' that He does not know particulars cannot arise.

> It is established that His knowledge of all things is a simple knowledge and their presence in Him is a simple reality . . . Knowledge is only an expression for being on the condition that it not be mixed with matter.[40]

Thus simplicity defines the nature of God's knowledge.

The doctrine of the simple reality has two further roles. First, it provides a proof for the existence of God by perfection, as the most intense limit case, given that simplicity is an attribute of perfection.[41] Second, it affirms his necessity in every sense thus negating the famous doubt of Ibn Kammūna [d. 1284] of the postulation of two necessary beings.[42] Simplicity denies any contingent facet to God, who is necessary in every sense.[43] God is simple being as He is uniquely necessary in and by Himself.[44]

Competing hierarchies in reality

Thus far, we have considered the reality of being at the level of the One. In this section, we discuss the descent of being in phenomenal reality in competing hierarchies of descent from the One, defined in terms of intensity.

Modalities

The approach to metaphysics that divides existents into the modalities of necessity and contingency is associated with Avicenna. They are defined in his work, *al-Mabda'*.

> The Necessary being is that existent for which the supposition of non-being (*farad ʿadamihi*) entails impossibility. The contingent being is that for which the supposition of either being or non-being does not entail impossibility. The Necessary being is logically necessary (*darūrī*), and the contingent is that in which there is no necessity of any sort, either of being or privation . . .[45]

Modalities provide a means for establishing a hierarchy of being and reality that places the One, the Necessary at the apex and contingents below it. All non-necessary and non-actual beings are a means of affirming his 'metaphysics of radical contingency'.[46]

However, Ṣadrā concurs with Leibniz on the necessity of everything.[47] This follows a basic metaphysical maxim of Islamic philosophy: whatever is not necessary cannot exist (*mā lam yajib [bi-ghayrih] lam yūjad*).[48] Everything is a necessary outcome of divine providence (*ʿināya*) due to the essential goodness of God.[49] It is this providence that is the cause of being, that overflows God's being into the universe as the contents of His mind become manifest.[50] He makes their existence in His mind manifest in extra-mental reality.[51] Thus the cosmos becomes necessary. Being is perfect procession so each degree of being proceeded is necessary.[52] Unlike the mechanistic emanating One of Neoplatonism, Ṣadrā 'saves' the Qur'anic account through a volitional theory of providence that insists upon the freedom and purpose of God.[53] God's self-intellection and conception of a perfect order in His mind is a cause for the procession of the cosmos, and not a desire (*al-shawq*) for the sensible that occurs in the *nous* of Neoplatonism.[54] Necessity defines existence, given the axiom that 'that thing that is not necessary, does not exist'.[55] But this does not entail a hard determinism. It is not the case that all possible outcomes are realised.[56] Rather, all contingents that are realisable and realised are necessary. It is still possible for some conceivables to be pure contingents (with respect to their quiddities) that languish in non-being.[57] Nor does it entail a violation of the uniqueness of the Necessary being.[58]

Fundamental to this hierarchy of reality is the concept of dependent contingency (*imkān faqrī*) as opposed to essential contingency (*imkān māhuwī*). The former relates contingency to the being of the contingent and the latter to its quiddity that is indifferent to being or privation.[59] Conventionally, 'contingency of quiddities means the negation of the necessity of being and the privation of (being) a thing (*maʿná l-imkān fī-l-māhiyyāt salb ḍarūrat al-wujūd wa-l-ʿadam ʿan al-shay'*)'.[60] But in dependent contingency, contingents are by virtue of their dependence upon the One existentially.[61] Each contingent, following the existence–essence distinction, has an aspect of quidditative contingency and existential contingency.[62] The point of dependent contingency is that the ipseity of things relates to the One, and nothing can exist if its being is not attached to the One.[63] The individuation of a particular contingent depends on being (through which it is necessary) and not upon a sufficient reason that will draw the quiddity out of its indifference to being and privation.[64] This dependence, this existential poverty in comparison with the True One is a source of shame for contingents to refer to themselves or be called 'existent'. Ṣadrā quotes a saying of the Prophet that 'Poverty is shame [darkness of the face] in this world and the next'.[65]

This concept of existential poverty is found in the Avicennan formulation where the cause and sustenance of the contingent is existential.[66] It suggests a monistic intent on the part of our author.[67] In fact, on this point as Ṣadrā quotes him, Avicenna seems to affirm intensification in modalities.[68] Existential poverty has strong Neoplatonic roots. The One of the *Enneads* preserves all things in existence, and is 'that on which everything depends'.[69] He is the existential cause of everything.[70] His being establishes and sustains all other.[71]

A traditional Avicennan approach to modalities depends upon the concept of sufficient reason (*tarjīḥ*), a preponderating agent that brings a privative quiddity out of its indifference to being and quiddity and existentiates it. This view can then function like a cosmological proof for the existence of God.[72] Although Ṣadrā allows for the possibility of cosmological proofs, he prefers ontological ones since the cosmos as degrees of the same reality of being concerns the apriority of being, then arguments about its nature and origin are ontological. Modulation is thus neither incompatible with modalities nor with emanationist monorealism.[73]

Another feature of the Sadrian approach to modalities is that the vertical hierarchy of being is regulated by noble contingency (*al-imkān al-ashraf*).[74] Suhrawardī explains this principle in *Ḥikmat al-ishrāq*:

> If a baser contingent exists, a nobler contingent must already have existed . . . The dominating light – that which is entirely incorporeal – is nobler than the managing light; being further from connections with darkness, it is thus nobler. Thus its being must be prior.[75]

The Illuminationist roots of the doctrine are significant.[76] Noble contingency posits co-dependence; whatever is higher in the hierarchy of contingent being depends on that which is lower for its manifestation, and that which is lower depends on what is higher for its realisation. This affirms the existence–essence distinction. Noble contingency describes reality as a continuum that as a totality is contingent and dependent upon the One, the apex of the modulated scale of being:

> The rule of noble contingency requires that there be between the First Principle and what is supposed to be the closest of existents to it an essential connection and similarly between any existent and what is proximate to it and so forth until the culmination of pure entities and lights. So the totality is like a single essence and a single connection differentiated in degrees of intensity of illumination and perfection of being (*shiddat al-ishrāq wa-kamāliyyat al-wujūd*) and it possesses an ascending aspect that is infinite in intensity and a descending aspect that is finite in intensity.[77]

Modulation defines noble contingency: the higher contingent is more intense than the lower.[78] This follows from Ṭūsī, for whom modalities are different degrees of being by modulation, entailing a hierarchy of being defined by intensification.[79]

Intensification

> Existents have degrees in existentiality, and being has different domains, some of which are more perfect and noble and other more imperfect and more base.[80]

Modulation by intensity occurs within the circle of being, from the arc of descent (*qaws al-nuzūl*) from the One to the arc of ascent (*qaws al-ṣuʿūd*) back to the One.[81] As Ṣadrā's student, Fayḍ says,

> Being descends from the heaven of absoluteness (*samāʾ al-iṭlāq*) to the earth of limitation (*arḍ al-taqyīd*) in *degrees*. It starts from the most noble and ends with the basest. Thus a descending path (*silsilat al-nuzūl*) makes its way in it [being]. Then it [being] takes an ascent (*ṣuʿūd*), and it continues to progress from the lowest to the most excellent, until it ends with the most excellent in this ascending order.
>
> Whatever is closer to its Originator, Glorified may He be, is closer to simplicity, unity and independence, and further from differentiation, complexity and dependence.[82]

God is the limit case of absolute perfection, intensity and the point of origin and return in the circle of being.[83]

The beatific and ecstatic experience of the 'doffing metaphor' of *Enneads* IV.8.1 is associated in the Illuminationist tradition with veils and degrees of light in a vertical hierarchy ascending up to the One. Ṣadrā in his *scholia* on the *Sharḥ Ḥikmat al-ishrāq* of Quṭb al-Dīn Shīrāzī [d. 1311] uses this to explain modulation:

> Know that the reality of being is graded in levels, one above the other and the higher comprehends all under it in a real sense (*ma'nawī*) . . . So everything that is more potent, is more intense in its comprehension and its rank is more enveloping. Everything that is less potent inclines towards what is more perfect than it. All levels of being are veils that prevent one from noticing the most perfect, the highest being that comprehends everything (*al-wujūd al-atamm al-a'lá al-muḥīṭ 'alá kulli shay'*). All being is light except that it is differentiated in its luminosity that becomes physical and corporeal forms, forms that are tenebrous in comparison to the higher [incorporeal] intellects and souls, since they are contaminated with privation.[84]

Veils of light are degrees of contingent being graded in intensities from the One, a translunary hierarchy that traverses the division between the sensible and intelligible realms.[85] The closer that a degree of being is to the One, the more intense it is, and the more distant it is, the weaker in intensity. Perfection in the scale of being is what tends towards simplicity and unity (and indeed the One) and what is most removed from complexity.[86] Every being thus has two aspects: one is a veil that hides the divine by confusing the perceiver into accepting what appears phenomenally before him, but the other is a manifestation of the divine. The former is its quidditative aspect and the latter its existential aspect. This is why beings that are devoid of quidditative features are purer lights that indicate the divine through their existence.

Intensification posits degrees of being that constitute modulation in degrees of perfection and participation.[87] The latter dynamic is significant for the Neoplatonic roots of the problem. Damascius affirmed that being *qua* soul constantly changes because the forms within it differ through differing levels of participation (*metexis*).[88] Perfect participation is perfect being, that is God who is the Agent of this hierarchy.[89] Beings participate in the general 'pool of being' sharing in the very roots of being, and differing in their degrees of participation by perfection and imperfection, independence and dependence, and priority and posteriority.[90] The concept of intensification is taken from the Illuminationist tradition's vision of the hierarchy of lights. The Illuminationist tradition considers quiddities as universals to undergo intensification as well, a concept that Ṣadrā then applies to being.[91] Ṣadrā explicitly tells us that he is reversing the Illuminationist position.[92] Modulation only applies to being since different intensities of being still permit causality but if modulation were to occur in quiddity, one quiddity of a different intensity could not be a cause for another.[93] Quiddity cannot undergo modulation because a quiddity defines a certain nature with essential and accidental properties that are true of all its portions and individuals. If it could be more intense, then all those individuals would be so, and so for debilitation. So quiddity cannot undergo modulation. What defines a quiddity is thus quite strict and what marks out a being is more 'fuzzy' and naturally open to modulation. The law of Indiscernibles does not apply equally to both quiddity and being.[94]

Ṣadrā affirms intensity in substances with three degrees in each substance, a logical, an intelligible and a material and the whole thing is a manifestation of the divine essence through its sustaining agency.[95] Substantial motion is a concomitant of being. Just as God's agency brings things into being so does it bring about substantial motion.[96] The relationship between being and motion is described as follows.

> Being permits intensification and debilitation (*al-ishtidād wa-l-taḍaʿʿuf*) meaning that it permits intensifying motion. Substance in its substantiality, that is its substantial being, allows for essential change. The parts of motion are continuous but they are not in actuality distinct, but rather exist in a single being . . . The quiddities that correspond to them do not exist in actuality as distinct . . .[97]

In the Sadrian doctrine substance undergoes intensification and modulation because it is in motion.[98] Two examples are given for this. First, water when boiled turns into steam not by changing from a definite substance water to a definite substance steam through a shifting intensity in its substantiality. Rather, the being intensifies and the substance undergoes a change and modulation.[99] The vortex of events of that being that is watery remains the substrate of that change. The other famous example is that of the sperm in the womb that develops and becomes an embryo. Substantial motion occurs in bodily substances through the flux of being and the constant layering of ipseities with forms one after another.[100] It is constant renewal of forms since hylomorphism demands that matter never be free of form.[101] The ipseity that undergoes the change remains a constant vortex.[102] The question of substantial motion was raised in Neoplatonism, as Ṣadrā knew well. Motion and being are identical concepts in Plotinus with the same reference in reality as properties of intellect.[103] But they are mentally distinct as intentional objects and cognitive activity. Both Iamblichus [d. *c.* 326] and Damascius [d. after 529] held that the soul in its descent into the body and then its ascending reversion undergoes substantial change without violating its unity and identity because it changed itself.[104] All the 'lives' of the human soul are so many faculties or manifestations of the same substance.[105] What is also useful for us is the 'architectonic' approach of later Neoplatonism to the hierarchy of being, shunning the monistic tendencies of both Plotinus and Porphyry.[106]

However, in the Aristotelian and mainstream Neoplatonic tradition, ousia *qua* substance does not admit of more or less.[107] Avicenna denies intensity in being or more specifically substance.[108] 'Being *qua* being does not differ in intensity or allow of more or less. It only differs in priority, posteriority, independence and dependence, necessity and contingency'.

The primary sense of being is substance.[109] Substance cannot undergo intensification and debilitation because it has no opposite and intensity requires opposition and contrariness.

> Substance does not allow of more intense and weaker Intensification and debilitation is negated with the negation of opposition in which it is not possible to change from one to another through motion . . . Rather opposition in substance occurs simultaneously and not through motion. Motion does not occur in substances and it is unlike the change from blackness to whiteness.[110]

Bahmanyār makes the link between the denial of intensity and the denial of substantial motion that is critical for intensification. Intensification and debilitation occur where there is motion but one substance cannot be more intense than another nor weaker than another. This does not mean that a substance cannot be prior in substantiality to another. First substance is prior in substantiality to second but is not more intense. Priority is attached to the being of substantiality and intensity to the quiddity of substantiality.[111] Although substances are divided into primary (that is, individuals) and secondary ('man'), this distinction in their substantiality is not by grades of intensity or modulation since the distinction is not essential.[112] Substance cannot undergo motion.[113]

The Sadrian counter-argument runs as follows. Substance is extra-mental self-sufficient being. It is not a genus and like being undergoes modulation. Being is more primary than substance.[114] Things exist in grades of intensity and existential priority and posteriority. For example, 'father' does not precede 'son' either causally or in humanity, but rather existentially.[115] The distinction in substances and substantiality is not through the modulation of substantiality as the Illuminationists suggest.[116] Rather, substantiality is a singular undifferentiated concept, but it is the being of the substance that is modulated in grades of intensity.[117] This pertains to the horizontal hierarchy as well. Humans are prior and more intense than beasts in being and not by virtue of 'greater substantiality'.[118]

The Peripatetics held that being cannot remain single with grades of intensity (and hence must be multiple in reality) because intensity does not differentiate one from the other and it leads to two problems within the metaphysics of radical contingency.[119] First, there can be no causality, because there is no greater or lesser in potency and a cause must be present with its effect but also more potent than its effect through essential priority and not greater intensity.[120] Causality functions with other scales of prior and posterior but not with intensity.[121] As Bahmanyār says,

> It works for priority and posteriority because the cause exists in the first instance and the effect in the second. [It works for] independence and dependence because the cause does not depend for its being on the effect but rather exists in itself or through another cause. The effect depends on the cause . . . [It works for] necessity and contingency because the being of the effect in itself is not necessary since if it were, then it would be necessary without

> a self-sufficient cause. So its essence is contingent being and only necessary through its cause.[122]

Second, there can be no sufficient cause or preponderance as no one side of a potential contingent, whether existence or non-existence, dominates.[123]

The Illuminationist response is to deny causality altogether since the hierarchy of lights is not causally related, and concepts such as substances and being are merely intentional.[124] For Ṣadrā, being has no cause since it must be necessary to exist.[125]

> Being exists by itself. It is the determination of itself and the being of its essence. With respect to itself, it is not attached to anything; rather [it is attached to other things] with respect to its accidental determinations and developments following it. So being *qua* being does not have an agent by which it is established, nor does it have matter which is impossible for it, and no substrate in which it is found, nor any form in which it is clothed, nor does it have any *telos*.
>
> Being is too great to be attached to any cause since it has been disclosed that it has no cause at all, nor any cause by which it is, nor any cause from which (*minhu*) it is . . . nor any cause in which it is, nor any cause which it has.[126]

Thus the hierarchy of being is not a causal hierarchy. Hence there is no sufficient cause or preponderance.[127] Contingents exist not through such agency but because they exist by virtue of the Necessary. They cannot be non-existent or indifferent and then emerge as existents.[128] The cause of being is the One but there is no causality within the realm of being.[129]

Furthermore, degrees of intensity for the Peripatetics entail different species.[130] But intensification is not differentiated in actual being since if it were it would entail composition in motion of momentary entities that are infinite and that is impossible.[131] The Peripatetic mistakes distinctions as occurrent in essences; thus he posits different species. But in fact being is what is considered.[132] The Peripatetic argument is rejected as follows:

> The nature of being accepts intensity and debilitation in its simple essence. There is no difference between individuals by an essential differential distinction (*mumayyiz faṣlī dhātī*) or by an accidental type (*muṣannif ʿaraḍī*) or by a feature of species (*mushakhkhiṣ*) that is additional to the ground of its nature. Their individuals and units only differ by essential intensity and debilitation (*al-shidda wa-l-ḍuʿf*), priority and posteriority, nobility and baseness (*al-sharaf wa-l-khissa*). Universal concepts that are true of them [referents]

modulation occurs in being, not only in terms of priority and precedence but also in terms of intensity.[134] In concession to Avicenna, he does not permit intensity within causality but does within other divisions of being including Necessary and contingent.[135] He argues that since quiddity cannot undergo intensity yet occurs in different modes, this suggests that the differences are existential instances of quiddity that differ in intensity. It is not quiddity that intensifies.[136] The Peripatetic doctrine holds that distinction by intensity occurs in quiddities through their differentiae. But this is rejected because differentiae are not grades of intensity and quiddity does not undergo intensification.[137] Being is not distinguished by differentiae since it is not a universal.[138] Ṭūsī is already part of a processist turn in Islamic philosophy because he does not automatically consider substance to be the primary referent and sense of being, unlike the other Peripatetics.

In the *Asfār*, Ṣadrā adjudicates at length between the Peripatetics and Illuminationists on intensity and modulation. The first issue is how things differ: do they differ by the whole of their quiddities, by parts of their quiddities, by extrinsic properties or by their existence? The Illuminationists pick the first option and the Peripatetics a mixture of the second and third. But the correct position is to assert that beings differ by intensity in their being.[139]

The second issue deals with varieties of 'more or less'. The first argument considers essences and individuals. The Peripatetics deny any modulation by precedence, priority or perfection within a essence. The Illuminationists permit such distinction. Ṣadrā takes the Illuminationist position and provides the example of light that is graded, intensifies and affects other by itself.[140] The individuation of beings and essences is precisely in such a hierarchy of intensity, precedence, excellence and perfection.[141] Against the Illuminationists he makes the point that the distinction between two black bodies is not that one is a more intensely black species than the other but rather that one's being is more intense, which manifests itself in being more black.[142] The unity of the thing is not compromised in intensifying motion since substance is not the primary ontic unit.[143]

The second argument of the Peripatetics is that intensity and modulation in being entails species distinction between individuals. This is a logical impossibility. The Illuminationists deny distinction by species or differentia. This is then related to the third argument that intensity and motion only occur in the categories of quantity and quality that are distinct types of modulation. Peripatetics deny intensity or motion in substance.[144] Ṣadrā broadly agreeing with the Illuminationists makes three objections. First, the Peripatetic argument on the distinction of scales of quantity and quality refers to ordinary and conventional language use. But these recourses do not amount to a philosophical proof. The Peripatetics distinguish between the two in a circular fashion entailing a *petitio principii*. In fact, both intensity and more or

tions of forms are of a lower ontological class and indeed 'less real'.[146] Ultimately, the Necessary is more intense than contingents.[149] One final point though not an argument that Ṣadrā makes is to accuse Avicenna of inconsistency since the latter affirms that some existents are more puissant and more intense than others and within being, both time and motion are scales of intensity.[150]

Does intensification entail composition in the divine? Two objections to modulation can be raised in this context. If we take God as the highest degree who is the Necessary and is equal to His attributes, then that entails composition in God. Second, if the actual supposition of modulation is applied to God as the highest and contingents below, then God is limited by the contingents. Since all share being and identity-in-difference, God is confined and bounded by the highest contingent degree. This is a problem, as we know that the being of God is pure and undetermined.[151] These objections are resolved in the following manner. First,

> The chain of existents (*silsilat al-mawjūdāt*) in degrees of being with the supposition of modulation do not have accidental being such that each degree has a border with the other . . . Each higher degree is not distinguished from the lower by boundaries that are fixed. Rather the chain of degrees is vertical and causal. Each higher degree is the cause of the lower and the lower the effect of the higher . . . The being of all the modular degrees in the chain contains all the perfections below it but not vice versa.[152]

Second,

> The essence of the Necessary who is the highest degree in the chain has all the perfections of the degrees below it *in actu* existing in him . . . For the philosophers all contingent degrees exist truly and are effects of higher degrees, ultimately of God and they indicate the greatness and glory of God. But for the mystics, being is exclusive to the essence of the Truth and all contingents are merely shadows and manifestations of him. The attribution of being to them [contingents] is thus figurative.[153]

The final point about modulation by intensification is that there are two axes of intensification, a vertical hierarchy that traverses the domains of being, intelligible, sensible and intermediary, and a horizontal hierarchy that organises this sublunary world of *sensibilia*. The horizontal hierarchy of being also undergoes intensification.[154] There is a gradual intensifying scale from the lowest being that is a mineral through the vegetable and animal until one arrives at the human, the most intense type of natural being, of which the most intense is the Perfect Man, the holder and deployer of *wilāya* (sanctified rank and proximity to the One).[155] The unity of the structure of reality is expressed using a common Neoplatonic and Hermetic metaphor of referring to the macrocosm as a 'living animal'.[156] But this animal is not a contiguous, atomic composed organism.

> The truth is that the circle of being (*dawr al-wujūd*) is one.[157] The whole cosmos is a single living great animal, whose limbs are connected one to the other,

> not in the sense of being quantitatively contiguous in surface and extension but in the sense that every perfect degree of being must be contiguous to a degree adjacent to it in existential perfection, either above it in intensity or below it in debilitation, without any other degree mediating between the two.[158]

The metaphor of the macrocosm is then reintegrated to the metaphor of the microcosm, man.

> Man . . . is a single existent possessing many faculties, some of which are intellectual, some psychic and some physical. All these [faculties] are degrees differing in excellence within their class. But the whole is still one essence.[159]

The vertical hierarchy moves from the basest most passive level of sensibility through the intelligibles to God in a scale of gradation of perfection and modulation of intensity.[160] This is a unified multiplicity in which each level of being is connected and ultimately dependent upon God.[161] The vertical scale also cuts across the modes of being: the concept and word are the least intense, mental being is higher but the reality of being is most intense.[162] The scale intensifies from pure privation to Pure Being. This is the 'limit case' proof for the existence of God as well.[163] This hierarchy also traverses time and the 'domains of being' across the distinction between this world and the afterlife. The beings of the afterlife are 'more permanent, more intense and more perfect'.[164] People also possess levels of being of which their being in the afterlife is more intense. Of such people, the person who is most intense in his being across all modes of being and all worlds and times is the Perfect Man.

The Akbarian and Shiʿi concepts of God's 'togetherness' (maʿiyya) with creatures

An alternative hierarchy of reality is conditioned by 'togetherness'. The concept of 'togetherness' (*maʿiyya*) is a significant meditation in the school of Ibn ʿArabī on the Qur'ānic verse 57:4, 'God is with you wherever you are'.[165] There are three central features of this concept. First, this relationship is existential. God existentially sustains all things based on a reading of the *ḥadīth*, 'God was and there was nothing with Him'.[166] The relationship between God and man is one of 'sustaining togetherness' (*maʿiyya qayyūmiyya*).[167] This relationship is at all levels of being-time, since God, to complete the *ḥadīth*, 'is as He was'.[168] God is with things and they are not with Him; the relationship is not equivalent.[169] This nearness is graded. Degrees of being are arranged according to their proximity to the One.[170] God bestows this togetherness on beings as a grace or revelation.[171] But it can also be petitioned through worship.[172] This type of sustaining togetherness is causal, thus the togetherness of God with creation is more potent and more excellent than vice versa since the cause is greater than the effect.[173]

Second, it is a principle of unity and inter-relationship.[174] Togetherness affirms 'hypostatic unity' (*waḥdat al-wujūd*) along with a recognition of plurality of each level of 'togetherness'.

> God is with all things. Nothing is prior to Him and nothing is posterior to Him. This property does not belong to other-than-God. That is why He has a specific face toward each thing, for He is the occasion of each existent thing. Each existent thing is one and cannot be two. He is also One so nothing proceeds from Him but one, for He is in the unity of every one thing. If multiplicity is found, this is in respect to the unity of time, which is the container. After all, in this multiplicity the *wujūd* of the Real is in the unity of every one.[175]

This illustrates the intimacy of man and God, given that God is qualified by His relationship with His creatures.[176] It reveals the paradox of He/not He explained by Chittick.[177] The cosmos is He, insofar as it cannot be if He did not sustain. But it is also not He because it is not identical to Him nor is it a pantheist reality. Our philosopher expresses this in the following way.

> The necessary Being is necessary in every sense and orientation . . . It is with every existent in every sense without [entailing] delimitation and multiplicity. He is in everything and not in everything. He is every moment and not in every moment. He is every place and not in every place. Rather He is all things and not all things.[178]

Third, paradoxically, it is a principle of God's transcendence. Togetherness is determined by God and not us. It does not mean that the being of the world or our being in any way delimits True being.[179] One cannot be together with the divine essence that is utterly ineffable.[180] Fourth, the relationship is sustaining like a flow or like light illuminating creatures, since following Qur'ān 24: 35, 'God is the light of the heavens and the earth'.[181] On this verse, Ṣadrā comments: 'The togetherness of the True One (*al-wāḥid al-ḥaqq*) to all existents – a sustaining togetherness – is through the comprehension of the light of being through all things'.[182] It is through God's togetherness that things become manifest from His awareness and presence with them when they were not manifest.[183]

Ṣadrā uses the fourth verse from *Sūrat al-Ḥadīd* to discuss togetherness. First, in an Akbarian vein, he shows how it suggests that divine causality underlies and is the reality behind all causality that occurs. As God is omnipresent, then the agency of Zayd is not a figurative agency but in reality is divine agency because 'there is no power or might save God's'.[184] Second, his stress on omnipresence provides a proof for the existence of God, which is 'obvious and needs no proof' because 'He is with you wherever you are'.[185] Third, he relates this verse to the proof of God as the simple reality. In this mode, God is the 'plenitude of all things' (*tamām al-ashyā'*)

two famous sayings of Imam 'Alī.[188] This tradition of discussing togetherness is prefigured in the work of the thirteenth-century Sufi ʿAzīz-i Nasafī, who puts it to monist use and uses it to illustrate a hierarchy of being sustained by (with) God, arranged in order of priority and posteriority.[189] The intensity of each entity is different and hence its togetherness is qualitatively different. The first text is 'I did not see anything except that I saw Allah before it and with it and in it'.[190] This text is discussed by Ṣadrā as critical to his cosmology and view of a modulated reality.[191] It also provides a cosmological proof for the existence of God because no one can deny that they 'see' God because He is omnipresent.[192] It also shows how togetherness is epistemic.[193] God knows things presentially so they are with them and exist.[194] The fact that it is the Imam enunciating this shows that he is the proof of God and indicator of Him. It is he who is the key to understanding God, the world and the text that is revealed, the key (*ta'wīl*) that unlocks the codes immanent in these 'texts' through a hermeneutic of being and togetherness.[195]

The second saying comes from the very first sermon in the collection of the Imam's discourse, *Nahj al-balāgha* (Peak of eloquence) compiled by Sayyid Raḍī [d. 1015], that plays such a critical role in Shiʿi thought. The context is an affirmation of God by *via negativa* that safeguards His alterity.

> He is without being originated. He exists without being brought into being from non-being. He is with everything without being joined with them (*lā bi-muqāranatin*) and not everything without being separate from them (*lā bi-muzāyalatin*).[196]

Maytham Baḥrānī [d. 1300] in his commentary makes two points about this.[197] First, that it emphasises God's utter transcendence and immanence, balancing monism and pluralism in our terms. His own monism stresses that in fact things are merely His effects and acts and cannot thus be separated from His because the effect is not existentially separate from the cause.[198] For Ṣadrā, togetherness shows that the hierarchy of being and its order of priority is ultimately not one of causality, but rather one thing is related to another as relations of togetherness (ultimately with God) as modulating modes and emanating circles of being.[199] Togetherness is existential and not temporal and refers to the existential poverty and dependence of creation upon God, and in this sense it is top-down.[200] Divine being is with the cosmos and sustains it. It is not a universal in which cosmic particulars share.[201] It is like light that flows through beings without being identical to them through the Law of Indiscernibles.[202] But the ontological distinction through this report remains paradoxical.[203] There is no complete separation in the longitudinal hierarchy of being. As the Imam says, 'To make Him unique is to

omnipresence and not His omnipresence, a theme that is Plotinian.[204]

Modulation and Akbarian hypostatic monism (waḥdat al-wujūd al-shakhṣiyya): critique or assimilation?

Akbarian monism is a strong influence upon the thought of Mullā Ṣadrā.[208] The latter accepts the Akbarian threefold division of being into pure, determined and deployable.[209] The same three levels of being, high, lower and intermediate are posited in a variety of Neoplatonic works and can be found in Ibn ʿArabī's *Kitāb al-azal* (On preternity).[210] Monism in the Akbarian tradition is implied by Qur'ān 28:88 which indicates ontological *tawḥīd* in opposition to the generally understood theological notion of the unity of the divine.[211] In the Akbarian tradition, there is no modulation in the reality of being that is identical to God, but rather modulation occurs in the manifestation of being.[212] Modulation and shared semantic content of being are not rejected outright.[213] Essentially there are two types of being: real and correlational (*iḍāfī*), the former is God and the latter all else.[214]

Pure being is God considered in Himself, determined being is God considered through the cosmos, and deployable being is an isthmus of concepts and means and divine names through which to reach God.[215] It is merely through different considerations and through a language of manifestations and divine self-disclosures that one can conceive of multiplicity in a metaphorical sense. Ṣadrā quotes ʿAlā' al-Dawla Simnānī [d. 1336] as a source for the threefold division of being in the monist tradition. 'True being (*al-wujūd al-ḥaqq*) is God, and absolute being (*al-wujūd al-muṭlaq*) is His action and limited being (*al-wujūd al-muqayyad*) His effects'.[216]

The first level of being is pure uniqueness, negative conditionality (*bi-sharṭ lā*), in which being is neither conditioned by a quiddity, nor by a certain mode of existence. This is the level of the divine.[217] It is what the Sufis call Pure Being or God.[218]

> The first is the existent whose being is not attached to another, and the being, which is not limited by any delimitation. It is called by the mystics the 'Unseen ipseity' (*al-huwiyya al-ghaybiyya*) and the unseen aspect of Ipseity (*ghayb al-huwiyya*), and the absolute Unseen (*al-ghayb al-muṭlaq*) and the Singular Essence (*al-dhāt al-aḥadiyya*). It is the essence of the Most High Truth considered without any determination (*al-lātaʿayyun*), and this level is marked by pure transcendence (*al-tanzīh al-ṣarf*). He has no name, has no attribute and is not available to cognition or perception. Everything that has a name, a description or an attribute, or is available to cognition and perception is a concept existing in the mind or in the estimative faculty, and He is not like that, since He is Unseen, Absolute and Unknown . . .
>
> The concomitants of His essence are conditions of His manifestation, and not causes of His being, which would entail imperfection and shortcoming and dependence upon another, utterly transcendent is He above what the unjust and the deniers say . . .[219]

This level of being is totally devoid of any attribute, quality or characterisation. In fact, even its 'effects' are not causal results but manifestations since causality would place God within the world process and entail imperfection.[220]

The second level is conditioned and limited being (*bi-sharṭ al-shay'*), that is, contingent being that occurs *in re* that are identified with divine effects.[221]

> The second degree is the existent that is attached to another, which is delimited being (*al-wujūd al-muqayyad*), and includes intellects, souls, spheres, elements, composites among humans, insects, trees, minerals and all other specific existents.[222]

This degree of being encompasses both supra-lunary and sub-lunary worlds.

The third level is the first thing emanating from Him and the true ground of being that is all-encompassing. This is unconditioned being (*lā bi-sharṭ*) that is identified with divine acts.[223] It is this level which is deployed in manifestations and theophanies of the One that undergo modulation.[224] It is the same as the primordial cloud *ʿamā'* that is the source of phenomenal being in the Akbarian tradition.[225] This is the pure relation that is the cosmos.[226]

> The third degree is absolute being that is deployable (*al-wujūd al-munbasiṭ al-muṭlaq*), whose generality is not a universality . . . Deployable being is not confined to a specific characterisation or determined quality . . . Rather with respect to itself, it is not associated with anything . . . Extra-mental realities spring from its level and are modes of its determinations . . . It is the ground of the cosmos. It is called the reality by which one creates (*al-ḥaqq al-makhlūq bihi*) in the language of the Sufis and the reality of realities . . .
>
> It should be clear that [this mode of] being is not the common abstracted notion of being that is *a priori* and conceived in the mind as a secondary intelligible and an intentional concept.[227]

An important corollary of monism is an affirmation of the unreality of quiddities.[228] What exists is merely a manifestation of the Real.

> The Necessary True being's theophanies (*tajalliyyāt al-wujūd al-ḥaqq al-wājibī*) are the forms of entities of the cosmos in itself, and the first of its manifestations is its theophany in the singular substance and the singular reality described in the form of all the 'permanent archetypes' (*aʿyān thābita*). They have no being except through it . . . So He is manifest in the form of the cosmos, and hidden in the forms of His entities.[229]

Ṣadrā also affirms this position on unreality.[230] Because quiddities are contingents, they are unreal and remain non-existent.[231] The Akbarian tradition extrapolates this from Qur'ān 88:28, 'everything perishes except His countenance'.[232] They interpret it to mean that God alone is being and all else, all contingents, all quiddities are purely privative. It is a conceit to suggest that contingent quiddities exist as such as opposed to being merely manifestations and reflections of True Being and Unitive Light.[233] Quiddities are merely mentally posited senses for predicates that have reference in the being of the thing predicated.[234] Being is affirmation but quiddities are privation.[235]

But the problem is that one needs to start by considering quiddities. Metaphysics is defined as the study of the essential accidents of being *qua* being. 'Quiddities are among the primary essential accidents of the reality of being (*al-aʿrāḍ al-awwaliyya al-dhātiyya li-ḥaqīqat al-wujūd*)'.[236] Multiplicity is still affirmed in the Sadrian approach and pure monism is not acceptable. Hypostatic unity is rejected while affirming ontological *tawḥīd*.[237] The Sadrian critique of monorealism in the Akbarian sense is encouraged by the Illuminationist rejection of it.[238]

The tension between monism and pluralism

Rahman notices a tension between monism and pluralism at the heart of Sadrian philosophy.[239] Monistic tendencies are clearly manifest in his work especially the *Asfār*.[240]

> His being is the being of all existents as it is the pure reality of being . . . He is the ground and reality in existentiality, and all else are His affairs and modes. He is the essence, and all else are His names, and His self-disclosures and manifestations. He is light and all else are his shadows and rays. He is the truth and all else apart from His gracious countenance is unreal.[241]

The idea that the totality of existence is the divine names and that God is identical with His creatures is a Hermetic ideal.[242] But it had been suggested that this affirmation only applies to the concept of being and not its reality.[243]

> Everything perishes in the Unity of the True Divine Being (*aḥadiyyat al-wujūd al-ḥaqq al-ilāhī*). . . He is the Necessary Being, the Subsistent in Himself and by Whom others subsist. He is described by the divine names, qualified by lordly qualities, and called upon the tongues of the Prophets and the saints, guides of His creation to His essence. He reveals through their tongues His identity with everything without entering in it or being separate from it and through His reality there is nothing separate. His creation of things is His concealment in them while manifesting them. His making them privative in the Greater resurrection is His manifestation in His oneness and his wrath to them through the effacement of their determinations and their marks and their making.[244]

Determination and distinction in being occurs by its ipseities coinciding in the very essence of reality, some prior to others essentially and in reality, and by degrees of modulated differentiation, by precedence, by priority and posteriority, by intensification and debilitation. So being that has no cause has precedence in its existentiality over others and is prior to all existents by essential priority. In fact all existents are like reflections and rays of the light of its being.[245]

Ṣadrā discusses four different positions on unity, which are then glossed perceptively by Sabzawārī. 'Beings are multiple and distinguished only as degrees of the determinations of the True One, and manifestations of His light and affairs of His essence. [They are] not independent things and divisible essences'.[246] This is his doctrine, the first view that there is a unity of being and existents in their very diversity. This was the position, he claims as do his followers, of the 'ancient Persian sages' (*Fahlawiyyūn*).[247] He then criticises an important view prevalent in his time associated with a theosist philosophical approach (*dhawq al-ta'alluh*) of Davānī.

> Some people have come to the conclusion that real being is one individual that is the Essence of the Creator the Most High, and quiddities are real things whose existentiality is an expression for their relation to necessary Being and their connection to Him the Most High. So being . . . is a universal, possessing numerous individuals that are existents. They relate this doctrine to the direct experience of the theosist philosophers (*dhawq al-muta'allihīn*).[248]

According to this view, the Necessary is the true referent of being but the particulars share in that being as 'portions' (*ḥiṣaṣ*).[249] This view undergoes a thorough criticism in three parts.

First, he criticises the notion of being as a universal whilst retaining its unity by arguing that being cannot be like a universal and can only be differentiated *whilst retaining its unity* through modulation.[250]

> [To say that] the entity of the essence of the Necessary in itself is a being for all quiddities, both substances and accidents, is not correct . . . Some individual existents are undifferentiated with respect to their quiddity while some are prior to others through being. The priority of some over others cannot be intellected with the being of being in everything as one, being real oneness related to all. If an excuse is given that distinction, with respect to priority and posteriority, is not in real being, instead it is in their connection and relation to it, such that the relation of some to real existence is more prior than others, we say that relation *qua* relation is an intentional factor that does not occur and is not differentiated in itself, but only with respect to one of the two things related. Thus, if what is related to it is a unitive essence, the related [thing] is a quiddity that with respect to itself cannot be necessary by priority or posteriority or causality, nor the priority of one of their individuals with analogy to another due to the lack of their occurrence and their actuality in themselves and with respect to their quiddity. So how can any distinction occur between the individuals of one reality through priority and posteriority in relation to the Necessary and posteriority in it?[251]

This is a thoroughly anti-pantheistic statement. Beings therefore, the cosmos and all that there is, does not exist *in* God as parts of God.

Second, the relationship between being and existents cannot be through an illuminative correlation since that would entail that being is other than what it is correlated to.[252]

> Their relation to the Creator is either unitive (*ittiḥādiyyatan*) necessitating that the being of the Necessary, the Most High, possesses quiddities . . . that

> are multiple and differentiated . . . Or the relation between them [quiddities] and the Necessary the Most High is by an attachment – the attachment of one thing to another is subordinate to their existence and their realisation – which necessitates that every quiddity possesses a specific being prior to their relation and attachment. As there is no doubt that their realities are not expressed by attachment to other-than-them, then however many quiddities we conceive and we doubt their connection to the First Truth, its attachment by it will differ through beings. Hence it is possible for it to be said that their connection and attachment do not differ since contentment is not possible by a mode of being except in the sense of knowledge of the reality of its cause and its Maker.[253]

This is an anti-essentialist statement ranged against the Illuminationist position on the cosmos as a collectivity of quiddities correlated to God.

Third, being is the very locus of existentiality and such is the relationship of existents.[254]

> Beings are multiple like existents. Existents are real things and some beings are real such as the existence of the Necessary, and some are intentional such as the existence of contingents. There is no difference between this doctrine and the famous doctrine of the later scholars who claim that the existence of contingents is intentional, and the existence of the Necessary is concrete/actual. [This is] because He the Most High in Himself is the [only] referent predicated by existent, in opposition to contingents. Except that the abstracted thing called the being of the contingents is expressed by relation, attachment and copulation (*bi-l-intisāb aw al-taʿalluq aw al-rabṭ*). So the argument is that being in this way is one real individual and existent is a universal multiple apart from another method that has no face apparently. Instead, we claim that that there is difference between these two doctrines such that the existentiality of things and their being is an intentional meaning and a universal concept that includes all existents . . . If one applies being in the other sense, that is the Truth subsisting in itself, then it is so through commonality [of meaning].[255]

Returning to our fourfold division, the third view is commonly associated with the Peripatetics: the multiplicity of being *and* existents. Sabzawārī describes this as a view of the common people, of the masses for whom unity (of God) is something accepted on the tongue and not fully recognised.[256] The problem with this view is that they still consider being to be a unified and common notion. But how can it be if there is no actual unity to justify the semantic unity?[257]

The fourth view is the 'vulgar' Sufi doctrine of hypostatic unity that considers our phenomenal experience of multiplicity to be illusory.[258] Being is one person and that is God.[259] It cannot be modulated nor synonymous since synonymy and modulation are logical concepts predicated of universals along in a logical (and nominalist) sense.[260] 'Abd al-Ghanī Nābulusī [d. 1731], Ibn 'Arabī's commentator, also clarifies that the univocal application of being to God does not mean that all existents are God but rather that only God is true being.[261] The Akbarian tradition qualifies this monism by distinguishing two senses of unity.[262] The first is the absolute sense that is predicated of God, the divine essence alone who is the True One. This is henadic unity (*aḥadiyya*), the unity of the intelligible world, between the divine essence and its attributes.[263] This is the level of the divine names oriented towards the divine essence.[264] The second is a relational oneness of entities in which oneness ultimately refers back to the True One through the relation of entities to it, almost in the sense of the togetherness (*maʿiyya*) mentioned above.[265] This is monadic unity (*wāḥidiyya*) that encompasses these attributes deployed in the circle of being.[266] The divine names at this level are the grounds for existence and acts deployed in the world.[267] When Ṣadrā criticises hypostatic unity, he understands being as extra-mental being that encompasses everything, that is deployable being, not being in the mode of uniqueness or Pure Being as understood by Sufis. Thus, he allows modulation.[268]

One possibility is that instead of monorealism being an immature doctrine along with the synonymy of being, in fact it is modulation that is a pedagogical tool on the way to unitive awareness.[269]

> From that it must be known that our affirmation of many degrees of being and our concessions in the interests of pedagogy (*al-taʿlīm*) conceiving the diversity and multiplicity of being does not exceed what we shall explain as before God-willing concerning the affirmation of the unity of being and the existent as an essence and in reality. Such is the doctrine of the saints and the mystics among the great of the people of revelation and certainty.[270]

He certainly wants to hold on to monorealism. At the same time, Ṣadrā holds different views on unity,[271] sometimes even in the same paragraph.[272]

Do particular existents really exist? Or are they mere relations and modes of the Real?[273] Rahman argues that modulation and 'unity-in-diversity' are incompatible with the forms of monism espoused in the text.[274] One can find textual evidence for both positions. First, on particulars as mere modes of being one recognises their existential dependence and deficiency.[275] In fact it is impious to suggest that particulars are independent beings.[276] This follows from the doctrine of 'existential contingency'. Second, modulation is real and particulars are real and not figurative existents. They are not illusory, contrary to what the Sufis think.[277]

So what is the solution? Modulation circumvents the principle of Non-contradiction, thus allowing paradoxical juxtaposition of doctrines and negating binarism of possibilities. The being of Zayd is real in itself and is related to Zayd in its reality not metaphorically, yet this necessity is entailed by it being a mode of the real.[278] Iqbal described the Sadrian system as proposing that reality was all things and yet none of them.[279] This is the Akbarian He/Not He that describes the cosmos.[280] Modulation of being thus absorbs monism and yet remains an alternative option in the market-place of metaphysical doctrines.

The God–World Relationship

God as the focal meaning of being is critical to any discussion. Ṣadrā discusses this in his commentary on *Sūrat al-jumʿa* by the statement that 'all existents are oriented towards the Truth [i.e. God]'.[281] Monistic tendencies are shown here too: 'every existent is like a drop in the ocean of His being, and a grain attached in the illumination of His manifestation and ray of His light'.[282] In this section I want to consider two issues. First, I want to examine the Sadrian proofs for the existence of God, especially the 'proof of the truthful' (*burhān al-ṣiddīqīn*). Second, we need to appreciate the God–world relationship in his work as expressed through the doctrine of 'making'.

Ontological proof

There are many proofs for the existence of God because as Ṣadrā says there are many signs that indicate Him and facets about Him. *Kalām* cosmological proofs began with the intuition of phenomenal existence requiring a cause; there was a creation which needed a cause to be. There had to be a reason why there was something rather than nothing. Avicenna's famous proof for the Necessary Being began with the concept of existence, proceeded with a modal distinction between necessity and contingent, and arrived at the exigency of a Necessary Being.[283] Avicenna himself called his argument the 'proof of the veracious' (*burhān al-ṣiddīqīn*) and his commentator Ṭūsī provided a typology of three proofs for the existence of a Creator, which in turn are the *kalām* cosmological argument, the proof from motion that derives from Aristotle's *Physics*, and the Avicennan ontological argument:

> The systematic theologians (*al-mutakallimūn*) infer from the origination of bodies and properties [pertaining to them] the existence of the Creator and from considering the states of the creation to his attributes one after another.
>
> The natural philosophers (*al-ṭabīʿiyyūn*) also infer from the existence of motion a Mover and from the impossibility of linking motive beings in a chain infinitely the existence of the First Mover (*muḥarrik awwal*) who is unmoved. Then from that they infer the existence of the First Principle (*mabda' awwal*).
>
> However, the divine philosophers (*al-ilāhiyyūn*) infer from their reflection upon being that it is either necessary or contingent to prove the Necessary. Then by reflecting upon what is entailed by necessity and contingency, they infer his attributes and from his attributes they infer the nature of the emanation of his acts from him one after another.
>
> The master mentioned the preponderance of this method over the others because it is more reliable and nobler. That is because the more excellent of demonstrations is one that yields certainty and it is the inference from the cause to the effect; however, its opposite which is the inference from the effect to the cause may yield certainty and that is if the thing sought has a cause that can only be discerned through it as has been explained in *apodeixis*. These two levels are posed in his saying – exalted is He: 'We shall show them our signs in the

> horizons and in their souls until it is clear to them that He is the Truth. Is it not enough that your Lord is witness for everything?' [Q. 41 52][284]

Ṭūsī mentions two types of argumentation that the tradition describes as assertoric proof (*burhān innī*) and demonstrative proof (*burhān limmī*), the former is an inference from effect to cause and the latter is from cause to effect. The demonstrative proof for Ṣadrā is the one that is 'most reliable, most illuminating and most noble' and it involves an inference of reality by taking God, Being as a witness to the totality of Being. This is what he calls the 'way of the veracious' (*sabīl al-ṣiddīqīn*).[285] What he means by *ṣiddīq* is not the same as Avicenna and the gap in meaning is a good illustration of the difference in their philosophical method. For Mullā Ṣadrā, the *ṣiddīq* is one who possesses intuition and inner disclosure that is attained through grace and spiritual exercise. In the exegesis of Q. 57:19 on the phrase 'those who believe in God and His messengers are the veracious ones and witness before their Lord', Ṣadrā argues that the *ṣiddīq* is characterised by witnessing the truth through inner revelation:

> What is meant by faith in God and his messengers is a perfect degree of knowledge that is only realised in true knowers. True, inner revealed faith is meant which the saints and mystics (*li-l-awliyā' wa-l-ʿurafā'*) possess especially because they are the veracious ones and witnesses due to the utmost level of their attestation [of truth] acquiring through inner revelation (*kashf*) and due to their self-annihilation acquired due to their inner spiritual struggle against the carnal forces of their souls.[286]

For Mullā Ṣadrā, the Avicennan argument was insufficient because it provided an assertoric not a demonstrative proof and because it engaged with the concept but not the concrete reality of being.[287] The Sadrian proof of the veracious is a natural corollary to his monorealism.[288] It is compatible with modulation; in fact the latter is significant for its proof.[289] 'Being is a concrete reality that is simple and unique and there is no distinction among its individuals essentially except by perfection and imperfection and intensity and debilitation'.

These degrees of being are acts of the divine essence such that even cosmological proofs are ultimately ontological.[290] Ontological proofs depend on the intelligibility of the concept of being, which must be shared between our notion of our being and God's being.[291] This is precisely the point made earlier about the possibility of theology depending upon the concept of modulation. Being has three modes: positively conditioned, unconditioned and negatively conditioned. Mystics of the Akbarian school consider God, the Pure Being (*al-wujūd al-muṭlaq*), to be unconditioned even by the condition of being unconditioned.[292] The divine essence must be in this mode because it is utterly ineffable. This position is articulated against what was the prevailing view of being after the fourteenth century and before our philosophy, that of unrealism, of being as an unreal concept.[293] For Ṣadrā, God, the divine essence, is being negatively conditioned at the level of pure henadic unity (*al-aḥadiyya*).[294] This proof follows from the Illuminationist proof from the intensifications of light towards the Light of Lights.[295] Safar III of the *Asfār* begins with a discussion of the ways of proving the existence of God. Having discussed previous cosmological and ontological proofs, he expresses his own 'method of the veracious' (*manhaj al-ṣiddīqīn*) in the following manner as a 'detailed thought experiment':

> The reality of Being (*ḥaqīqat al-wujūd*), by virtue of its being a simple thing (*amran basīṭan*), not possessing a quiddity or a constituent property or a means of being defined, is identical to the Necessary, requiring the most complete perfection that is infinitely intense, because every other degree [of being], which is weaker in intensity is not the pure reality of Being. Rather, it is being with deficiency since the deficiency of everything is other than that thing necessarily. The deficiency of being is not being itself but rather its privation and this privation is merely attached to being concomitantly and not the foundation of being, due to its actuality in a subsequent degree [of being] and what comes after that. Deficiencies and privations comprise secondary [entities] insofar as they are secondary, but the First is its complete perfection, which has no definition and nothing may be conceived that is more perfect than it. Deficiency and ontological indigence issue from emanation and existentiation (*min al-ifāḍa wa-l-jaʿl*) and are perfected by it [the Necessary]. The haecceity of these secondaries is attached to the First. So he treats their deficiencies with his perfection and their ontological indigence with his ontological richness (*iftiqārihā bi-ghināʾihi*).
>
> Thus through this demonstration is the being of the Necessary proven.[296]

The Sadrian argument may be summarised as follows:[297]

1 There is being
2 Being is a perfection above which no perfection may be conceived
3 God is perfection and perfection in being
4 Being is a singular and simple reality
5 That singular reality is graded in intensity in a scale of perfection.
6 That scale must have a limit point, a point of greatest intensity and of greatest being.
7 Hence God exists (= being).

Thus the proof begins with the concept and reality of being and of God and ends with it.

This proof originates in the famous proof for the Necessary being in Avicenna.[298] The Avicennan proof focuses on the concept of the being that is necessary by virtue of itself, a concept suggested by Aristotle.[299] The proof is not a demonstration because it starts with the posterior and infers the prior, that is, its middle term is an effect and not a cause of the presence of the major term in the minor term.[300] There is a certain debate about whether this proof is ontological or cosmological. Davidson describes it as cosmological because it begins with the intuition of contingent being, and contingency is defined by dependence upon another.[301] There are two major premisses of the argument: first, that there is existence, and second, that an infinite ranked series of units in a causal relationship in reality is impossible, that is the impossibility of a real infinite regress.[302] It postulates a being that is necessary because the supposition of its non-being entails a logical impossibility.[303] Avicenna formulates this argument in the following succinct way.

> There is no doubt that there is being. Every being is either necessary or contingent. If it is necessary, then it is valid that it is the being of the Necessary, which is sought. If it is contingent, then we have shown that the being of the contingent culminates in the Necessary being.[304]

What this proof actually does is to suggest that the reality is entailed by the concept, but it does not mean that the concept of the Necessary Being is true in itself.[305] This is a feature of an ontological argument that purports to be an *a priori* inference.[306] It is more authentically Sadrian to regard the proof as ontological. The intuition of being refers to being *qua* being and every contingent is as we have seen ultimately necessary in reference to One True Being.

Nevertheless, the Sadrian proof remains susceptible to the common criticisms of ontological proofs. It actually seems to be tautological. Because Ṣadrā argues that the reality of being eludes human ability to confine it to discourse, it is not perhaps surprising that the *manhaj al-ṣiddīqīn* is not *in strictu sensu* an apodeictic proof. In a perceptive gloss, ʿAllāma Ṭabāṭabāʾī, the eminent philosopher and commentator, argues that Mullā Ṣadrā does not provide a *burhān limmī* but rather an assertoric argument because in effect all proofs for the existence of God begin with his effects and deduce his existence as the cause of those effects. This is because for Ṭabāṭabāʾī, as for Ṣadrā, being is an *a priori* intuition that all sound intellects possess and within that intuition, the existence of a Necessary Being is logically necessary (*ḍarūrī*). Proofs for the existence of God, therefore, are not attempts at producing demonstrations that convince or even fulfil the scientific parameters within proof theory, but are mere reminders (*tanbīhāt*) to what we already know in our souls and hence corroborate and support faith in the One.[307] This perhaps is why Ṣadrā never refers to his argument as a 'demonstration' (*burhān*) but as a way (*manhaj*, *sabīl*) of understanding and as a thought experiment (*tadhkira*). Thus the 'argument' may be a useful means for the exposition of a theistic viewpoint but does not fall into the category of persuasion.[308]

'Making' (al-jaʿl)

The world is pure correlation for Ṣadrā.[309] Contingent ipseities are mere connectives to the Emanator of being that is beyond any determination.[310] This reflects the Peripatetic doctrine of differentiation as a relational factor, such as less and more, big and small and so on, as well as contingent existential dependence.[311] Making (*al-jaʿl*) relates to being since God's relationship with the world directly is existential; it is the act of divine existential agency.[312] This is because He has no quiddity.[313] What emanates from Him and is 'made' by Him is being, and quiddity is an accident of that process.[314]

Making posits a sustaining role for the One who 'is the ground of being' (*huwa-l-aṣl fī-l-wujūd*).[315] He states that 'His being and activity bring existents into being and make ipseities manifest and the being-a-thing of something is only by virtue of the mercy of the attributes'.[316]

Thus His activity brings about their being, and His attributes bring about quiddities that allow for the identification of specific entities.

The first ontological level of making is that 'source of being' from which everything issues: it is deployable being (*wujūd munbasiṭ*) that safeguards God's distinction from the cosmos. This hypostasis is pure act of being, unlike matter's pure passivity, and from it are all things fashioned.[317] Yet this deployment is not totally separate from God (we already know this from the doctrine of togetherness) but is its shadow since it is equivalent in the language of the Akbarian tradition to the Breath of the Merciful (*nafas al-raḥmān*).[318] Ibn ʿArabī makes the connection in his work.[319] This doctrine is recognisably Proclean and (at least ps.-)Empedoclean.[320] Ṣadrā relates this breath of the Merciful and deployable being to the Muḥammadan reality and the primordial 'point'.[321] In this Shiʿi cosmology, according to the saying of the first Imam ʿAlī, the totality of the Qur'ān, that is the cosmos itself, is encompassed in the primary letter of the *basmala*, and he the Imam is the point underneath.[322] The simplicity of the 'point' ensures that it is all things according to the doctrine of the simple reality.[323] The letter *bā'* enunciates the majesty of God and manifests Him as the cause of causes. As He is ineffable, so our intellects are too weak to see beyond the black of the ink of the words of the Qur'ān.[324] But if one's intellect is guided by God, illuminated by the simple intellect, one can see beyond the ink and recognise that the reality of the Qur'ān is all things. The Book is the deployable being, and is in fact identical of the Imam, the 'clear Imam' (*al-imām al-mubīn*) that is the heart of the Qur'ān (*Umm al-kitāb*).[325] The Imam, who is the Perfect Man, is the 'comprehensive book' and a microcosmic disclosure of God and cosmos.[326] So where does distinction arise? Again we return to the complementarity between the Book of God and of the Cosmos.

> The differentiation of forms of existents and the difference in their properties and contrariness of these states [reflect] great signs for cognition of the inner Qur'ān and lights of His beauty and rays of His signs, and bring knowledge of His names and attributes.[327]

Thus this first emanation, first existent and the Book and cosmos are cosmological proofs for the existence of God, of which the most potent proof is the comprehension of it all, the point and essence of the Qur'ān and the Face of God, the Imam.[328]

world (*tajassum, bashariyya*).[330] The [primordial] point [who is the Imam] is an expression for the descent of Pure Being that is manifested'.[331] The reflexivity of him as the agent and proof of God, as God's revelation with the Book is a major theme of Imamology-cosmology and hermeneutics.[332]

For Rahman, a problem with this account of the divine attributes is that it seems to place quiddities in the mind of God as archetypes and reifies and ontologises them as necessities; this contradicts his normal denial of reality to quiddities.[333] But as we have suggested, there are two chains of causality, one essential and existential, and the other quidditative.[334] The attributes and divine forms determine the identification of quiddity through the traditional account of hylomorphism, but their reality is merely divine being and existence. Things occur because the divine agent act yields them. Following the mainstream Mu'tazilite reading of Shi'i theology, Ṣadrā realises that attributes and names are conceptual reflections of the reality of being.[335] Quoting the Imam: 'The perfection of monotheism is sincerity to Him and perfection of that sincerity is negating attributes of Him'.

He then comments on this phrase.

> All else is not a simple reality as a simple reality has nothing that can be negated of it (which is a sign of existential perfection). Negation of being is not affirmation of being. If one negates an existential reality of Him, that entails composition in His essence. But since He is simple that is absurd.
>
> '. . . negating the attributes' means those whose being is other than the being of His essence, since His essence is the referent for all perfect attributes and qualities of the divine, and they do not subsist through another. So His knowledge, His power and so on exist through the existence of His unitive being, while they are differing notions and concepts.[336]

The attributes too undergo modulation, but not in a real sense rather in a conceptual sense, *pace* Rahman.[337]

Wilāya and the Perfect Man

Finally, we come to the return to the One, the process by which man and the whole cosmos reverts to the One and the circle of being becomes complete. This is the arc of ascent.

Man has differing levels. 'Intelligible man', that is, the form 'man' encompasses all realities since they all participate in Him.[338] It is this man that is the lord of creation. This is precisely the concept of the Perfect Man. The motif of the Perfect

the intelligible and sensible domains of being because he belongs to both.[341] The most intense level of man, the Perfect Man/Imam/Walī is the last degree of being before the One.[342]

The Perfect Man is the primordial point and that point is the secret of *wilāya*.[343] On this, Ṣadrā draws on the Shiʿi discussion of the fourteenth-century mystic, Rajab Bursī in his *Mashāriq anwār al-yaqīn fī asrār Amīr al-Mu'minīn*:[344]

> Beings culminate in a single point that is the quality of the essence and the cause of existents, and it is known by many terms. In the words of the Prophet it is the intellect: 'the first thing that God created was the intellect'. Also in his words it is the Muḥammadan presence: 'the first thing that God created was my light', thus in this respect it is the first thing emanated from God the most High without any mediation that is called the First Intellect. But insofar as things acquire from it the faculty of intellection it is the Agent Intellect. Insofar as intellect flows to all existents from it such that they perceive through it the realities of things it is called the Universal Intellect. It is known through a clear proof that the Muḥammadan presence is the point of light that is the First manifestation, the reality of beings, the origin of existents, the pole of all orbits. Its outward nature is a divine attribute and its inward the divine unseen. It manifests the greatest name, and is the form of the remaining cosmos. It transcends belief and unbelief. His [the Prophet's] spirit is a copy of henadic unity (*aḥadiyya*) in the divine realm, and his body is the form of meanings in the visible and invisible realms (*al-mulk wa-l-malakūt*), and his heart is the treasure of the Living who does not die. This is because when God first spoke with a word it became a light, then it became a spirit. The spirit entered the light and made it a veil so that His word and its light and its spirit are veils. Their flow in the world is like that of the point in letters and bodies and the one in the numbers and the *alif* in speech.[345]

Imams partake in the modulation of being. The Muḥammadan reality is singular and each Imam partakes of it and manifests it.[346] The realm of *wilāya* is the most intense grade of being in both vertical and horizontal hierarchies and the first emanation closest to the One, being the *logos* of it.[347] It is both ontologically and epistemologically prior. Knowing the Imam is the epistemological *sine qua non* of knowledge just as being has to be intuited for the possibility of knowledge of syllogistic chains and definitions.[348] He is the last indicating his role in the *eschaton* of our *epochē*.[349] He is thus the instrument of return to the One.

The hierarchy of being and the role of *wilāya* at the culmination of the pyramid of being suggests a direction that Mullā Ṣadrā takes. His ontology begins with the semantics of the term being and the epistemological distinction between the concept and reality of being (whether mental or extra-mental) but seems to finds its completion in the eschatology of the reversion of all beings that exist to their principle the One. The central role of *wilāya* as the hermeneutics of being, its unfolding and its folding demonstrates that confluence of Shiʿi thought and Neoplatonism in the critical synthesis of Mullā Ṣadrā's vision of metaphysics.

Conclusion

Is *tashkīk al-wujūd* in Mullā Sadrā an adequate account of reality and a successful argument? Is it a satisfactory semantic theory and ontology? Christopher Shields argues that the use of homonymy in Aristotle is a failure because the Stagirite fails to demonstrate his case. Being for Aristotle is thus synonymous and always means *ousia* as substance.[1] Yet substance itself retains an elusive quality. The quest for the *tertium quid* as a means for articulating a desire to reconcile an ideal unity in existence with the phenomenal pluralism that we encounter remains beyond the possibilities of Aristotelian science.

The absence of demonstration follows from the intuition of being that is central to Islamic philosophical traditions. However, unlike Aristotle, Ṣadrā does not indulge in ousiological reduction; that is, he does not essentialise being as 'substance'. He does not consider metaphysics to be the study of being *qua ousia*, but being insofar as it is a process of becoming and unfolding of being. The Aristotelian focus on (primary) substance is discarded in favour of processes and acts of being as becoming. Mullā Ṣadrā conceives of being as a process that characterises reality and manifests itself in the three modes examined in this study. However, an element of doubt in the certainty of our perception and its discursive articulation means that in the very act of our claim to have grasped 'being', we falsify, reify and essentialise it. Hence being evades us.

I have argued that starting from the semantics of unity-in-diversity, or predication of being by *pros hen* homonymy, Ṣadrā commits himself not only to a threefold sense of being, but also postulates modulation within each of these modes of being. Thus modulation by intensity of being has two levels. First, there are three senses of being related to one another with a focal sense of the real or the One that is most intense. 'Pure Being is God the Most High . . . It is the light of God's being that illuminates all others . . . from the highest level of being to the lowest, all unified as correlations to the One'.[2]

Intensifying modulation characterises the relationship between these different modes of being, from the most intense that is God, down through being that is realised, through to the less intense senses of being such as mental being and being-in-language. The pyramid of being is a singular, simple reality that consists of all that exists in grades and degrees of intensity. The most intense point within this pyramid is God the Necessary Being. While one might argue that Aristotle and later

Avicenna signalled the conflation of ontology and theology into an onto-theology of Necessary Being, they still managed to keep the notion of a divine, uncaused being separate from our intuition of our selves. Mullā Ṣadrā's monistic tendency within the hermeneutics of modulation means that he wishes to place God within the pyramid of being and at the same time considers God to be beyond that object of metaphysical analysis.

The second step in the postulation of modulation is that each sense of being is marked by intensification, of more or less. The reality of being is the classic paradigm for this process.

> The nature of being permits intensity and debilitation in its simple essence . . . Their individuals and units only differ by essential intensity and debilitation (*bi-l-shidda wa-l-ḍuʿf*), essential priority and posteriority, and essential nobility and baseness (*al-sharaf wa-l-khissa*).[3]

Modulation of being by intensity is thus marked by certain critical characteristics:

1 It posits a unity of being, or a unified mode of being.
2 This unity is graded in degrees differentiated by intensification and debilitation.
3 The principle of unity and differentiation in each mode of being is being itself.
4 Each grade of being, that is not by virtue of itself the *arche* or the One, that is the focal sense of being, is privative considered in itself and existentially dependent upon the One.
5 This hierarchy of being is dynamic as the degrees of being are in constant substantial motion and progress from lower to higher levels.

What emerges, therefore, is a vision of reality that is processist, hierarchical and dynamic. It is a fresh attempt at describing a reality that is at once One and many.

Does Ṣadrā fail to make his case for the modulation of being? One of the central problems in the Sadrian approach is the lack of a definitive argument or demonstrative proof (*burhān limmī*). One might defend this lacuna by stating that any argument about an *a priori* such as being must also necessarily elude demonstration in the technical sense. But this seems unsatisfactory. What the Sadrian method does is actually posit a pedagogical method and grounds for argument and debate, having provided the student with an exhaustive consideration of previous theories. The inadequacy of modulation to forge a middle path between monorealism of the

more recently in the twentieth century, Ṣāliḥ Ḥāʾirī Māzandarānī rejected Sadrian modulation in favour of metaphysical pluralism, an ontology of substances, and criticised the 'second-rate' synthesis of Mullā Ṣadrā as having been patched together from previous thinkers who were not properly acknowledged.[4] Māzandarānī in his defence of Avicennism entitled *Ḥikmat-i Bū ʿAlī* focused his attack on Ṣadrā and the 'dishonesty' of his synthesis and the inefficacy of his doctrines of the ontological primacy and modulation of being. While his debt to previous thinkers is clear, it is, however, somewhat unfair to accuse Ṣadrā of failing to cite his influences: as we discussed above, the *Asfār* is a key source for understanding the history of Islamic philosophy and the new editions produced by SIPRIn make his sources clear.

At the other end of the intellectual spectrum, monists and adherents of Ibn ʿArabī such as Mīrzā Muḥammad Riḍā Qumshihī [d. 1888], another of the pillars of the school of Tehran, rejected modulation in favour of monorealism in his *risāla fī waḥdat al-wujūd*, his glosses on the *Faṣṣ* of Seth from the *Fuṣūṣ al-ḥikam* and in his *scholia* on the *Tamhīd al-qawāʿid* of Ṣāʾin al-Dīn Ibn Turka Iṣfahānī [d. 1433].[5] Clearly, for these critics Sadrian modulation had failed to articulate an adjudicated position between monism and pluralism and hence they had lapsed into these two existing visions and descriptions of reality. Notwithstanding these critiques, the Sadrian school has remained hegemonic through the important contributions of Qajar thinkers such as Mullā Hādī Sabzawārī [d. 1873] and Āqā ʿAlī Zunūzī [d. 1889]; the modern philosopher Sayyid Muḥammad Ḥusayn Ṭabāṭabāʾī [d. 1981], whose glosses on the *Asfār* are truly insightful; and the current prayer leader (*imām-jumʿeh*) of Qom and philosopher Āyatullāh ʿAbd Allāh Javādī Āmulī, whose voluminous commentary on the *Asfār* is a real asset in understanding critically Mullā Ṣadrā's thought.[6]

Potentially more problematic for Sadrian approaches to metaphysics are two critiques posed by rival schools of thought, namely, the philosophy of Shaykh Aḥmad al-Aḥsāʾī [d. 1826] and the modern 'school of the separation of the sciences' (*maktab-i tafkīk*) founded by Āyatullāh Mīrzā Mahdī Gharawī Iṣfahānī [d. 1365Q/1946] and Shaykh Mujtabá Qazvīnī [d. 1386/1966] in Mashhad and their students Shaykh Muḥammad Riḍā Ḥakīmī and Āyatullāh Muḥammad Bāqir Malikī Miyānjī.[7] Aḥsāʾī consistently critiques the two core ideas of Mullā Ṣadrā: the ontological primacy and modulation of being. In a short treatise responding to questions posed to him by Mīrzā Muḥammad ʿAlī Mudarris, he argues that because contingent entities are real composites of being and quiddity, it must be the case that in the cosmos, being and quiddity come together as coeval principles and hence are both 'ontologically primary'. Similarly, there is only a lexical commonality between the term 'being' applied to God and to creatures since Aḥsāʾī wishes to adhere to a strict ontological distinction.[8] His more systematic critiques emerged in

and the contingent because they are radically distinct.[10] The 'true doctrine' of the

Imams and of the Shiʿi ʿulema is that God's being is utterly different, while contingent being is susceptible to division into substance and accident, cause and effect, prior and posterior, more intense and more weak. Modulation may well apply to the totality of contingent beings but the 'pyramid of being' cannot and must not include God. This is a clear rejection of monorealism associated with 'the killer of the faith' (*mumīt al-dīn*) Ibn ʿArabī and he stresses that the doctrine of *waḥdat al-wujūd* is manifest unbelief according to the scholarly consensus of the Shiʿi ʿulema.[11] Aḥsāʾī suggests that Mullā Ṣadrā's thinking has become corrupted by the influence of the school of Ibn ʿArabī and by its distance from the true teachings of the Imams. He clinches his argument by adducing a saying of the first Shiʿi Imam ʿAlī b. Abī Ṭālib on the nature of being which he interprets to denote extra-mental being. A conflation of mental and extra-mental being, of the concept and reality of being, of the Necessary and the contingent in a singular continuum represents ignorance and not true knowledge.[12] Ultimately, Aḥsāʾī's critique is not philosophically sophisticated and has the rhetorical appearance of a philosophical argument. Its recourse to scripturalism suggests a critique of 'philosophy' grounded in the method of the ancient Greeks in favour of a wisdom that is Prophetic and Imamic.

The *maktab-i tafkīk* shares with Aḥsāʾī this basic criticism of Sadrian inquiry. They agree that, contrary to Mullā Ṣadrā's claims of rooting his philosophy in prophetic teachings, his philosophical positions are incompatible with the true teachings of the Prophet and the Shiʿi Imams. The school is also characterised by its incessant assault on the philosophical consensus that promotes Sadrian thought as the 'definitive Shiʿi philosophy'. Iṣfahānī in his major work *Abwāb al-hudá* argues against following the philosophers, as they represent Greek thought that was promoted to suppress the teachings of the Imams:

> For whoever is cognisant of the policy of the caliphs, it will become as clear as daylight that the reason for the translation of Greek philosophy and promotion of the way of the Sufis that both derived from Greece was merely a policy to suppress the knowledge and teachings of the Family of the Prophet.[13]

Although he does not mention Mullā Ṣadrā by name, he does criticise philosophers for posing analogy between God and creation, and Sufis for monorealism.[14] In *Tawḥīd al-imāmiyya*, his student Miyānjī attempts to construct a rigorous philosophical theology on the basis of interpretations of the narrations of the Imams and engages in a lengthy debate and polemic against philosophers such as Avicenna and especially Mullā Ṣadrā. He argues that the book sets out to expound transcendent knowledge about the nature of God and unlock explanations of the divine essence and activity gleaned from the Qur'ān and the narrations of the Holy family according to the Twelver Shiʿa.[15] Miyānjī seeks to establish an authentic Shiʿi philosophy and theology that is uncontaminated by foreign, Hellenic methods and ideas. He explicitly rejects ontological arguments for the existence of God and affirms the exclusive validity of defining and describing the divine through the scriptural texts available in the Shiʿi tradition.[16] He takes to task Mullā Ṣadrā and his famous student Muḥsin Fayḍ Kāshānī for affirming that being is a singular modulated reality differentiated by degrees of intensification and debilitation.[17] First, being is merely a term that is shared by the Necessary and contingents; there is no shared semantic content. The only commonality between them is that we use the same words to describe aspects of them in very different senses (i.e. *ishtirāk lafẓī*). Second, modulation is based on the postulation of a singular pyramid of being that incorporates God and creation, but such a position relegates God to an individual within a larger class and practically places God at the same level as creation. Third, modulation is predicated on monorealism (*waḥdat al-wujūd*) and this is manifest heresy. If being is a singular but graded reality, it should be possible for a lower grade to aspire to a higher grade, but scripture tells us that one cannot become divine. For Miyānjī all these features of modulation are in direct contradiction to the scripture and must be rejected. True philosophy and understanding of reality can only be acquired from a meditation upon scripture. These critiques demonstrate how the field of philosophy and especially metaphysics has become the ground for the debate on authentic culture and knowledge in the Shiʿi tradition. Nevertheless, the philosophical traditions within the Shiʿi seminary, particularly in Iran, remain under the dominance of the Sadrian school. Monists, Avicennans, *tafkīkīs* and Shaykhīs are relegated to the margins. The theory of modulation is debated, refined, critically analysed and modified. Ultimately, modulation by intensity of being is a working theory, an explanation (*bayān*) of truth but not truth itself. The latter exists but is not so easily available to us through discourse or analysis. The problem of ineffability remains unavoidable. The limits to human knowledge are thus clearly delineated. Arguments, proofs, thought-experiments and rhetoric guide students, corroborate intuitions and 'confirm faith'. They often are persuasive without being demonstrative, complete or even rationally sound.[18] This does not imply that Mullā Ṣadrā lapses into an unsatisfactory 'mysticism' that is inaccessible to any form of intellect, discourse or cognitive content. Rather, it signals a continuation of the aporetic method, recognition of a reality in constant flux and a hermeneutics of *tashkīk* in which reality, being, truth are affirmed and negated simultaneously. The Sadrian method is not a closed system in which modulation is the final word on the structure of reality. It is thus that modulation (*tashkīk*) is itself *mushakkak*. Since all being in its processes of becoming in the cosmos is subject to change and flux, then it follows that this applies to understanding, explanation, discourse and argumentation as well. The explanation is not fixed but open to modification and revision as any conceptualisation differs from reality. 'The concept of being is quite separate from its reality and cannot grasp its reality'.[19]

Mullā Ṣadrā makes precisely this point when he stresses that any conceptualisation or notion of being that we may conceive is necessarily a 'falsification' of its true nature, since representation can never truly mirror reality: 'Whatever is described by being in the soul, is not the reality of being but rather an appearance, an aspect'.[20]

Appearances can mislead precisely because the senses, physicality and our phenomenal world may fail to yield the true nature of being to us. Indeed, as Mullā Ṣadrā writes in the *Asfār*, 'beings are meanings whose names are unknown'.[21] The realities of essences can only be intellected by 'ontic presence' and through 'illuminative vision'.[22] Phenomenal experience is communicable through language and definitions, but it seems that true reality can be known through mystical intuition, non-discursive thought and 'immediate knowledge' but remains in some way ineffable.[23] Our human limitations display the sheer contingency of our ways of disclosing reality – it is no coincidence that Mullā Ṣadrā and other philosophers before him held that the philosophical enterprise sought cognition of reality 'insofar as is humanly possible'. Perhaps only once we have achieved some 'enlightenment', some direct encounter and 'taste' of reality, can we comprehend what being truly is. But in the mean while, our struggle to define, understand and control being is without an end and constantly iterated and differed. Ultimate explanation constantly eludes us. *Apophasis* and negation dominate *kataphasis* and affirmation.

This is precisely why modulation is such a successful explanation because it avoids closure whilst being a comprehensive account open to doubt and change. Being is in constant flux and modulation. Its explanation, which as we have seen must necessarily be a falsification of its nature, should attempt to duplicate this state of change and revision and be able to develop. This is why the Sadrian tradition itself has thrown up thinkers who are profoundly at odds with Ṣadrā's method of explanation, yet who are still able to work within the paradigm of modulation. It is for this reason that the perceptive glosses of the late 'Allāma Ṭabāṭabā'ī on the *Asfār* are so illuminating, as is the commentary of Javādī Āmulī. It is for the Sadrians of the present generation and beyond to work towards better explanations of truth, and posit arguments that have a greater intensity than those put forward by Mullā Ṣadrā. Many of them have stayed faithful to the Sadrian theme of ineffability as well as modulation as the best explanation for reconciling unity and multiplicity.

The philosophical quest remains live and exciting. *Tashkīk* demands at least this of us and rejects imitation and rehearsal of arguments. But the central problematic of being remains one of the inadequacy of explanation, the ineffability of the *explanandum* before the *explanans*. As Mullā Ṣadrā says of being:

> It is the most manifest of things in realisation and essence such that it is said of it that it is *a priori*. It is the most hidden of all things in reality and inner-reality such that it is said that it is purely intentional, although nothing is realised in the mind or in external reality except by it.[24]

Notes

Introduction

1 Ṣadrā (1382 Sh*a*: 19–20), *al-Shawāhid al-rubūbiyya*.
2 I will not provide a biographical context for Mullā Ṣadrā. I would refer interested readers to Khāminihī (2000), Rizvi (2005*b*) and (2007).
3 As I shall refer to it henceforth. Cf. Ṣadrā (1967: 23) and (1961*a*: 131–2). The standard bibliographical references: *GAL*, S II: 588–89; Ṭihrānī (1936, II: 60); Kaḥḥāla (1961, VIII: 203).
4 Throughout this work, I use Sadrian as an adjective to describe the method of Mullā Ṣadrā.
5 Henceforth Avicenna.
6 Ṭūsī in Avicenna (1375 Sh, I: 21) and (1992*a*: 18). It crops up in Baḥrānī (1958, I: 21). This fourfold scheme is found in the thought of the Illuminationist (*ishrāqī*) philosopher, Suhrawardī [d. 1191] based upon the principle of *tashkīk* – see Dīnānī (1366 Sh: 143–4). One finds this tropic fourfold division of being in the work of the thirteenth-century Sufi ʿAzīz-i Nasafī (1998: 355). Other Sufi occurrences include Shaʿrānī [d. 1565] in his (1998, I: 128) and earlier *Inshā' al-dawā'ir* of Ibn ʿArabī [d. 1240] (1919: 78). cf. T(a)hānawī (1963–77, II: 1457). Ṣadrā's commentator, Sabzawārī [d. 1873] (1995, II: 94–9) recognises this fourfold division. Among contemporary scholars, Anvār in Surūsh (1360 Sh: 68) notes the four fundamental modes of being. Other philosophers, such as Mullā Ṣadrā's commentator Hādī Sabzawārī [d. 1873], have proposed an alternative schema of five modes of being: essential (*dhātī*) which is directly perceived in extra-mental reality, sensible (*ḥissī*) which denotes sense data, imaginal (*khayālī*) which renders meanings and 'intentions' abstracted from things in extra-mental reality, intelligible (*ʿaqlī*) which denotes the forms of the sense data abstracted, and figurative (*shibhī*) which refers to non-existents whose sense is similar to things that possess form and reality. See Sabzawārī (1995: 244–7).
7 Ṣadrā (1378 Sh*a*: 19).
8 For a discussion of Sadrian metaphysics within the paradigm of considering philosophy as a way of life, see Rizvi (2005*a*).
9 Avicenna (1960: 10–16) defines sciences by which mode of being they investigate.
10 Böwering, ''Erfān', *Enc. Ir.* VIII: 553.
11 Ṣadrā (1303 Q: 256), quoted in Bīdārfar's introduction to Ṣadrā (1987, I: 21); cf. Ṣadrā (1382 Sh*b*, I: 70, 145, 148).
12 E.g. Amīn (1986).
13 Nasr (1977*a*: 12). His importance in India is attested by the centrality of his *Sharḥ al-hidāya* of Abharī to the Dars-i Niẓāmī curriculum of North India from the eighteenth century – see Rizvi (1986, II: 218); Malik (1997: 153, 527); Robinson (1997: 151–84); S̲ubūt (1996, 1380 Sh). It is also attested in the number of *scholia* (23 extant) in numerous manuscripts that were composed on it in India – see Maʿṣūmī (1961: 40–1).

14 Hodgson (1974, I: 96).
15 Muṭahharī (n.d., chapter 5).
16 *Ḥikmat* (here used in its Persian transliteration) is a semantically rich concept, which covers a range and hierarchy of concepts of philosophical, noetic and mystical inquiry. It is a synonym for *falsafa* in the classical period of Islamic philosophy [Jolivet (1991)], connotes a study and understanding of the *sunna* in the work of early scholars such as Shāfiʿī, and describes wisdom literature [Gutas (1981)]. For the Qur'ānic incidence of the term and a traditional Safavid interpretation, see Fayḍ Kāshānī (1979, I: 275), commenting upon Qur'ān 2:269. In this study, I concentrate on the sense of the term that connotes an intellectual inquiry and practice that reconciles intellectual and mystical approaches.
17 Izutsu (1983: 3), in Izutsu and Mohaghegh (1983).
18 *Asfār* II: 326.
19 Ṣadrā (1982: 4).
20 Horten (1912*a*) and (1913).
21 Gobineau (1933: 79–90).
22 Gobineau (1933: 86–7).
23 For further discussion on his 'persecution', see Rizvi (2007: 31–6).
24 Wild in Wahba and Abousenna (1996: 161); Daiber (1999: xxiv).
25 Horten (1906) and (1907).
26 Horten (1912*a*) and (1912*b*).
27 Horten (1913: i, vi–vii); cf. Rahman (1975: 13–14).
28 Two main works: the magisterial *EII* (1971–2) and (1993*a*). An excellent example of a work influenced by Corbin (for the better) is Hernández (1981), in which philosophy in the East is given extensive coverage, while a work contemporary to it, Fakhry (1980), still only devotes one chapter to the same material.
29 Nasr (1981) and (1996*a*).
30 Nasr wrote the first major piece on Ṣadrā in English in Sharif (1966, II: 932–61).
31 *EII* I: xvi.
32 *EII* I: 24.
33 For a strong critique of 'theosophy', see Żiā'ī (1993).
34 Wasserstrom (1999: 35–6).
35 Gutas (2002: 18), although he does go a bit too far with his dismissal of mysticism as 'adolescent talk'. Mysticism is a proper area of study, respectable and serious on its own, as indeed is the philosophy of mysticism.
36 Mahdi (2001) is perhaps the paradigmatic example of a Straussian work in the study of Arab-Islamic philosophy. On Leo Strauss [d. 1973] and his hermeneutics of Arabic philosophy, see Gutas (2002: 19–24).
37 Morris (1981: 6, 11).
38 Morris (1981: 16, 42–4).
39 Rahman (1975: 14–15, 296) focuses on the central tension between monism and pluralism.
40 Z. Moris (2003: 5).
41 Sharif (1966, II: 938–9).
42 Genequand, in his article, 'Metaphysics' in Nasr (1996*b*, II: 798), argues that the only way philosophical inquiry could survive in Islam after Averroes was through a merger with mysticism and Shiʿi esotericism.
43 Sharif (1966, II: 941), quoting the text in Ṣadrā (1885: 279–86). Chittick (2004: xvii) has already noted that the *Iksīr* is in fact a paraphrase of the *Jāwidān-nāma* of Bābā Afḍal Kāshānī [d. *c.* 1213] so Nasr's scheme is based on a text that is not really Sadrian. It has also been argued that Nasr's privileging of the other-worldly, the intangibility of mysticism and transcendence is associated with his own ideology of the Pahlavi imperium – see Boroujerdi (1996: 122–30).
44 Nasr (2006: 223–33).

45 In which he was followed by Açikgenç (1993).
46 Corbin (1938). See 'De Heidegger à Sohravardi' in Jambet (1981).
47 Corbin (1981*a*). For Corbin's defence against the charge of ahistoricity, see his *EII* I: 159–76, which, if anything, actually confirms the charge for his critics!
48 Corbin (1993*a*: 275).
49 Açikgenç (1993: xii–xiv).
50 Açikgenç (1993: 12).
51 Heidegger (1959: 1–51) and (1996: 3). Nader el-Bizri's comparative work (2000 and 2001) on Avicenna and Heidegger reveals this problem of the difference of ontological assumptions.
52 Kamal (2006: 4). Incidentally, the rendition of *al-ḥikma al-mutaʿāliya* as 'transcendent philosophy' in any dialogue with the analytic and continental traditions of European philosophy is problematic given the Kantian overtones of the term.
53 Kamal is currently completing another monograph (to be published probably by Edinburgh University Press in 2010) that compares Mullā Ṣadrā and Heidegger more explicitly on issues of being, time, change and knowledge as responses to Platonism; the structure and concerns, he contends, go far beyond Açikgenç's work.
54 I am thinking particularly of Gerson (2005) and his reassessment of Aristotle, and Moravcsik (1992).
55 *EII* IV: 158. Followed by Mūsawī (1978: 213–6); Mishkāt al-dīnī (1355 Sh).
56 *EII* IV: 92; Corbin (1990: 164–70).
57 Professor Sarah Hutton at the University of Wales, Aberystwyth is one of the few More specialists around.
58 Jambet (2002: 15). On the *Ūthūlūjiyā* (*Theologia Aristotelis*), see Adamson (2003).
59 Jambet (1983).
60 Plato (1997: 58); cf. Domański (1996: 6); Kindī (1950, I: 172–4); cf. Jolivet (1991: 37–8). For a Safavid discussion, see Ashkiwarī (1999: 99–100).
61 Jambet (2002: 15, 16, 96).
62 Nasr (1996*b*, I: 638–9).
63 Ṣadrā (1992: 9).
64 Morewedge (1995: xii–xiii).
65 Morewedge (1995: xiii). On Process philosophy, see Rescher (1996).
66 Rahman (1975: 1–2).
67 Rahman (1975: 4).
68 Rahman (1975: 5).
69 Rahman (1975: 15).
70 Rahman (1975: 19).
71 Shehadi (1982).
72 Derived from *al-shaykh al-akbar*, a popular title for the Sufi Ibn ʿArabī [d. 1240].
73 Izutsu (1994). His translation with Mohaghegh of the ontology of Sabzawārī in Izutsu (1983) is an excellent contribution to our understanding of *ḥikmat*.
74 Bonmariage (1998). This has now (2007) been published by Librairie Vrin in Paris.
75 Boroujerdi (1996). Dabashi (1993) shows how Ṣadrā remains at the heart of the traditionalist discourse in Iran.
76 Āshtiyānī (1980).
77 Nasr (1996*b*, I: 639). Ḥā'irī (1981), (1992) and especially (1982). Cf. Nasr (1996*b*, II: 1042).
78 Cooper *et al.* (1998*a*: 41) note that the *Asfār* was a critical influence on the formation of the thought of this controversial Iranian thinker. Cf. Matin-asgari (1997).
79 Surūsh (1978). This work, along with (1980), was written while Surūsh was participating in the formative discourse of Islamic ideology that influenced revolutionary rhetoric in Iran. Surūsh (1989) and (1991) develops a sociology of religion based upon the concept of substantial motion and on the Sufi psychology of the expansion and contraction of mystical states. The latter work is his controversial manifesto for

(post-)modernist thought in Islam. However, his position on Ṣadrā and *ḥikmat* has shifted as a result of his constructivist reading of *tashkīk* and substantial motion as he explained at his talk entitled 'Is there an Islamic epistemology?' at the Philosophy Group of the Association of Muslims Researchers, London, 19 December 1998.

80 Surūsh (1991: 81–2, 99).
81 Khorassani (1976).
82 Boroujerdi (1996: 163–70).
83 Khorassani (1976: 110).
84 Khatami (1996). It has now been published – Khatami (2004).
85 It seems that these two terms are rather convoluted expressions for the Sadrian doctrines of the unity and primacy of being.
86 Ahmadi (1998: 31–3).
87 Ahmadi (1998: 31); Fashahi (1995) is similarly naïve.
88 On Khomeini and the philosophical tradition of Mullā Ṣadrā, see Dabashi (1993: 463–6), Knysh (1992), Brumberg (2001: 46–8), Moin (1994: 66–77), and Martin (2000).
89 A philosophical school originating with Suhrawardī.
90 For example, Corbin in Ṣadrā (1964: 13–14); Khājavī (1988: 26–32). For a short introduction to this thinker, see Chittick, 'Ebn al-'Arabī', *Enc. Ir.* VII: 664–70.
91 The only translations of his work available are either mystical or Qur'anic such as Morris (1981), Chittick (2004) and Peerwani (2004). I have been commissioned by Edinburgh University Press to provide a philosophical reader which should, *in shā' allāh*, be available by the beginning of 2011.

1 Methodological concerns

1 Gadamer (2004: 278).
2 By hard contextualism, I mean the approach of Quentin Skinner who argues that 'a rational agent will be someone who . . . believes what he or she ought to believe', and 'understanding of texts presupposes the grasp of what they were intended to mean and how that meaning was intended to be taken' – Skinner (2002: 31, 86). I favour a softer contextualism, even a holism, inclining towards the position of Mark Bevir (1997), (1999), (2000).
3 On the issue of knowledge/power and strategy that concerns us here, see Foucault (1980: 135–45).
4 Chamberlain (1994: 5–11, 21–5); Motahhedeh (1981: 1–7). Unfortunately, the same sorts of analyses have yet to be applied to the intellectual history and analysis of the transmission of knowledge in Safavid Iran. Nasr in Lockhart and Jackson (1986: 656–97) does not particularly tell us much about the relationship between knowledge and its dissemination, power and elites.
5 On the Avicennan dissemination, see Wisnovsky (2004) and (2005).
6 Ṣadrā as an affluent scholar owned copies of all of these texts – see Rizvi (2007: 117–35) for details of his personal library.
7 'Plato's Pharmacy' in Derrida (1972). Nehamas (1999: 345–47) shows that the debate is about attitudes and communication and not about privileging one over the other. On the other hand, Spade (1996: 60, 78) suggests that the mediaeval privileging of the spoken over the written was due to an idea that one could not know or read a language that one did not speak.
8 Plato (1997: 762), *Protagoras*, 329 a 3–4.
9 Hadot (1995: 62).
10 See Zanjānī-Khū'ī (1375 Sh, I: 118–47) for a discussion of the transmission; cf. Dakake (1998, especially 4–5). This work was actually transmitted at his deathbed, contrary to the deathbed phenomenon that Cook (1997: 479), notes at which point the (Sunni) transmitter would destroy his books to ensure the continuity of oral transmission.
11 Kulaynī (1968, I: 52, ḥadīth 149).

12 Ṣadrā (1988, II, 276).
13 Kulaynī (1968, I: 52, *ḥadīth* 148).
14 Ṣadrā (1988, II, 275).
15 Robson, 'Ḥadīth', *EI*[2] III: 27.
16 Ernst in Katz (1992: 191).
17 Plato (1997: 1658–62) *Epistles* 344a–345c. On the Islamic discussion of this, see Walbridge (2000: 174–6).
18 Nasr (1992: 11).
19 I owe this piece of information to a conversation with Prof. Hossein Modarressi at St Antony's College, Oxford in May 1998.
20 Barnes (1976: 14–15).
21 A recent example is the transcription by Shaykh Muḥammad Isḥāq Fayyāḍ of the lectures on *uṣūl al-fiqh* of Sayyid al-Khū'ī (1988–95). The genre of *taqrīrāt* is very common in Shi'i seminaries in the field of jurisprudence.
22 Carruthers (1990: 7–14). The same point is made for Islamic scholarly culture by Mahdi in Atiyeh (1995: 8).
23 Eickelman (1978: 485–516); Goody and Watt (1963: 304–45).
24 Cf. Chamberlain (1994: 144–5).
25 Goody and Watt (1963: 327–31), discussing Plato's *Seventh Epistle*.
26 Mahdi in Vyronis (1975: 3–15).
27 Nasr (1992: 6) argues that the writing of critical commentaries such as Ṣadrā's notes on *Ḥikmat al-Ishrāq* would be inconceivable without the oral tradition.
28 Bausani in Boyle (1968: 538–49).
29 Madelung (1985); Schmidtke (2000); Shīdiyān (1376 Sh); Muvaḥḥid (1995).
30 Nasr (1981: 171–2). I use 'philosophies' because it is clear that the nature of the intellectual inquiry, how it is defined and its ends are not the same across different traditions within Islamic theology, discursive and mystical philosophies.
31 Introduction to Ṣadrā (1362 Sh: 34).
32 Introduction to Ṣadrā (1362 Sh: 43).
33 Introduction to Ṣadrā (1362 Sh: 6).
34 Introduction to Ṣadrā (1362 Sh: 17).
35 *Asfār* I: 68–9. Cf. Taftazānī (1294 Q: 13–14) on Ibn 'Arabī in his *Risāla fī waḥdat al-wujūd*, (Istanbul), quoted in Knysh (1999: 155).
36 Khorassani (1976: 46).
37 E.g. *Asfār* I, 59; VI: 86. A number of the works of the Dashtakī family have recently been published. See the bibliography for further details.
38 Ashkiwarī (1999–2003, II: 265).
39 In the collection of the Raza Library in Rampur, there is an extremely valuable manuscript copy (MS 3476) of *al-Shifā'* of Avicenna dated 1318 which contains tables and *marginalia* in the hand of various members of the Dashtakī family – 'Arshī (1963–2000, IV: 440–3). The manuscript was brought to India by Mīr Fatḥ Allāh Shīrāzī [d. 1589], the famous philosopher and scientist credited with introducing the study of philosophy to the Mughal court; he had studied in Shiraz with Ghiyāth al-Dīn Dashtakī.
40 For a brief discussion of some of these influences, see Rizvi (2007: 153–4).
41 Cf. Walbridge (2000: 39).
42 Hadot (1995: 265).
43 Aristotle (1984, II: 1736) *Nicomachean Ethics* 1098 b 21.
44 Nock and Festugière (1945–54, III: 13) *Corpus Hermeticum Stobaean Fragments* II.8.
45 *Asfār* IX: 121.
46 Ṣadrā (1961*b*: 55–8).
47 Usener (ed.) (1887) *Epicurea*, Leipzig, 221 quoted in Nussbaum (1994: 13).
48 Ashkiwarī (1999, I: 248–50). Cf. Walbridge (2000: 81); Netton (1991: 91); Kingsley (1995: 335ff.).

49 *Asfār* I: 20. This definition draws upon Avicenna (1952: 12), and his *Risāla fī aqsām al-ʿulūm* in Avicenna (1908: 104–5). In earlier times, this meant a quidditative inquiry into the essences of things. Cf. Versteegh (1989: 69); Aristotle (1984, I: 169), *Topics* 101 b 39; Badawī (1948–9, II: 474), Zajjājī (1959: 46); Tawḥīdī (1970: 316). But Ṣadrā is no essentialist; for him, reality denotes an underlying process.

50 I want to insist upon a distinction between our use of the term 'Sufi' and 'mystic', although this does not amount to an apologetic separation of *taṣawwuf* and *ʿirfān à la* Muṭahharī. I would therefore reject Spencer Trimingham's all-encompassing definition of Sufi in his (1971), partly on the Sadrian grounds that a science must have a clearly articulated subject, precisely defined essential properties that one wishes to study, and clearly expressed goals, all of which are lacking in Trimingham's account of Sufism. For me, a Sufi inhabits a cultural space that is defined by notions of putative genealogical inheritance from the Prophet of sanctity and authority through a chain of initiation and grace. A Sufi must therefore have some affiliation with an order that clearly Ṣadrā lacks as far as our evidence allows us to speculate. A mystic is more difficult to define. It remains a highly problematic concept that makes a virtue of its vagueness, used for a range of noetic, non-discursive arguments.

51 Cf. Alston in Katz (1992: 80).

52 Morewedge (1973).

53 Ṣadrā (1362 Sh: 4).

54 Ṣadrā (1362 Sh: 6). This definition is in Avicenna (1954: 16) and Bahmanyār (1375 Sh: 279). Aristotle defines metaphysics as the study of being *qua* being in *Metaphysics* 1003 a 20-1, quoted in Barnes (1995: 69). Cf. Averroes (1938–52, I: 296).

55 Babayan (1993: 244) argues that his account of his inner revelation sounds like those popular among the Sufiesque *ghulāt*. But there is certainly no antinomian thread in his thought or in his epistemology.

56 Such claims are often succeeded by voluminous descriptions of mystical states – see Katz (1992: 3–41). For an argument on the theological significance of apophasis, see Turner (1994).

57 Matilal in Katz (1992: 151–3).

58 Matilal (1977: 6).

59 Rist (1967: 185) of Plotinus.

60 Hadot (1997: 116).

61 Cf. Fowden (1986: 97) on this theme in Hermeticism and later Neoplatonism, quoting the Nag Hammadi Codices. The circle of philosophers in this tradition is 'hermetically sealed' – see Nock and Festugière (1945–54, II: 204) *Corpus Hermeticum* XIII.9.

62 Hadot (1995: 57).

63 This is a strong Neoplatonic aim of the curriculum – see Siorvanes (1996: 114–16) and Lloyd and Blumenthal (1990: 4–6).

64 *Asfār* I: 22; cf. Hadot (1995: 83) and (1997: 74); Nussbaum (1994: 46–7).

65 Nussbaum (1994: 485).

66 Corbin (1986: 232–3). Ashkiwarī (1999, I: 100) quotes a maxim popular among Safavid philosophers: 'asceticism is a requisite for (successful) philosophy/wisdom (*al-ḥikma*)'.

67 Hadot (1995: 59).

68 Quoted by Āmulī in his introduction to Iṣfahānī (1372 Sh: 13) from Āmidī (1960, I: 238). It is also a feature of Pythagorean late Neoplatonism exemplified in Iamblichus' comments upon the *Carmina Aurea* – see Daiber (1995: 66–8).

69 *Asfār* I: 11–12.

70 Ṣadrā (1363 Sh: 132).

71 Avicenna (1375 Sh, III: 399). The word '*rāsikhūn*' is an important Qur'anic term derived from Qur'ān 3:7.

72 Avicenna (1375 Sh, III: 401).

73 Bahmanyār (1375 Sh: 816). I do not wish to enter the debate upon mystical knowledge

in Avicenna and his tradition – on this question, see Gutas (2006*a*, 2006*b*) and Adamson (2004).

74 Āshtiyānī (1370 Sh: 280). Qayṣarī (1978: 15) castigates those who do not understand as being 'veiled from this higher wisdom'.

75 Cf. *Asfār* VI: 263.

76 This is a sort of knowledge that is directly inspired by God in the heart of the knower, and alludes to the hidden knowledge of Khiḍr that was not available to Moses in their encounter in Qur'ān 18:76.

77 Ṣadrā (1984*b*: 41).

78 Amir-Moezzi (1994: 69). There are innumerable *aḥādīth* on this subject, which can be gauged by studying the first book of *al-Uṣūl min al-Kāfī* – see Ṣadrā (1988, I: 1–386). The idea of gnosis elevating the soul is also Hermetic – see Fowden (1986: 146) and Nock and Festugière (1945–54, I: 50) *Corpus Hermeticum* IV. 3–4.

79 Ṣadrā (1984*b*: 142).

80 *Asfār* IX: 108.

81 Avicenna (1375 Sh, III: 99–100). However, *pace* Nasr and Leaman (1996*b*, I: 247), he is no *ishrāqī*. See Gutas (2000) on the debate on Avicenna's 'Oriental' philosophy.

82 *Asfār* III: 514: one of his definitions of 'wisdom' is this *assimilatio* or *theosis*. This is the goal of life in the Plotinian scheme – see Wallis (1995: 85); O'Meara (1995: 102). Druart in van Ophuijsen (1999: 163) argues that this ideal from Plato's *Theaetetus* 176 b is based on the idea of imitating the Demiurge of *Timaeus* 29e, a rational and ordered actor who desires for all things to be like him, *as far as possible* (*ho ti malista*) – Plato (1975: 54–5). Proclus in his commentary in Festugière (1966–8, I: 225) says that this means that the divine is participable. On Platonic *theosis*, see Alcinous (1993: 37–8), *Didaskalikos* 28; O'Meara (2003: 31–9); Annas (1999: 52–71); Armstrong (2004); Dürlinger (1985); Sedley (1999). Mahoney (2005) criticises Sedley for negating the moral virtue aspect of theosis.
However, in the Islamic tradition, this desire is related to the *ḥadīth* '*takhallaqū bi-akhlāq Allāh*' (adorn yourselves with the qualities of God), that is, strive for high moral values and implement them in your lives – see *Asfār* I: 21–2; Majlisī (1392 Q, 61: 129). But the demiurge of the *Timaeus* would also have been familiar to Muslims through the Arabic version of Galen's epitome – see Walbridge (2000: 90–1).

83 Dillon in Gerson (1996: 320). The roots of *theosis* lie in Egyptian Hermeticism and later theurgic Neoplatonism that stressed the importance of the Chaldaean rites and of the philosopher as magus – see Fowden (1986: 26, 131); Wallis (1992: 100–5).

84 Plato as cited in Sedley (1999: 312).

85 Badawī (1948: 21).

86 Alcinous (1993: 38).

87 Sedley (1999) and Armstrong (2004) stress the former, and Baltzly (2004) discusses the two trends and the other-worldly moral pursuit.

88 See Shaw (1995).

89 On *riyāḍa* and philosophy, see Suhrawardī (1999: 162); *Asfār* I: 22. Festugière (1983, III: 48) shows the importance of theurgy in later Neoplatonism exemplified in Iamblichus' *De mysteriis Aegyptiorum*. On the conjunction of Iamblichean theurgy and the Islamic concept of spiritual and philosophical invocation through the tradition of Ḥarrān, see Ḥamad (1998: 110).

90 *Asfār* VI: 6. Islamic Neoplatonisms stayed with the Plotinian and Iamblichean stress on a moral life and self-purification as a means to *theosis* – see Daiber (1995: 110); Fowden (1986: 132).

91 *Asfār* IX: 108.

92 *Asfār* II: 315.

93 Ṣadrā (1885: 294) *Iksīr*. Cf. Ḥamad (1998: 103); Salaman *et al.* (1999: 109); Nock and Festugière (1945–54, I: 179–80) *Corpus Hermeticum* XII.14.

94 Ṣadrā (1363 Sh: 132–3).

95 Ṣadrā (1988, I: 170); cf. *Asfār* IV: 275.
96 *Asfār* I: 9–12.
97 *Asfār* VI: 6.
98 *Asfār* III: 446.
99 Rahman (1975: 12).
100 Açikgenç (1993: 38).
101 Ṣadrā (1988, I: 399–538) *Kāfī, K. al-ʿaql wa-l-jahl.* Ṣadrā makes it clear in a short logic text that various epistemological terms are *mushakkak* – see Ṣadrā (1996: 198) *Tanqīḥ.*
102 *Asfār* III: 266–8.
103 In Ṣadrā (1377 Sh: 192), he argues that contingency is univocal in mental being, but differentiated and graded in extra-mental being.
104 Jambet (1983: 47–8).
105 See the introduction to Iṣfahānī (1976: 12–77).
106 Frede (1987: xiv).
107 Ḥā'irī (1981) and (1982).
108 Ashkivarī (1986).
109 Liddell and Scott (1968: 215) *A Greek-English Lexicon* (Oxford: Clarendon Press).
110 Kahn (1996: 94–101).
111 Kahn (1996: 178–80, 100).
112 Aristotle (1998: 9) *Metaphysics* 982 b 13–15.
113 Booth (1983).
114 Owens (1978: 211–58), chapter 6 on the aporematic treatment of causes.
115 Aristotle (1984, II: 1554) *Metaphysics* 982 b 12–22.
116 Aristotle (1984, II: 1572) *Metaphysics* 995 a 27. Cf. Averroes (1938–52, I: 165).
117 Wittgenstein (1953, § 123).
118 Rescher (1987: 283–97).
119 Rescher (1987: 283).
120 Kenny (1973: 14–15) states that this is the main preoccupation of the *Philosophical Investigations*. Cf. Derrida (1982), 'La différance' and 'Plato's pharmacy' in (1972: 69–172) on language play.
121 Hintikka (1983: 443–68, especially 458–9).
122 For answers in the negative, see Goldman (1987) and Hartman (1986).
123 Quine (1966: 3).
124 Quine (1966: 5).
125 Shayegan (1990: 41). For a discussion of this concept more Generally in European esotericist circles, see Wasserstrom (1999: 67–82).
126 Martin (1995); Corbin (1981*a*: 19–23).
127 In the Arabic translation of Aristotle's *Metaphysics* Book β in Badawī (1948–9, I: 4).
128 Forman (1990); Katz (1978).
129 See Ḥillī (1988: 281–93).
130 Cf. Sells (1994: 2–3).
131 Morewedge (1995: xvi). Rescher (1996: 5). Processual is a neologism that he has coined to express 'process-oriented'. My understanding of process metaphysics and the paradigm shift in later Islamic philosophy is informed and influenced by

138 Hamid (1998: 25).

139 Surūsh (1978: 52–3).
140 *Asfār* III: 61–2.
141 Corbin (1972: 119).
142 Cf. Ha'iri (1992: 25) and Cooper (1998*b*).
143 Bonaud (1997: 56–63) has an important description of the text and its place in the *madrasa* curriculum.
144 Hadot (1987) and De Smet (1995: 18–19).
145 Aristotle (1984, II: 1587) *Metaphysics* IV.3, 1005 b 7–14, makes it clear that analysis, the syllogistic and axioms of logic are properly metaphysical issues. Cf. Averroes (1938–52, I: 341).
146 In taking such a position, I disagree with Ḥā'irī (1993: 709) who insists on the systematic nature of his approach. But I would draw a distinction between comprehensive and authoritative surveys of ideas and his goal.
147 Ṣadrā (1380–3, I, 18) *Asfār*.
148 Tilimsānī (1413 Q: 380–2).
149 Shams al-Dīn Khafrī, *Risāla fī asfār arbaʿa*, MS Raza Library (Rampur) 1027, fol. 49r.
150 In *al-Maṭālib al-muhimma min ʿilm al-ḥikma*, Ibn Kammūna (1382 Sh: 77) considers the problem of proving that there can only be one Necessary Being. He concludes by stating that his argument only demonstrates that there cannot be two Necessary Being sharing a singular essence (*fa-qad bāna min hādhā istiḥālat wujūd wājibayn mutashārikayn fī-l-māhiyya*). It was Khafrī (1382 Sh: 209) who accused him of formulating this objection and hence named him the 'pride of the satans' (*iftikhār al-shayāṭīn*) and from this source, Mullā Ṣadrā took up the notion of the *shubhat Ibn Kammūna* and his critique of the objection is entitled 'stoning the satan' (*rajam al-shayṭān*) – *Asfār* I: 131–2. For a discussion of the argument of Ibn Kammūna and its reception, see Schmidtke and Pourjavady (2006: 37–47); Rahman (1975: 134–6); Mūsawī (1381 Sh).
151 *Man ʿarafa nafsahu faqad ʿarafa rabbahu* – see Majlisī (1392 Q, 70: 72).
152 Rahman (1975: 10).
153 Morris (1981: 22–9).
154 Ashkiwarī (1999, I: 118–22).
155 Ashkiwarī (1999, I: 135).
156 Ashkiwarī (1999, I: 161–9).
157 Ashkiwarī (1999, I: 161–2). Cf. Shahrazūrī (1976, I: 49, 61, 64). The myth of the three Hermes in Arabic probably originates with the astrologer Abū Maʿshar but does have precedents in late antiquity in the Graeco-Roman and Iranian cultural contexts – see the discussion in van Bladel (2004: 128–71).
158 Ashkiwarī (1999, I: 195, 206).
159 Walbridge (2000: 30). See De Smet (1998) on the importance of Empedocles to late Antique Neoplatonism. The dissemination of philosophy from Adam is related to the chain of *wilāya* (sanctity, authority) that runs from him to our age – Ṣadrā (1992: 3–5).
160 Ashkiwarī (1999, I: 208–36).
161 Ṣadrā (1378 Sh*b*: 153–4).
162 Rudolph (1989: 24–32) argues for the centrality of Shahrastānī as the main source for

Pythagoras and popular in later Neoplatonism. Daiber (1995); Jambet in Corbin (1986:

26); Walbridge (2000: 60–2, 75). The Peripatetic tradition saw him as a commentator on Aristotle only – see Ibn al-Nadīm (1970, II: 599, 614) and Qifṭī (1903: 60).

167 Ibn al-Nadīm (1970, II: 607–9); Qifṭī (1903: 89).

168 Ashkiwarī (1999, I: 258).

169 Massignon (1983) is one inventory. The best and most up to date account is van Bladel (2004: 303–3). Mostly, Hermetic texts remain in manuscript form. A few examples include MS British Museum Or 5591 and 5907, MS India Office 4616 and 473.

170 Qifṭī (1903: 7ff.); Shahrazūrī (1976, I: 64ff.); Ashkiwarī (1999, I: 165ff.). See van Bladel (2004: 178–301) for a complete listing of wisdom sayings attributed to Hermes.

171 *Asfār* II: 48 on the issue of Platonic realism. Qifṭī (1903: 2); Shahrazūrī (1976, I: 48). Cf. *EII* II: 24; Massignon (1975, II: 329).

172 *EII* II: 24, 144–5, 151, 153; Massignon (1975, I: 62). Qifṭī (1903: 1); Shahrazūrī (1993: 572) and (1976, I: 55); Walbridge (2000: 70).

173 *Asfār* V: 206; Qāshānī (1987: 43–4); *EII* II: 36, 51, 142; Walbridge (2000: 62, 48, 182). The philosophical tradition of the Syrian city of Ḥarrān that mixed Pythagorean Neoplatonism with Hermeticism was immensely influential – see Ḥamad (1998: 43–7, 87ff.). On the Ḥarrānian conduit for Hermetic texts, see van Bladel (2004: 83–127).

174 *Asfār* I: 411, II: 60, V: 163, VIII: 308.

175 Ashkiwarī (1999, I, 162).

176 Shahrazūrī (1976, I: 84, 86–9) whose Ṭāṭ evokes the Tat of the *Hermetica*. Cf. Ashkiwarī (1999, I: 169ff.); Gutas (1998: 104). Shahrazūrī (1976, I: 59) places the Hermetic line in Egypt (Memphis to be precise) whence it moved to Syria.

177 *Asfār* II: 50, 60, 123, V: 245; Ṣadrā (1382 Sh*a*: 192); Suhrawardī (1945: 108), *Talwīḥāt*. Cf. Corbin (1978: 50–2); *EII* II: 296, 300–4, (1976: 386–7); Walbridge (2000: 32, 104). For the original text, see Nock and Festugière (1945–54, I: 7ff.) *Corpus Hermeticum* I.1ff.

178 Shahrazūrī (1976, I: 8).

179 Shahrazūrī (1976, I: 2).

180 Ḥamad (1998: 110, 149).

181 Ṣadrā (1380–3 Sh, VIII: 357–75); cf. Ṣadrā (1382 Sh*a*: 259–62) for a briefer version.

182 Ṣadrā (1380–3 Sh, VIII: 375).

183 Ṣadrā (1380–3 Sh, VIII: 360–3).

184 Cf. Badawī (1948: 22) *mīmar* I; Armstrong (1966–88, IV: 397).

185 Badawī (1948: 23); Armstrong (1966–88, IV: 397).

186 Here, Ṣadrā has significantly changed the authority; both the *Theologia* and the *Enneads* cite Pythagoras – Badawī (1948: 23); Armstrong (1966–88, IV: 399).

187 Badawī (1948: 24); cf. Armstrong (1966–88, IV: 399); cf. Plato (1997: 524–5) *Phaedrus* 246 c–e.

188 Adapted from Badawī (1948: 24–5); cf. Armstrong (1966–88, IV: 401); cf. Plato (1997: 1241) *Timaeus* 37 d.

189 See Mīrī and ʿIlmī (1374 Sh) for an idea of the range of authors and texts that he drew upon.

190 *Asfār* I: 5.

2 The modulation of being (*tashkīk al-wujūd*)

1 Munitz (1974: 206).

2 At least from the Pre-Socratics – see Stokes (1971: 3–6).

3 Siorvanes (1996: 49).

4 Kindī (1998: 45–51) on how the categories are plural and yet retain their unity. Cf. Jolivet (1979: 56–7), quoting the connection with Proclus (1968–87, I: 4–9).

5 Vlastos (1981: 58–75). Some scholars such as Morrison (1987) even find a doctrine of degrees of reality in Aristotle.

6 Shields (1999: 118–19). My modification in italics.
7 Ṣadrā (1996: 107) *Tanqīḥ*. Cf. T(a)hānawī (1862: 1457).
8 Quoted by Waismann in Flew (1953: 16). Williams (1981: 35) points out its use for a modal logic.
9 Owen in Barnes (1979: 13–32); Kńuuttila and Hintikka (1986 100).
10 Rahman (1975: 34–5), followed by his student, Açikgenç (1993: 28, 55).
11 Klima (2000: 195).
12 Cf. Heer in Jāmī (1979: 197). Legenhausen and Sarvdalir in Miṣbāḥ (1999: 236) render *tashkīk* as 'graduation' and *mushakkak* as 'graduated'.
13 Nasr (1996*b*, I: 647) and (1972*b*: 155).
14 *EII*, IV: 78.
15 Monnot (1998, III i: 1441).
16 Jambet (2000: 9).
17 In Sabzawārī (1969: 602–3).
18 Izutsu (1983: 35).
19 Izutsu (1983: 39).
20 Leaman (1999: 92–3); Ḥusayn (1998: 72); Ziai in Nasr (1996*b*, I: 472); Khorassani (1976: 110).
21 Avicenna (1960: 466).
22 This is also true of Aristotle for whom the *pros hen* homonymy of being is an argument for the unity of a science of metaphysics. See Aristotle (1998: 80–2) *Metaphysics* book Γ, especially 1003 a 21–6 and 1003 a 34–b 10. Cf. Averroes (1938–52, I: 296, 300–1); Shields (1999: 1).
23 Wolfson (1938: 151–2).
24 Aristotle (1984, I: 184). Cf. Badawī (1948–9, II: 508–9).
25 Alexander (1891: 152, II.7.8) *In Topica*. Cf. Wolfson (1938: 171); Gyekye (1979: 197) on ambiguity.
26 Bonmariage (1998: 68–9); she comments that sometimes the term is found as *mushakkik* and at others as *mushakkak* but she follows the former as that it is the choice of the *Avicenna Latinus* project that is based in Louvain. Madkur (1969: 61) uses the same vocalisation to translate 'équivoque'.
27 Bonmariage (1998: 67), following Bonaud (1997).
28 Kahn (1973: 1–2) and (1981: 105–34).
29 Heidegger (1996: 7).
30 Heidegger (1996: 1–3). This critique is part of his counter-foundationalism and critique of traditional concepts of epistemology that was later taken up by Rorty (1980).
31 Jurjānī (1969: 270); Chittick (1989: 6). I shall translate this term as being and not existence as others do, not because, like Corbin (Ṣadrā 1967: 63), I regard *ex-sistere* to be a poor root for the 'act of being', but because I use existence for being *in concreto* and not for *ab alio sistere* or other modes of being. Being is a more comprehensive term than existence and covers the other modes of mental reality and propositional occurrence, despite contemporary philosophy's aversion to the term. From a slightly different perspective, Gilson (1946) and (1952: 3) suggests that while existence is something inconceivable [rather as Suhrawardī holds], being is always directly intuited by us. Owens in Kretzmann (1993: 45) concurs. The distinction between being and existence occasions a distinction between being as a general notion or infinitive *einai* and the act of being, *to on*, that stands apart – see Hadot (1999: 72). Ṣadrā, however, does not make such a distinction: *wujūd*, *mawjūd*, *mawjūdiyya* and *wujūdiyya* are completely synonymous terms.
32 Āmulī (1367 Sh: 407).
33 Ibn ʿArabī (n.d., II: 579).
34 Kāshānī (1991: 26).
35 Kāshānī (1991: 23, 27).
36 Kāshānī (1991: 28).

37 Hamid (1998: 90) describes this concept of apriority as 'ousiological intuition'.
38 T(a)hānawī (1862: 1456).
39 *Asfār* I: 23, 27, 37–8; Ṣadrā (1362 Sh: 7); (1976: 10); (1967: 7); (1979: 56); Lāhījī (n.d.: 16–19). Earlier references to this doctrine include: Ibn Sīnā (1952: 8–9) and (1960, I: 29). Cf. Marmura (1984: 219, 225); Bahmanyār [d. 1066] (1375 Sh: 280); Lawkarī [d. 1123] (1995: 27). For Baghdādī [d. 1164] (1415 Q, III: 63) what is *a priori* is not so much a general concept of being but the awareness of one's personal existence. Cf. Pines (1979: 295). Fakhr al-Dīn Rāzī [d. 1209] (1343 Q, I: 10); Baḥrānī [d. 1274] (1406 Q: 38); Taftazānī [d. 1389] (n.d., I: 327–8). Aristotle (1984, II: 1609) *Metaphysics* 1060 b 4 states that 'being is predicated of all things (*estin ousiai ta onta*)', and thus is the most general of concepts. The most general concept is also the most prior in the mind – Aristotle (1984, II: 1675) *Metaphysics* 1018 b 32. For the Arabic, especially in terms of the commentaries on book *Lambda* by Alexander and Themistius, see Averroes (1938–52, III: 1396–7, 1401). The Arabic translation consistently uses '*huwiyya*' for being (*on, ousia*). Plotinus argues for the same point based on the fact that the One is infinite, amorphous and beyond *ousia* in Armstrong (1966–88, V: 173 and VII: 185), *Enneads* V.5.6.5, VI.7.32.9. This follows Plato (1997: 1130) who asserts that the form of the Good is beyond *ousia* both in terms of rank and power in *Republic* 509 b 8–10.
40 *Asfār* I: 84. Aristotle (1984, I: 152) *Posterior Analytics* B 7, 92 b 14. Cf. Badawī (1948–9, II: 323). Thus being is not a universal – see Avicenna (1973: 183, 186).
41 Definition yields the *māhiyya* and being has no *māhiyya*. For the former, see Aristotle (1984, I: 169), *Topics* 101 b 39; cf. Badawī (1948–9, II: 474); Bahmanyār (1375 Sh: 46). For the latter, see Corbin (1986: 481); Ṣadrā (1313 Q*b*: 304).
42 Ṣadrā (1992: 31).
43 *Asfār* I: 120–1.
44 Bahmanyār (1375 Sh: 813).
45 *Asfār* IV: 269, I: 25; Sabzawārī (1995, II: 42). Cf. Heidegger (1996: 127, 142).
46 Ṣadrā (1964: 6). On the apriority of both the concept and reality of being, see Ṣadrā (1976: 10); *Asfār* I: 343.
47 *Asfār* I: 53, 61, VI: 230.
48 *Asfār* I: 412–13.
49 Ṭūsī (1985: 437) *Risālat qawāʿid al-ʿaqā'id*.
50 *Asfar* I: 335; Sabzawārī (1995, II: 67–8).
51 Aristotle (1984, II: 1623) *Metaphysics* 1028 a 10. Cf. Averroes (1938–52, II: 745).
52 Aristotle (1984, I: 176) *Topics* 106 a 9. Cf. Badawī (1948–9, II: 491); Alexander (1891, 97, II.22–3) *In Topica*.
53 Dooley and Madigan (1993: 43).
54 Brentano (1975: 4); Shields (1999: 216); Aristotle (1984, II: 1620) *Metaphysics* 1026 a 34–b 2. Cf. Averroes (1938–52, II: 715).
55 *Risāla fī jawāb masā'il su'ila ʿanhā* in Fārābī (1890: 88).
56 Martin (1995: 169–70).
57 Lloyd (1990: 138).
58 Ebbesen in Sorabji (1990: 162–5).
59 Siorvanes (1996: 123–5) on Proclus' *Platonic Theology III*; Lloyd (1982: 19). In this section one finds the enumerative list of what there is according to Proclus. Cf. Jolivet

(1969: 60).

64 Ibn Sīnā (1952: 50–1); Bahmanyār (1375 Sh: 467–71); Ṭūsī in Avicenna (1375 Sh, III: 109–10); Ṣadrā (1313 *Qa*: 230), *Asfār* III: 261, and (1967: 59). Following Aristotle (1984, II: 1608–9) *Metaphysics* 1018 b 9–35. Cf. Badawī (1948–9, II: 48–9); Alexander in Dooley (1993: 60–2).
65 Bahmanyār (1375 Sh: 467); Lawkarī (1995: 125, 142); Avicenna (1960: 163). Ṣadrā (1313 *Qa*: 231) and *Asfār* III: 260–1, quoting the *Shifā'* and confirming his point about focal meaning and modulation by stressing that these types of priority are 'arranged in order' and with 'reference to a single principle'. Cf. Sabzawārī (1969: 118–19); Izutsu (1983: 130–2).
66 Avicenna (1992*a*: 332).
67 See Chapter 5, pp. 102–130.
68 This is critical – see ʿAṣṣār (1391 Q: 10). This shift from *pros hen* homonymy to intensifying predication of more or less and of prior–posterior is found in Plotinus as well – see Gerson (1994: 105) quoting Armstrong (1966–88, VI: 15) *Enneads* VI.1.1.25–8. cf. Nock and Festugière (1945–54, I: 53) *Corpus Hermeticum* IV.11, where an intensifying scale applies to contingents but not the Father.
69 *Asfār* I: 36, cf. I: 427, 430–2.
70 This would not be acceptable to the Avicennan tradition because things are essentially differentiated but common through a general notion. Thus the principle of commonality cannot be the same as the principle of differentiation because things would not be distinct and because of the principle of Non-contradiction. See Avicenna (1375 Sh, III: 28, 30).
71 Aristotle (1998: 60–1) *Metaphysics* 996 a 6–14. Cf. Averroes (1938–52, I: 166).
72 Lloyd (1990: 76–8) quotes Armstrong (1966–88, VII: 147) *Enneads* VI.7.18.36.
73 Schubert (1995: 86–93).
74 Avicenna (1958, III: 458–9). However, Rāzī (1343 Q, I: 13–22) seems to accept predication by *tashkīk* but since this is an early work, he may have left that view later in life.
75 Avicenna (1958, III: 435–6).
76 See *Asfār* I: 19 on this.
77 Avicenna (1375 Sh, III: 32–4).
78 Baḥrānī (1992: 52–3, 76); cf. Oraibi (1992: 63), though he does stress that the concept of modulation is a logical one with respect to the term 'be'. Ṣadrā (1340 Sh: 19) also stresses the levels of soul and its multiple faculties while remaining a unity. Cf. Morris (1981: 131). There are strong Neoplatonic precursors for this. Although some of Plotinus' followers proposed monopsychist arguments about the soul and insisted that the totality of the hypostatic soul/intellect was homogenous (*homoiomenes*), Iamblichus insisted upon degrees and ontological levels within the soul to safeguard multiplicity in the world, while allowing for everything to be psychically present in the hypostatic soul. Thus soul is hierarchically arranged and contains within it both the principle of unity and differentiation. See Steel (1978: 25, 155).
79 Suhrawardī (1952: 107–9) *Ḥikmat al-ishrāq*. Cf. Aminrazavi (1992: 25).
80 Suhrawardī (1952: 119) *Ḥikmat al-ishrāq*. Cf. Sabzawārī (1969: 72–3); Āshtiyānī (1980: 26). Specifically on intensity, see Suhrawardī (1998: 43).
81 Suhrawardī (1945: 293–301) *Mashāriʿ*.
82 *Asfār* I: 433.

85 Suhrawardī (1945: 156) *Muṭāraḥāt* on intensity in blackness quoted in *Asfār* I: 436.

Ḥasanzāda suggests such a reading based *tashkīk ittifāqī* in Ṣadrā (1995–, I: 101), *Asfār*.

86 *Asfār* I: 427–46. A succinct statement on the gradual intensification within the chain of being can be found in Ṣadrā (1988, II: 502–3). cf. Lāhījī (n.d.: 52).

87 Ṣadra (1967: 135–6); cf. Bonmariage (1998: 86–9).

88 Avicenna (1960: 276); Bahmanyār (1375 Sh, 307–8, 529–30).

89 Ṭūsī in Avicenna (1375 Sh, III: 33–4).

90 Jīlī (n.d.). This is a critical source for the concept of modulation as suggested by ʿAbd al-Haq (1967: 271).

91 Ibn ʿArabī (1997: 425).

92 Ibn ʿArabī (1997: 395).

93 Āmulī (1367 Sh: 438).

94 Āmulī (1969: 631–2).

95 Āshtiyānī (1370 Sh: 141); Āmulī (1969: 634).

96 Fanārī (1363 Sh: 14).

97 Iṣfahānī (1976).

98 Nābulsī (1995: 91–3, 143).

99 Kāshānī (1375 Sh: 11). This follows Ṣadrā (1885: 132) *Sarayān*.

100 Dāmād (1998: 261).

101 Chittick (1982: 108). Cf. *Asfār* III: 502. An alternative Sufi account of levels of existence is found in Ghazālī's *Fayṣal al-tafriqa* as quoted in Ṣadrā (1976: 403). Ṣadrā posits an Akbarian three modes (or realms) of being at various points – see *Asfār* II: 310, 320, 330, III: 363, IX: 61.

102 Kāshānī (1991: 59).

103 Qāshānī [*sic*] (1987: 11). For a brief introduction to the concept, though marked by the influences of British idealism, see Nicholson (1921: 77–161); Massignon (1947); Takeshita (1988). The concept has its roots in the Hermetic tradition's *anthrōpos teleios* – see Nock and Festugière (1945–54, I: 10) *Corpus Hermeticum* I.12.

104 Kazimirski (1860: 1257); Wehr (1961: 481). No entry for *tashkīk*.

105 Dozy (1967, I: 777).

106 Ibn Manẓūr (1301 Q: 337–8); Lane (1984, II: 1582).

107 Martin (1995: 180, 189) uses *aphairēsis* to describe the systematic negation of the grades of being in Neoplatonic logic and ontology. In *tashkīk*, each grade of reality is being but also insofar as it is becoming and not the One, it is essentially privative and self-negating. This self-negation might be the reason why Ṣadrā is so insistent on affirming the possibility of the self-negation of the impossible-in-itself, that is the contingent – see *Asfār* I: 150–3.

108 Aristotle (1984, II: 1621), *Metaphysics* 1026 b 21. Cf. Averroes (1938–52, II: 716–17).

109 Avicenna (1959: 9–12), (1954: 117). Cf. Afnan (1969: 129). Baḥrānī (1958, I: 9) uses these terms. It is surprising that Rahman (1975: 34) does not consider a third possibility within the Aristotelian and the Avicennan tradition.

110 Avicenna (1959: 10–11). Shahrastānī [d. 1087] attributes the term *mushakkak* to an Avicennan invention that had not existed in logic before him – *Muṣāraʿat al-falāsifa* in Ṭūsī (1405 Q: 46–7); for the original text, see Shahrastānī (2001: Arabic 30–2). Ṭūsī himself holds that the predication of being is modulated in Avicenna (1958, III: 435). On these texts and issues, see Madelung (1976: 250–9). However, it is clear that it is a term that connotes the *tertium quid* of Aristotelian logic, even if the term was not translated in the Arabic Aristotle, though Ṭūsī (1405 Q: 60) says it was. In the *Metaphysics* of the *Dānishnāma* (Avicenna 1952: 38), Avicenna categorically states that being is neither synonymous nor homonymous as such. In fact Avicenna (1992*b*: 232) says that being is not *mushtarak* but *mushakkak*. The lack of an explicit emergence of the *tertium quid* in the Arabic Aristotle could be attributed to Aristotle's own semantics – see Owen (1986: 192), though Shields (1999) makes a good case

for stating the importance of core dependent homonymy in Aristotle's philosophical discourse. The musical analogy that allows one to use modulation in this sense is apposite because modulation of being refers to a variation in frequency, that is intensity, within the scale of being.

111 Aristotle (1984, I: 3), *Categories* 1 a 1–15. Cf. Badawī (1948–9, I: 33).

112 Evangeliou in Harris (1982: 74). For Plotinus, the inadequacies of Aristotle's system lie in the fact that his categories only consider the *sensibilia* and not the *intelligibilia* and as such the 'list' cannot possibly be exhaustive. In Armstrong (1966–88, VI: 15) *Enneads* VI.1.1.24, Plotinus wonders whether being is applied homonymously to both the sensible and intelligible realms.

113 Arguably true synonyms are rare since different terms have different shades of meaning, such as the many words which denote 'lion' in Arabic and yet have differing senses such as 'young lion', 'ferocious lion' and 'wounded lion'. This is similar to the issue of the denotation and senses in Indian Nyāya philosophy. See Matilal (1968: 48), (1990: 15) and Mohanty (2000: 147) on how 'blue pot' and 'pot' have the same reference but different senses. This distinction of sense and reference is raised due to the problem of identicals.

114 Shields (1999: 11).

115 Suhrawardī (1952: 64), *Ḥikmat al-ishrāq*, and Suhrawardī (1945: 17), *al-Talwīḥāt*.

116 Kahn (1966: 265–6).

117 Owens (1978: 303) on this point about Aristotle. Cf. Ferejohn (1980); Owen (1986: 181); Bäck (1987: 366).

118 Avicenna (1992*a*: 234). Sibawayh (1991, I: 24) considered being (or more precisely the verb 'wujida') to be merely homonymous in that it had multiple occurrences in the same form but with different meanings. Gyekye (1975: 98–9) and (1979: 82–3) shows that earlier logicians in Islam before Avicenna recognised that being was neither homonymous nor synonymous but something 'intermediate', but did not equate this '*tertium quid*' with *pros hen* homonymy but rather with a sort of '*ab uno*' homonymy since all existents issued from the same principle.

119 Bahmanyār (1375 Sh: 23, 28).

120 Avicenna (1959: 10) and (1992*b*: 232, 692).

121 Shields (1999: 11). See Aristotle (1984, I: 176–9), *Topics* I, 15, 106 a 1–107 b 38 on discrete homonymy; cf. Badawī (1948–9, II: 490–8) and Avicenna (1959: 11).

122 Precedents for this example include Porphyry, *in Cat.*, 1.4, 67.10–68.1 in Strange (1992: 47–8) and Simplicius, *in Cat.*, 33 in Hadot (1990, III: 25).

123 Shields (1999: 11–12).

124 Aristotle (1998: 167), *Metaphysics* Z 1, 1028 a 10. Ackrill uses 'multivocal' to express this idea of 'saying' in many senses in Stern (1972: 19). Shields (1999: 22–3) suggests that multivocity is not the same as homonymy (or ambiguity) adducing Aristotle (1984, II: 1584), *Metaphysics* 1003 a 33–34 and (1984, I: 184), *Topics* 110 b 16–32 as evidence. Cf. Badawī (1948–9, II: 510); Averroes (1938–52, I: 300, II: 745).

125 Porphry, *In Cat.*, in Strange (1992: 45–6). All types of homonyms fit into two broad categories of homonyms by chance (discrete) and by thought. Cf. Simplicius, *in Cat.*, 31–3, in Hadot (1990, III: 22–4).

126 On this definition, see Ṭūsī in Avicenna (1375 Sh, III: 33).

127 *Asfār* I: 258. Hamade (1992: 243) is unnecessarily restrictive in allowing only two choices of 'analogy' and 'univocity'. Cf. Ṭūsī (1405 Q: 46) on the importance of modulation defined by non-uniformity of predication.

128 Lloyd (1990: 41). See Porphyry, *in Cat.*, 57.29–58.3 in Strange (1992: 33–4).

129 *Asfār* I: 29. Ṣadrā (1313 *Qa*: 220).

130 *Asfār* V: 4, 175; VI: 68–9. Cf. Lloyd (1990: 39), citing Olympiodorus, *in Cat.* 41.12, Elias, *in Cat.* 103.14, Ammonius, *in Ana. Pr.* 1.7–11, and Dexippus, *in Cat.*, 7–10 in Dillon (1990: 25–9). It was universally agreed in Islamic philosophy following Aristotle (1984, II: 1577, I: 152, I: 203), *Metaphysics* 998 b 22, 1001 a 5, 1040 b 18;

Posterior Analytics 92 b 14; *Topics* 121 a 16–19, that being was not a genus, though it could metaphorically be referred to as the 'genus of genera'. Cf. Badawī (1948–9, II: 554); Averroes (1938–52, I: 220, 260, II: 999); Shields (1999: 1); Owens (1978: 417); Ibn al-Muqaffaʿ (1978: 4–5); Gyekye (1975: 95–8) and (1979: 79–83).

131 *Asfār* II: 38, quoting Avicenna's *al-Shifā'*.

132 *Asfār* IV: 7, V: 88–91.

133 Steinschneider (1893: 36–7, 97, 99, 103, 106). Cf. Shahrastānī (1984, II: 357–62).

134 Rahman (1975: 17) quoting *Asfār* I: 134. However, the text upholds not mere ambiguity but *ishtirāk maʿnawī.*

135 Rāzī (1343 Q, 15, 568); Ṭūsī (1985: 74); Baḥrānī (1958, I: 9) and (1406 Q: 39).

136 Suhrawardī (1945: 26) *Talwīḥāt*; (1952: 66) *Ḥikmat al-Ishrāq*; and (1945: 125) *Muqāwamāt*.

137 Suhrawardī (1957: 57–8).

138 Owens in Munitz (1973: 23); Gilson (1952: 3).

139 Jāmī (1979: 34–6, 43).

140 A thirteenth-century partisan of Suhrawardī in his commentary on *Ḥikmat al-ishrāq* (1993: 168); cf. Shahrazūrī (2004, III: 29). See Chapter 3, pp. 57–76.

141 Mīr Dāmād (1977: 37) and (2006: 5).

142 Sijistānī (1949: 12); Shahrastānī (2001: 71–4). Cf. Netton (1994: 216, 224–5); Walker (1993: 37–8); Halm (1996: 78–9). Daftary (1990: 234–46) and Fenton in Kraye (1986: 155–6) argue that the doctrine of the *hyperousion* is connected to the *Plotiniana Arabica* and the influence of Neoplatonic thought in Ismaili circles. One also finds this doctrine in some Sufi thinkers such as ʿAlā' al-Dawla Simnānī (*Asfār* II: 335) where he is credited with holding that the essence of the Necessary is beyond both being and non-being. Elias (1995: 62–3) stresses his doctrine of the utter transcendence of God that, in common with most Sufi thinkers, insists upon the term 'being' exclusively referring to God.

143 For the Hermetic roots of this doctrine, see Nock and Festugière (1945–54, III: 2) *Corpus Hermeticum, Stobaean Fragments* I.1.

144 De Smet (1995: 38, 41); Sijistānī (1980: 28–9); Kirmānī (1967: 129–30, 131–4). A peculiar feature of this theological school is their doctrine of double-negation. Not only is God not being, He is also not non-being – see De Smet (1995: 75–83).

145 Armstrong (1966–88, V: 173) *Enneads*, V.5.6. Cf. De Smet (1995: 65).

146 Armstrong (1966–88, V: 119, VII: 307) *Enneads* V.3.13, VI.9.2.

147 Aristotle (1984, II: 1606) *Metaphysics* 1017 a 22–27. Cf. Averroes (1938–52, II: 555).

148 De Smet (1995: 42). God was not *mu'ayyis* though this term is used in Kindī (1950, I: 182–3), and later by Avicenna (1960, I: 266) of the existentiation of things (*ta'yīs al-ashyā'*).

149 Badawī (1948: 24). This reflects the pseudo-Dionysian way of ignorance that stipulated that one was closer to the truth when one maintained that one did not know the nature of God than when one describes him as such and such – see d'Ancona Costa (1997: 422–3).

150 Avicenna (1331 Sh: 21). Cf. De Smet (1999: 476–7). This is the first cause that is not God as such but depends upon him. See Kirmānī (1967: 130); De Smet (1995: 40). For the distinction between the utterly transcendent *deus absconditus* and the immanent *deus revelatus* in the Hermetic tradition, see Nock and Festugière (1945–54, I: 87) *Corpus Hermeticum* VIII.2, on the distinction between the 'first' and 'second' gods. This distinction between two levels of the deity is common in apophatic writings, Being God-in-himself and God-in-creatures, or in Eckhart's terms between God and 'God'. See Sells (1994: 2).

151 Qummī (1373–8 Sh, II: 245–6). Cf. *EII*, IV: xvi and in Fahd (1970: 150); Madelung (1977: 63).

152 That is, true being is only God, while 'figurative' being that applies to contingents, applies homonymously. See Āshtiyānī and Corbin (1972–8, I: 239ff.).

153 Corbin's introductions to Āshtiyānī (1972–8, I: 109–11, II: 91–6, 121–31).
154 Armstrong (1966–88, III: 397) *Enneads* III, 8.10.29–30, denies all predication to the One. Being is also associated with activity (*energeia*), as argued by Aristotle (1984, II: 1693) *Metaphysics* 1071 b 19–20. Cf. Averroes (1938–52, III: 1563). The One is similarly above all activity as described in *Enneads* VI.7.17.10, VI.8.16.16, VI.8.20.15 – see Armstrong (1966–88, VII: 141, 281, 293). It is interesting that Ṣadrā himself equivocates on the question of God and being: in *Asfār* I: 423 he suggests that God is both utterly unlike anything, even being and yet He must be or else nothing would be. Thus He is and is not, a rather classic apophasis that, as he notes, violates and shows up the inadequacies of the Law of Non-contradiction. See Āmulī in Iṣfahānī (1372 Sh: 753).
155 Aḥsā'ī (1856, fol. 3) and (2006, I: 79–86). But he does not fail to use the language of being and nor does he fail to refer to the One as being – see Aḥsā'ī (1856: fols. 15–18, 33–5, 124–35).
156 *Fā'ida fī-l-wujūdāt al-thalātha*, in Aḥsā'ī (1993: 156–7).
157 *Asfār* I: 93, 120; cf. Āshtiyānī (1980: 167).
158 Cf. Chapter 4, pp. 77–101.
159 D'Ancona Costa (1999: 60).
160 Badawī (1948: 21, 27, 132).
161 D'Ancona Costa (1997: 430–5); Badawī (1948: 157).
162 Badawī (1948: 19, 20, 112, 156).
163 D'Ancona Costa (1999: 60), *pace* Badawī (1948: 246). Zimmermann in Kraye (1986) vehemently attacks the Porphyrian provenance of the *Theologia*. Brague (1997: 381) focuses on non-Porphyrian doctrines in the text to show this.
164 Kindī (1998: 11).
165 Frank (1956: 188–91, 198). Badawī (1948: 246) does allow for the possibility of such a translation; Averroes (1938–52, III: 722). Alonso (1969: 61) argues that *anniyya* is not being or existence as such; rather it is what specifies, identifies and picks out a thing, and being (both *wujūd* and *ithbāt*) are signifying effects of it.
166 Avicenna (1960: 344); Hasnaoui in Matté (1998: 191–2).
167 Nock and Festugière (1945–54, I: 37–8, III: 90) *Corpus Hermeticum* II.14, *Stobaean Fragments* XXII.1.
168 On the question of whether the One of Plotinus is being or not, Anton and Deck take antithetical views in their respective contributions to Harris (1982). In the same collection, Bales (40–50) argues that the confusion of interpretations arises from Plotinus' three competing modes of discourse about the One: meontological (i.e. disontological), ontological and paradoxical (or apophatic). Arguably this equivocation is highlighted in the work of Porphyry – see Jambet (2000: 17).
169 A representative example of this tension is Baghdādī (1415 Q, III: 22, 66) who insists that being is a *mushtarak maʿnawī* but also that *in a real sense* existent exclusively refers to God. Avicenna (1960, I: 348–9) and (1958, III: 145) does it by insisting that God is a being quite unlike any other.
170 Corbin (1976*b*).
171 Sells (1994: 8).
172 Nasafī (1998: 108) talks about the paradox of God as being yet manifesting non-being, while the cosmos is non-being whilst manifesting being. He displays the confusion between the real and the phenomenal.
173 Dāmād (1998: 199, 202).
174 Avicenna (1958, III: 435–6); Ṭūsī (1405 Q: 124).
175 Ṭabāṭabā'ī (1403 Q: 11).
176 Ḥillī (1959: 6–8).
177 *Asfār* I: 77–8. Cf. Ṣadrā (1988, III: 209–10), *Kāfī*.
178 Shahrastānī, *Muṣāraʿat al-falāsifa* in Ṭūsī (1405 Q: 56).
179 Taftazānī, (n.d., I: 341).

180 Rāzī (1343 Q, I: 39) and in Ṭūsī (1985: 146–7). This is a fairly common *kalām* position – see Ṭūsī (1405 Q: 83); Frank (1978: 69).
181 Dashtakī (1386 Sh, I: 19).
182 Ṭabāṭabā'ī (1403 Q: 12). Cf. Sabzawārī (1969: 48); Izutsu (1983: 40–1); Āshtiyānī (1372 Sh: 144–5).
183 Ṭabāṭabā'ī (1362 Sh: 9).
184 Ṭabāṭabā'ī (1403 Q: 12).
185 Āshtiyānī (1372 Sh: 138).
186 Lawkarī (1995: 27–8); Bahmanyār (1375 Sh: 284, 282).
187 Bahmanyār (1375 Sh: 281).
188 Bahmanyār (1375 Sh: 36).
189 This reveals the mixed legacy of Avicenna on the issue.
190 T(a)hānawī (1963–77: 1460) upholds this form of 'commonality'.
191 Sha'rānī (1998, I: 44–51).
192 Ḥā'irī (1981: 50); Zunūzī (1376 Sh: 78).
193 Ha'iri (1992: 23, 25). He is followed in this by Juzi in Lewisohn (1999: 270) and Khatami (1996: 61–4). Gerson (1991: 333–4) points out that the concept of graded synonymy in Plotinus is a critique of *pros hen* homonymy in Aristotle.
194 Cf. Bonmariage (1998, I: 68). Although it is clear from the *Asfār* that being is a modulated concept and reality, in another work of Ṣadrā (1996: 182), *Aṣālat* he actually says that 'being possesses reality in a singular sense and meaning in which there is no distinction *except by term*'.
195 Bonaud (1997: 180) quotes Khumaynī (1410 Q: 272). However, Khumaynī is responding to Qayṣarī's rejection of this concept to demonstrate the synonymy of being!
196 Bonaud (1997: 190). Avicenna (1959: 9) denies the possibility of intensity in synonymy. Ha'iri, however, seems to be drawing upon Illuminationist semantics on this.
197 *Asfār* VI: 18.
198 *Asfār* I: 35.
199 This is apparently true of Simplicius, *in Cat.*, 30.16–22 in Hadot (1990, III: 21) – see Flannery (1999: 268–9). It is complicated by the possibility of certain words being predicated synonymously and homonymously; Avicenna (1959: 14) gives the example of '*aswad*' (meaning 'black') that is a man's name and describes his colour as well as the colour of tar.
200 Rahman (1975: 35).
201 On this point for Aristotle, see Shields (1999: 72).
202 Rahman (1975: 37). Cf. Siorvanes (1996: 59) on Proclean similarity (*homoiotēs*) that ensures a continuum within phenomenal diversity.
203 Ṣadrā (1885: 138, 142–3, 145), *Sarayān*, being an early work, shows that *tashkīk* is his mature doctrine because he rejects it for being. It seems that early on in his life monism was a more attractive position. Predication of being in this text is *ab uno* that is God.
204 Significantly Avicenna (1973: 144) insists that the 'onymies' only apply to terms and concepts. Homonymy concerns the definitions of things and not the thing itself. He thus shows himself to be careful with his ontological commitments.
205 Ṣadrā (1976: 10).
206 Ṣadrā (1967: 70).
207 Ṣadrā (1967: 66–7).
208 Ṣadrā (1982: 36, 21, 45–7).
209 E.g. *Asfār* I: 259.
210 This is asserted throughout Mullā Ṣadrā's œuvre e.g. *Asfār* I: 37.
211 Sabzawārī (1969: 72–3). A useful gloss on this extract is provided in Āshtiyānī (1372 Sh: 259–62), where he describes the two sorts of multiplicity as referring to 'specific' [i.e. reality] and 'general' [i.e. notion] *tashkīk*.

3 The semantics of modulation of being

1 Lloyd (1990); Martin (1995).
2 Fodor (1998: 27).
3 Cf. Avicenna (1970: 2–3). I shall not make a type–token distinction (a universal–particular distinction in effect) within being-in-language, as I collapse 'written' being with 'spoken' into being-in-language. Ṣadrā makes little distinction between spoken and written tokens of language in his discussions.
4 Ebbesen in Sorabji (1990: 146–9).
5 For Fārābī, see Zimmermann (1981: 11–3, 22–3).
6 Ibn al-Muqaffaʿ (1978: 25). This is repeated in Ṣadrā's section *Fī bārīmīnās* (De Interpretatione) in his logical treatise *al-Tanqīḥ* (1996: 207).
7 Aristotle (1984, I: 25). Cf. Badawī (1948–9, I: 59–60).
8 I am borrowing the term 'ontological commitment' from Quine. Williams (1981: 164) puts this in the following way: 'To be an entity is to be the value of a variable. So we commit ourselves ontologically by making things the values of our variables'. I am also aware of criticisms of Searle (1976: 17), who states that 'a theory is committed to those entities and only those entities which the theory says exist'. Similarly, I realise the problem with using a concept that assumes that being is synonymous, which is not the Sadrian position – see Putnam (1999: 179).
9 Sedley (1996: 87).
10 Kneale (1962: 45).
11 Dummett (1993*a*: 5). Putnam (1999: 119) is critical of this, preferring his semantic externalism in which the context of sentences is partly dependent on the determination of the reference in a particular context.
12 Miṣbāḥ (1405 Q: 18); Ḥā'irī (1981: 45). Cf. Dummett (1993*a*: 7–12) on the cognate sense–reference distinction of Frege in Moore (1993: 23–42). For the connection, see Ḥā'irī (1982: 94–5).
13 Dummett in Guttenplan (1975: 123).
14 Dummett in Blackburn (1999: 281).
15 Dummett in Guttenplan (1975: 99–101).
16 Dummett in Guttenplan (1975: 102).
17 Cf. Horwich (1999); Künne (2003) is the best all-round account of conceptions and arguments about truth in the contemporary analytical tradition. I am deliberately simplifying the typology and leaving aside deflationism ('it is a mistake to suppose that there is a property of truth that one attributes to propositions, statements, beliefs and/or sentences') and forms of minimalism ('one need assume no more about truth than what is expressed in instances of the propositional schema').
18 Both Putnam (1981) and Dummett (1991: 331) argue that truth-conditionality does not require correspondence. Cf. Blackburn (1999: 1).
19 Künne (2003: 170).
20 Putnam (1981); Dummett (1980).
21 Avicenna (1960: 48); Ṣadrā (1996: 315) *Rubūbiyya*; Davidson in Blackburn (1999: 309).
22 Avicenna (1960: 48, 278); Blackburn (1999: 7).
23 *Asfār* I: 89. Cf. Davidson (1984: 37); Putnam (1981: 54).
24 *Asfār* I: 249; Putnam (1981: 49). On veridical uses of being in Indian schools, see Mohanty (1992: 150); Halbfass (1997: 25).
25 Ṣadrā (1992: 7).
26 Avicenna (1992*a*: 20). Cf. Suhrawardī (1999: 12) *Ḥikmat al-ishrāq*.
27 Ṣadrā (1996: 207) *Tanqīḥ*.
28 Strawson (1974: 1).
29 Legenhausen (1996*b*: 150–1). In *Asfār* I: 76, he argues that the meanings that underlie the names are transcendent and not available to us.

30 Ṣadrā (1340 Sh: 13); Morris (1981: 117).
31 Ṣadrā (1340 Sh: 14); Morris (1981: 118).
32 Legenhausen (1996*b*: 151).
33 Avicenna (1992*a*: 21); Ṣadrā (1996: 208–9) *Tanqīḥ*. Cf. Frank in Morewedge (1982: 268).
34 Avicenna (1960: 129). Avicenna (1960: 48) says that 'what is understood by truth is a statement or tie that signifies a state of something in extra-mental existence (*fī-l-khārij*) that corresponds to it [the predication]'.
35 Bahmanyār (1375 Sh: 272). Akbarian (2000: 10).
36 Ṣadrā (1982: 10–11).
37 Ṣadrā (1967: 12).
38 This was also true of Fārābī (1968: 48–9), cited in Abed (1991: 61).
39 Ṣadrā (1992: 14).
40 Frank (1978: 15).
41 Dummett (1993*a*: 66).
42 Frege in Moore (1993: 28–9).
43 *Asfār* I: 37, 68, 217, and Ṣadrā (1967: 21). On this he follows amongst others, Qayṣarī in Āshtiyānī (1370 Sh: 126).
44 Corresponding to facts – see Lawkarī (1995: 33); Ṭabāṭabā'ī (1403 Q: 24); Āmulī in Iṣfahānī (1372 Sh: 177). In the phenomenological tradition, the truth of an object is independent of the facticity of the object – see Levinas (1998: 6). Cf. the Porphyrian formulation in Lloyd (1990: 53).
45 Sabzawārī (1969: 83); Izutsu (1983: 86). That '*nafs al-amr*' is like Dummett's categorisation of 'knowing it as God knows it' – see Dummett in Ayer (1979: 1) and Davidson (1984: 214). *Nafs al-amr* may be defined as 'the logical reference of a propositional subject that has no external reality' – Miṣbāḥ (1999: 158).
46 *Asfār* I: 414.
47 *Asfār* I: 43–4. Cf. Akbarian (2000: 13).
48 Künne (2003: 89) is one recent instance of an analytic philosopher's acceptance of truth as a real predicate.
49 Ṣadrā (1885: 117) *Ittiṣāf*. 'Our saying "man exists" means that the concept of humanity refers to an existent in extra-mental reality (*fī-l-khārij*), and the concept of humanity corresponds to its referent in reality'. 'Man exists' therefore means that 'there is at least one "man" who exists in reality.
50 *Asfār* I: 38. Āshtiyānī (1350 Sh: 11). Suhrawardī (1945: 160–5) *Muqāwamāt* and (1952: 64ff.) *Ḥikmat al-ishrāq*, on the failure of reference, Dīnānī (1366 Sh: 650) and Ziai (1990: 171) on the equation. Walbridge (1992: 40) insists that one avoid falling into the trap of equating light and being.
51 Ziai (1990: 167).
52 Horwich (1998: 4, 44).
53 This may have Stoic origins in the distinction between a pure thought and the thing. See Mates (1961: 2, 11). Sabra (1980: 758) asserts the connection, as does Wolfson (1943: 114). Cf. Annas (1992: 72). For an excellent recent sketch of the history of this pair of concepts, see Lameer (2006: 3–35).
54 Ṣadrā (1416 Q: 46–7); Lameer (2006: 103).
55 Ṣadrā (1885: 280–3) *Iksīr*; Chittick (2004: 5). These three levels evoke Frege's triad of context, conditions and assignations of knowledge – see Dummett (1993*a*: 5) and Guttenplan (1975: 5–6).
56 'Irāqī (1414 Q, I: 84); Khurāsānī (1990: 12). Quine (1960: 221) amongst others explicitly rejects such a mental language.
57 *Asfār* I: 175, 291, III: 257.
58 *Asfār* IV: 91, VIII: 58.
59 Munitz (1974: 168–9); Ṣadrā (1992: 11).
60 Russell (1918–19: 243–5).

61 Ṣadrā (1976: 52).
62 Pines (1979: 262) suggests that we might translate the title as 'the book of what has been established by personal reflection'.
63 Baghdādī (1415 Q, I: 34).
64 Ḥā'irī (1981: 51).
65 Ḥā'irī (1981: 52).
66 Davidson (1984: 201).
67 One finds a critical and detailed discussion of this issue in Khū'ī (1988–95, I: 219–32). For an earlier discussion, see Baḥrānī (1958, I: 5).
68 Ṣadrā is not a linguistic reductionist – see Sellars (1963: 160) quoted in Rorty (1980: 182).
69 *Asfār* II: 333–5.
70 Kant (1929: 504–5). For a good discussion of the debate on existence as a real predicate, see Oppy (1995: 130–61).
71 *Asfār* I: 38–44. On the contemporary debate, see Moore in Flew (1953: 94); Munitz (1974: 106); Williams (1981: 57).
72 *Asfār* II: 3.
73 Baḥrānī (1406 Q: 39).
74 Cf. Rahman (1975: 27).
75 Another philosopher with such disontological tendencies is the Buddhist Vasubhandu who similarly holds that existence is not a predicate because there is no difference between the existence of the thing and the thing itself – see Mohanty (1992: 158).
76 A tautology. Ṣadrā (1987, IV: 354) makes this point. Neoplatonists such as Dexippus (1888: 34)*, in Cat.*, in Dillon (1990: 69–70) also recognised this – see Hadot (1999: 80). Ibn 'Arabī (1919: 8) also seems to hold that being is not a predicate in his *Inshā' al-dawā'ir* when he argues: '[the concept of] Zayd exists in the mind and exists in speech, but does not exist *in re* (*fī-l-a'yān*) at all. So his qualification of being and non-being are conceived without reference to time. So it follows from this that being is not an attribute of the existent'. Ṣadrā would rebut that the Zayd in the mind or in being-in-language still exists within one of the four modes of being so the argument is invalid.
77 Suhrawardī (1945: 162, 346) *Muqāwamāt* and *Mashāri'* (1952: 66) *Ḥikmat al-Ishrāq*. Cf. Legenhausen (1994*a*: 211); Kneale (1962: 358); Quine (1953); Munitz (1974: 79–80); Williams (1981: 61).
78 Kant (1929: 504–5).
Cf. Plantinga (1965: 57–64); Oppy (1995: 143); Campbell (1974: 98); Alston (1960: 462).
79 Dāmād (1977: 37, 51–3); Āshtiyānī (1972–8, I: 20).
80 Dāmād (1977: 56, 71, 77).
81 Rescher (1966: 71–2); Shehadi (1982: 45); Abed (1991: 124) Langhade (1994: 366) says that existence is not a real predicate in Fārābī. Cf. Fārābī (1970: 212) on the thing's existence as distinct from its account. Morewedge (1970: 236) holds that Avicenna also does not consider existence to be analytic and hence not a real predicate.
82 Fārābī (1344 Q: 9). Cf. Akbarian (2000: 2). Rescher (1963: 39–41) holds that to say existence 'is not an informative predicate' is to assert the existence–essence distinction. The distinction between a method of analysis of concepts and an inquiry into the nature of actual existents is manifest in the existence–essence distinction – see Morewedge in Hourani (1975: 165).
83 Aristotle (1984, II: 1585) *Metaphysics* 1003 b 27; Cf. Averroes (1938–52, I: 310). This position is rejected by Owen (1986: 265), who argues that Aristotle's denial of being as a genus does not entail a belief that existence is not a predicate.
84 Cf. Narāqī (1365 Sh: 3).
85 Ṣadrā (1982: 29). This specific point is also made by Ṭūsī in Ḥillī (1988: 10) on the supervenience of existence over quiddity.

86 Bonmariage (1998: 56), quoting Ṣadrā (1885: 117) *Ittiṣāf*. Does this mean that singular terms and names do not refer? Or that abstracts only refer as universals?
87 Ṣadrā (1885: 110) *Ittiṣāf*.
88 Ṣadrā (1885: 113) *Ittiṣāf*.
89 Ḥā'irī (1982: 13). As such it is a secondary intelligible – see Sa'dī (1998: 56).
90 Miṣbāḥ (1405 Q: 20). Cf. Brentano (1975: 25–6) on Aristotle.
91 *Asfār* I: 79, 82.
92 Qazvīnī (1376 Sh: 209).
93 *Asfār* I: 80.
94 Ṣadrā (1967: 12).
95 *Asfār* I: 79, II: 333; Avicenna (1992*a*: 62).
96 Kahn (1973: 88).
97 Bäck (1987: 356).
98 *Asfār* I: 81–2. Cf. Kahn (1966: 254–7) and (1973: 88) on different senses of the copula in the classical Greek tradition.
99 *Asfār* II: 333, where this example is given along with the classic 'Homer is (*mawjūd*) a poet'.
100 Frank (1978: 21); Shehadi (1982: 4). Cf. Brown in Everson (1994: 233) on Aristotle.
101 Sabzawārī (1969: 94) and (1376 Sh: 411); Izutsu (1983: 98).
102 *Asfār* I: 82.
103 *Asfār* VI: 20.
104 Following Aristotle (1984, II: 1587), *Metaphysics* 1005 a 9; Cf. Averroes (1938–52, I: 331); Owens in Morewedge (1982: 45).
105 Modifying Abed (1991: 37), a predicate is literally a 'meaning-bearer'.
106 Dexippus, *in Cat.*, 7.1–3, in Dillon (1990: 25).
107 Lloyd (1990: 48) quoting *in Cat.*, 58.16–17 – see Strange (1992: 35).
108 Using Munitz (1974: 48). Cf. Kahn (1973: 42–4) adds a fourth type 'conceptual predication' or 'judgement predication' in which the subject and predicate are constituents of judgement and meanings of declarative sentences.
109 Avicenna (1960: 62).
110 Avicenna (1958, I: 15–16).
111 See Aristotle (1984, I: 4) *Categories* 1 b 10–12, 'when one thing is predicated of another, all that is predicated of the predicate will be predicable also of the subject'. Cf. Badawī (1948–9, I: 5).
112 Avicenna (1952: 28). Cf. Aristotle (1984, I: 3) *Categories* 1 a 20; Badawī (1948–9, I: 4); Menn (1999: 218); Abed (1991: 4, 29).
113 Ṣadrā (1996: 214) *Tanqīḥ*; Sabzawārī (1969: 150) and Izutsu (1983: 167). This is discussed with respect to the propositions 'Zayd is human' and 'Zayd exists' in Ṣadrā (1885: 115) *Ittiṣāf*. Cf. Kant (1977: 12).
114 Ṣadrā (1996: 201) *Tanqīḥ*; Sabzawārī (1969: 150); Izutsu (1983: 168). The Kantian analogy is made by Ḥā'irī (1981: 15) and (1982: 258–61). See Kneale (1962: 356–7); Ayer (1971: 103). For the Aristotelian discussion of essential and accidental predication, see Gillespie in Barnes (1975–9, III: 3).
115 Sabzawārī (1969: 151); Izutsu (1983: 169).
116 Carnap (1947: 19, 40–1).
117 Anton (1968: 315–26) and (1969: 1–18).
118 *Asfār* I: 35. The rejection of synonymy is critical because that is how some commentators read Aristotle and that is how even now some regard existence – see Quine (1960: 125, 127, 129); Oppy (1995: 152); Horwich (1998: 46–7); Hintikka (1986: 85, 258); Dancy in Hintikka (1986: 49); Hintikka (1971: 370–1) citing Aristotle (1984, I: 184), *Topics* 110 b 16ff.; cf. Badawī (1948–9, II: 509).
119 *Asfār* I: 38. *Pace* Suhrawardī (1999: 7) *Ḥikmat al-ishrāq*.
120 Marmura (1979: 35).
121 Abed (1991: 3).

122 *Asfār* I: 35. Ṣadrā (1885: 118–19) *Ittiṣāf.*
123 Ṣadrā (1967: 8–10).
124 Sadrian semantics owes more to the categorisation of Avicenna than of Suhrawardī, for the latter (1999: 8) only considers synonymy and homonymy and nothing in between. See the debate on Aristotelian *pros hen* homonymy in Brentano (1975: 3); Owens (1978: 118, 307); Kahn (1966: 248–52).
125 *Asfār* I: 35.
126 As held by Aristotle – see Gerson (1991: 335). Gerson (1990: 213) makes it quite clear that for Plotinus, being is neither synonymous as such nor homonymous. Being seems therefore to be a '*pros hen*' synonym for Plotinus.
127 *Asfār* I: 37. Ṭabāṭabā'ī comments on this by saying that the difference is between the referents of being and not between the portions conceived of its concept because *tashkīk* is a reality essential to the reality of being and not to its concept except accidentally.
128 *Asfār* I: 35
129 Dancy (1991: 3) makes the illuminating point that predication implies immanence. When something is predicated of a subject, it suggests that that predicate is immanent in the subject. This applies to the existence of things. Sadrian predication is not entirely immanentist because one can have accidental predication.
130 *'Ayn* is a good example of commonality of word and not meaning shared by different nouns.
131 This is a good illustration of *ishtirāk*. Usually the rhyme of a poem is not solely the final letter, but although it is permissible for the rhyme to be the same word repeated, it is regarded as a 'flaw' known as *īṭā'*. The word is permissible if the different instances of it have different shades of meaning – see Wright (1995, II: 357). Cf. Sadrā (1988, II: 5); Sabzawārī (1969: 49); Izutsu (1983: 42); Fārābī (1975: 49) and Zimmermann (1981: 229).
132 For a discussion of Neoplatonic parallels, see Lloyd (1990: 17, 21); Martin (1995: 170, 175).
133 *Asfār* I: 36.
134 *Asfār* IV: 181.
135 *Asfār* IV: 266, where he gives two examples, one of two lines, and the other of a father–son relationship between Zayd and 'Amr, for both of which intensity does not enter into their quiddity.
136 *Asfār* I: 35.
137 *Asfār* I: 74, II: 119.
138 Spade (1996: 61, 64). Aristotle (1984, I: 26) *De Interpretatione* 16 b 19–21. cf. Badawī (1948–9, I: 62). Cf. Zimmermann (1981: 34).
139 Spade (1996: 245).
140 Cf. Sedley (1996: 87) on Stoics and Epicureans.
141 Khū'ī (1988–95, I: 73). This is debated strongly in works on legal hermeneutics with 'Irāqī (1414 Q, I: 84) agreeing and Khurāsānī (1990: 12, 41) and Bihbahānī (1415 Q: 185) disagreeing.
142 Morewedge (1982: 287).
143 Evangeliou (1988); Avicenna (1973: 94).
144 Dunlop (1956: 127). Cf. Brentano (1975: 49) citing Aristotle (1984, II: 1627) *Metaphysics* 1030 b 11; Averroes (1938–52, II: 807).
145 Badawī (1948–9, II: 34). Cf. Owen (1986: 262).
146 Badawī (1948–9, II: 2). Cf. Barnes (1971: 65–80); Wedin (1997) for an approach that sees the onymies as grouping principles.
147 Frede (1987: 48). This instrumentalist reading is followed by Harrison in Anton (1992: 40).
148 Aristotle (1984, I: 3–4), *Categories* 1 a 20–b 6. Cf. Badawī (1948–9, I: 3–5). Fārābī follows this in his *Categories* – Abed (1991: 4). The enumerative approach is also

exemplified in the categoriology of *padārtha* theory among Vaiśeṣika philosophers – see Matilal in Morewedge (1982: 96) and Halbfass (1997).

149 Anton in Morewedge (1982: 64–5); Brentano (1975: 61) citing Aristotle (1984, II: 1728, 1733) *Metaphysics* 1093 b 18 and *Nicomachean Ethics* 1096 b 25.

150 Anton in Morewedge (1982: 76).

151 Evangeliou (1988: 164–5).

152 Badawī (1948–9, II: 3).

153 Waismann in Fodor and Katz (1964: 2).

154 Alston in Steinberg and Jacobvits (1971: 46–7).

155 Ṣadrā (1987, VI: 9).

156 Ṣadrā (1996: 199–200, 204) *Tanqīḥ*.

157 Carnap (1947: 1).

158 *Asfār* II: 82.

159 Ibn ʿArabī (1919: 6). They are expressions for truth and falsehood. The text, and indeed the title, is concerned with the relationship between language and the origination and procession of the cosmos. God writes/creates the wor(l)d – see *Asfār* I: 89, II: 257.

160 *Asfār* II: 106–7; Suhrawardī (1952: 312) *Mashāriʿ*. Cf. Yūsuf-i Sānī (1997: 44).

161 *Asfār* III: 297.

162 *Asfār* I: 387, 'the thing cannot be separated from being for what has no being, is not a thing'. Cf. Ṭabāṭabā'ī (1403 Q: 25); Wisnovsky (2000: 186).

163 Suhrawardī (1945: 199, 203) *Mashāriʿ* uses the argument about the possibility of a meaningful discourse of non-existents and fictionals to separate the concept of being-a-thing from being. Cf. Suhrawardī (1945: 4, 23), *Talwīḥāt* and (1945: 125) *Muqāwamāt*.

164 Ṣadrā (1988, III: 42ff.) on the chapter on 'saying that He is a thing'. Cf. Wisnovsky (2000: 186–7); McDermott (1978: 196–9).

165 Ṣadrā (1988, III: 44–5). Cf. Qummī (1373–8 Sh, II: 245ff.).

166 Narāqī (1365 Sh: 256).

167 *Asfār* I: 77.

168 Bahmanyār (1375 Sh: 286–90); Avicenna (1960: 29–34); Cf. Wisnovsky (2000: 212–19).

169 *Asfār* I: 75–6.

170 *Asfār* VIII: 252. Proclus (1968–87, I: 4, 14); Kindī (1998: 45). Avicenna (1973: 145) says that to state 'Zayd is a writer' is to say that 'there is (exists) one Zayd and he is a writer'. Cf. Jāmī (1979: 43).

171 *Asfār* II: 157, III: 68, 297, V: 196, VIII: 132. Cf. Ṣadrā (1967: 61).

172 *Asfār* II: 82.

173 Avicenna (1992*a*: 279).

174 *Asfār* II: 99.

175 *Asfār* II: 87.

176 Bahmanyār (1375 Sh: 365–6); Ṭūsī (1405 Q: 100).

177 *Asfār* II: 82, 157. Ṣadrā (1967: 62).

178 *Asfār* II: 88–9.

179 *Asfār* II: 82.

180 *Asfār* II: 82. Avicenna seems to deny the synonymy of the terms by arguing that the many *qua* the many exists therefore existence and unity cannot be synonymous, a

of light that is differentiated by degrees of perfection and imperfection within it. Cf.

Ṣadrā (1987, IV: 353); Ṭūsī in Avicenna (1375 Sh, III: 35). Is this an indication that Ṭūsī is an Illuminationist as claimed by Ziai in Nasr (1996*a*, I: 486)?

183 *Asfār* I: 63–4.
184 *Asfār* I: 108–9. Cf. Nasafī (1998: 106).
185 Ṣadrā (1987, IV: 356).
186 Cf. Avicenna (1973: 145).
187 Dāmād (1998: 215).
188 Campbell (1974: 96).
189 *Asfār* II: 10–11. Cf. *Asfār* V: 95 where he quotes with approval the view of Dashtakī that individuation and the act of being are the same in sense and occurrence but not identical (in terms of Leibniz's law of indiscernibles).
190 Ṣadrā (1967: 72).
191 Sabzawārī (1969: 142); Izutsu (1983: 158).
192 *Asfār* IX: 185.
193 This is the main thrust of his treatise on this topic – see Ṣadrā (1885: 120–31).
194 Hintikka (1959: 141). Langhade (1994: 363) argues for a paronymous relationship between the two terms in Fārābī.
195 Strange (1992: 46–50) translating Porphyry, *in Cat.*, 66.1–69.20.
196 Sabzawārī (1969: 47).
197 Quine (1953: 2, 5). Cf. Williams (1981: 40). The roots of the issue lie in Plato's *Sophist* – see Frede in Kraut (1992); Moravcsik (1992: 169–212).
198 *Asfār* I: 270; Russell (1905: 48). His solution is to reformulate the proposition as a negation.
199 Quine (1953: 8, 15) wants to avoid an ontology of what is not, but this is at odds with Plato's original point against Parmenides. Frede in Kraut (1992: 399, 403) argues that Plato insists at *Sophist* 255 e 8–257 a 12 on the possibility of asserting what is not. 'X is not Y' is a statement of not being, and not one of identity or difference.
200 Orenstein in Munitz (1973: 63).
201 Avicenna (1960: 33), and Marmura (1984: 229). Absolute privatives have neither sense nor reference but 'specific privatives' are intentional concepts in the mind that are meaningful as absences of presence/being – *Asfār* I: 345. Following Aristotle (1984, I: 33) *De Interpretatione* 21 a 22–4. Cf. Badawī (1948–9, I: 90).
202 *Asfār* I: 343.
203 *Asfār* I: 75.
204 *Asfār* I: 76; Frank (1978: 59).
205 For an overview of the Mu'tazilī position, see Klein-Franke (1994).
206 Frank (2000: 28).
207 *Asfār* IX: 165; Wolfson (1973–7, II: 338–58).
208 *Asfār* IX: 165.
209 Sabzawārī (1969: 74); Izutsu (1983: 75).
210 *Asfār* I: 76–7.
211 Avicenna (1960: 308).
212 Ṭabāṭabā'ī (1403 Q: 26–7).
213 Ṭūsī (1985: 30). The context is a critique of Fakhr al-Dīn Rāzī's denial that the principle of non-contradiction is not *a priori* (i.e. that affirmation and negation cannot both be the case).

220 *Asfār* I: 345.

221 *Asfār* VI: 357.
222 Khū'ī (1988–95, III: 27).
223 At the same time this law that states ¬(p & ¬p), does not hold literally given the possibility of intensity within being – see *Asfār* VIII: 73. Cf. Dummett (1993*b*: 66).
224 *Asfār* I: 342–3.
225 *Asfār* I: 32–5 makes this argument following Suhrawardī (1999: 84–5) where it is stated that the reality of light differs not by species but by 'perfection and deficiency'. Cf. Sabzawārī (1969: 71).
226 *Asfār* I: 343.
227 *Asfār* II: 4, 288: 'it is impossible to reconcile two contradictories (*naqīḍayn*) in an existence insofar as it exists, but not insofar as it does not exist (*ghayr mawjūd*)'. This is also true of Meinong and some of the early phenomenologists – see Simons (1998: 284).
228 Chakrabarti in Matilal (1985*b*: 320–1); Matilal (1985*a*: 83). Wolfson (1973–7, II: 342), where he also points out that the Stoics permitted the predication of non-existents and Democritus asserted the existence of a void.
229 *Asfār* II: 333.
230 Matilal (1985*a*: 79).
231 Matilal (1985*a*: 96, 112).
232 Avicenna (1960: 129).
233 Avicenna (1973: 30).
234 *Asfār* I: 365–6.
235 This type of proposition is 'infinite' and hence not a correct proposition – see Suhrawardī (1999: 15) *Ḥikmat al-ishrāq*.
236 *Asfār* II: 105–6. Cf. Alexander (1891: 327 on II.18–20) on the permissibility of saying 'wall is not seeing' but not the 'wall is blind' as the latter is nonsensical through habit. Cf. Wolfson (1973–7, II: 543, 555). Avicenna (1992*a*: 24) states that the latter type of proposition is where the subject does not occur, either because it is not actualised or because it is a universal.
237 Kātibī (1854: 10); Rescher (1966: 76).
238 *Asfār* I: 368.
239 *Asfār* I: 348.
240 *Asfār* I: 349.
241 Martin (1995: 192).
242 *Asfār* VI: 300.
243 *Asfār* I: 383.
244 *Asfār* III: 175.

4 Mental being

1 Nock and Festugière (1945–54, I: 7) *Corpus Hermeticum* I.1–3; Salaman *et al.* (1999: 19); cf. *Asfār* II: 50.
2 Rahman (1972: 146). Mental being is primarily cognitive and, unlike Strawson (1994: 154), not primarily experiential although cognition and experience in a presential mode of knowledge are indistinguishable.
3 Simons (1998: 283); Hamid (1998: 135).
4 A rare defender of dualism is Strawson (1994: 47), although he describes his position as 'mental *and* physical monism', adheres to soft token-token identity in the mind-body problem and definitely does not believe in a soul. Behaviourist attacks on dualism such as Ryle (1949) and identity theories have questioned whether the 'mental' means something 'in the mind'.
5 *Asfār* I: 321–2. Cf. Shakībā (1996*b*: 40); Āmulī (1374 Sh: 147).
6 Cf. Fodor (1998: 8).
7 *Asfār* III: 281. Cf. Rahman (1972: 141).

8 *Asfār* I: 263; Ṣadrā (1362 Sh: 33).
9 *Asfār* I: 271.
10 Āmulī (1374 Sh: 148).
11 *Asfār* I: 274.
12 Kindī (1998: 19); Avicenna (1973: 37) and (1960: 142) Cf. Shakībā (1996*a*: 66); Michot (1986: 85); Narāqī (1365 Sh: 232)
13 Baghdādī (1415 Q, I: 210, 225).
14 Rāzī (1343 Q, I: 131–2). Cf. Akbarī (1999: 39).
15 Dashtakī (1382 Sh: 102–5).
16 *Asfār* I: 263–4.
17 *Asfār* I: 264–6.
18 *Asfār* I: 266–8; cf. Ibn ʿArabī (1980: 88–90); Austin (1981: 102–3). The commentators clarify that the terms *qur'ān* and *furqān* here stand for the Sufi binary concept of union and separation (*al-jamʿ wa-l-farq*) which draws as Ibn ʿArabī so often does on an etymological analysis of the terms.
19 *Asfār* I: 268.
20 Akbarī (1999: 39).
21 *Asfār* I: 269 on Sabzawārī's correction. Cf. Akbarī (1999: 40).
22 *Asfār* I: 269–70.
23 Akbarī (1999: 40).
24 *Asfār* I: 275.
25 Dashtakī (1382 Sh: 108).
26 Akbarī (1999: 42). Cf. Dummett (1993*b*: 280); Dancy (1991: 61–101).
27 These are things that are *iʿtibārī*. On the use of the term 'intellectual fiction', see Walbridge (2000: 22).
28 Ziai's introduction to Suhrawardī (1999: xxv). Cf. Gyekye (1975: 56) and (1979: 41); Frank in Morewedge (1982: 261) on the *kalām* discussion of non-existents.
29 Marmura (1984: 230).
30 *Asfār* I: 269–70. Cf. Ṣadrā (1362 Sh: 39); Sabzawārī (1969: 58); Izutsu (1983: 54); Ṭabāṭabā'ī (1403 Q: 37); Leaman (1999: 95).
31 Michot (1985: 94).
32 *Asfār* I: 287. Cf. Black (1997: 429).
33 *Asfār* VIII: 238.
34 Black (1997: 428).
35 Evans (1982: 22–3, 30–1) argues that this issue is about sense without referent. He prefers the concept of 'descriptive names' for these, names whose reference is fixed by description even if the name is empty [i.e. not real].
36 *Asfār* IX: 191. One does not intellect *intelligibilia* through bodily or material means in the Peripatetic tradition – see Bahmanyār (1375 Sh: 490, 740).
37 *Asfār* VIII: 227. But the creative nature of the imagination is important for all intellects. However, it is only saints who, through their imagination in the form of spiritual concentration, can realise those forms in the imaginal realm, quoting Ibn ʿArabī – see *Asfār* I: 266.
38 *Asfār* VI: 152–4, 283–4. Cf. Shakībā (1996*b*: 46).
39 Rāzī (1343 Q, I: 439–41); Sabzawārī (1969: 59); Izutsu (1983: 55).
40 *Asfār* I: 272.
41 Sabzawārī (1969: 58); Izutsu (1983: 54).
42 Or perhaps conceptualism would be more accurate given that the names refer to concepts that exist in the mind as bearers of meaning.
43 *Asfār* I: 263–6; Ṣadrā (1967: 24–5).
44 *Asfār* I: 273–4.
45 Akbarī (1999: 43) on the passage in the text.
46 *Asfār* I: 273.
47 *Asfār* I: 274.

48 *Asfār* I: 274–5.
49 Crane in O'Hear (1998: 230–3); Dummett (1993*a*: 30); Levinas (1998: 13, 58).
50 Akbarī (1999: 45).
51 *Asfār* I: 275.
52 Cf. Honderich (1998: 138) on conscious events.
53 *Asfār* I: 343.
54 Cf. Ṭabāṭabā'ī (1403 Q: 31).
55 This is also not possible because the existence of the mind as an extra-mental reality and mental being are quite distinct. Cf. Ṣadrā (1992: 36); Dashtakī (1382 Sh: 109).
56 *Asfār* I: 276. Sabzawārī in his note gives the example of the first Shi'i Imam 'Alī in one of the early battles of Islam ripping open the gates of the fort Khaybar with the strength of his psychic and spiritual concentration becoming manifest *in re*.
57 *Asfār* VI: 149.
58 Āmulī (1374 Sh: 8, 147).
59 As Rahman (1975: 200) charges.
60 Idealism characterises the phenomenological and Platonic tradition that he inherited – see Levinas (1998: 138ff) and *EII*, volume II on the Platonists of Persia.
61 Strawson (1994: 153); Levinas (1998: 135).
62 Honderich (1998: 140).
63 Honderich (1998: 141, 154); Levinas (1998: 58).
64 This is certainly true of most Islamic philosophers from Avicenna onwards shown by his *homo volans* argument. See Pines (1979: 193); Marmura (1986).
65 However, from this one does not lapse into idealism. Rappe in Gerson (1996: 262) uses an illuminating discussion of the macro and microcosmic aspects of the world and our experience to explain this. From the macrocosmic point of view, the world is publicly available; from the microcosmic view, the same world is viewed from within the confines of an individual consciousness.
66 Amīn (1986: 52) indicates the subjectivist problem of mental being.
67 For Baghdādī (1415 Q, III: 20–1) what exists is what is capable of being apprehended. Cf. Pines (1979: 287).
68 Walbridge (2000: 220–1). Cf. Levinas (1998: 17). This is denied by Searle (1992: 149) who holds that one can jettison incorrigibility, introspection and privileged epistemic privacy along with foundationalism while still holding a concept of consciousness.
69 Levinas (1998: 13, 183). The term intentionality derives from the scholastic term *intentio*, translating the Arabic *ma'ná* in Avicenna (1960: 470) and denoting a mental entity that is oriented and intended towards an object *in re*.
70 Lloyd (1990: 182).
71 *Asfār* III: 507.
72 Ṣadrā (1376 Sh: 16). Cf. Avicenna (1973: 161) and (1992*b*: 224); Levinas (1998: 135). Searle (1992: 142) denies that a conscious being need be self-conscious.
73 Chalmers (1996: 3).
74 *Asfār* III: 515.
75 Chalmers (1996: 6, 26).
76 *Asfār* VII: 153 mentions this but the full argument is given by his commentator Sabzawārī in the *ta'līqa*. Cf. Ṣadrā (1987, VI: 148).
77 Lloyd (1990: 77) and (1976). Cf. Clark in Gerson (1996: 288). Minds are monads.

80 Rescher (1996: 125).

81 Avicenna (1960, III: 671). I owe this point to Paul Hardy.
82 A very Hermetic phrase! See Nock and Festugière (1945–54, I: 10) *Corpus Hermeticum* I.12 on *nous*.
83 *Asfār* VIII: 367–8.
84 *Asfār* VIII: 51. Also cf. VIII: 121, 123. Cf. ʿAbd al-Haq (1970: 176). This is a recognisably Pythagorean doctrine as attested in the Arabic Aëtius – see Daiber (1980: 190). Festugière (1983, III: 190) shows how it is also a feature of Iamblichus' Pythagorean Neoplatonism.
85 *Asfār* II: 44 on the soul being a simple reality quoting Suhrawardī. See Chapter 5, pp. 102–130.
86 See Sabzawārī's note at the bottom of *Asfār* VIII: 51. For the idea that the soul is *in a sense* all things, see Aristotle (1984, I: 686), *De Anima* 431 b 21 and Philoponus' commentary at *in De Anima* 567, 20 in Charlton (2000: 148). Cf. Badawī (1954: 78).
87 *Asfār* VIII: 267, the *psuchē* is such. On this theme in Plotinus, see Armstrong (1966–88, IV: 407, V: 43, 123, VI: 113, 143), *Enneads* IV.8.3.10, V.1.8.26, V.3.15.11, VI.2.2.2, VI.2.10.11. cf. Gerson (1994: 44). See also Proclus, *in Parm.*, 1148–9 in Dillon and Morrow (1987: 504).
88 Cf. *Asfār* III: 360, 362 on sense perception and *Asfār* IX: 21–2 on threefold objects of perception.
89 *Asfār* III: 368.
90 The simple intellect is non-discursive – see *Asfār* III: 369.
91 Nagel (1979: 181–2, 193).
92 McGinn (1996: 34).
93 Though most such theories reject emergence of cognitive states from complex entities as well – see Nagel (1979: 182).
94 McGinn (1996: 35).
95 Intensity within the soul is denied by the Peripatetics – see Bahmanyār (1375 Sh: 729).
96 Jambet (2000: 78); Rahman (1975: 195ff); Steel (1978).
97 *Asfār* VIII: 42, 136ff. This draws upon the growth argument in Aristotle (1984, I: 527), *De Generatione et Corruptione* 322 a 28–33 – see Sorabji in Crabbe (1999: 23).
98 *Asfār* VIII: 346, 380 on the soul being incorruptible. See *Asfār* VIII: 330–40 for the discussion defending Aristotelians against Platonists on this issue.
99 *Asfār* IX: 47; cf. Sorabji in Crabbe (1999: 11); Emilsson in Everson (1991: 155). Cf. Philoponus, *in De Anima* 481 in Charlton (2000: 56); Aristotle (1984, I: 648) *De Anima* I.3 407 a 2–3. Cf. Badawī (1954: 15). Body is defined by its extension – see Plotinus (1951–73, II: 179) *Enneads* IV.7.1; Badawī (1948: 121).
100 *Asfār* VIII: 389. Ṣadrā (1967: 195). Cf. Jambet (1997: 221). The union of the body and soul in a real sense is asserted in the Peripatetic tradition – see Bahmanyār (1375 Sh: 726). For the material origins of the soul in the Peripatetic school, see Lawkarī (1995: 144).
101 Steel (1978: 158–9).
102 *Asfār* IX: 21, 116.
103 *Asfār* VIII: 356.
104 *Asfār* VIII: 330–1, 348ff.

111 Strawson (1959: 56–7).

112 Ricoeur (1992: 130).
113 Rescher (1996: 62).
114 McGinn (1996: 47).
115 Kenny in Crabbe (1999: 40). Thus the language of self that I use, following Ha'iri (1992: 90ff), ought perhaps to be tempered.
116 *Asfār* III: 344–5. *Asfār* III: 291 criticises Suhrawardī for holding this for knowledge of others that are not separable lights.
117 Ryle (1949, chapter V); Matilal (1986: 102). *Asfār* III: 290 uses the term 'a relational quality of an essence'.
118 *Asfār* IV: 121. See Rāzī (1343 Q, I: 331) on knowledge as an *iḍāfa*. His point is that in the Avicennan doctrine, if God knows particulars, it entails plurality in the Godhead, which is avoided if one regards knowledge and its objects as correlations. This theory is also held by Baghdādī (1415 Q, III: 2); cf. Pines (1979: 275).
119 Sabzawārī (1969: 60).
120 *Asfār* III: 286–7.
121 *Asfār* III: 284, 345.
122 Rorty (1980: 319, 359) wants to replace this concept of the mirror with a pragmatic and minimalist concept of knowledge that focuses on self-description.
123 A more famous precursor is Plato (1997: 146) *Cratylus* 430 b–c: the name, like the picture, is an imitation of the thing. For objections to the picture theory, see Daitz in Flew (1966: 59–74).
124 *Asfār* III: 286, 297.
125 *Asfār* III: 288.
126 Ṣadrā (1967: 242).
127 *Asfār* III: 313. Cf. Ha'iri (1992: 35).
128 Putnam (1999: 43). His direct realism goes against most philosophers who hold a representational model of perception.
129 *Asfār* I: 391. Cf. Avicenna (1973: 34).
130 Ṣadrā (1964: 5–6); *Asfār* I: 61.
131 What is clear is that these models are essentially rationalist insofar as they regard the intellect or reason as the prime organ of perception and relegate sense perception to a lower level. But human epistemic experience cannot be so easily compartmentalised. One knows and experiences as a whole self and body in a holistic manner. One cannot divide knowledge into the perception of a certain sense or internal sense and distinguish it from another since it defies our ordinary experience. As such any distinction between the functions of specific senses, or sense perception more generally, and rationalist accounts, is misleading.
132 *Asfār* I: 413.
133 Ziai in Nasr (1996*b*, I: 438).
134 But not in the sense of being *anamnesis* on which he equivocates, affirming it in Ṣadrā (1340 Sh: 58–9); cf. Morris (1981: 219). This equivocation is typical of much of the Neoplatonic tradition after Porphyry that attempts a harmonisation between the philosophies of Plato and Aristotle.
135 Walbridge (2000: 178–9); Averroes (1974: 94–5) *Republic* 74.15–25. Cf. Plato (1997: 1132–4) *Republic* 514a–517a. It is important to avoid the fallacy of naturalism that reduces experience to sensory experience – see Levinas (1998: 9).
136 Plato (1997: 1113) *Republic* 490 b–c.
137 Ṣadrā (1996: 70) *Ittiḥād* and (1967: 244).
138 Cf. Matilal (1986: 108–9); Gilson (1952: 193).
139 *Asfār* III: 297–8; Rahman (1972: 143–6). cf. Armstrong (1966–88, III: 385) *Enneads* III.8.8.8, 'knowing and being are the same'. According to *Asfār* III: 285, 291, Suhrawardī holds that knowledge is light, hence being in the metalanguage of Sadrian philosophy.
140 *Asfār* VI: 85. Ṣadrā (1992: 30): 'the reality of being does not occur in any mind since

it is not a universal . . . Knowledge of the reality of being can only be [attained] through illuminative presence and actual vision [experience] such that there can be no doubt about its ipseity'.

141 *Asfār* VII: 252. Cf. Corbin (1972: 120); Hernández (1981, II 330).
142 Cf. Putnam (1999: 155).
143 Lloyd (1990: 141).
144 Lloyd (1990: 144, 184).
145 *Asfār* III: 278.
146 Walbridge (2000: 164–5, 169). Empiricist in the sense of not being realist in the mediaeval sense. Further, since the simple intellect is all things the 'problem' of God's knowledge of particulars is resolved – see Ṣadrā (1987, II: 297); *Asfār* VI: 110, VIII: 230.
147 *Asfār* III: 301. This goes against the Avicennan model of material images imprinted in the imagination – see Rahman (1975: 225).
148 *Asfār* VIII: 211, 227, 236. cf. Rahman (1975: 226–7).
149 Ziai in Nasr (1996*b*, I: 437).
150 Sabzawārī (1969: 571); Michot (1985: 102).
151 Ha'iri (1992: 153).
152 *Asfār* I: 288.
153 *Asfār* I: 289.
154 Badawī (1948: 22); Ibn ʿArabī (n.d., II: 219); Suhrawardī (1945: 112–13) *Talwīḥāt* and (1952: 162) *Ḥikmat al-ishrāq*; Shahrazūrī (1993: 399); Ṣadrā (1313 Q*b*: 378). Cf. Plotinus (1951–73, II: 225) *Enneads* IV.8.1; Nock and Festugière (1945–54, I: 7) *Corpus Hermeticum* I.1–2; Zimmermann in Kraye (1986: 138–9).
155 Marmura (1986: 383); cf. Rappe in Gerson (1996: 252); Hadot (1997: 28).
156 *Asfār* III: 450. Walbridge (2000: 225) from Suhrawardī (1945: 70–4), *Talwīḥāt*. Cf. Ha'iri (1992: 183–9). Self-knowledge as a foundation for epistemology and metaphysics also draws upon the famous *khabar* '*man ʿarafa nafsahu faqad ʿarafa rabbahu*' which Ṣadrā invokes – see *Asfār* VI: 302, 377, VII: 21, VIII: 35, 306; Āmidī (1960, V: 194); Bursī (1978: 188); Majlisī (1392 Q, 70: 72).
157 Cf. Avicenna (1973: 79).
158 *Asfār* III: 318, 353ff.
159 Leaman (1999: 70).
160 Walbridge (2000: 26–7).
161 *Asfār* III: 447. Cf. Ṣadrā (1967: 211).
162 *Asfār* III: 457. The pre-epistemic doubt does not arise.
163 Translated and quoted by Ha'iri (1992: 55), slightly modified by me.
164 For a Plotinian parallel, see Emilsson in Gerson (1996: 224).
165 Cf. Evans (1982: 123–4). The way that we experience ourselves is a mental process, a conceptual 'imagining' that is virtual in Sadrian terms; this mental 'self' is not therefore a being as such – see Strawson in Crabbe (1999: 129, 132–3).
166 *Asfār* I: 74, 'the real nature of something is different from what the intellect understands by it'. *Asfār* III: 453. The concept of the thing is an intellectual fiction – see Baghdādī (1415 Q, III: 39) and Pines (1979: 289).
167 Bermúdez (1998: 5) recognises this distinction, drawing on Wittgenstein in his two concepts of 'I'-thought. Cf. Evans (1982: 185).
168 *Asfār* III: 295–96.
169 'Taste' when considered in pre-Renaissance thought is not the subjective and idiosyncratic judgement of an individual that we know. Rather, it is an accurate apperception of reality, and when understood in terms of mediaeval aesthetics is the act of perception (*aesthesis*). As such one cannot dispute the 'dictates of taste'; as the mediaeval saying goes, '*de gustibus non est disputandum*'.
170 Bermúdez (1998: xi, 24).
171 Porphyry (2005, I: 372–5), *Sentences* 44; Ṣadrā (1340 Sh: 11); *Asfār* VI: 165–6;

cf. Morris (1981: 113) and Hamade (1992: 623). The roots of this doctrine are in Aristotle's anti-sceptical postulation of the unity of the perceiving subject and object in Aristotle (1984, I: 683), *De Anima* III.4 430 a 4–5: 'what thinks and what is thought are identical; for speculative knowledge and its object are identical'. Cf. Badawī (1954: 74) for Arabic: *al-ʿāqil wa-l-maʿqūl minhā shay' wāḥid*. Cf. Hadot (1999: 267–69). For Philoponus' commentary, see Charlton (2000: 113, 119).

172 Siorvanes (1996: 166) quoting Proclus, *in Parm.*, 901. Cf. Dillon and Morrow (1987: 261). Armstrong (1966–88, I: 280–1, III: 380–1, V: 72–3, 154–63), *Enneads* I.8.2.7–21, III.8.8.1–30, V.3.1.1–9, V.5.1–2; Wallis in Harris (1976: 125); Emilsson in Everson (1991: 165); Blumenthal in Sorabji (1990: 313); Baghdādī (1415 Q, III: 2); T(a)hānawī (1963–77, I: 1061–2).

173 Armstrong (1966–88, V: 96–7), *Enneads* V.3.8.21–24, quoted in Crystal (1998: 283).

174 O'Meara (1995: 41).

175 Crystal (1998: 268).

176 Suhrawardī (1945: 68–9), *Talwīḥāt*.

177 *Asfār* III: 323.

178 Avicenna (1375 Sh, III: 292–5).

179 Avicenna (1375 Sh, III: 295) and *Asfār* III: 323. Ṣadrā affirms the truth of the Porphyrian doctrine and criticises those who attack him – see *Asfār* VI: 188–9.

180 Ṣadrā (1996: 92), *Ittiḥād*; *Asfār* III: 321.

181 Avicenna (1375 Sh, III: 293).

182 *Asfār* VI: 170.

183 Avicenna (1960: 356) and (1984: 6); Ṭūsī (1405 Q: 96, 116).

184 It is significant that though he considers Avicenna's criticism of the union of intellection, he does not deal with objections to presential knowledge as such.

185 *Asfār* III: 324, VI: 171.

186 Ṣadrā (1996: 82) *Ittiḥād*.

187 *Asfār* III: 366.

188 Ṣadrā (1996: 83) *Ittiḥād*; *Asfār* III: 325.

189 Avicenna (1960: 329).

190 Muḥaqqiq Dāmād (1997: 62). Cf. *Asfār* III: 313.

191 *Asfār* VI: 180–1. Cf. Bonmariage (1998: 147).

192 Sabzawārī (1969: 66); Izutsu (1983: 66).

193 *Asfār* VI: 264. cf. Ṣadrā (1987, II: 216). For Avicenna, the simple intellect is an abstracted higher form that is the basis for detailed knowledge – see Rahman (1975: 235). Yet Avicenna (1992*b*: 301–2) concurs with the Sadrian position.

194 Emilsson in Gerson (1996: 234).

195 *Asfār* III: 371–2.

196 Cf. Gerson (1996: 279); Bussanich (1997: 199).

197 *Asfār* III: 372.

198 Ṣadrā (1987, II: 143). This level is that same as the content of the divine mind and not the same as mental being itself, *contra* Iṣfahānī (1372 Sh: 156). The distinction of the facts themselves and actuality is similar to the processist distinction between facts obtaining and the existence of things – see Rescher (1996: 87).

199 *Asfār* III: 306, VIII: 65, IX: 71. He quotes the *Theologia* as authority for this doctrine.

200 *Asfār* III: 373. Cf. Wallis (1992: 55, 69), drawing on Plato (1997: 1236) *Timaeus* 30 c.

201 The Plotinian tradition identifies this Active Intellect with the divine or the One that is the simple intellect here – see Emilsson in Gerson (1996: 238).

202 Fowden (1986: 101); cf. Nock and Festugière (1945–54, I: 7, 50) *Corpus Hermeticum* I.3, IV.4.

203 Walbridge (2000: 165).

204 *Asfār* VI: 265–6. Cf. Sabzawārī (1969: 66); Izutsu (1983: 66); Gerson (1997: 14) from Armstrong (1966–88, V: 118–19), *Enneads* V.3.13.13–17.

205 *Asfār* III: 326.
206 This is true of Plotinus – see Wallis (1992: 89).
207 *Asfār* III: 337.
208 *Asfār* III: 335. Cf. Bahmanyār (1375 Sh: 792).
209 *Asfār* III: 346–7.
210 Badawī (1948: 94) quoted in Ṣadrā (1996: 75, 100) *Ittiḥād*; *Asfār* III: 317.
211 Ṣadrā (1996: 101–2) *Ittiḥād*.
212 Badawī (1948: 98), and Ṣadrā (1996: 103) *Ittiḥād*. Philoponus, *in De Anima* 533, 20ff on *DA* 429 b 30–1 in Charlton (2000: 112): 'The intellect *in potentia* is all the objects of intellect'. Cf. Badawī (1954: 74). Later in *in DA* 535 he quotes Alexander on the doctrine that all things are in the Active Intellect, their source – see Charlton (2000: 114). For the Arabic Alexander's *Peri Nou*, see Finnegan (1956: 187).
213 Since such matters supervene upon the soul/intellect – see *Asfār* VIII: 52.
214 Things do not exist in the simple intellect as forms impressed upon it but by unitive presence. Since they are the same and identical, there can be no doubt about what the simple intellect knows. Furthermore, Ṭabāṭabā'ī glosses the point by saying that this knowledge and infallibilism is communicable to us. We do not doubt what we receive from the simple intellect because of the union and also because the level of the simple intellect is in the world of ***intelligibilia*** that is free from corruption and evil such as deception. See *Asfār* VII: 280–1. Cf. Iṣfahānī (1372 Sh: 163). *Contra* Alston (1983: 77).
215 Gerson (1997: 2).
216 *Asfār* III: 377. This capacity is infinite.
217 *Asfār* III: 373, VIII: 148. I am grateful to Paul Hardy for pointing this out to me. Cf. Lloyd (1986: 259). This is also true of the Peripatetic tradition – see Bahmanyār (1375 Sh: 815).
218 Lloyd (1986: 259).
219 Bussanich (1997: 202); Ha'iri (1992: 161).
220 Ha'iri (1992: 176).
221 Wittgenstein (1953, § 243), quoted in Candlish (1998: 693).
222 McDowell in Moore (1993: 260).
223 Candlish (1998: 694); Dummett (1993*b*: 166). Putnam (1999: 25) urges caution in our assuming that this means that knowledge claims about the external are subject to communal approval. Further, Strawson (1994: 26) is equally sceptical about claims of public observability for the non-mental.
224 McDowell in Moore (1993: 263, 276).
225 Katz (1992: 5, 22).
226 Putnam (1999: 47). Cf. Alston (1983: 73).
227 Putnam (1981); Searle (1992: 65).
228 Arguably Cartesian personhood depends on the twin supports of the mind's self-transparency and the privacy of mental states. Both these conditions are actually met by Plotinus – see Rappe in Gerson (1996: 251). They are also met by Avicenna in his famous *homo volans* argument.
229 McDowell in Moore (1993: 284) considers this as a case of anti-realism.
230 Ha'iri (1992: 108, 113).
231 A more immediate defence is the postulation of *a priori* concepts that are innate in humans, or axioms that are logically and mathematically primitive and cannot be doubted, immediate and devoid of discursive content.
232 Davidson in Guttenplan (1975: 9).
233 McGinn (1996: 84).
234 *Asfār* III: 420.
235 McGinn (1996: 102, 105).
236 Fodor (1998: 63) famously champions this.
237 Cf. 'Alīzāda (1998: 96).

238 Khurāsānī (1990: 35).
239 *Asfār* VI: 63.
240 *Asfār* I: 37. In the Akbarian tradition, the concept of being *qua* being is unreal – see Qayṣarī in Āshtiyānī (1370 Sh: 111); Āmulī (1969: 631).
241 *Asfār* I: 111–12, 340, II: 329, 333, 346, III: 453, VI: 19. Concepts mediate between thought, mind and world but often are themselves devoid of propositional content as they do not exist as such. Cf. Fodor (1998: 28).
242 *Asfār* I: 49.
243 Dummett (1993*a*: 37).
244 On the three terms, 'logical', 'mental' and 'natural' universals, see Avicenna (1952: 65–8); Rāzī (1343 Q, I: 448); Ṭūsī in Avicenna (1958, I: 204). Logic is the study of secondary intelligibles – see Arnaldez (443), Avicenna (1960: 10) and (1973: 167); Sabra (1980: 753); Narāqī (1365 Sh: 48).
245 Avicenna (1952: 68); Marmura (1979: 42).
246 Avicenna (1992*b*: 169) on being *qua* being as a pure concept.
247 *Asfār* I: 78–82. This is rejected by 'Irāqī (1414 Q, I: 86) among other *uṣūlīs*, who insist that concepts exist in the mind as beings correlated to extra-mental reality.
248 Ṣadrā (1996: 182) *Aṣālat*.
249 Khurāsānī (1990: 193).
250 Muẓaffar (1411 Q: 111).
251 *Asfār* I: 37; Bahmanyār (1375 Sh: 286–7).
252 *Asfār* VI: 85; Ḥā'irī (1981: 44).
253 *Asfār* I: 401, 406.
254 Sabzawārī (1969: 67); Izutsu (1983: 67).
255 *Asfār* I: 335. Cf. Sa'dī (1998: 53).
256 The Sadrian view following the later Illuminationist doctrine is a radical departure from the Avicennan one that regards the concept of being as a primary intelligible. Being and its like are epistemologically prior for Avicenna – see Marmura (1984: 220). But the later traditions consider primary intelligibles as what refer to primary substances that are epistemologically prior such as quiddities.
257 Levinas (1998: 51).
258 *Asfār* I: 323.
259 *Asfār* I: 332–3. Cf. Owens in Morewedge (1982: 44).
260 *Asfār* I: 335.
261 *Asfār* I: 336–7.
262 *Asfār* I: 338–9.
263 *Asfār* III: 453.
264 Ḥā'irī (1981: 51–2) explaining the Sadrian view.
265 *Asfār* I: 337.
266 *Asfār* I: 339.
267 *Asfār* I: 37; Ṣadrā (1992: 8).
268 Cf. Matilal (1986: 309) on the Buddhist parable of the magician and the tiger's bones that is a warning against relying upon false concepts and images to 'make' our reality.
269 Ṣadrā (1987, II: 143); Fayḍ Kāshānī (1375 Sh: 8).
270 All thought intends something and that is its object – see Levinas (1998: 4) following the Brentano thesis.
271 *Asfār* II: 1–2.
272 For *inniyya* as existence, see Abed (1991: 68).
273 *Asfār* I: 413.
274 *Asfār* I: 74.
275 Such notions are by consensus agreed to be non-existent and non-occurrent *in re*. When one says that a quiddity occurs, one merely qualifies it with being *in re*. See *Asfār* I: 139–40.

276 *Asfār* II: 119–20.
277 Avicenna (1960: 292), Anawati (1978, II: 42). Marmura (1979: 44) on Avicenna (1952: 37–41). Cf. *Asfār* II: 16–17.
278 Dīnānī (1372 Sh, II: 459–69).
279 Avicenna (1952: 34).
280 *Asfār* II: 3, III: 281. Khū'ī (1988–95, V: 355ff).
281 The latter term became common in nineteenth-century Shiʿi legal hermeneutics and is not attested in Sadrian philosophy – see Khū'ī (1988–95, V: 355–6); Ḥā'irī (1982: 211–12).
282 *Asfār* II: 5.
283 *Asfār* II: 8. This is specifically what is known as the *muqsimī* sub-mode, a more absolute form of non-conditionality – see Izutsu (1974: 153–6, 160).
284 Ṣadrā (1992: 34).
285 *Asfār* II: 8–9.
286 Putnam (1999: 151). But our philosopher, though he accepts the possibility of such mediated perception, is really a direct realist, a position.
287 Lloyd (1990: 67). This question is related to the one of unallocated species in Simplicius, *in Cat.*, 10.3–4. cf. Booth (1983: 106); Avicenna (1952: 28–9).
288 Lloyd (1990: 70).
289 Fayḍ Kāshānī (1375 Sh: 9).
290 Ṣadrā's *scholia* on the *Ḥikmat al-ishrāq* – see Corbin (1986: 491).
291 Marmura (1979: 35).
292 Plato (1997: 1660) *Seventh Epistle* 343 c 3–4 on the distinction between what a thing is and how it is. Aristotle (1984, I: 152) *Posterior Analytics* 92 b 3–10 on the distinction between what a man is and that a man is. Cf. Badawī (1948–9, II: 422–3). Goichon (1937: 132); Avicenna (1960: 31); Rahman (1958) and (1981). For the background to the distinction, see Rizvi (2000: 72–8). Some theologians such as Abū-l-Ḥasan Ashʿarī [d. *c.* 941] and Abū-l-Ḥusayn Baṣrī [d. 1044] deny any distinction – see Ḥillī (1988: 25), Sabzawārī (1969: 48) and Izutsu (1983: 41).
293 Avicenna (1958, III: 443). Cf. Gilson (1952: 75).
294 *Asfār* I: 171; Cf. I: 61, 243–9, II: 310, III: 234–5, 248, 281, 306.
295 This is critical to the proof of mental being in the later tradition. If being were not ontologically fundamental but merely a concept, then there would be no distinction between mental and extra-mental realms of being. See Ṭabāṭabā'ī (1403 Q: 15).
296 Ṣadrā (1992: 10–21). These arguments as in the *Asfār* I: 53ff are ranged against Suhrawardī's claims of the unreality of being and its lack of reference, for which see Rizvi (2000: 90–5).
297 *Asfār* I: 69. Cf. Rahman in Hourani (1975: 246).
298 Ṣadrā (1964: 6, 9).
299 *Asfār* I: 61, 243, 249, 403, III: 131, 433, IV: 229, VI: 271, VIII: 13.
300 Ṣadrā (1967: 110, 139); *Asfār* I: 66, 245, III: 354, 444, IV: 254, V: 155, VI: 50; Dīnānī (1372 Sh, II: 470–82). This means that their realisation is identical –see Ḥasanzāda in Ṣadrā (1995–, I: 387) *Asfār*.
301 Ṭūsī in Avicenna (1958, III: 462).
302 *Asfār* I: 446.
303 *Asfār* I: 291.
304 *Asfār* II: 289.
305 Hamade (1992: 246).
306 *Asfār* I: 243–4.
307 *Asfār* II: 11; Rahman (1975: 46).
308 *Asfār* III: 348.
309 *Asfār* II: 35.
310 *Asfār* II: 352; Intiẓām (1998: 80). Ḥasanzāda in Ṣadrā (1995–, I: 343) *Asfār*, comments that quiddities are prior in the mind but this does not mean that they are ontologically

prior *per se*. Rather, they are posterior to their concepts in the mode of the 'fact-itself' that is in the mind of God.

311 Khorassani (1976: 110).

312 On Plotinus, see Crystal (1998: 272), quoting Armstrong (1966–88, VII: 90–1) *Enneads* VI.7[38].2.25–7.

313 Ricoeur (1992: 27–8).

314 *Asfār* I: 415; Ṭūsī (1405 Q: 189).

315 This division might also follow a division of identity into *ipse* identity that picks out the ipseity, that is the being of a thing, and *idem* identity that picks out sameness and can pick out same types of things – see Ricoeur (1992: 2–3).

316 *Asfār* II: 289.

317 *Asfār* I: 414; Ṣadrā (1992: 46). His insistence that it is being that is made and emanated directly from the One is in direct criticism of the mainstream Illuminationist position that it is quiddity that emerges from the One and is made by it. See Suhrawardī (1952: 186), *Ḥikmat al-ishrāq*.

318 *Asfār* I: 38–40. Cf I: 48, 54, 60–1, 65, 101–3, 112, 119, 172, 259, 340, 418, III: 87, 122, 257, 324, IV: 270, VI: 81.

319 *Asfār* IX: 185.

320 *Asfār* I: 45, II: 290–1, IX: 185.

321 *Asfār* I: 334–5.

322 Goodman (1992: 66–7).

323 *Asfār* II: 347.

324 Gerson (1994: 29–32) quoting Armstrong (1966–88, V: 33, 117, 141) *Enneads* V.1.6.41–6, V.3.12.39ff, V.4.1.1–5.

5 Reality and the circle of being

1 *Asfār* I: 259–60.

2 Iṣfahānī (1372 Sh: 281).

3 Since a multiplicity of senses does not entail a multiplicity of referents – see *Asfār* III: 352, 356.

4 Ṣadrā (1313 Q*a*: 223).

5 Āshtiyānī (1350 Sh: 17) and (1980: 10).

6 *Asfār* VI: 148.

7 Ṣadrā (1961*b*: 73); *Asfār* I: 47, II: 327.

8 Ṣadrā (1885: 137) *Sarayān*. Cf. Ibn ʻArabī (1996: 422–3).

9 *Asfār* I: 146, 381, VI: 155, 187, 268, 277, 334. On Neoplatonism, see Proclus, *in Parm.*, 1039ff., 1199–201 in Dillon and Morrow (1987: 400ff., 546–7). Cf. Siorvanes (1996: 49).

10 *Asfār* VIII: 81. Cf. Siorvanes (1996: 57).

11 Jambet (2000: 9).

12 This Sadrian position evokes the views of Anaximander and Empedocles – see Ashkiwarī (1999, I: 207–8); Kirk *et al.* (1983: 132, 296); Walbridge (2000: 49–50).

13 Cf. Davidson (1980: 164) on the ontology of events; Levinas (1998: 96).

14 Davidson (1980: 174). I am using the language of Davidson and phenomenology to explain these processes in the Sadrian theory of the process of being. There is no Arabic equivalent for 'vortices' used by our author; but his concept of an existent is close to the phenomenological concept of a vortex.

15 *Asfr* III: 83, 183, VIII: 80–93. This is in sharp contrast to the rigid and stable hierarchy of the Neoplatonic Great Chain of Being. Cf. Lovejoy (1936: 242); Nasr (1996*b*, II: 647).

16 *Asfār* III: 183. Cf. Rahman in Hourani (1975: 233–4).

17 *Asfār* III: 37, 126, 160. Cf. Davidson (1980: 177).

18 Hamid (1998: 265).

19 *Asfār* V: 191, VI: 292, 301.
20 A p-series is an ordered series whose units or monads are held in common and the units are the same as the first member of the series. The classic example is that of a number series – see Lloyd (1990: 76, 84); Vlastos (1981).
21 Tr. O'Meara (1995: 44). Cf. Armstrong (1966–88, V: 141). The theme of the simple unconditioned (*apeiron*) principle that is the source of all in a form of monism is found in Anaximander and may be another source for the Sadrian doctrine filtered through doxographical literature such as the Arabic Aëtius – see Daiber (1980: 96). Cf. Ḥamīd (1995: 819–21); Kirk (1983: 107, 108, 115).
22 Ṣadrā (1996: 63) *Ittiḥād*. However, in Plotinus, the One has all the forms in it indistinctly (*mē diakekrimena*) – Armstrong (1966–88, V: 125), *Enneads* V.3.15.31. Cf. Gerson (1994: 33).
Iṣfahānī (1372 Sh: 173) quotes the eighth *mīmar* of the *Theologia*; Qayṣarī (1416 Q, I: 12–13); cf. Badawī (1948: 32, 68, 134). Cf. Armstrong (1966–88, V: 59), *Enneads* V.2.1.1–5. These texts are quoted in *Asfār* II: 66, VI: 278.
23 Ṣadrā (1996: 93) *Ittiḥād*.
24 *Asfār* VII: 272–3. Cf. *Asfār* VI: 277. Badawī (1948: 134); cf. Armstrong (1966–88, V: 159), *Enneads* V.2.1.
25 *Asfār* VII: 273.
26 Lloyd (1990: 82).
27 *Asfār* II: 368.
28 Ṣadrā (1340 Sh: 5–6) *'Arshiyya*; Morris (1981: 98–9); *Asfār* II: 368, VI: 110.
29 *Asfār* VI: 124; cf. Ṣadrā (1377 Sh: 201). As such, they are also necessary. Cf. Āshtiyānī (1376 Sh: 177).
30 *Asfār* VI: 100. On the simplicity of the One, see Badawī (1948: 134). Cf. Armstrong (1966–88, II: 225, V: 59, VII: 203, 321) *Enneads* II.9.1.3, V.2.1.4, VI.7.37.19, VI.9.5.24. Cf. Gerson (1994: 7).
31 *Asfār* VI: 23–4. On God not having a quiddity, see Avicenna (1960: 489).
32 *Asfār* VI: 101. Cf. Fanārī (1363 Sh: 52).
33 *Asfār* VI: 103. Cf. Āshtiyānī (1376 Sh: 305).
34 *Asfār* VI: 280, VIII: 121. Cf. Qummī (1373–8 Sh, II: 420); Fanārī (1363 Sh: 63); Āshtiyānī (1376 Sh: 192).
35 As noted by Nūrī in his *risāla* on this topic in Āshtiyānī and Corbin (1972–8, III: 546).
36 On negative attributes, see *Asfār* II: 301, VI: 118. Cf. Ḥillī (1988: 292–301).
37 Nūrī in Āshtiyānī and Corbin (1972–8, III: 547).
38 Cf. *Asfār* VI: 111–12.
39 *Asfār* V: 295.
40 Cf. *Asfār* III: 40, VI: 280; Iṣfahānī (1372 Sh: 409).
41 *Asfār* I: 123, VI: 116.
42 *Asfār* VI: 63. Here he says that this doubt is first raised by Suhrawardī in *al-Talwīḥāt* and only taken up later by his commentator Ibn Kammūna.
43 *Asfār* I: 132, 135, VI: 58; Ṣadrā (1964: 47) and (1967: 37). Cf. Intiẓām (1998: 86).
44 *Asfār* VI: 215.
45 Avicenna (1984: 2–3).
46 Goodman (1992: 66–7); Verbeke (1977: 42*–62*).
47 Cf. Davidson in Morewedge (1979: 173). Mason (1997: 51–4) shows how this holds for Spinoza as well. For Leibniz, see Rescher (1991: 18–19, 23–5); cf. Miṣbāḥ (1405 Q: 42) on the Sadrian concept.
48 *Asfār* I: 221.
49 Legenhausen (1995*b*: 162). This process of necessitation is attested by the theory of the 'divine spark' in man beloved of both Near Eastern Hermeticism and late Neoplatonism – see Daiber (1995: 105); Nock and Festugière (1945–54, I: 11) *Corpus Hermeticum* I.11. The best study of theodicy in Mullā Ṣadrā arising from the notion of providence is Kalin (2007).

50 *Asfār* I: 225. Cf. Rahman (1975: 77).
51 *Asfār* VI: 301.
52 Lloyd (1990: 104).
53 *Asfār* I: 224. This also implies a critique of Avicenna (1984: 32) for whom Being of the One does not entail volitional creation but a necessary emanation.
54 *Asfār* II: 251. Badawī (1948: 19).
55 *Asfār* I: 53–4; Dīnānī (1372 Sh, II: 295ff). This principle has a venerable history and was known to be Parmenidean in the Arabic Aëtius – see Daiber (1980: 132).
56 Hintikka in Knuuttila (1981: 4).
57 *Asfār* I: 83.
58 *Asfār* VI: 124.
59 *Asfār* I: 86, 206; Avicenna (1375 Sh, III: 18, 19) on quidditative contingency. Cf. Imām-jum'e-ī (1997: 48); Mason (1997: 59–62) on Spinoza. Bäck (1992: 226–7) sees the distinction in terms of temporal and atemporal contingents.
60 Ṣadrā (1377 Sh: 191).
61 Ṣadrā (1377 Sh: 192); cf. Avicenna (1375 Sh, III: 19–20).
62 Imām-jum'e-ī (1997: 50).
63 *Asfār* I: 87, 412.
64 Sabzawārī (1969: 106); Izutsu (1983: 115). On the use of the term 'sufficient reason' from Leibniz, see Rescher (1991: 21–2).
65 *Asfār* I: 69; Ṣadrā (1982: 23). Cf. 'Aṣṣār (1391 Q: 18).
66 Avicenna (1973: 177–9); *Asfār* I: 46. Existential poverty is a major theme in the Akbarian tradition as well – see Āmulī (1969: 662).
67 He quotes a verse of Shabastarī stating this, and Ḥasanzāda states that this is indeed the Sadrian view – Ṣadrā (1995–, I: 107–8), *Asfār*.
68 *Asfār* I: 46, quoting Avicenna (1992*b*: 41).
69 Armstrong (1966–88, I: 281) *Enneads* I.8.2.2–4. Cf. Gerson (1994: 9).
70 Armstrong (1966–88, V: 125) *Enneads* V.3.15.27–29; Badawī (1948: 177); Gerson (1994: 27).
71 Nābulusī (1995: 29).
72 Cf. Legenhausen (1994*b*: 123).
73 Sabzawārī (1969: 48); Izutsu (1983: 40).
74 *Asfār* II: 307, VII: 243–53. Cf. Khāliqānī (1999: 74).
75 Suhrawardī (1999: 107).
76 Suhrawardī (1945: 435) *Muṭāraḥāt*, and (1952: 154) *Ḥikmat al-ishrāq*. Cf. Badawī (1948: 54); *Asfār* VII: 244–5; Dāmād (1977: 372, 378–80); Khāliqānī (1999: 72).
77 *Asfār* IX: 245.
78 *Asfār* VII: 258.
79 Avicenna (1375 Sh, III: 35).
80 *Asfār* VI: 277.
81 Siorvanes (1996: 106). Cf. *Asfār* V: 347; Ṣadrā (1987, III: 66).
82 Fayḍ Kāshānī (1375 Sh: 14).
83 *Asfār* I: 253. Ṣadrā (1961*b*: 63) and (1992: 58). Cf. Armstrong (1966–88, V: 207) *Enneads* V.6.2.13; Āshtiyānī (1376 Sh: 277).
84 Ṣadrā (1313 Q*b*: 379).
85 *Asfār* VI: 300.
86 Suhrawardī (1945: 293) *Mashāri'* and (1952: 87) *Ḥikmat al-ishrāq*. Cf. Dīnānī (1372 Sh, III: 104–5).
87 Cf. Bonmariage (1998: 83–4).
88 Steel (1978: 108–9). It is important to note that this is a feature of Iamblichean Neoplatonism, since most other Neoplatonists reject it.
89 *Asfār* I: 443; Ṣadrā (1885: 118) *Ittiṣāf*. The Agent is more perfect than its effects following an old Aristotelian rule – see *Asfār* III: 250; Ṣadrā (1964: 44).
90 *Asfār* VI: 86.

91 *Asfār* I: 441, 443, IV: 270, V: 92. Cf. Suhrawardī (1945: 13, 22) *Talwīḥāt* and (1945: 299) *Mashāriʿ*.
92 *Asfār* I: 427; Ṣadrā (1967: 134–6).
93 *Asfār* VI: 21, 390.
94 The Leibnizian Law of Indiscernibles postulates that 'if a is identical to b, whatever is true of a is true of b' – see Russell (1905: 47).
95 *Asfār* II: 313.
96 *Asfār* VIII: 256.
97 *Asfār* IX: 186.
98 *Asfār* IV: 273.
99 *Asfār* IV: 274.
100 *Asfar* II: 96–7.
101 *Asfār* II: 112. He draws on the Akbarian tradition for the doctrine of the renewal of forms (*tajaddud al-amthāl*). See Humā'ī (1997: 14) and Chittick (1998: 57–66).
102 *Asfār* III: 96, 101, IV: 273.
103 Gerson (1994: 99) quoting Armstrong (1966–88, VI: 183) *Enneads* VI.3.2.21–2.
104 Steel (1978: 157–8); Shaw (1995: 98–102). Steel (1978: 55–6) shows how Priscianus uses Theophrastus on this point against his thesis in the commentaries on the *De Anima*.
105 Steel (1978: 62), quoting Priscianus.
106 Steel (1978: 155).
107 Evangeliou (1988: 66), quoting Porphyry's *in Cat.*, 2 b 7–22 in Strange (1992: 84).
108 Avicenna (1960: 276); Bahmanyār (1375 Sh: 529); Ḥillī (1988: 29). Cf. *Asfār* II: 188–9.
109 Avicenna (1960: 57); Bahmanyār (1375 Sh: 304). Cf. Verbeke (1977: 83*).
110 Bahmanyār (1375 Sh: 307–8).
111 Bahmanyār (1375 Sh: 308).
112 *Asfār* IV: 263.
113 *Asfār* III: 229.
114 *Asfār* I: 260.
115 *Asfār* IV: 247–48.
116 *Asfār* IV: 265. They do affirm intensity in substance – see Suhrawardī (1945: 13), *Talwīḥāt*; cf. Ḥasanzāda in Ṣadrā (1995–, I: 696) *Asfār*.
117 *Asfār* IV: 269.
118 *Asfār* IV: 269.
119 Intiẓām (1998: 79).
120 Avicenna (1960: 269).
121 Avicenna (1960: 277).
122 Bahmanyār (1375 Sh: 529–30). Cf. Avicenna (1960: 277–78).
123 Avicenna (1960: 278).
124 Suhrawardī (1999: 120). *Asfār* IV: 265.
125 *Asfār* I: 53. Cf. Ḥasanzāda in Ṣadrā (1995–, I: 88).
126 *Asfār* I: 54.
127 Ḥasanzāda in Ṣadrā (1995–, I: 206ff); Sabzawārī (1969: 106); Izutsu (1983: 115).
128 *Asfār* I: 221.
129 *Asfār* I: 401.
130 *Asfār* II: 187; Ṭūsī (1405 Q: 58).
131 *Asfār* IV: 276.
132 *Asfār* II: 188.
133 *Asfār* IX: 186.
134 Avicenna (1375 Sh, III: 33).
135 Avicenna (1375 Sh, III: 34).
136 Ṣadrā (1996: 306) *Rubūbiyya*.
137 Ṣadrā (1996: 322) *Rubūbiyya*.

138 *Asfār* I: 50.
139 *Asfār* I: 427–31.
140 *Asfār* I: 432–3.
141 *Asfār* I: 433.
142 *Asfār* I: 436, III: 83, 434.
143 *Asfār* VIII: 71–4, 80–93, 257.
144 *Asfār* III: 85, 95.
145 *Asfār* I: 433, 438.
146 *Asfār* I: 437.
147 Vlastos (1981: 65).
148 Vlastos (1981: 73).
149 *Asfār* I: 440–1.
150 *Asfār* II: 189, III: 252.
151 Ṭihrānī (1417 Q: 211).
152 Ṭabāṭabā'ī in Ṭihrānī (1417 Q: 212).
153 Ṭabāṭabā'ī in Ṭihrānī (1417 Q: 213–14).
154 *Asfār* V: 342ff. Cf. III: 131, 402, 500, 502.
155 *Asfār* V: 345–7.
156 Armstrong (1966–88, IV: 407), *Enneads* IV.8.3.14–16. Cf. Shaykh al-Yūnānī translated by Lewis in Plotinus (1951–73, II: 235). It draws upon the Neoplatonic concept of the world-soul. See Gerson (1994: 63), Clark in Gerson (1996: 285); Walbridge (2000: 92).
157 The lithograph has '*dawr*' while the edition has '*dār*' (abode).
158 *Asfār* V: 343.
159 *Asfār* V: 343.
160 *Asfār* V: 79, VI: 117. Miṣbāḥ (1405 Q: 43–4) denies any modulation in the vertical hierarchy of being.
161 *Asfār* V: 349. Cf. Ṭihrānī (1417 Q: 210).
162 *Asfār* I: 263.
163 *Asfār* V: 343.
164 *Asfār* IX: 175.
165 Chittick (1989: 392).
166 Chittick (1989: 88) quoting Ibn ʿArabī (n.d., II: 56); Murata (1992: 221); Qummī (1373–8 Sh, I: 442).
167 Qayṣarī (1416 Q, I: 513); Fanārī (1363 Sh: 283); Iṣfahānī (1976: 169); *Asfār* I: 261, III: 146. Cf. Hamid (1998: 148).
168 This is disputed by Dāmād (1998: 246) for whom this togetherness occurs at the ontological level of *dahr*, of that temporal stage that is beyond the sublunary world and below the pure level of the Divine essence in itself.
169 Murata (1992: 70).
170 Izutsu in Nasr (1977*c*: 130–2) on ʿAyn al-Quḍāt Hamadānī [d. 1132]. Cf. Gerson (1994: 46) quoting Armstrong (1966–88, VII: 303), *Enneads* VI.9.1ff.
171 Ibn ʿArabī (n.d., II: 94, 153, 404, III: 484, IV: 120).
172 Ibn ʿArabī (n.d., II: 486, III: 153, 177, IV: 97). Or *dhikr* – see Qummī (1373–8 Sh, III: 86).
173 *Asfār* V: 151. On the principle, see *Asfār* I: 440, III: 257. Cf. Lloyd (1976). This

from Him; they are not He because it is in abiding by himself that he gives them'.

179 Ibn ʿArabī (n.d., I: 90, 183); Iṣfahānī (1976: 40).
180 Ibn ʿArabī (n.d., II: 119).
181 Chittick (1998: 37).
182 Ṣadrā (1987, III: 303).
183 Chittick (1998: 21) quoting Ibn ʿArabī (n.d., IV: 424).
184 *Asfār* VI: 374. Cf. Qummī (1373–8 Sh, I: 616).
185 *Asfār* III: 400. On the theme of the omnipresence of the One, see Armstrong (1966–88, III: 391, V: 180–3) *Enneads* III.8.9.25, V.5.8.24, V.5.9.18–19.
186 *Asfār* II: 372. Cf. Qummī (1373–8 Sh, I: 195–9).
187 Ṣadrā (1987, VI: 171). An important consequence of this is that the conventional philosophical view of the eternity of the world with the eternity of its principle cannot hold.
188 Āshtiyānī (1376 Sh: 180ff).
189 Nasafī (1998: 104, 106). Cf. Landolt (1996: 189–90).
190 Ṣadrā (1982: 46). Cf. Qummī (1373–8 Sh, I: 14, 221, 445); Ibn ʿArabī (n.d., III: 116).
191 ʿAṣṣār (1391 Q: 14) argues that this position is concomitant with modulation.
192 *Asfār* I: 117.
193 Ibn ʿArabī (n.d., II: 56, 383).
194 *Asfār* V: 27, VIII: 73. Cf. Ṣadrā (1982: 46).
195 Corbin (1962*a*: 63).
196 Imām ʿAlī (1967: 40, 273 for different version). Cf. Qummī (1373–8 Sh, II: 420, III: 510, 513).
197 Baḥrānī (1958, I: 128).
198 On his monism that is quite independent of the Akbarian tradition, see Oraibi (1992: 177). On the causality point, see *Asfār* I: 219.
199 *Asfār* III: 257–8.
200 *Asfār* III: 268–71 and Ṣadrā (1885: 138) *Sarayān*. Cf. Qummī (1373–8 Sh, II: 502).
201 Ṣadrā (1984*b*: 322).
202 *Asfār* IX: 141.
203 *Asfār* I: 261.
204 Sabzawārī (1969: 114); Izutsu (1983: 126).
205 Ṣadrā (1313 Q*a*: 375) and (1976: 32).
206 *Asfār* VII: 274.
207 Gerson (1994: 18) quoting Armstrong (1966–88, VI: 283) *Enneads* VI.4.3.18. Cf. Lewis in Plotinus (1951–73, II: 352–3) and Hadot (1997: 39). It is also Hermetic – see Festugière (1983, IV: 65), quoting Nock and Festugière (1945–54, I: 65) *Corpus Hermeticum* V.11.
208 Monism has good Near Eastern credentials and can be noticed in the *Corpus Hermeticum* 12.23 in Nock and Festugière (1945–54, I: 183). 'He is All and the All pervades and encompasses everything'.
209 Khorassani (1976: 126–8).
210 Ibn ʿArabī (1997: 154). See also these three modes in the Hallajian concept of God as reality (*al-ḥaqq*), essence (*ḥaqīqa*) and realisation (*taḥaqquq*) in Massignon (1975, II: 85–6).
211 Āmulī (1969: 351, 361).
212 Āshtiyānī (1370 Sh: 39, 138, 187, 194, 262). Qaysarī (1375 Sh: 15, 19). Fanārī (1363

Ashtiyānī (1972–8, I: 73–6); Corbin (1981*b*: 66–9); Hamade (1992: 264).

217 Zunūzī (1378 Sh, I: 242).
218 Lāhījī (n.d.: 40). Pure being (*wujūd muṭlaq*) for Ṭūsī is not God but rather that conceptual source of being that encompasses everything and is metaphilosophically speaking identical to 'deployable being' – see Avicenna (1375 Sh, III: 36). The debate on this term reveals the tension between monists who deny a distinction between *hyparxis* and *ousia* and pluralists or Peripatetics who affirm it – see Festugière (1983, IV: 6), quoting Nock and Festugière (1945–54, I: 113–14) *Corpus Hermeticum* X.2; Hadot (1999: 82–4).
219 Ṣadrā (1982: 5–6).
220 *Asfār* II: 327.
221 *Asfār* I: 299. Cf. Zunūzī (1378 Sh, I: 244). Aḥsā'ī modifies this by placing both negatively conditioned and conditioned being in limited being since they are both outcomes of divine acts – see Hamid (1998: 97).
222 Ṣadrā (1982: 6).
223 Zunūzī (1378 Sh, I: 243).
224 Āshtiyānī (1376 Sh: 211ff).
225 Qayṣarī (1375 Sh: 157).
226 Attas (1995: 290).
227 Ṣadrā (1982: 6–7). Cf. Āmulī (1969: 635); Āshtiyānī (1370 Sh: 153).
228 *Asfār* II: 342; Rahman (1975: 82–3).
229 Qāshānī (1987: 74). Cf. Qayṣarī (1375 Sh: 47).
230 *Asfār* I: 71. Cf. Mu'ayyadī (1996: 70).
231 Ṣadrā (1982: 15). Cf. Mu'ayyadī (1996: 72).
231 *Asfār* II: 342.
233 *Asfār* II: 291.
234 *Asfār* IV: 227.
235 Qayṣarī (1416 Q, I: 51).
236 *Asfār* I: 25.
237 *Asfār* II: 292, VI: 368.
238 Walbridge (1992: 193). Cf. Knysh (1999: 153–7) on an earlier *kalām* refutation with similar themes. On parallels in Anaximander, see Ḥamīd (1995: 823, 825, 828); Kirk (1983: 115).
239 Rahman (1975: 14–15, 266); Ḥusayn (1998: 28).
240 *Asfār* I: 53, 71, 433, II: 291, 300, 305, 318, 335, 339, VI: 18, 24.
241 Ṣadrā (1961*b*: 70–2).
242 Ṣadrā (1961*b*: 65). Cf. Gersh in Wallis (1995: 134–5), referring to *Asclepius* 33.344.22–3; Festugière (1983, II: 59), quoting Nock and Festugière (1945–54, I: 182–3) *Corpus Hermeticum* XII.20–2.
243 Āmulī in Iṣfahānī (1372 Sh: 48) quoting *Asfār* I: 330.
244 *Asfār* I: 261–2.
245 Ṣadrā (1313 Q*a*: 305).
246 *Asfār* I: 71.
247 Sabzawārī (1969: 54); Izutsu (1983: 48). Cf. Āshtiyānī (1376 Sh: 195–7); Qazvīnī (1376 Sh: 128–9).
248 *Asfār* I: 71–3. Cf. Sabzawārī (1969: 56); Izutsu (1983: 51).
249 'Aṣṣār (1391 Q: 9).
250 Sabzawārī in *Asfār* I: 72. Beings are modes of being and not portions or parts of a whole – *Asfār* VIII: 369, IX: 186.
251 *Asfār* I: 73.
252 *Asfār* I: 72.
253 *Asfār* I: 74.
254 *Asfār* I: 73.
255 *Asfār* I: 74. The quotations are from Sabzawārī's *scholia* on the *Asfār*.
256 *Asfār* I: 71.

257 Sabzawārī (1969: 55); Izutsu (1983: 50).
258 *Asfār* I: 71. Sabzawārī tries to reconcile these four views as merely four levels of unity, each of which in itself is not incorrect. Cf. Ṣadrā (1313 *Qa*: 298–9).
259 *Asfār* II: 333–34 quoting the Persian poets on this. Cf. Jāmī (1979: 35–36); Iṣfahānī (1372 Sh: 461); Qazvīnī (1376 Sh: 127); Dīnānī (1366 Sh: 286).
260 Qayṣarī (1375 Sh: 37).
261 Nābulusī (1995: 11).
262 Āmulī (1969: 51). Cf. Chittick (1998: 173).
263 *Asfār* II: 305, 310, 327, V: 232.
264 *Asfār* VI: 143, 144.
265 Iṣfahānī (1372 Sh: 213).
266 Corbin (1976*b*: 83–4).
267 *Asfār* VI: 146; Ṣadrā (1987, II: 324, IV: 55).
268 Āshtiyānī's comment in Qayṣarī (1375 Sh: 31, 172).
269 Nasr (1972*b*: 159) argues this.
270 *Asfār* I: 71.
271 *Asfār* I: 73–4, II: 292, VI: 86; Ṣadrā (1313 *Qa*: 277); cf. Sabzawārī (1969: 56–7).
272 *Asfār* I: 65.
273 This is a central problematic of modulation as noticed by Rahman (1975: 37–41) and Bonmariage (1998: 174).
274 Rahman in Hourani (1975: 250–1).
275 *Asfār* I: 206, II: 138, 319.
276 *Asfār* I: 220, II: 223.
277 *Asfār* I: 65, 406, IX: 159.
278 *Asfār* VI: 374. Cf. Bonmariage (1998: 177).
279 Iqbal (1908: 175).
280 Chittick (1998: 29–31).
281 Ṣadrā (1987, VII: 144).
282 Ṣadrā (1987, VII: 144–5).
283 Avicenna (1375 Sh, III: 18–22); Mayer (2000) is the best analysis of the argument.
284 Avicenna (1375 Sh, III: 66–7).
285 *Asfār* VI: 13.
286 Ṣadrā (1987, VI: 229) *Tafsīr*. I am grateful to Janis Esots for alerting me to this reference.
287 Avicenna (1375 Sh, III: 66–7).
288 Ṣadrā (1885: 139), *Sarayān* and (1964: 68). The name of the proof comes from Avicenna (1375 Sh, III: 67). Cf. Iṣfahānī (1372 Sh: 739–40).
289 *Asfār* VI: 14–16; Ṣadrā (1964: 69) and (1967: 35–6).
290 *Asfār* VI: 16.
291 Iṣfahānī (1372 Sh: 742).
292 Iṣfahānī (1372 Sh: 276, 743). Cf. *Asfār* II: 336. The Sadrian proof draws upon the Akbarian tradition – see A'vānī (1374 Sh: 155).
293 Iṣfahānī (1372 Sh: 191). This shows the success of the Illuminationist agenda in philosophy before the Safavid period.
294 *Asfār* VI: 284.
295 *Asfār* VI: 17; Suhrawardī (1999: 87–9). Sabzawārī considers the Sadrian proof to be more comprehensive and better than the Illuminationist proof because it considers everything both in the vertical and horizontal hierarchy to be an intensity of being from the One, while in the Illuminationist account bodies and other base beings in the horizontal hierarchy of light are not lights at all.
296 *Asfār* VI: 23–4.
297 *Asfār* VI: 14–26.
298 Avicenna (1375 Sh, III: 146), (1992*a*, II: 89), (1984: 22, 33).
299 Aristotle (1984, II: 1694–5) *Metaphysics* 1072 b 10–14); cf. Averroes (1938–52, III:

1608–9). Davidson (1987: 289). It is also suggested by *kalām* arguments about the being that cannot not be – see Baḥrānī (1406 Q: 34).

300 Avicenna (1960: 6); cf. Davidson (1987: 299).

301 Davidson in Morewedge (1979: 169).

302 Davidson (1987: 336). This follows Aristotle (1984, II: 1570), *Metaphysics* 994 a 1–19; cf. Averroes (1938–52, I: 16–19). Arguably the proof can work in an unconditioned mode without the presumption of the impossibility of infinite regress – see Davidson (1987: 308).

303 *Asfār* I: 83.

304 Avicenna (1984: 22).

305 Legenhausen (1994*a*: 217).

306 Legenhausen (1994*a*: 210).

307 *Asfār* VI: 29, n. 1 and 14–15, n. 3.

308 Cf. Oppy (1995: 186).

309 Ṣadrā (1885: 133) *Sarayān*. Rahman (1975: 77). Aḥsā'ī actually goes as far as stating that contingents are correlational accidents – see Hamid (1998: 258).

310 Dāmād (1998: 234).

311 Bahmanyār (1375 Sh: 362).

312 Ṣadrā (1992: 55) and (1987, I: 49).

313 *Asfār* I: 96. His quiddity, in the sense of 'that by which something is', is His specific being, His very ipseity.

314 *Asfār* I: 397. Cf. Sabzawārī (1969: 88); Izutsu (1983: 94).

315 Ṣadrā (1377 Sh: 179).

316 Ṣadrā (1984*b*: 265–6).

317 *Asfār* II: 328.

318 *Asfār* II: 312–13, 314, 329–31. Ṣadrā (1967: 70) and (1964: 41). Cf. De Smet (1999: 476–7).

319 Ibn ʿArabī (1919: 53) *ʿUqlat* and (n.d., III: 443–4).

320 Proclus (1963: 68, 72). Cf. Walbridge (2000: 49).

321 Cf. Qummī (1373–8 Sh, I: 522, II: 132, 602). This is because the Muḥammadan reality is that through which divine mercy flows – see Jilveh in Qayṣarī (1375 Sh: 213).

322 *Asfār* VII: 32. Ṣadrā (1984*b*: 21). For the *khabar* of the Imam *'anā-l-nuqṭa taḥt al-bā'*, see Majlisī (1392 Q, 40: 165). There is a further saying attributed to the Prophet that all existents are manifested by this point – see Ibn ʿArabī (n.d., I: 102); Āmulī (1374 Sh: 210–11). These sayings can be related to the previous discussion on *maʿiyya* since it is also reported that the Prophet said, 'I did not see anything without seeing the point of the *bā'* written upon it' – see Ibn ʿArabī (n.d., I: 102); Āmulī (1374 Sh: 211).

323 *Asfār* VII: 33.

324 *Asfār* VII: 33. Ṣadrā (1984*b*: 22).

325 *Asfār* VII: 34.

326 *Asfār* VI: 296, quoting the famous verse of Imam ʿAlī.
Wa-nta l-kitābu l-mubīnu lladhī, bi-aḥrufihi yaẓharu l-muḍmar
a-tazʿamu nnaka jirmun ṣaghīr, wa fīka nṭawā l-ʿālamu l-akbar
See Imam ʿAlī (n.d., 45). On the microcosm theme, see Murata (1992: 45–6).

327 Ṣadrā (1984*b*: 23).

(1373–8 Sh, II: 336, 340). On deployable being as the logos, see Ashtiyānī (1370

Sh: 161). On the Hermetic roots, see Festugière (1983, II: 55), quoting Nock and Festugière (1945–54, I: 61–3) *Corpus Hermeticum* V.3–8.
330 Ṣadrā (1988, II: 394). Cf. Corbin (1962*a*: 58).
331 Bursī (1978: 23).
332 Amir-Moezzi (1994: 24).
333 Rahman (1975: 88). Certainly the Akbarian tradition regards quiddities as forms of attributes – see Āshtiyānī (1370 Sh: 158).
334 *Asfār* II: 250.
335 Following the famous sermon of Imam ʿAlī (1967: 212), true unity involves negating the attributes – *Asfār* VI: 135, 145. Cf. Āmulī (1969: 638); Sabzawārī (1969: 114); Izutsu (1983: 126).
336 *Asfār* VI: 140. Ṣadrā (1982: 6) on Akbarian authority for this.
337 *Asfār* VI: 125. Rahman (1975: 142).
338 Ṣadrā (1967: 256, 712).
339 For some comparative references, see Amir-Moezzi (1996: 193–4).
340 Āshtiyānī (1370 Sh: 219); *Asfār* VIII: 140.
341 Ṣadrā (1967: 355).
342 The discussion of the ontological and cosmological role of *wilāya* is interspersed throughout Ṣadrā's commentary on *kitāb al-ḥujja* of *Uṣūl al-Kāfī* – see Ṣadrā (1988, II: 388–95) for a representative sample.
343 Bursī (1978: 158).
344 This is not to say that he quotes him directly. Rather, the intellectual tradition of Shiʿi mystical and philosophical thought and its meditation upon the concept of *wilāya* permeates its thought and finds an appropriate precursor in the thought of Bursī.
345 Bursī (1978: 30–1). Cf. Ṣadrā (1988, II: 417ff).
346 Corbin (1962*a*: 51).
347 *Asfār* II: 315, IX: 175. Cf. Ṣadrā (1988, II: 508ff).
348 Morris (1981: 84); *Asfār* I: 25–6.
349 *EII* I: 173. Corbin (1962*b*: 158) notes that Shiʿi philosophy such as Ṣadrā's is inherently eschatological.

Conclusion

1 Shields (1999: 266–7).
2 *Asfār* V: 349.
3 *Asfār* IX: 186.
4 Nasr (2006: 245–6). For an excellent study and collection of his treatises and glosses, see Jilveh (1385 Sh); for the latter thinker, see Ḥāʾirī Māzandarānī (1956).
5 Nasr (1996*a*: 304–19) and (2006: 242–4); Iṣfahānī (1976).
6 Nasr (2006: 235–42); Dabashi (1993: 273–323); Javādī Āmulī (1996–2002).
7 For basic introductions to this intellectual tendency, see Muʿīnī (n.d.), Ḥakīmī (1373 Sh), Raḥīmiyān-i Firdūsī (1383 Sh).
8 Aḥsāʾī (1993: 45, 51). For a general account of Aḥsāʾī's critical engagement with Ṣadrā, see Bayat (1982: 37–58).

17 Miyānjī (1415 Q: 211–20).

18 This is true of the classic Avicennan ontological proof for the existence of God – see Legenhausen (1994*a*: 209).
19 *Asfār* II: 329.
20 *Asfār* I: 37.
21 *Asfār* I: 49.
22 *Asfār* I: 412–13.
23 Walbridge (2000: 68) makes it clear that such an emphasis is a sign of Pythagoreanising Neoplatonism such as that of Iamblichus.
24 *Asfār* I: 260. Cf. Sabzawārī (1969: 4); Izutsu (1983: 31).

Glossary of philosophical terms

Analytic proposition in Kantian philosophy, this refers to a proposition in which the predicate concept is subsumed in the subject concept, e.g. 'God exists'

Apophasis a process of reasoning by denial; used in theology to describe God in a negative manner through attributes that are not true of him

Aporetic a method of teaching through posing seemingly insoluble problems

Aporia a philosophical puzzle or impasse

Assertoric proof (*burhān innī*) an inference from effect to cause

Copula a connecting word that links the subject and the predicate; usually used for the verb 'to be' in propositions

Demonstrative proof (*burhān limmī*) an inference from cause to effect

Divinalia issues in theology or God-talk

Elenctic/Socratic method a philosophical inquiry that attempts to arrive at understanding through forcing the student to question his beliefs and positions

Existential analytic Heideggerian concept that all experience is grounded in existence in this world and 'care' for other things, in opposition to Husserl's contention that all experience is intentional

Future contingency modal possibility in the future relating to things that do not exist in extra-mental reality at the present time

Hyparxis process, existence

Inexistence a mediaeval scholastic term used by Brentano to express existence of objects in the mind only (and not in extra-mental reality)

Intelligibilia objects that can only be perceived through the intellect, and which exist in the higher ontological realm of the nous

Intension property connoted by a term, its meaning

Kataphasis a process of reasoning by affirmation (opposite of apophasis); used in theology to describe God through attributes that can be predicated of him

Meinong object an mental object that has no existence in extra-mental reality, but can be predicated

Metempsychosis transmigration of souls between bodies

Modulation variation by degrees of intensity within a singular scale as in music

Name of second imposition a term that only signifies ambiguous arbitrary signs

Ontological commitment the articulation of a proposition in which the existence of a thing is presupposed or implied

P-series term used for a type of harmonic series in mathematics whose units or monads are held in common and these units are the same as the first member of the series

Principle of plenitude in Platonic philosophy the contention that in a perfect cosmos, possibilities must be as full as possible; in effect, everything that is possible and can happen, will become necessary and will happen

Privation absence of existence

Processist a process metaphysician who privileges processes and events over substances as the basic foundational units of existence

Processual pertaining to process metaphysics

***Pros hen* homonymy** systematic ambiguity of terms in which various instances are related to a focal meaning

Quiddity whatness, essence of a thing, the bundle of properties that define a thing

Seinsfrage articulated by Heidegger; the formal question of being and discerning its structure based on rejecting previous philosophy's neglect of the question (due to the assumption that being is a given and beyond definition)

Sensibilia objects that can be grasped by sense perception

Summum genera the ultimate *genus* (in the technical sense used in the predicables of Porphyry) or class of thing

Synonymy different terms used with the same meaning; terms possessing the same 'intensional' content

Synthetic proposition a proposition in which the predicate concept adds meaning to the subject concept; upholders of the ontological argument held that 'God exists' is a synthetic proposition but Kant denied it

Tertium quid a third way of asking 'how' a term denotes, between synonymy and homonymy

Theosis (*ta'alluh*) becoming divine, god-like; assimilation to divine virtues

Bibliography

Mullā Ṣadrā's works

Mullā Ṣadrā, Ṣadr al-Dīn Shīrāzī (1865) *al-Ḥikma al-muta'āliya fī-l-asfār al-'aqliyya al-arba'a*, copied by Muḥammad Ṣādiq Gulpāyiganī, ed. 'Alī Dāmghānī, Tehran lithograph.

—— (1865, repr. 1971) *Sharḥ uṣūl al-Kāfī* with *Mafātīḥ al-ghayb* in margins, Tehran lithograph.

—— (1885) *Rasā'il*, Tehran lithograph. Includes

: *Fī ḥudūth al-'ālam* (2–109).

: *Fī ittiṣāf al-māhiyya bi-l-wujūd* (110–19).

: *Fī-l-tashakhkhuṣ* (120–32).

: *Fī sarayān wujūd al-ḥaqq (or Ṭarḥ al-kawnayn)* (132–48).

: *Fī-l-qaḍā' wa-l-qadar* (148–237).

: *Fī-l-wāridāt al-qalbiyya fī ma'rifat al-rubūbiyya* (238–77).

: *Iksīr al-'ārifīn fī ma'rifat ṭarīq al-ḥaqq wa-l-yaqīn* (278–340); tr. W. Chittick (2004) *The Elixir of the Gnostics*, Provo, UH: Brigham Young University Press.

: *Fī-l-Ḥashr* (341–71).

—— (1303 Q) *Ta'līqa 'alá-l-ilāhiyyāt min kitāb al-Shifā'* of Avicenna [d. 1037], Tehran: Dār al-Funūn lithograph.

—— (1313 Q*a*) *Sharḥ al-hidāya* of Athīr al-Dīn Abharī [d. 1264], copied 'Abd al-Karīm Shīrāzī, ed. Aḥmad Shīrāzī, Tehran lithograph, facsimile repr. Qum: Intishārāt-i Bīdār.

—— (1313 Q*b*) *Ta'līqa 'alá Sharḥ Ḥikmat al-Ishrāq* of Quṭb al-Dīn Shīrāzī [d. 1311], copied by Muḥammad b. Mīrzā 'Abd al-'Alī Darjazīnī, ed. Asad Allāh Hirātī under the direction of Sayyid Ibrāhīm Ṭabāṭabā'ī, Tehran lithograph.

—— (1340 Sh) *al-Ḥikma al-'Arshiyya*, ed./tr. Ghulām Āhanī, Isfahan: Isfahan University Press; tr. J.W. Morris (1981) as *The Wisdom of the Throne*, Princeton: Princeton University Press.

—— (1961*a*) *Kasr aṣnām al-jāhiliyya fī dhamm al-mutaṣawwifīn*, ed. M.T. Dānishpazhūh, Tehran: Tehran University Press.

—— (1961*b*, 1377 Sh) *al-Maẓāhir al-ilāhiyya fī asrār al-'ulūm al-kamāliyya*, ed. Sayyid Jalāl al-Dīn Āshtiyānī, Mashhad: Mashhad University Press, repr. Qum: Markaz-i intishārāt-i daftar-i tablīghāt-i islāmī.

—— (1961*c*) *Risāla-yi Sih aṣl*, ed. Sayyid Ḥ. Naṣr, Tehran: University Faculty of Theology.

—— (1964) *Kitāb al-Mashā'ir: Le livre des pénétrations métaphysiques*, ed./tr. H. Corbin with the Persian translation of Mīrzā 'Imād al-Dawla, Tehran: Institut Français d'Iranologie de Téhéran.

—— (1967) *al-Shawāhid al-rubūbiyya fī manāhij al-sulūkiyya*, ed. S.J. Āshtiyānī with *marginalia* of Sabzawārī, Mashhad: Mashhad University Press.

—— (1976) *al-Mabda' wa-l-ma'ād*, ed. S.J. Āshtiyānī with *marginalia* of Sabzawārī, Tehran: Imperial Iranian Academy of Philosophy.

—— (1979) *al-Wāridāt al-qalbiyya fī ma'rifat al-rubūbiyya,* ed. A. Shafī'īhā, Tehran: Anjuman-i falsafa-yi Īrān.

—— (1980) *Fī-l-taṣawwur wa-l-taṣdīq*, tr. M. Ḥā'irī as *Āgāhī va gavāhī*, Tehran: Anjuman-i Ḥikmat.

—— (1981) *al-Ḥikma al-muta'āliya fī-l-asfār al-'aqliyya al-arba'a*, eds R. Luṭfī, I. Amīnī, and F. Ummīd, 3rd edn, Beirut: Dār iḥyā' al-turāth al-'arabī.

—— (1982) *Īqāẓ al-nā'imīn*, ed. M. Mu'ayyadī, Tehran: Mu'assasa-yi muṭāla'āt va taḥqīqāt-i farhangī.

—— (1362 Sh) *Rasā'il-i falsafī*, ed. S.J. Āshtiyānī, Qum: Markaz-i intishārāt-i daftar-i tablīghāt-i Islāmī. Includes

: *al-Masā'il al-qudsiyya fī-l-ḥikma al-muta'āliya (or Al-qawā'id al-malakūtiyya)* (3–72).

: *Mutashābihāt al-Qur'ān* (75–121).

: *Ajwibat al-masā'il aw jawāb masā'il ba'ḍ al-khillān* (125–98).

—— (1363 Sh) *Tafsīr Sūrat al-Wāqi'a*, ed. M. Khājavī, Tehran: Intishārāt-i Mawlá.

—— (1984*a*) *Asrār al-ayāt wa-anwār al-bayyināt*, ed. M. Khājavī with *marginalia* of 'Alī Nūrī, Tehran: Mu'assasa-yi muṭāla'āt va taḥqīqāt-i farhangī.

—— (1984*b*) *Mafātīḥ al-ghayb*, ed. M. Khājavī with the *scholia* of 'Alī Nūrī, Tehran: Mu'assasa-yi muṭāla'āt va taḥqīqāt-i farhangī.

—— (1366 Sh) *Risāla fī-l-ḥashr,* ed./tr. M. Khājavī, Tehran: Intishārāt-i Mawlá.

—— (1987) *Tafsīr al-Qur'ān al-Karīm*, ed. M. Khājavī 7 vols, Qum: Intishārāt-i Bīdār; partial translation by Latimah-Parvin Peerwani (2004) *On the Hermeneutics of the Light Verse of the Qur'an* (*Tafsīr āyat al-nūr*), London: ICAS Press.

—— (1988) *Sharḥ Uṣūl al-Kāfī*, ed. M. Khājavī, 3 vols, Tehran: Mu'assasa-yi muṭāla'āt va taḥqīqāt-i farhangī.

—— (1992) *Kitāb al-Mashā'ir: The Metaphysics of Mulla Sadra*, tr. P. Morewedge, New York: SSIPS.

—— (1995–) *al-Ḥikma al-muta'āliya fī-l-asfār al-'aqliyya al-arba'a,* edited with *scholia* of Ḥasanzāda Āmulī, 2 vols, Tehran: Wizārat al-thaqāfa wa-l-irshād al-Islāmī.

—— (1996) *Majmū'a-yi Rasā'il-i falsafī-yi Ṣadr al-muta'allihīn*, ed. Ḥ.N. Iṣfahānī, Tehran: Intishārāt-i Ḥikmat. Includes

: *Fī ittiḥād al-'āqil wa-l-ma'qūl* (63–103).

: *Ajwibat masā'il Mullā Shamsā Gīlānī [d. 1670]* (107–21).

: *Ajwibat masā'il Mullā Muẓaffar Ḥusayn Kāshānī* (125–60).

: *Ajwibat masā'il al-Naṣīriyya* (163–77).

: *Aṣālat ja'l al-wujūd* (181–91).

: *Al-tanqīḥ fī-l-manṭiq* (195–236).

: *Al-khulsa* (265–66).

: *Al-Shawāhid al-rubūbiyya* (283–341).

: *al-Fawā'id* (345–61).

: *Ḥal shubhat al-jadhr al-aṣamm* (467–78).

: *Al-wujūd* (453–63).

—— and Quṭb al-Dīn Taḥtānī Rāzī (1416 Q) *Risālatān fī-l-taṣawwur wa-l-taṣdīq*, ed. Mahdī Sharī'atī, Qum: Mu'assasa-yi Ismā'īliyān; tr. Joep Lameer (2006) *Conception and Belief in Ṣadr al-Dīn Shīrāzī*, Tehran: Iranian Institute of Philosophy.

—— (1376 Sh) *Risāla-yi Sih aṣl*, ed. M. Khājavī, Tehran: Intishārāt-i Mawlá.

—— (1377 Sh) *Risāla fī ḥudūth al-ʿālam*, ed./tr. M. Khājavī, Tehran: Intishārāt-i Mawlá.
—— (1378 Sh*a*) *al-Tanqīḥ fī-l-manṭiq*, ed. G.-R. Yāsīpūr, Tehran: SIPRIn.
—— (1378 Sh*b*) *Risālat al-ḥudūth*, ed. S.Ḥ. Mūsavīyān, Tehran: SIPRIn.
—— (1999) *al-Maẓāhir al-ilāhiyya fī asrār al-ʿulūm al-kamāliyya*, ed. S.M. Khāmanihī, Tehran: SIPRIn.
—— (1380–3 Sh) *al-Ḥikma al-mutaʿāliya fī-l-asfār al-ʿaqliyya al-arbaʿa maʿ taʿlīqāt Mullā Hādī Sabzawārī*, eds G. Aʿvānī, N. Ḥabībī, M. Muḥammadī, R. Akbariyān, ʿA. Rashād, A. Ahmadī and R. Muḥmmadzāda, Tehran: SIPRIn.
—— (1381 Sh) *al-Mabdaʾ wa-l-maʿād*, eds M. Dhabīḥī and J. Shāh-Naẓarī, 2 vols, Tehran: SIPRIn.
—— (1382 Sh*a*) *al-Shawāhid al-rubūbiyya fī manāhij al-sulūkiyya*, ed. Sayyid Muṣṭafā Muḥaqqiq-Dāmād, Tehran: SIPRIn.
—— (1382 Sh*b*) *Taʿlīqāt ʿalá-l-ilāhiyyāt min Kitāb al-Shifāʾ*, ed. N. Ḥabībī, 2 vols, Tehran: SIPRIn.

Primary sources

Aḥsāʾī, Shaykh Aḥmad (1856) *Sharḥ al-Fawāʾid*, Tehran lithograph.
—— (1993) *Rasāʾil al-ḥikma*, Beirut: al-Dār al-ʿālamiyya.
—— (1999) *Sharḥ al-ziyāra al-jāmiʿa*, 4 vols, Beirut: Dār al-Mufīd.
—— (2006) *Sharḥ al-ʿarshiyya*, ed. Ṣāliḥ b. Aḥmad al-Diyāb, 3 vols, Beirut: Muʾassasat al-balāgh.
Alcinous (1993) *Didaskalikos or The Handbook of Platonism*, tr. J. Dillon, Oxford: Clarendon Press.
Alexander of Aphrodisias (1891) *In Aristotelis metaphysica commentaria*, ed. M. Hayduck, Berlin: Reimer; trs W. Dooley and A. Madigan (1989–93) *Metaphysics 1–5*, London: Duckworth.
Āmidī, ʿAbd al-Wahid (1960) *Ghurar al-ḥikam wa-durar al-kalim*, Najaf: al-Maṭbaʿa al-Ḥaydariyya.
Āmulī, Ḥaydar (1969) *Jāmiʿ al-asrār wa-manbaʿ al-anwār* and *Risālat naqd al-nuqūd fī maʿrifat al-wujūd* in *La Philosophie Shīʿite*, eds H. Corbin and O. Yahia, Tehran: L'Institut Franco-Iranien.
—— (1367 Sh) *al-Muqaddimāt min Kitāb Naṣṣ al-Nuṣūṣ fī Sharḥ Fuṣūṣ al-Ḥikam*, eds H. Corbin and O. Yahia, repr. Tehran: L'Institut Franco-Iranien.
—— (1374–80 Sh) *Tafsīr al-Muḥīṭ al-Aʿẓam wa-l-baḥr al-khiḍam*, ed. S.M. Mūsawī Tabrīzī, 4 vols, Tehran: Vizārat-i farhang va irshād-i Islāmī.
Anawati, G. (tr.) *al-Shifāʾ: ilāhiyyāt*, (1978), 2 vols (Paris, Librairie Vrin).
Aristotle (1984) *The Complete Works of Aristotle. The Revised Oxford Translation*, 2 vols, gen. ed. J. Barnes, Princeton: Princeton University Press.
—— (1998) *The Metaphysics*, tr. H. Tancred-Lawson, London: Penguin.
Armstrong, A.H. (tr.) (1966–88) *Plotinus: Enneads*, 7 vols, Cambridge, MA: Harvard University Press.
Asadābādī, Qāḍī ʿAbd al-Jabbār (1960–) *al-Mughnī fī abwāb al-ʿadl wa-l-tawḥīd*, ed. I. Madkūr, A. Zāyid, G. Anawātī, M.M. al-Ḥilmī, A. al-Ghunaymī, A.F. al-Ahwānī, M.M. al-Khuḍayrī, M.A. al-Najjār and M. al-Saqqa, 16 vols, Cairo: al-Hayʾa al-ʿāmma al-Miṣriyya li-l-Kitāb.
Ashkiwarī, Quṭb al-Dīn (1999–2003) *Maḥbūb al-qulūb*, 2 vols, eds I. Dībājī and Ḥ. Ṣidqī, Tehran: Āyīna-yi Mīrāth.
Āshtiyānī, S.J. (ed.) (1376 Sh) *Rasāʾil-i Ḥakīm-i Sabzavārī*, repr. Tehran: Intishārat-i Usva.

Austin, R.J. (tr.) (1981) *The Bezels of Wisdom*, New York: Paulist Press.
Averroes, *see* Ibn Rushd
Avicenna, *see* Ibn Sīnā
Badawī, ʻA.-R. (ed.) (1948–9) *Manṭiq Arisṭū*, 2 vols, Cairo: Maṭbaʻat Dār al-Kutub al-Miṣriyya.
—— (1948, 1413 Q) (ed.) *Ūthūlujiyā: Aflūṭīn ʻind al-ʻArab [Theologia Aristotelis]*, Cairo: L'Institut Français, repr. Qum: Intishārāt-i Bīdār.
—— (ed.) (1954) *Arisṭūṭālīs: Fī-l-nafs*, Cairo: Maktabat al-nahḍa al-miṣriyya.
Baghdādī, Abū-l-Barakāt (1415 Q) *al-Kitāb al-Muʻtabar fī-l-ḥikma*, 3 parts, ed. S. Yaltkaya, Hyderabad: Osmania Oriental Publications Bureau, 3rd printing repr.: Isfahan University Press.
Bahmanyār b. Marzubān (1375 Sh) *Kitāb al-Taḥṣīl*, ed. M. Muṭahharī, 2nd printing, Tehran: Tehran University Press.
Baḥrānī, Maytham (1958) *Sharḥ Nahj al-balāgha*, 5 vols, Tehran: al-Maṭbaʻa al-Ḥaydariyya.
—— (1406 Q) *Qawāʻid al-marām fī ʻilm al-kalām*, ed. S.A. Ḥusaynī, Qum: Maktabat al-Marʻashī.
—— (1992) *Sharḥ mi'at kalima li-l-Imām Amīr al-Mu'minīn*, ed. Sayyid Jalāl al-Dīn Urmawī, Beirut: Mu'assasat al-aʻlamī li-l-maṭbūʻāt.
Bihbahānī, Muḥammad Bāqir Waḥīd (1415 Q) *al-Fawā'id al-Ḥā'iriyya*, Qum: Majmaʻ al-fikr al-Islāmī.
Bursī, Rajab (1978, 1375 Sh) *Mashāriq anwār al-yaqīn fī asrār Amīr al-Mu'minīn*, Beirut: Mu'assasat al-aʻlamī, repr. Qum: Intishārāt al-Maktaba al-Ḥaydariyya.
Charlton, W. (tr.) (2000) *'Philoponus', On Aristotle on the Soul 3*, London: Dukworth.
Chittick, W. (tr.) (2004) *The Elixir of the Gnostics*, Provo, UH: Brigham Young University Press.
Daiber, H. (ed.) (1980) *Aëtius arabus. Die Vorsokratiker in arabischer Überlieferung*, Wiesbaden: Franz Steiner.
—— (ed.) (1995) *Neuplatonische Pythagorica in arabischem Gewande. Der Kommentar des Iamblichus zu den Carmina aurea*, Amsterdam: Koninklijke Akademie.
Dāmād, Mīr Muḥammad Bāqir (1977) *Kitāb al-qabasāt*, eds T. Izutsu, M. Mohaghegh and S.M. Mūsawī Bihbahānī, Tehran: Tehran University Press.
—— (1998) *Taqwīm al-īmān*, ed. ʻA. Awjabī, Tehran: Institute of Islamic Studies.
—— (2003) *Muṣannafāt-i Mīr Dāmād I: rasā'il, nāma-hā va ijāzāt*, ed. ʻA. Nūrānī, Tehran: Anjuman-i āṯār va mafākhir-i farhangī.
—— (2006) *Muṣannafāt-i Mīr Dāmād II: al-Ufuq al-mubīn*, ed. ʻA. Nūrānī, Tehran: Anjuman-i āṯār va mafākhir-i farhangī.
Dashtakī, Mīr Ghiyāth al-Dīn Manṣūr (1382 Sh) *Ishrāq hayākil al-nūr li-kashf ẓulumāt shawākil al-ghurūr*, ed. ʻA. Awjabī, Tehran: Mīrāṯ-i Maktūb.
—— (1386 Sh) *Muṣannafāt*, ed. ʻA. Nūrānī, 2 vols, Tehran: Anjuman-i āṯār va mafākhir-i farhangī.
Dexippus (1888) *In Aristotelis Categorias commentarium*, ed. A. Busse Berlin: Reimer; tr. J. Dillon (1990) *Dexippus: On Aristotle's Categories*, London: Duckworth.
Dillon, J. (tr.) (1990) *Dexippus: On Aristotle's Categories*, London: Dukworth.
Dillon, J.M. and G.R. Morrow (trs) (1987) Proclus' Commentary on Plato's Paramenides, Princeton: University Press.
Dooley, W. and A. Madigan (trs) (1989–93) *Alexander of Aphorodisias on Aristotle's Metaphysics 1–5*, London: Duckworth.
Fanārī, Muḥammad b. Ḥamza (1363 Sh) *Miṣbāḥ al-uns bayn al-maʻqūl wa-l-mashhūd*, Tehran: Fajr.

Fārābī (1890) *Alfārābīs philosophische Abhandlungen*, ed. F. Dieterici, Leipzig.
—— (1344 Q) *Risāla fī masā'il mutafarriqa*, Hyderabad: Osmania Oriental Publications Bureau.
—— (1968) *Kitāb al-alfāẓ al-mustaʿmala fī-l-manṭiq*, ed. Muḥsin S. Mahdī, Beirut: Dar el-Machreq.
—— (1970) *Kitāb al-ḥurūf*, ed. Muḥsin S. Mahdī, Beirut: Dar el-Machreq.
—— (1975) *Fī-l-ʿibāra*, eds S. Kutsch and G. Morrow, Beirut: Dar el-Machreq.
—— (1981) *Taḥṣīl al-saʿāda*, ed. J. Āl Yāsīn, Beirut: Dār al-Andalus; tr. M. Mahdi in *Alfarabi: Philosophy of Plato and Aristotle*, revised edn (2001), Ithaca, NY: Cornell University Press, 13–50.
—— (1993*a*) *Fuṣūl muntazaʿa*, ed. F. Najjār, Beirut: Dar el-Machreq.
—— (1993*b*) *Kitāb al-siyāsa al-madaniyya al-mulaqqab bi-mabādi' al-mawjūdāt*, ed. F. Najjār, Beirut: Dar el-Machreq.
—— (1999) *al-Jamʿ bayn ra'yay al-ḥakīmayn Aflāṭūn al-Ilāhī wa Arisṭūṭālīs*, ed. F. Najjār with French translation D. Mallet, Damascus: L'Institut Français.
Festugière, A.-J. (tr.) (1966–8) *Proclus: Commentaire sur le Timée*, 5 tomes, Paris: Librairie philosophique J. Vrin.
Finnegan, J. (ed.) (1956) 'Texte arabe du Περι Νου d'Alexandre d'Aphrodise', *Mélanges de l'Université Saint Joseph* (Beirut) XXXIII, 2: 159–202.
Hadot, I. (tr.) (1990) *Simplicius: Commentaire sur les catégories*, 3 tomes, Leiden: Brill.
Ḥā'irī, ʿAlī Yazdī (1977) *Ilzām al-nāṣib fī ithbāt al-ḥujja al-ghā'ib*, 2 vols, Beirut: Mu'assasat al-Aʿlamī li-l-maṭbūʿāt.
Ḥillī, Ibn Muṭahhar (1959) *Īḍāḥ al-maqāʿid min ḥikmat ʿayn al-qawāʿid*, ed. ʿA. Munzawī, Tehran: Tehran University Press.
—— (1988) *Kashf al-murād fī sharḥ Tajrīd al-iʿtiqād*, Beirut: Mu'assasat al-aʿlamī li-l-maṭbūʿāt.
Iamblichus of Apamea (2003) *De mysteriis Aegyptiorum [Les mystères d'Égypte]*, ed./tr. E. des Places, Paris: Les Belles Lettres.
Ibn ʿArabī (1919) *Kleinere Schriften des Ibn al-ʿArabī [Inshā' al-Dawā'ir, ʿUqlat al-mustawfiz, al-Tadbīrāt al-ilāhiyya]*, ed. H.S. Nyberg, Leiden: Brill.
—— (n.d.) *al-Futūḥāt al-Makkiyya*, 4 vols, Beirut: Dār Ṣādir.
—— (1980) *Fuṣūṣ al-ḥikam*, ed. ʿA. ʿAfīfī, Cairo: Dār al-kitāb al-ʿarabī; tr. R.J. Austin (1981) *The Bezels of Wisdom*, New York: Paulist Press.
—— (1997) *Rasā'il*, ed. S. ʿArabī, Beirut: Dār Ṣādir.
Ibn Manẓūr (1301 Q) *Lisān al-ʿArab*, Cairo: Būlāq.
Ibn al-Muqaffaʿ (1978) *al-Manṭiq wa ḥudūd al-manṭiq li-Ibn Bihrīz*, ed. M.T. Dānishpazhūh, Tehran: Imperial Iranian Academy of Philosophy.
Ibn al-Nadīm (1970, 1997) *Fihrist*, ed. I. Ramaḍān, Beirut: Dār al-maʿrifa; tr. B. Dodge, 2 vols, New York: Columbia University Press.
Ibn Rushd/Averroes (1938–52) *Tafsīr mā baʿd al-ṭabīʿa*, ed. M. Bouyges, 4 vols, Beirut: Imprimerie Catholique.
—— (1974) *Averroes on Plato's Republic*, tr. R. Lerner, Ithaca, NY: Cornell University Press.
Ibn Sīnā/Avicenna (1908) *Tisʿ Rasā'il fī-l-ḥikma wa-l-ṭabīʿiyya*, Cairo: Maṭbaʿat Hindiyya.
—— (1952) *Ilāhiyyāt-i Dānishnāma-yi ʿAlā'ī*, ed. M. Muʿīn, Tehran: Tehran University Press; tr. P. Morewedge (1973) *The Metaphysica of Avicenna*, London: Routledge, Kegan & Paul.
—— (1331 Sh) *Risāla-yi ḥaqīqat va kayfiyyat-i silsila-yi mawjūdāt va tasalsul-i asbāb va musabbibāt*, ed. M. Ummīd, Tehran: Tehran University Press.

—— (1952) *al-Shifā': manṭiq 1 – al-madkhal*, eds M. Khuḍayrī, G. Qanawātī and F. Ahwānī, Cairo: Wizārat al-ma'ārif al-'umūmiyya li-l-idārat al-'āmma li-l-thaqāfa.

—— (1954) *'Uyūn al-ḥikma*, ed. 'A.-R. Badawī, Cairo: L'Institut Français.

—— (1958) *al-Ishārāt wa-l-tanbīhāt*, 3 vols, ed. S. Dunyā, Cairo: Dār al-Ma'ārif.

—— (1959) *al-Shifā': manṭiq 2 – al-maqūlāt*, eds M. Khuḍayrī, G. Qanawātī, S. Zāyed and F. Ahwānī, Cairo: Wizārat al-thaqāfa wa-l-irshād al-qawmī.

—— (1960) *al-Shifā': ilāhiyyāt*, eds G.C. Anawātī and S. Zāyed, Cairo: al-Hay'a al-miṣriyya al-'āmma; tr. G. Anawati (1978) 2 vols, Paris: Librairie Vrin; tr. M. Marmura (2005) *The Metaphysics of the Cure*, Provo, UH: Brigham Young University Press.

—— (1970) *al-Shifā': manṭiq 3 – al-'ibāra*, ed. M. Khuḍayrī, Cairo: al-Hay'a al-miṣriyya al-'āmma.

—— (1973) *al-Ta'līqāt*, ed. 'A.-R. Badawī, Cairo: al-Hay'a al-miṣriyya al-'āmma.

—— (1984) *al-Mabda' wa-l-ma'ād*, ed. 'Abd Allāh Nūrānī, Tehran: McGill Institute of Islamic Studies.

—— (1992*a*) *al-Najāt min al-manṭiq wa-l-ilāhiyyāt*, ed. 'Abd al-Raḥmān 'Umayra, Beirut: Dār al-Jīl.

—— (1992*b*) *al-Mubāḥathāt*, ed. M. Bīdārfar, Qum: Intishārāt-i Bīdār.

—— (1375 Sh) *al-Ishārāt wa-l-tanbīhāt* with commentaries of Fakhr al-Dīn Rāzī, Naṣīr al-Dīn Ṭūsī, and Quṭb al-Dīn Rāzī, ed. M. Shihābī, 3 vols, Tehran: Tehran University Press, repr. Qum: Nashr al-balāgha.

—— (1383 Sh) *al-Shifā' (al-ilāhiyyāt) ma' zubdat al-ḥawāshī*, ed. Ḥāmid Nājī Iṣfahānī, vol I, Tehran: Anjuman-i āṯār va mafākhir-i farhangī.

Imām 'Alī b. Abī Ṭālib (1967) *Nahj al-balāgha*, compiled by Sayyid Raḍī, ed. Ṣ. Ṣāliḥ, Qum: Mu'assasat Dār al-hijra.

—— (n.d.) *Dīwān al-mansūb ilā l-Imām 'Alī*, Beirut: Mu'assasat al-a'lamī li-l-maṭbū'āt.

Iṣfahānī, Ibn Turka (1976) *Tamhīd al-qawā'id*, ed. S. J. Āshtiyānī, Tehran: Imperial Iranian Academy of Philosophy.

—— (1372 Sh) *Taḥrīr Tamhīd al-Qawā'id*, ed./tr. Javādī Āmulī, Tehran: Intishārāt-i Zahrā'.

Jabre, F. (ed.) (1999) *al-Naṣṣ al-kāmil li-manṭiq Arisṭū*, 2 vols, Beirut: Dār al-Fikr al-Lubnānī.

Jāmī, 'Abd al-Raḥmān (1979) *al-Durra al-fākhira: The Precious Pearl with Glosses and Commentary of 'Abd al-Ghafūr Lārī*, tr. N. Heer, Albany: SUNY Press.

Jīlī, 'Abd al-Karīm (n.d.) *Marātib al-wujūd wa-ḥaqīqat kulli mawjūd*, ed. Badawī Ṭāhā 'Allām, Cairo: Maktabat al-Jandī.

Jilveh, Mīrzā Abū-l-Ḥasan (1385 Sh) *Majmū'a-yi āṯār-i ḥakīm Jilveh*, ed. Ḥ. Riżāzādeh, Tehran: Intishārāt-i Ḥikmat.

Jurjānī, Sayyid 'Alī (1969) *Kitāb al-ta'rīfāt*, ed. A. Sprenger, repr. Beirut: Maktabat al-Lubnān.

Kant, I. (1929) *The Critique of Pure Reason*, tr. N. Kemp Smith, London: Macmillan.

—— (1977) *Prolegomena to any Future Metaphysics*, tr. P. Carus, revised by J. Ellington, Indianapolis, IN: Hackett.

Kāshānī, 'Abd al-Razzāq (1991) *Iṣṭilāḥāt al-ṣūfiyya*, ed. A. Sprenger, repr. in *A Glossary of Sufi Technical Terms*, London: Octagon Press.

Kāshānī, Muḥsin Fayḍ (1979) *Tafsīr al-Ṣāfī*, ed. Ḥ. A'lamī, 5 vols, Mashhad: Dār al-Murtaḍá.

—— (1375 Sh) *Uṣūl al-Ma'ārif*, ed. S.J. Āshtiyānī, repr. Qum: Daftar-i tablīghāt-i Islāmī.

Kashfī, Sayyid Ja'far (1873) *Tuḥfat al-mulūk*, 2 vols, Tehran lithograph.

Kātibī, Dabīrān Qazwīnī (1854) *al-Risāla al-Shamsiyya*, ed./tr. A. Sprenger as *The Logic of the Arabians*, 1st Appendix to Biblioteca Indica no. 76, Calcutta: Bengal Military Orphan Press.

Khafrī, Shams al-Dīn (1382 Sh) *Ta'līqa bar ilāhiyyāt-i Sharḥ-i Tajrīd-i Mullā 'Alī Qūshjī*, ed. F. Sā'atchīyān, Tehran: Mīrāṯ-i Maktūb.

Kindī, Abū Yūsuf Ya'qūb (1950) *Rasā'il al-Kindī al-falsafiyya*, ed. M. Abū Rīda, 2 vols, Cairo.

—— (1998) *Oeuvres philosophiques et scientifiques d'al-Kindi*, eds/trs R. Rashed and J. Jolivet, vol II, Leiden: Brill.

Kirk, G.S, J.E. Raven and M. Schofield (eds) (1983) *The Presocratic Philosophers*, 2nd edn., Cambridge: Cambridge University Press.

Kirmānī, Ḥamīd al-Dīn (1967) *Rāḥat al-'aql*, ed. M. Ghālib, Beirut: Dār al-Andalus.

Kulaynī, Abū Ja'far Muḥammad b. Ya'qūb (1968) *al-Uṣūl min al-Kāfī*, ed. 'A.-A. Ghaffārī, 2 vols, Tehran: Dār al-Kutub al-Islāmiyya.

Lāhījī, 'Abd al-Razzāq (1372 Sh) *Shawāriq al-ilhām fī sharḥ Tajrīd al-kalām*, Tehran lithograph, repr. Isfahan: Intishārāt-i Mahdavī.

Lameer, Joop (tr.) (2006) *Conception and Belief in Ṣadr al- Dīn Shīrazī*, Tehran: Iranian Institute of Philosophy.

Lawkarī, Abū'l-'Abbās (1995) *Bayān al-ḥaqq bi-ḍiman al-ṣidq: al-'ilm al-ilāhī*, ed. I. Dībājī, Tehran: ISTAC.

Majlisī, Muḥammad Bāqir (1392 Q) *Biḥār al-anwār*, 128 vols, Qum: Intishārāt-i Ismā'īliyān.

Marmura, M. (tr.) (2005) *The Metaphysics of the Cure*, Provo, UH: Brigham Young University Press.

Morewedge, P. (tr.) (1973) *The Metaphysica of Avicenna*, London: Routledge, Kegan & Paul.

Nābulsī, 'Abd al-Ghanī (1995) *al-Wujūd al-ḥaqq wa-l-khiṭāb al-ṣidq*, ed. B. Aladin, Damascus: L'Institut Français.

Narāqī, Mahdī (1365 Sh) *Sharḥ al-ilāhiyyāt min Kitāb al-Shifā'*, ed. M. Mohaghegh, Tehran: McGill Institute of Islamic Studies.

Nasafī, 'Azīz al-dīn-i (1998) *Kitāb al-insān al-kāmil (majmū'a-yi rasā'il)*, ed. M. Molé, Tehran: Ṭāhūrī, repr. Institut Franco-Iranien.

Nock, A.D and A.-J. Festugière (eds/trs) (1945–54) *Corpus Hermeticum*, 4 tomes, Paris: Collections des Universités de France; trs C. Salaman, D. van Oye and W.D. Wharton (1999) *The Way of Hermes*, London: Duckworth.

Peerwani, Latimah-Parvin (2004) *On the Hermeneutics of the Light Verse of the Qur'an (Tafsīr āyat al-nūr)*, London: ICAS Press.

Philoponus, John (1897) *in De Anima*, ed. M. Hayduck, Berlin: Reimer; tr. Charlton (2000) *'Philoponus', On Aristotle on the Soul 3*, London: Duckworth.

Plato (1975) *Timaeus*, ed./tr. R.G. Bury, Cambridge, MA: Harvard University Press.

—— (1997) *Complete Works*, ed. J.M. Cooper, Indianapolis, IN: Hackett.

Plotinus (1951–73) *Plotini opera*, 2 vols, eds P. Henry and H.R. Schwzyer with *Plotiniana Arabica*, tr. G. Lewis, Brussels: Desclée de Brouwer; tr. A.H. Armstrong (1966–88) *Plotinus: Enneads*, 7 vols, Cambridge, MA: Harvard University Press.

Porphyry (1887) *Isagoge et in Aristotelis categorias commentarium*, ed. A. Busse, Berlin: Reimer; tr. S. Strange (1992) *On Aristotle's Categories*, Ithaca, NY: Cornell University Press.

—— (2003) *Porphyry: Introduction*, tr. J. Barnes, Oxford: Clarendon Press.

—— (2005) *Porphyre: Sentences*, ed. Luc Brisson avec études d'introduction, commentaire, texte grec, traduction française et traduction anglaise de John Dillon, 2 vols, Paris: Librairie philosophique Vrin.

Proclus (1864) *In Platonis Parmenidem*, ed. V. Cousin, Paris: Durand; trs J.M. Dillon and G.R. Morrow (1987) *Proclus'Commentary on Plato's Parmenides*, Princeton: Princeton University Press.
—— (1903–6) *Procli in Platonis Timaeum commentaria*, ed. E. Diehl, 3 vols, Leipzig: Teubner; tr. A.-J. Festugière (1966–8) *Proclus: Commentaire sur le Timée*, 5 tomes, Paris: Librairie philosophique J.Vrin.
—— (1963) *The Elements of Theology*, ed./tr. E. Dodds, Oxford: Clarendon Press.
—— (1968–87) *Théologie Platonicienne*, eds/trs H.D. Saffrey and M. Westerink, 5 tomes, Paris: Les Belles Lettres.
Qāshānī [*sic*] [='Abd al-Razzāq Kāshānī] (1987) *Sharḥ ʿalá Fuṣūṣ al-ḥikam*, 3rd printing, Cairo: Muṣṭafā al-Bābī al-Ḥalabī.
Qayṣarī, Dā'ūd (1978) *Rasā'il-i Qayṣarī*, ed. S.J. Āshtiyānī, Tehran: Anjuman-i ḥikmat.
—— (1416 Q) *Maṭlaʿ khuṣūṣ al-kalim fī maʿānī Fuṣūṣ al-ḥikam*, ed. M.H. Saʿīdī, 2 vols, Tehran: Manshūrāt anwār al-hudá.
—— (1375 Sh) *Sharḥ Fuṣūṣ al-ḥikam ba-kūshish-i Sayyid Jalāl al-Dīn Āshtiyanī*, Tehran: Intishārāt-i ʿilmī va farhangī.
Qifṭī, ʿAlī b. Yūsuf (1903) *Ta'rīkh al-ḥukamā'*, ed. J. Lippert, Leipzig: Dieterische Verlagsbuchhandlung.
Qummī, Qāḍī Saʿīd (1373–8 Sh) *Sharḥ Tawḥīd al-Ṣadūq*, ed. Najafqulī Ḥabībī, 3 vols, Tehran: Wizārat al-thaqāfa wa-l-irshād al-islāmī.
Rāzī, Fakhr al-Dīn (1343 Q) *al-Mabāḥith al-mashriqiyya*, 3 vols, Hyderabad: Osmania Oriental Publications Bureau.
Rudolph, U. (1989) *Die Doxographie des Pseudo-Ammonios. Ein Beitrag zur neuplatonischen Überlieferung im Islam*, Wiesbaden: Franz Steiner.
Sabzawārī, Mullā Hādī (1969) *Sharḥ Ghurar al-Farā'id maʿrūf bih Sharḥ Manẓūma-yi ḥikmat, qism umūr ʿāmma wa jawhar wa ʿaraḍ*, eds M. Mohaghegh and T. Izutsu, Tehran: McGill Institute of Islamic Studies.
—— (1995) *Sharḥ Ghurar al-Farā'id: qism al-ḥikma*, ed. M. Ṭālibī with *scholia* of Ḥasanzāda Āmulī, 2 vols, Tehran: Nashr-i Nāb.
—— (1376 Sh) *Rasā'il-i Ḥakīm-i Sabzavārī*, ed. S.J. Āshtiyānī, repr. Tehran: Intishārat-i Usva.
Shahrastānī, Muḥammad b. ʿAbd al-Karīm (1984) *al-Milal wa-l-niḥal (Le livre des religions et des sectes)*, trs J. Jolivet and G. Monnot, Louvain: Peeters.
—— (2001) *Kitāb al-muṣāraʿa*, eds/trs W. Madelung and T. Mayer as *Struggling with the Philosopher: A Refutation of Avicenna's Metaphysics*, London: I.B. Tauris.
Shahrazūrī, Shams al-Dīn Muḥammad (1976) *Nuzhat al-arwāḥ wa-rawḍat al-afrāḥ fī ta'rīkh al-ḥukamā' wa-l-falāsifa*, ed. S.K. Aḥmad, 2 vols, Hyderabad: Osmania Oriental Publications Bureau.
—— (1993) *Sharḥ Ḥikmat al-ishrāq*, ed. Ḥ. Żiā'ī, Tehran: Mu'assasa-yi muṭālaʿāt va taḥqīqāt-i farhangī.
—— (2004) *Rasā'il al-shajara al-ilāhiyya fī ʿulūm al-ḥaqā'iq al-rabbāniyya*, ed. N. Görgün, 3 vols, Istanbul: Elif Yayınları.

—— (1980) *Kitāb al-iftikhār*, ed. M. Ghālib, Beirut: Dār al-Andalus.

Simplicius (1907) *In Aristotelis categorias commentarium*, ed. C. Kalbfleisch, Berlin: Reimer; tr. I. Hadot (1990) *Commentaire sur les catégories*, 3 tomes, Leiden: Brill.

Strange, S. (tr.) (1992) *On Aristotle's Categories*, Ithaca, NY: Cornell University Press.

Suhrawardī, Shihāb al-Dīn (1945) *Opera metaphysica et mystica, tome I*, ed. H. Corbin, Istanbul: Maarif Matbasi.

—— (1952) *Opera metaphysica et mystica, tome II*, ed. H. Corbin, Tehran: L'Institut Franco-Iranien.

—— (1957) *Hayākil al-nūr*, ed. M. Abū Rayyān, Cairo: al-Maktaba al-tujjāriyya al-kubrá.

—— (1998) *The Book of Radiance (Partaw'nāma)*, ed./tr. Ḥ. Żiā'ī, Costa Mesa, CA: Mazda Publishers.

—— (1999) *The Philosophy of Illumination (Ḥikmat al-Ishrāq)*, eds/trs J. Walbridge and H. Żiai, Salt Lake City, UH: Brigham Young University Press.

Tabrīzī, Shams al-Dīn, *al-Bawāriq al-nūriyya*, MS Delhi Arabic [Asian and African Studies, British Library, London] 1778.

Taftazānī, Sa'd al-Dīn (n.d.) *Sharḥ al-maqāṣid*, ed. 'A.-R. 'Umayra, 2 vols, Cairo: Maktabat al-kulliyya al-Azhariyya.

T(a)hānawī, M.'A. (1862) *Kashshāf iṣṭilāḥāt al-funūn* in *Biblioteca Indica*, eds 'Abd al-Ḥaqq, Ghulām Qādir and Aloys Sprenger, Calcutta: W.N. Lees Press.

—— (1963–77) *Kashshāf iṣṭilāḥāt al-funūn*, eds Luṭfī 'Abd al-Badī' and 'Abd al-Na'īm Ḥasnayn, 4 vols, Cairo: Ministry of Culture.

Tawḥīdī, Abū Ḥayyān (1970) *al-Muqābasāt*, ed. M.T. Ḥusayn, Baghdad: Jāmi'at Baghdād.

Tilimsānī, 'Afīf al-Dīn (1413 Q) *Sharḥ manāzil al- sā'irīn*, Tehran: Intishārāt-i ḥikmat.

Ṭūsī, Naṣīr al-Dīn (1985) *Talkhīṣ al-Muḥaṣṣal*, ed. 'Abd Allāh Nūrānī, Beirut: Dār al-aḍwā'.

—— (1405 Q) *Muṣāri' al-muṣāri'*, ed. Ḥ. Mu'izzī, Qum: Maktabat Āyatullāh al-Mar'ashī.

Zajjājī, 'Abd al-Raḥmān (1959) *al-Īḍāh fī 'ilal al-naḥw*, ed. M. Mubārak, Cairo: Maktabat Dār al-'Urubba.

Zanjānī-Khū'ī, Muḥammad Bāqir (ed.) (1375 Sh) *Kitāb Sulaym b. Qays al-Hilālī*, 3 vols, Qum: Nashr al-Hādī.

Zunūzī, 'Alī (1376 Sh) *Badāyi' al-ḥikam*, ed. A. Vā'iẓī, Tehran: Intishārāt-i Zahrā'.

—— (1378 Sh) *Majmū'a-yi musannafāt-i Ḥakīm-i mu'assis Āqā 'Alī Mudarris Zunūzī*, ed. M. Kadīvar, 3 vols, Tehran: Intishārāt-i Iṭṭilā'āt.

Secondary sources in Arabic, Persian and Urdu

Akbarī, R. (1999) 'Vujūd-i dhihnī az manẓar-i dīgar', *Ṣadrā* 14: 37–48.

'Alīzāda, B. (1998) 'Māhiyyat-i maktab-i falsafī-yi Mullā Ṣadrā', *Ṣadrā* 10: 90–101.

Amīn, S.Ḥ. (1986) *Afkār-i falsafī-yi Mullā Ṣadrā*, Exeter: Intishārāt-i gurūh-i taḥqīq va nashr va farhang-i Īrān.

Āmulī, Ḥasanzāda (1374 Sh) *al-Nūr al-mutajallī fī-l-ẓuhūr al-ẓillī*, Qum: Maktab al-i'lām al-islāmī.

Ashkivarī, H. (1986) 'Risāla fī l marātib al khams', ed. S. Sāwī, *Taḥqīqāt i Islāmī* 1: 117

Khurāsān.

—— (1980, 1376 Sh) *Hastī az naẓar-i falsafa va ʿirfān*, Tehran: Nahżat-i zanān-i musalmān.
—— (1370 Sh) *Sharḥ-i muqaddima-yi Qayṣarī bar Fuṣūṣ al-Ḥikam*, Tehran: Intishārāt-i Amīr-i Kabīr.
ʿAṣṣār, Sayyid Kāẓim (1391 Q) *Thalāth rasā'il fī-l-ḥikma al-islāmiyya*, ed. S. Ṣāwī, Tehran: al-Maktaba al-Murtaḍawiyya.
Aʿvānī, G. (1374 Sh) 'Mas'ala-yi vujūd dar maktab-i Ibn-i ʿArabī', in Gulshanī (1374 Sh: 133–59).
Dīnānī, G. Ibrāhīmī (1366 Sh) *Shuʿāʿ-yi andīsha va shuhūd dar falsafa-yi Suhravardī*, Tehran: Intishārāt-i Ḥikmat.
—— (1372 Sh) *Qavāʿid-i kullī-yi falsafī dar falsafa-yi islāmī*, 3 vols, 2nd edn, Tehran: Mu'assasa-yi muṭālaʿāt va taḥqīqāt-i farhangī.
Gulshanī, M. (ed.) (1374 Sh) *Āyat-i ḥusn: jashn-nāma-yi buzurgdāsht-i Ustād Ḥasanzāda Āmulī*, Tehran: Pazhūhishgāh-i ʿulūm-i insānī va muṭālaʿāt-i farhangī.
Ḥā'irī Māzandarānī, Muḥammad Ṣāliḥ (1956) *Ḥikmat-i Bū ʿAlī Sīnā*, 4 vols, Tehran: Intishārāt-i Islāmiyya.
Ḥā'irī Yazdī, M. (1981) *Kāvush-hā-yi ʿAql-i naẓarī*, Tehran: Shirkat-i sihāmī-yi intishār.
—— (1982) *Hiram-i hastī*, Tehran: Mu'assasa-yi muṭālaʿāt va taḥqīqāt-i farhangī.
—— (1993) 'Dar āmadī bar Kitāb-i Asfār', *Īrānshenāsī* IV.4: 707–12.
Ḥakīmī, Muḥammad Riḍā (1373 Sh) *Maktab-i tafkīk*, Qum: Markaz-i bar-rasī-hā-yi Islāmī.
Ḥamad, M.ʿA.-Ḥ. (1998) *Ṣābi'at Ḥarrān wa-Ikhwān al-ṣafā'*, Damascus: al-Ahālī.
Ḥamīd, Ḥ. (1995) 'Pāra-yi ʿanāṣir-i Anāksīmāndres [Anaximander] dar naẓariyya-yi vujūd-i Mullā Ṣadrā', *Īrānshenāsī* VI.4: 817–32.
Humā'ī, J. (1997) *Dū risāla dar falsafa-yi islāmī*, Tehran: Institute of Humanities and Cultural Studies.
Ḥusayn, S.M. 'Yād' (1998) *Mullā Ṣadrā kā qābil-e ʿamal falsafa*, Lahore: al-Razzāq Publications.
ʿAbd al Haq, M. (1967) 'Mullā Ṣadrā's concept of being', *Islamic Studies* 6: 268–76.
Imām-Jumʿe-ī, S.M. (1997) 'Az imkān-i vujūdī-yi Ibn Sīnā tā imkān-i vujūdī-yi Mullā Ṣadrā', *Ṣadrā* 5 and 6: 48–53.
Intiẓām, S.M. (1998) 'Ibtikārāt-i falsafī-yi Ṣadr al-muta'allihīn', *Ṣadrā* 12: 78–86.
ʿIrāqī, Ḍiyā' al-Dīn (1414 Q) *Maqālāt al-Uṣūl*, eds M. ʿIrāqī and M. Ḥakīm, 2 vols, Qum: Majmaʿ al-fikr al-islāmī.
Iṣfahānī, Mīrzā Mahdī (1363 Sh) *Abwāb al-hudá*, Mashhad: Chāpkhāna-yi Saʿīd.
Javādī Āmulī, ʿAbd Allāh (1996–2002) *Raḥīq-i makhtūm: sharḥ-i ḥikmat-i mutaʿāliya*, 10 vols, Qum: Markaz-i nashr-i Isrā'.
Kaḥḥāla, ʿU.R. (1957–61) *Muʿjam al-mu'allifīn: tarājim muṣannifiyy al-kutub al-ʿarabiyya*, 15 vols, Damascus: Maṭbaʿat al-taraqqī.
Khājavī, M. (1988) *Lavāmiʿ al-ʿārifīn fī aḥvāl Ṣadr al-Muta'allihīn*, Tehran: Intishārāt-i Mawlá.
Khāliqānī, F. (1999) 'Qāʿida-yi imkān-i ashraf', *Ṣadrā* 14: 71–8.
Khāminihī, Sayyid Muḥammad (2000) *Mullā Ṣadrā: zindagī, shakhṣiyyat va maktab-i Ṣadr al-muta'allihīn*, Tehran: SIPRIn.
Khāqānī, M. Āl Shabbīr (1412 Q) *ʿAnāṣir al-ʿulūm: dirāsāt fī-l-taʿrīf wa-l-mawḍūʿ wa-l-ghāya*, Damascus.
Khū'ī, Sayyid Abū-l-Qāsim (1988–95) *Muḥāḍarāt fī uṣūl al-fiqh*, transcribed by Shaykh Muḥammad Isḥāq Fayyāḍ, 5 vols, Beirut: Mu'assasat Āl al-bayt.
Khumaynī, Sayyid Rūḥullāh (1410 Q) *Taʿlīqa ʿalá Sharḥ Fuṣūṣ al-ḥikam wa Miṣbāḥ al-uns*, Qum: Daftar-i tablīghāt-i Islāmī.

Khurāsānī, Ākhūnd Muḥammad Kāẓim (1990) *Kifāyat al-uṣūl*, Beirut: Mu'assasat Āl al-Bayt li-iḥyā' al-turāth.

Kintūrī, Sayyid I'jāz Ḥusayn (1330 Q) *Kashf al-ḥujub wa-l-astār 'an asmā' al-kutub wa-l-isfār*, ed. M.H. Ḥusayn, Calcutta: Baptist Mission.

Ma'ṣūmī, A. (1961) 'Ṣadr al-Dīn Shīrāzī: ḥayātuhu wa ma'thūruhu', *Indo-Iranica* (Calcutta) XIV: 27–42.

Mīrī, S.M. and M.J. 'Ilmī (1374 Sh) *Fihrist-i mawḍū'ī-yi Kitāb al-ḥikma al-muta'āliya fī-l-asfār al-arba'a-yi Ṣadr al-Muta'allihīn*, Tehran: Intishārāt-i ḥikmat.

Miṣbāḥ-i Yazdī, Muḥammad-Taqī (1405 Q) *Ta'līqa 'alá Nihāyat al-ḥikma*, Qum: Dar Rāh-i Ḥaqq.

—— (1999) *Āmūzish-i falsafa*, trs M. Legenhausen and A. Sarvdalir as *Philosophical Instructions*, Binghamton NY: SSIPS and Global Publications at Binghamton University.

Mishkāt al-dīnī, 'A. (1355 Sh) *Naẓarī ba falsafa-yi Ṣadr al-Dīn Shīrāzī*, Tehran: Intishārāt-i bunyād-i farhangī-yi Iran.

Miyānjī, Muḥammad Bāqir Malikī (1415 Q) *Tawḥīd al-imāmiyya*, Tehran: Wizārat al-thaqāfa wa-l-irshād al-islāmī.

Mu'ayyadī, M. (1996) 'Ṣadrā va 'adamiyyat-i mumkināt', *Ṣadrā* 3: 58–72.

Muḥaqqiq Dāmād, Muṣṭafá (1997) 'Favā'id-i chand dar masā'il va mafāhīm-i ḥikmiyya', *Ṣadrā* 5 and 6: 61–6.

Mu'īnī, M (n.d.) 'Tafkīk', *Dā'irat al-ma'ārif-i tashayyu' (Tehran)* 5: 7–10.

Mūsawī, Mūsā (1978) *al-Jadīd fī falsafat Ṣadr al-Dīn al-Shīrāzī*, Baghdad: al-Dār al-'Arabiyya li-l-ṭibā'a.

Mūsawī, S.Ḥ. (1381 Sh) 'Mullā Ṣadrā u Ibn Kammūna', in *Mullā Ṣadrā va muṭāla'āt-i taṭbīqī: Majmū'a-yi maqālāt-i hamāyish-i jahānī-yi ḥakīm Mullā Ṣadrā*, Tehran: SIPRIn, 5: 46–53.

Muṭahharī, M. (n.d.) *Āshnā'ī bā 'ulūm-i Islāmī*, Qum: Intishārāt-i Ṣadrā.

—— (1374 Sh) *Maqālāt-i falsafī*, Qum: Intishārāt-i Ṣadrā.

Muvaḥḥid, Ṣ. (1995) 'Ibn Abī Jumhūr', *Dā'irat al-ma'ārif al-islāmī* (Tehran) II: 634–7.

Muẓaffar, Muḥammad Riḍā' (1411 Q) *Uṣūl al-fiqh*, 2 parts in 1 vol. Qum: Maktab al-i'lām al-islāmī.

Qazvīnī, Abū-l-Ḥasan Rafī'ī (1376 Sh) *Ghawṣī dar baḥr-i ma'rifat*, Tehran: Intishārāt-i Islām.

Raḥīmiyān-i Firdūsī, Muḥammad 'Alī (1383 Sh) *Muta'allih-i qur'ānī: Shaykh Mujtabá Qazwīnī Khurāsānī*, Qum: Dalīl-i mā.

Sa'dī, 'A. (1998) 'Ma'qūlāt-i thāniyya dar ḥikmat-i muta'āliya', *Ṣadrā* 13: 51–6.

Shakībā, 'A. (1996*a* and *b*) 'Shinākht az dīdgāh-i Ṣadr al-muta'allihīn I and II', *Ṣadrā* 3: 61–7; 4: 40–6.

Shīdiyān, G. (1376 Sh) 'Zindagī-nāma-yi Ibn Abī Jumhūr', *Kayhān-i andīsha* 72: 101–9.

Ṣubūt, A. (1996) 'Sharḥ-i Hidāya-yi Ṣadrā', *Ṣadrā* 3: 100–7.

—— (1380 Sh) *Faylasūf-i Shīrāzī dar Hind*, Tehran: Markaz-i bayn-al-milalī-yi guftagū-yi tamaddun-hā.

Surūsh, 'Abd al-Karīm (1978, 1378 Sh) *Nihād-i nā-ārām-i jahān*, Tehran: Qalam; repr. Tehran: Ṣirāṭ.

—— (1980) *Az tā'rīkh-parastī tā khudā-parastī*, Tehran.

—— (ed.) (1360 Sh) *Yādvāra-yi Mullā Ṣadrā*, Tehran: Nahżat-i zanān-i Musalmān.

—— (1989) *'Ilm chīst, falsafa chīst?* Tehran: Ṣirāṭ.

—— (1991) *Qabż va basṭ-i ti'ūrīk-i sharī'at*, Tehran: Ṣirāṭ.

Ṭabāṭabā'ī, Sayyid Muḥammad Ḥusayn (1403 Q) *Bidāyat al-ḥikma*, 3rd printing, Qum: Daftar-i tablīghāt-i islāmī.

—— (1362 Sh) *Nihāyat al-ḥikma*, Qum: Mu'assasat al-nashr al-islāmī.

Ṭihrānī, Āqā Buzurg (1936–52) *al-Dharīʿa ilá taṣānīf al-shīʿa*, 22 vols, Najaf: Maṭbaʿat al-Gharrá.

Ṭihrānī, Sayyid Muḥammad Ḥusayn Ḥusaynī (1417 Q) *Mihr-i tābān: yādnāma va muṣābiḥāt-i tilmīz va ʿAllāma-yi . . . Ṭabāṭabā'ī*, Mashhad: Intishārāt-i ʿAllāma-yi Ṭabāṭabā'ī.

Yūsuf-i S̱ānī, M. (1997) 'Taqābul-i salb va ījāb va mājarā-yi ān', *Ṣadrā* 5 and 6: 42–7.

Żiā'ī, Ḥ. (1993) 'Ṣadr al-dīn Shīrāzī va bayān-i falsafī-yi ḥikmat-i mutaʿāliya', *Īrānshenāsī* V.2: 353–64.

Secondary sources in European languages

ʿAbd al-Ḥaq, M. (1967) 'Mullā Ṣadrā's concept of being', *Islamic Studies* 6: 268–76.

—— (1970) 'The psychology of Mullā Ṣadrā', *IS* 9: 173–81.

—— (1972) 'Mullā Ṣadrā's concept of substantial motion', *IS* 11: 79–91.

Abed, S. (1991) *Aristotelian Logic and the Arabic Language in Alfarabi*, Albany: SUNY Press.

Açikgenç, A. (1993) *Being and Existence in Sadra and Heidegger*, Kuala Lumpur: ISTAC.

Adamson, P. (2002) 'Before essence and existence: al-Kindī's conception of being', *JHP* 40.3: 297–312.

—— (2003) *The Arabic Plotinus: A Philosophical Study of the 'Theology of Aristotle'*, London: Duckworth.

—— (2004) 'Non-discursive thought in Avicenna's commentary on the *Theology of Aristotle*', in J. McGinnis (ed.) (2004) *Interpreting Avicenna: Science and Philosophy in Medieval Islam,* Leiden: Brill, 87–111.

—— and R. Taylor (eds) (2005) *The Cambridge Companion to Arabic Philosophy*, Cambridge: Cambridge University Press.

—— (2006) *Al-Kindī,* New York: Oxford University Press.

Afnan, S. (1969) *A Philosophical Lexicon in Persian and Arabic*, Beirut: Dar el-Machreq.

Ahmadi, N. and F. (1998) *Iranian Islam: The Concept of the Individual*, Basingstoke: Macmillan.

Akbarian, R. (2000) 'Existence as a predicate in Kant and Mulla Sadra', *Transcendent Philosophy* 1.3: 69–88.

Alonso, M. (1969) 'Concordia entre el Divino Platón y el Sabio Aristóteles', *Pensamiento* 25: 21–70.

Alston, W.P. (1960) 'The ontological argument revisited', *Philosophical Review* 69: 452–74.

—— (1983) 'What's wrong with immediate knowledge?' *Synthese* 55: 73–95.

Aminrazavi, M. (1992) 'Suhrawardī's metaphysics of illumination', *HI* 15: 19–36.

Amir-Moezzi, M.A. (1994) *The Divine Guide in Early Shiʿism*, tr. D. Streight, Albany: SUNY Press.

—— (1969) 'Ancient interpretations of Aristotle's doctrine of Homonyma', *JHP* 7: 1–18.

—— and A. Preus (eds) (1992) *Essays on Ancient Philosophy V. Aristotle's Ontology*, Albany: SUNY Press.

Armstrong, A.H. (ed.) (1970) *The Cambridge History of Later Greek and Early Medieval Philosophy*, Cambridge: Cambridge University Press.

Armstrong, J.M. (2004) 'After the ascent: Plato on becoming like God', *OSAP* 26: 171–83.

Arnaldez, R. 'Māhiyya', *EI^2* V: 1261–3.

—— 'Manṭiq', *EI^2* VI: 442–52.

ʿArshī, I. (1963–2000) *Catalogue of the Arabic Manuscripts in the Raza Library*, 6 vols, Rampur: Raza Library Trust.

Asad, T. (1993) *Genealogies of Religion: Discipline and Reasons of Power in Christianity and Islam*, Baltimore, MD: Johns Hopkins University Press.

Ashtiyani, S.J., Hideichi Matsubura, Akiro Matsumoto and Takashi Iwami (eds) (2000) *Consciousness and Reality. Studies in Memory of Toshihiko Izutsu*, Leiden: Brill.

Atiyeh, G.N. (ed.) (1995) *The Book in the Islamic World*, Albany: SUNY Press.

Attas, S.N. (1995) *Prolegomena to the Metaphysics of Islam*, Kuala Lumpur: ISTAC.

Aubenque, P. (1978) 'Les origines de l'analogie de l'être: Sur l'histoire d'un contresens', *Études Philosophiques* 53: 3–12.

Austin, J.L. (1962) *Sense and Sensibilia*, ed. G. Warnock, Oxford: Clarendon Press.

Ayer, A.J. (1971) *Language, Truth and Logic*, London: Penguin.

—— (ed.) (1979) *Perception and Identity*, London: Macmillan.

Bäck, A. (1987) 'Avicenna on existence', *JHP* 25: 351–67.

—— (1992) 'Avicenna's conception of the modalities', *Vivarium* 30: 217–55.

Baltzly, D. (2004) 'The virtues and "becoming like god": Alcinous to Proclus', *OSAP* XXVI: 297–321.

Bär, Erika (1994) *Bibliographie zur deutschsprachigen Islamwissenschaft und Semistik vom Anfang des 19. Jahrhunderts bis heute*, band 3, Wiesbaden: Ludwig Reichert Verlag.

Barnes, J. (1971) 'Homonymy in Aristotle and Speusippus', *Classical Quarterly* 25: 65–80.

—— (ed.) (1975–9) *Articles on Aristotle*, 4 vols, London: Duckworth.

—— (1976) 'Introduction', in *Aristotle: Ethics*, London: Penguin.

—— (ed.) (1995) *The Cambridge Companion to Aristotle*, Cambridge: Cambridge University Press.

Bayat, M. (1982) *Mysticism and Dissent: Socioreligious Thought in Qajar Iran*, Syracuse, NY: Syracuse University Press.

Bermúdez, J.-L. (1998) *The Paradox of Self-consciousness*, Cambridge, MA: MIT Press.

Bernal, M. (1987) *Black Athena: The Afro-Asiatic Roots of Classical Civilisation*, vol. 1, New Brunswick, NJ: Rutgers University Press.

Bevir, M. (1997) 'Mind and method in the history of ideas', *History and Theory* 36: 167–89.

—— (1999) *The Logic of the History of Ideas*, Cambridge: Cambridge University Press.

—— (2000) 'Meaning and intention: a defence of procedural individualism', *New Literary History* 31: 385–403

Cambridge: Cambridge University Press.

Boroujerdi, M. (1996) *Iranian Intellectuals and the West*, Syracuse, NY: Syracuse University Press.
Bourdieu, P. (1990) *The Logic of Practice*, tr. R. Nice, Stanford, CA: Stanford University Press.
Böwering, G. '‘Erfān', *Enc. Ir.* VIII: 553.
Boyle, J.A. (ed.) (1968) *The Cambridge History of Iran Volume 5: The Saljuq and Mongol Periods*, Cambridge: Cambridge University Press.
Brague, R. (1997) 'La philosophie de la *Théologie d'Aristote* par l'inventaire', *Documenti* 8: 365–87.
Brentano, F. (1975) *On the Several Senses of Being in Aristotle*, ed./tr. R. George, Berkeley, CA: University of California Press.
Brockelmann, C. (1937–42) *Geschichte der arabischen Litteratur*, 2 Bd and 2 Suppl, Leiden: Brill.
Brown, L. (1986) 'Being in the *Sophist*', *OSAP* 4: 49–70.
Brumberg, D. (2001) *Reinventing Khomeini: The Struggle for Reform in Iran*, Chicago: University of Chicago Press.
Bussanich, J. (1997) 'Non-discursive thought in Plotinus and Proclus', *Documenti* VIII: 191–210.
Calmard, J. 'Gobineau, Joseph Arthur de', *Enc. Ir.* XI: 20–4.
Campbell, R. (1974) 'Real predicates and "exists"', *Mind* 83: 95–9.
Candlish, S. (1998) 'Private language argument', in Craig (1998, 7: 693–8).
Carnap, R. (1937) *The Logical Syntax of Language*, New York: Harcourt & Brace.
—— (1947) *Meaning and Necessity*, Chicago: University of Chicago Press.
Carruthers, M. (1990) *The Book of Memory*, Cambridge: Cambridge University Press.
Chalmers, D. (1996) *The Conscious Mind*, Oxford: Oxford University Press.
Chamberlain, M. (1994) *Knowledge and Social Practice in Medieval Damascus*, Cambridge: Cambridge University Press.
Chittick, W.C. 'Ebn al-ʿArabī', *Enc. Ir.* VII: 664–70.
—— (1981*a*) 'Ṣadr al-Dīn al-Qūnawī on the oneness of being', *IPQ* 21: 171–84.
—— (1981*b*) 'Mysticism versus philosophy in earlier Islamic philosophy', *Religious Studies* 17: 87–104.
—— (1982) 'The five divine presences: from al-Qūnawī to al-Qayṣarī', *MW* 72: 107–28.
—— (1989) *The Sufi Path of Knowledge: Ibn ʿArabī's Metaphysics of Imagination*, Albany: SUNY Press.
—— (1998) *The Self-disclosures of God: Principles of Ibn ʿArabī's Cosmology*, Albany: SUNY Press.
Cook, M. (1997) 'The opponents of the writing of tradition in early Islam', *Arabica* 44: 437–530.
Cooper, J. R. Nettler and M. Mahmoud (eds) (1998*a*) *Islam and Modernity: Muslim Intellectuals Respond*, London: I.B. Tauris.
—— (1998*b*) 'Mulla Sadra', in Craig (1998, 6: 595–9).
Corbin, H. (1938) *Qu'est-ce que c'est la métaphysique?* Paris: Gallimard.
—— (1962*a*) 'De la philosophie prophétique en Islam Shîʿite', *Eranos Jahrbuch* XXXI: 49–116.
—— (1962*b*) 'La place de Mollâ Sadrâ Shîrâzî dans la philosophie iranienne', *SI* 18: 81–113.
—— (1964) *Histoire de la philosophie Islamique*, Paris: Gallimard.
—— (1967) 'Face de Dieu et face de l'homme', *Eranos Jahrbuch* XXXVI: 165–228.
—— (1971) 'L'idée du Paraclet en philosophie iranienne', in *La Persia nel medievo*, Roma: Accademia Nazionale dei Lincei, 37–68.

—— (1971–2) *En Islam Iranien*, 4 tomes, Paris: Gallimard.

—— (1972) 'For the concept of Irano-Islamic philosophy', *Philosophical Forum* 4: 114–23.

—— (1976*a*) *L'archange empourpré*, Paris: Fayard.

—— (1976*b*) 'Le paradoxe du monothéisme', *Eranos Jahrbuch* 45: 69–133.

Corbin (1978) *The Man of Light in Iranian Sufism*, Boulder, CO: Shambala Publications.

—— (1981*a*) *The Concept of Comparative Philosophy*, tr. P. Russell, Ipswich: Golgonooza Press.

—— (1981*b*) *La philosophie iranienne islamique aux XVII*e *et XVIII*e *siècles*, Paris: Buchet Chastel.

—— (1986) *Le livre de la sagesse orientale*, ed. C. Jambet, Paris: Verdier.

—— (1990) *Spiritual Body and Celestial Earth: From Mazdean Iran to Shīʿite Iran*, tr. N. Pearson, London: I.B. Tauris.

—— (1993*a*) *History of Islamic Philosophy*, tr. P. Sherrard, London, Kegan Paul International.

—— (1993*b*) *Itinéraire d'un enseignement. Résumé des conférences à l'École Pratique des Hautes Études 1955–79*, ed. C. Jambet, Tehran: Institut Français.

—— (1995) *Swedenborg and Esoteric Islam*, tr. Fox, West Chester, PA: Swedenborg Foundation.

Crabbe, J.C. (ed.) (1999) *From Soul to Self*, London: Routledge.

Craig, E. (1998) (gen. ed) *The Routledge Encyclopaedia of Philosophy*, 10 vols, London: Routledge.

Crow, K.D. 'Mullā Ṣadrā's Sharḥ of al-Ṣādiq's *Ḥadīth al-ʿAql wa-l-jahl*', Website of Mulla Sadra Congress URL: http://www.mullasadra.org/papers/karim_d_crow.htm

Crystal, I. (1998) 'Plotinus on the structure of self-intellection', *Phronesis* 43: 264–86.

Dabashi, H. (1993) *The Theology of Discontent: The Ideological Foundations of the Islamic Revolution in Iran*, New York: New York University Press.

Daftary, F. (1990) *The Ismailis: Their History and Doctrines* Cambridge: Cambridge University Press.

—— (ed.) (1996) *Medieval Ismaili History and Thought*, Cambridge: Cambridge University Press.

Daiber, H. (1999) 'What is the meaning of and to what end do we study the history of Islamic philosophy?', in *A Bibliography of Islamic philosophy*, vol. 1, Leiden: Brill, xi–xxxiii.

Dakake, M. (1998) 'Hidden Knowledge and the Written Text: Kitāb Sulaym b. Qays and Shiʿite Counter-history', unpublished paper, Chicago, MESA annual meeting.

D'Ancona Costa, C. (1997) 'Divine and human knowledge in the *Plotiniana Arabica*', in J.J. Cleary (ed.) *The Perennial Tradition of Neoplatonism*, Leuven: Leuven University Press, 419–42.

—— (1999) 'Porphyry, Universal soul and the Arabic Plotinus', *ASP* 9: 47–88.

Dancy, R.M. (1991) *Two Studies in the Early Academy*, Albany: SUNY Press.

Davidson, D. (1980) *Essays on Actions and Events*, Oxford: Clarendon Press.

—— (1984) *Inquiries into Truth and Interpretation*, Oxford: Clarendon Press.

Davidson, H.A. (1987) *Proofs for Eternity, Creation and the Existence of God in Medieval Islamic and Jewish Philosophy*, New York: Oxford University Press.

Derrida, J. (1972) *La dissémination*, Paris: Éditions du Seuil.

—— (1982) *Marges de la philosophie*, tr. A. Bass, Brighton: Harvester Press.

—— (1981) *Dissemination*, tr. B. Johnson, Chicago: Chicago University Press.

De Smet, D. (1995) *La quiétude de l'Intellect, Néoplatonisme et gnose ismaélienne dans l'oeuvre de Ḥamīd al-Dīn al-Kirmānī*, Louvain: Peeters.

—— (1998) *Empedocles arabus. Une lecture néoplatonicienne tardive*, Bruxelles: Koninklyke Akademie.

—— (1999) 'Le souffle de Miséricordieux (*Nafas al-Raḥmān*): un élément pseudo-empédocléen dans la métaphysique de Mullā Ṣadra aš-Šīrāzī', *Documenti* X: 467–86.

Dillon, J. (2003) *The Heirs of Plato: A Study of the Old Academy (347–274 BC)*, Oxford: Clarendon Press.

Domański, J. (1996) *La philosophie, théorie ou manière de vivre? Les controverses de l'Antiquité à la Renaissance*, Fribourg: Éditions universitaires.

Dozy, R. (1967) *Supplément aux dictionnaires arabes*, 2 tomes, 3e édn, Paris: Maisonneuve et Larose.

Dummett, M. (1980) *Truth and Other Enigmas*, London: Duckworth.

—— (1991) *The Logical Basis of Metaphysics*, London: Duckworth.

—— (1993*a*) *Origins of Analytical Philosophy*, London: Duckworth.

—— (1993*b*) *The Seas of Language*, Oxford: Clarendon Press.

Dunlop, D.M. (1956) 'Al-Fārābī's Eisagoge', *Islamic Quarterly* 3: 117–38.

—— (1957) 'Al-Fārābī's introductory risālah on logic', *Islamic Quarterly* 3: 224–35.

Dürlinger, J. (1985) 'Ethics and the divine life in Plato's philosophy', *Journal of Religious Ethics* 13: 312–31.

Eickelman, D. (1978) 'The art of memory and Muslim education', *Comparative Studies in Society and History* 20: 485–516.

Eliade, M. (1987) (gen. ed) *The Encyclopaedia of Religion*, 12 vols, Chicago: Macmillan Press.

Elias, J. (1995) *The Throne Carrier of God: The Life and Thought of ʿAlāʾ al-Dawla Simnānī*, Albany: SUNY Press.

El-Bizri, N. (2000) *The Phenomenological Quest between Avicenna and Heidegger*, Binghamton, NY: Global Publications.

—— (2001) 'Avicenna and essentialism', *Review of Metaphysics* 54: 753–78.

Evangeliou, C. (1988) *Aristotle's Categories and Porphyry*, Leiden: Brill.

Evans, G. (1982) *The Varieties of Reference*, ed. J. McDowell, Oxford, Clarendon Press.

Everson, S. (ed.) (1991) *Companion to Ancient Thought 2: Psychology*, Cambridge: Cambridge University Press.

—— (ed.) (1994) *Companion to Ancient Philosophy: 3. Language*, Cambridge: Cambridge University Press.

Fahd, T. (ed.) (1970) *Le shiʿisme imâmite*, Paris: Presses universitaires de France.

Fakhry, M. (1980) *A History of Islamic Philosophy*, 2nd edn, New York: Columbia University Press.

Fashahi, M.R. (1995) *Aristote de Baghdad: de la raison grecque à la révélation coranique*, Paris: L'Harmattan.

Ferejohn, M. (1980) 'Aristotle on focal meaning and the unity of science', *Phronesis* 25: 117–28.

Festugière, A.-J. (1983) *La révélation d'Hermès Trismégiste*, 2nd edn, 4 tomes, Paris: Les Belles Lettres.

Flannery, F.L. (1999) 'The synonymy of homonyms', *Archiv für Geschichte der Philosophie* 81: 268–89.

Flew, A. (ed.) (1953 and 1955) *Logic and Language, 1st and 2nd series*, Oxford: Blackwell.

—— (ed.) 1966) *Essays in Conceptual Analysis*, London: Macmillan.

Fodor, J. and J. Katz (eds) (1964) *The Structure of Language: Readings in the Philosophy of Language*, New Jersey: Prentice-Hall Inc.

—— (1998) *In Critical Condition*, Cambridge, MA: MIT Press.

Forman, R.K.C (ed.) (1990) *The Problem of Pure Consciousness*, New York: Oxford University Press.

Foucault, M. (1972) *The Archaeology of Knowledge*, tr. A.M. Sheridan Smith, London: Tavistock.

—— (1977) *Language, Counter-memory, Practice*, ed./tr. D.F. Bouchard, Ithaca, NY: Cornell University Press.

—— (1980) *Power/Knowledge*, ed. C. Gordon, London: Harvester Press.

Fowden, G. (1986) *The Egyptian Hermes: A Historical Approach to the Late Pagan Mind*, Cambridge: Cambridge University Press.

Frank, R.M. (1956) 'The origin of the Arabic philosophical term anniyya', *Cahiers de Byrsa* VI: 181–201.

—— (1978) *Being and their Attributes: The Teaching of the Basrian School of the Muʿtazilah in the Classical Period*, Albany: SUNY Press.

—— (1980) 'The non-existent, the existent and the possible in the teaching of Abū Hāshim and his followers', *MIDEO* 14: 185–209.

—— (2000) 'The non-existent and the possible in classical Ashʿarite teaching', *MIDEO* 24: 1–37.

Frede, M. (1987) *Essays in Ancient Philosophy*, Oxford: Clarendon Press.

Gadamer, H.-G. (1980) *Dialogue and Dialectic: Eight Hermeneutical Studies on Plato*, tr. P. Christopher Smith, New Haven: Yale University Press.

—— (2004) *Truth and Method*, 2nd revised edn, trs J. Weinsheimer and D.J. Marshall, London: Continuum.

Gardet, L. 'al-Burhān', *EI²* I: 1326–7.

Gaskill, T.E. (1997) 'The complementarity of reason and mysticism in Avicenna', in J.J. Cleary (ed.) *The Perennial Tradition of Neoplatonism*, Leuven: Leuven University Press, 443–57.

Gerson, L.P. (1990) *God and Greek Philosophy*, London: Routledge.

—— (1991) 'Causality, univocity and First Philosophy in *Metaphysics* ii', *Ancient Philosophy* 11: 331–49.

—— (1993) 'Plotinus' metaphysics: emanation or creation?' *Review of Metaphysics* 46: 559–74.

—— (1994) *Plotinus*, London: Routledge.

—— (ed.) (1996) *The Cambridge Companion to Plotinus*, Cambridge: Cambridge University Press.

—— (1997) '*Epistrophē prōs eauton*: history and meaning', *Documenti* VIII: 1–32.

—— (2005) *Aristotle and Other Platonists*, Ithaca, NY: Cornell University Press.

Gibb, H.A. and C.E. Bosworth (ed.) (1966–99) *Encyclopaedia of Islam*, new edition, 9 vols, CD-ROM, v.1.0, Leiden: Brill.

Gilson, E. (1946) 'Notes sur le vocabulaire de l'être', *MS* 8: 150–8.

—— (1952) *Being and Some Philosophers*, 2nd edn, Toronto: Pontifical Institute of Mediaeval Studies.

Gobineau, Comte Joseph Arthur de (1933) *Les philosophies et religions de l'Asie centrale*, Paris: Gallimard.

Goichon, A.-M. 'Ḥikma', *EI²* III: 377–8.

—— (1937) *La distinction de l'essence et de l'existence d'après Ibn Sīnā*, Paris: Desclée de Brouwer.

—— (1938) *Lexique de la langue philosophique d'Ibn Sīnā*, Paris: Desclée de Brouwer.

Goldman, A. (1987) *Epistemology and Cognition*, Cambridge, MA: Harvard University Press.

Goodman, L.E. (1992) *Avicenna*, London: Routledge.
Goodman, N. (1978) *Ways of Worldmaking*, Indianapolis, IN: Hackett.
Goody, J. and I. Watt (1963) 'The consequences of literacy', *Comparative Studies in Society and History* 5: 304–45.
Graham, A.C. (1965) 'Being in linguistics and philosophy', *Foundations of Language* 1: 223–31.
Gutas, D. (1981) 'Classical Arabic wisdom literature', *JAOS* 101: 49–86.
—— (1988) *Avicenna and the Aristotelian Tradition*, Leiden: Brill.
—— (1998) *Greek Thought, Arabic Culture: The Graeco-Arabic Translation Movements in Baghdad and Early 'Abbasid Society*, London: Routledge.
—— (2000) 'Avicenna's Eastern ("Oriental") philosophy: Nature, contents, transmission', *ASP* 10: 159–80.
—— (2002) 'The study of Arabic philosophy in the twentieth century', *British Journal of Middle Eastern Studies* 29: 5–25.
—— (2006*a*) 'Intellect without limits: The absence of mysticism in Avicenna', in M.C. Pacheco and J.F. Meirinhos (eds) (2006) *Intellect and Imagination in Medieval Philosophy: Actes du XIe Congrès International de Philosophie Médiévale de la Société Internationale pour l'Etude de la Philosophie Médiévale (SIEPM)*, Turnhout: Brepols, 351–72.
—— (2006*b*) 'Imagination and transcendental knowledge in Avicenna', in J. Montgomery (ed.) (2006) *Arabic Theology, Arabic Philosophy From the Many to the One: Essays in Celebration of Richard M. Frank*, Leuven: Peeters, 337–54.
Guttenplan, S. (ed.) (1975) *Mind and Language*, Oxford: Clarendon Press.
Gyekye, K. (ed.) (1975) *Ibn al-Ṭayyib's Commentary on Porphyry's Eisagoge*, Beirut: Dar el-Machreq.
—— (1979) *Arabic logic, Ibn al-Ṭayyib's Commentary on Porphyry's Eisagoge*, Albany: SUNY Press.
Hadot, I. (1987) 'Les introductions aux commentaires exégètiques', in M. Tardieu (ed.) *Les règles de l'interpretation*, Paris: Presses Universitaires de France, 99–122.
Hadot, P. (1995) *Philosophy as a way of life*, tr. M. Chase, Oxford: Blackwell.
—— (1997) *Plotin ou la simplicité du regard*, Paris: Gallimard.
—— (1999) *Plotin, Porphyre: études néoplatoniciennes*, Paris: Les Belles Lettres.
Ha'iri Yazdi, M. (1992) *The Principles of Epistemology in Islamic Philosophy: Knowledge by Presence*, Albany: SUNY Press.
Halbfass, W. (1988) *India and Europe*, Albany: SUNY Press.
—— (1991) *Tradition and Reflection: Explorations in Indian Thought*, Albany: SUNY Press.
—— (1997) *On Being and What There Is*, Albany: SUNY Press.
Halm, H. (1996) 'The cosmology of the pre-Fāṭimid Ismā'īliyya', in Daftary (1996: 75–83).
Harris, R. Baine (ed.) (1976) *The Significance of Neoplatonism*, Norfolk, VA: SUNY, for International Society for Neoplatonic Studies.
—— (ed.) (1982) *The Structure of Being*, Norfolk, VA: SUNY, for International Society for Neoplatonic Studies.
Hartman, G. (1986) *Change in View*, Cambridge, MA: Bradford Books.
Heidegger, M. (1959) *An Introduction to Metaphysics*, tr. R. Manheim, New Haven: Yale University Press.
—— (1996) *Being and Time. A Translation of Sein und Zeit*, tr. J. Stambaugh, Albany: SUNY Press.
Heinaman, R. (1983) 'Being in Plato's Sophist', *Archiv für Geschichte der Philosophie* 65: 1–17.

Hernández, M.C. (1981) *Historía del pensamiento en el mundo Islámico*, 2 vols, Madrid: Alianza.

Hintikka, J. (1959) 'Aristotle and the ambiguity of ambiguity', *Inquiry* 2: 137–51.

—— (1971) 'Different kinds of equivocation in Aristotle', *JHP* 9: 368–72.

—— (1983) 'Semantical games, alleged ambiguity of "is" and Aristotelian Categories', *Synthese* 54: 443–68.

Hodgson, M. (1974) *The Venture of Islam: Civilisation and History in a World Civilisation,* 3 vols, Chicago: Chicago University Press.

Honderich, T. (1998) 'Consciousness as existence', in O'Hear (1998: 137–55).

—— (1999) 'Consciousness as existence again', Website of the Mulla Sadra Congress

URL: http://www.mullasadra.org/papers/ted_honderich.htm

Horten, Max (1906) *Das Buch der Ringsteine Al-Farabis*, Munster Beiträge zur Geschichte der Philosophie des Mittelalters.

—— (1907) *Kitāb aš-Šifā'. Das Buch der Genesung der Seele: eine philosophische Enzyklopädie Avicennas*, Halle: Abhandlungen zur Philosophie und ihrer Geschichte.

—— (1912*a*) *Die Gottesbeweise bei Schirāzī*, Bonn: Friedrich Cohen Verlag.

—— (1912*b*) *Die Philosophie der Erleuchtung nach Suhrawardī*, Halle: Abhandlungen zur Philosophie und ihrer Geschichte.

—— (1913) *Das philosophische System von Schirazi*, Strassburg: Trübner.

Horwich, P. (1998) *Meaning*, Oxford: Clarendon Press.

—— (1999) 'What is truth?' Website of the Mulla Sadra Congress URL: http://www.mullasadra.org/papers/paul_horwich.htm

Hourani, G.F. (ed.) (1975) *Essays on Islamic Philosophy and Science*, Albany: SUNY Press.

Iqbal, M. (1908) *The Development of Metaphysics in Persia*, London: Luzac.

Ivry, A. (1974) *al-Kindi's Metaphysics*, Albany: SUNY Press.

Izutsu, T. and M. Mohaghegh (eds/trs) (1983) *The Metaphysics of Sabzavari*, Tehran: Iran University Press.

—— (1974) 'The problem of quiddity and the natural universal', in O. Amine (ed.) *Études Philosophiques*, Cairo: GEBO, 131–77.

—— (1983) *La logique des orientaux: Henry Corbin et la science des formes*, Paris: āditions du Seuil.

—— (1994) *Creation and the Timeless Order of Things*, Ashland, OR: White Cloud Press.

Jambet, C. (ed.) (1981) *Cahiers de l'Herne: Henry Corbin*, Paris: Éditions de l'Herne.

—— (1997) 'L'âme humaine d'Aristote à Mollâ Ṣadrâ Shîrâzî', *SI*? 26: 211–36.

—— (2000) *Se rendre immortel suivi du Traité de la résurrection de Mollâ Sadrâ Shîrâzî*, Paris: Fata Morgana.

—— (2002) *L'acte d'être: La philosophie de l révélation chez Mollâ Sadrâ*, Paris: Fayard; (2006) *The Act of Being*, tr. J. Fort, New York: Zone Books.

Jolivet, J. (1979) 'Pour le dossier du Proclus Arabe: al-Kindi et la Théologie Platonicienne', *SI* 49: 55–75.

—— (1991) 'L'Idée de la sagesse et sa fonction dans la philosophie des 4e et 5e siècles', *ASP* 1: 31–65.

Kahn, C. (1966) 'The Greek verb "to be" and the concept of being', *Foundations of Language* 2: 245–65.

—— (1973) *The Verb 'Be' in Ancient Greek*, Volume 6 of *The Verb 'Be' and its Synonyms. Philosophical and Grammatical Studies*, Dordrecht: D. Reidel Publishing Co.

—— (1981) 'Some philosophical uses of "to be" in Plato', *Phronesis* 26: 105–34.

—— (1996) *Plato and Socratic Dialogues*, Cambridge: Cambridge University Press.

Kalin, I. (2007) 'Mullā Ṣadrā on theodicy and the best of all possible worlds', *JIS* 18: 183–201.

Kamal, M. (2006) *Mulla Sadra's Transcendent Philosophy*, Aldershot: Ashgate.

Katz, S.T. (ed.) (1978) *Mysticism and Philosophical Analysis*, Oxford: Oxford University Press.

—— (ed.) (1992) *Mysticism and Language*, New York: Oxford University Press.

Kazimirski, A.D. (1860) *Dictionnaire Arabe Français*, 2 tomes, Paris: Maisonneuve.

Kenny, A.J. (1973) *Wittgenstein*, London: Penguin.

Khatami, Mahmoud (2004) *From a Sadrean Point of View: Toward an Ontetic Elimination of the Subjectivistic Self*, London: London Academy of Iranian Studies.

Kingsley, P. (1995) *Ancient Philosophy, Mystery and Magic: Empedocles and the Pythagorean Tradition*, Oxford: Clarendon Press.

Klein-Franke, R. (1994) 'The non-existent is a thing', *Le Muséon* 107: 375–90.

Klima, G. (2000) 'Aquinas on the one and many', *Documenti* 11: 195–215.

Kneale, W. and M. (1962) *The Development of Logic*, Oxford: Clarendon Press.

Knuuttila, S. (ed.) (1981) *Reforging the Great Chain of Being*, Dordrecht: D. Reidel Publishing Co.

Knuuttila, S. and J. Hintikka (eds) (1986) *The Logic of Being: Historical Studies*, Dordrecht: D. Reidel Publishing Co.

Knysh, A.D. (1992) ''Irfan revisited: Khomeini and the legacy of Islamic mystical philosophy', *Middle East Journal* 46: 631–53.

—— (1999) *Ibn ʿArabi in the Later Islamic Tradition. The Making of a Polemical Image in Medieval Islam*, Albany: SUNY Press.

Kostman, J. (1973) 'False logos and Not-being in Plato's *Sophist*', in J. Moravcsik (ed.) *Patterns in Plato's Thought*, Dordrecht: D. Reidel Publishing, 192–212.

Kraut, R. (ed.) (1992) *The Cambridge Companion to Plato*, Cambridge: Cambridge University Press.

Kraye, J., W.F. Ryan and C.B. Schmitt (eds) (1986) *Pseudo-Aristotle in the Middle Ages. The* Theology *and Other Texts*, London: Warburg Institute.

Kretzmann, N. and E. Stump (eds) (1993) *The Cambridge Companion to Aquinas*, Cambridge: Cambridge University Press.

Künne, W. (2003) *Conceptions of Truth*, Oxford: Clarendon Press.

Lameer, J. (1994) *al-Fārābī and Aristotelian Syllogistics. Greek Theory and Islamic Practice*, Leiden: Brill.

Landolt, H. (1996) 'Le paradoxe de la "face de Dieu": ʿAzīz-e Nasafī (VIIe/XIIIe siècle) et le monisme ésotérique', *SIr.* 25: 163–92.

Lane, E.W. (1984) *An Arabic English Lexicon*, ed. S.L. Poole, 2 vols repr, Cambridge: Islamic Texts Society.

Langhade, J. (1994) *Du Coran à la philosophie: La langue arabe et la formation du vocabulaire philosophique de Fārābī*, Damascus: Institut Français.

Leaman, O. (1980) 'Does the interpretation of Islamic philosophy rest upon a mistake?' *IJMES* 12: 525–38.

—— (1985) *An Introduction to Medieval Islamic Philosophy*, Cambridge: Cambridge University Press.

—— (1999) *A Short Introduction to Islamic Philosophy*, Cambridge: Polity Press.

Lee, E. (1972) 'Plato on negation and not-being in the *Sophist*', *Philosophical Review* 81: 267–304.

Legenhausen, M. (1994*a*) 'The contemporary revival of the philosophy of religion in the

United States part 2, Lectures 4 & 5: Prima facie justification and ontological arguments', *Al-Tawḥīd* XI, 1 & 2: 185–231.

—— (1994*b*) 'The contemporary revival of the philosophy of religion in the United States part 3, Lecture 6: A cosmological argument', *Al-Tawḥīd* XI, 3 & 4: 122–50.

—— (1995*a*) 'The contemporary revival of the philosophy of religion in the United States part 6, Lecture 10: Eternity', *Al-Tawḥīd* XII, 3: 109–37.

—— (1995*b*) 'The contemporary revival of the philosophy of religion in the United States part 7, Lectures 11 & 12: Omnipotence and goodness', *Al-Tawḥīd* XII, 4: 153–71.

—— (1996*a*) 'The contemporary revival of the philosophy of religion in the United States part 8, Lecture 13 & 14: Evil & God is not a person', *Al-Tawḥīd* XIII, 1: 161–75.

—— (1996*b*) 'The contemporary revival of the philosophy of religion in the United States part 9, Lecture 16: The Trinity', *Al-Tawḥīd* XIII, 2: 149–65.

Levinas, E. (1998) *Discovering Existence with Husserl*, trs R.A. Cohen and M.B. Smith, Evanston, IL: Northwestern University Press.

Lewis, F. (1976) 'Plato on not', *California Studies in Classical Antiquity* 9: 89–115.

Lewisohn, L. (ed.) (1999) *The Heritage of Sufism Volume III: The Legacy of Medieval Persian Sufism*, Oxford: Oneworld.

Lloyd, A.C. (1976) 'The principle that the cause is greater than the effect', *Phronesis* 21: 146–56.

—— and H. Blumenthal (eds) (1982) *Soul and the Structure of Being in Late Neoplatonism: Syrianus, Proclus and Simplicius*, Liverpool: Liverpool University Press.

—— (1986) 'Non-propositional thought in Plotinus', *Phronesis* 31: 258–65.

—— (1990) *The Anatomy of Neoplatonism*, Oxford: Clarendon Press.

Lockhart, L. and P. Jackson (eds) (1986) *The Cambridge History of Iran Volume 6: The Timurid and Safavid Periods*, Cambridge: Cambridge University Press.

Lovejoy, A.D. (1936) *The Great Chain of Being: A Study of the History of an Idea*, Cambridge, MA: Harvard University Press.

McDermott, M.J. (1978) *The Theology of al-Shaikh al-Mufīd*, Beirut: Dar el-Machreq.

McDowell, J. (1982) 'Falsehood and not-being in Plato's Sophist', in M. Schofield and M. Nussbaum (eds) *Language and Logos*, Cambridge: Cambridge University Press, 115–34.

—— (1994) *Mind and World*, Cambridge, MA: Harvard University Press.

—— (1998) 'Evans, Gareth', in Craig (1998, 3: 459–61).

MacEoin, D. 'Mullā Ṣadrā Shīrāzī', *EI*[2] VII: 547–8.

McGinn, C. (1996) *The Character of the Mind*, Oxford: Oxford University Press.

MacIntyre, A. (1988) *Whose Justice? Whose Rationality?* London: Duckworth.

—— (1997) *After Virtue: A Study in Moral Theory*, 2nd edn, London: Duckworth.

Madelung, W. (1976) 'Aš-Šahrastānīs Streitschrift gegen Avicenna und ihre Widerlegung durch Naṣīr al-Dīn aṭ-Ṭūsī', in A. Dietrich (ed.) *Akten des VII. Kongressen für Arabistik und Islamwissenschaft (Göttingen 1974)*, Göttingen: Vanderhoek und Ruprecht.

—— (1977) 'Aspects of Ismāʿīlī theology: The prophetic chain and the God beyond being', in Nasr (1977*d*: 53–65).

—— (1985) 'Ibn Abī Ǧumhūr al-Aḥsā'ī's synthesis of kalām, philosophy and Sufism', in *Religious Schools and Sects in Medieval Islam*, London: Variorum.

Madkur, I. (1969) *L'Organon d'Aristote dans le monde Arabe*, Paris Librairie philosophique J. Vrin.

Mahdi, M.S. (2001) *Al-Farabi and the Foundations of Islamic Political Philosophy*, Chicago: University of Chicago Press.

Mahoney, T.A. (2005) 'Moral virtue and assimilation to God in Plato's *Timaeus*', *OSAP* XXVIII: 77–91.

Malik, J. (1997) *Islamische Gelehrtenkultur in Nordindien. Entwicklungsgeschichte und Tendenzen am Beispiel von Lucknow*, Leiden: Brill.

Marmura, M.E. (1979) 'Avicenna's chapter on universals in the *Isagoge* of his *Shifā*'', in A.T. Welch and P. Cachia *Islam: Past Influence and Present Challenge*, (eds) Edinburgh: Edinburgh University Press, 34–56.

—— (1984) 'Avicenna on primary concepts in the Metaphysics of his *al-Shifā*'', in *Logos Islamikos: Studia Islamica in honorem Georgii Michaelis Wickens*, Toronto: Pontifical Institute of Mediaeval Studies, 219–39.

—— (1986) 'Avicenna's flying man in context', *Monist* 69: 383–95.

—— (1991) 'Plotting the course of Avicenna's thought', *JAOS* 111: 333–42.

—— (2005) *Probing in Islamic Philosophy*, Binghamton, NY: Global Publications.

Martin, J.N. (1995) 'Existence, negation and abstraction in the Neoplatonic hierarchy', *History and Philosophy of Logic* 16: 169–96.

Martin, V. (2000) *Creating an Islamic State: Khomeini and the Making of a New Iran*, London: I.B. Tauris.

Mason, R. (1997) *The God of Spinoza*, Cambridge: Cambridge University Press.

Massé, H. (ed.) (1956) *Mélanges Louis Massignon*, 3 tomes, Damascus: Institut Français.

Massignon, L. (1947) 'L'homme parfait en Islam et son originalité eschatologique', *Eranos Jahrbuch* 15: 287–353.

—— (1975) *La passion de Hallaj, martyr mystique de l'Islam (nouvelle édition)*, 4 tomes, Paris: Gallimard.

—— (1983) 'Inventaire de la littérature Hermétique Arabe', in Festugière (1983, I: 384–400, 438–9).

Mates, B. (1961) *Stoic Logic*, Berkeley, CA: University of California Press.

Matilal, B.K. (1968) *The Navya-Nyāya Doctrine of Negation*, Cambridge, MA: Harvard University Press.

—— (1977) *The Logical Illumination of Indian Mysticism*, New Delhi: Oxford University Press.

—— (1985*a*) *Logic, Language and Reality: An Introduction to Indian Philosophical Studies*, New Delhi: Motilal Banarsidass.

—— and J.L. Shaw (eds) (1985*b*) *Analytical Philosophy in Comparative Perspective. Exploratory Essays in . . . Meaning and Reference*, Dordrecht: D. Reidel Publishing Co.

—— (1986) *Perception: An Essay in Classical Indian Theories of Knowledge*, Oxford: Clarendon Press.

—— (1990) *The Word and the World*, New Delhi: Oxford University Press.

—— (1998) *The Character of Logic in India*, eds J. Ganeri and H. Tiwari, Albany: SUNY Press.

Matin-asgari, A. (1997) 'Abdul Karim Surush and the secularization of Islamic thought in Iran', *IrS*. 30: 85–115.

Matté, J.-F. (1998) (gen. ed.) *Encyclopédie Philosophique Universelle*, 4 tomes, Paris: Presses universitaires de France.

Mayer, T. (2000) 'Ibn Sīnā's *Burhān al-ṣiddīqīn*', *Journal of Islamic Studies* 20: 18–39.

Menn, S. (1999) 'The Stoic theory of Categories', *OSAP* XVII: 215–47.

Michot, J. (1985) 'Avicenna's "Letter on the disappearance of the vain intelligible forms after death"', *Bulletin de Philosophie Médiévale* 27: 94–103.

—— (1986) *La destinée de l'homme selon Avicenne*, Louvain: Peeters.

Mohanty, J.N. (1992) *Reason and Tradition in Indian Thought*, Oxford: Clarendon Press.

—— (2000) *Classical Indian Philosophy*, Oxford: Rowman & Littlefield.
Moin, B. (1994) 'Khomeini's search for perfection', in *Pioneers of Islamic Revival*, ed. A. Rahnema, London: Zed Books, 66–77.
Monnot, G. (1998) 'Mollā Ṣadrā Shīrāzī', in Matté (1998, III, i: 1440–1).
Moore, A.W. (ed.) (1993) *Meaning and Reference*, Oxford: Oxford University Press.
Moravcsik, J. (1992) *Plato and Platonism*, Oxford: Blackwell.
Morewedge, P. (1970) 'Ibn Sina (Avicenna), Malcolm and the ontological argument', *Monist* 54: 234–49.
—— (ed.) (1979) *Islamic Philosophical Theology*, New York: SUNY Press.
—— (ed.) (1981) *Islamic Philosophy and Mysticism*, New York: Caravan Books.
—— (ed.) (1982) *Philosophies of Existence Ancient and Medieval*, New York: Fordham University Press.
—— (ed.) (1992) *Neoplatonism and Islamic Thought*, Albany: SUNY Press.
—— (1995) *Essays in Islamic Philosophy, Theology and Mysticism*, Oneonta, NY: SUNY Press.
Moris, M. (2003) *Mullā Ṣadrā's Doctrine of the Primacy of Existence (aṣālat al-wujūd)*, Kuala Lumpur: ISTAC.
Moris, Z. (2003) *Revelation, Intellectual Intuition and Reason in the Philosophy of Mullā Ṣadra: An Analysis of al-Ḥikma al-ʿArshiyya*, London: RoutledgeCurzon.
Morris, J.W. (1981) *The Wisdom of the Throne*, Princeton, NJ: Princeton University Press.
Morrison, D. (1987) 'The evidence for degrees of being in Aristotle', *Classical Quarterly* 37: 382–401.
Motahhedeh, R. (1981) *Loyalty and Leadership in an Early Islamic Society*, Princeton, NJ: Princeton University Press.
—— (1985) *The Mantle of the Prophet: Religion and Politics in Iran*, London: Penguin.
Munitz, M. (ed.) (1973) *Logic and Ontology*, New York: New York University Press.
—— (1974) *Existence and Logic*, New York: New York University Press.
Murata, S. (1992) *The Tao of Islam*, Albany: SUNY Press.
Nagel, T. (1979) *Mortal Questions*, Cambridge: Cambridge University Press.
Nasr, S.H. (ed.) (1961) *Sadra Commemoration Volume*, Tehran: Faculty of Theology.
—— (1967) 'Mullā Ṣadrā', *Encyclopaedia of Philosophy* 5: 411–13.
—— (1971) 'Ḥikmat and kalām', *SI* 34: 139–49.
—— (1972*a*) 'Philosophy in Islam', *SI* 37: 57–80.
—— (1972*b*) 'Mullā Ṣadrā and the doctrine of the unity of being', *Philosophical Forum* 4: 153–61.
—— (1977*a*) *Sadr al-Din Shirazi and his Transcendent Theosophy*, Tehran: Imperial Iranian Academy of Philosophy.
—— (1977*b*) 'Post-Avicennan Islamic philosophy and study of being', *IPQ* 17: 265–71.
—— (ed.) (1977*c*) *Mélanges offerts à Henry Corbin*, Tehran: Tehran University Press.
—— (ed.) (1977*d*) *Ismāʿīlī Contributions to Islamic Culture*, Tehran: Imperial Iranian Academy of Philosophy.
—— (1981) *Islamic Life and Thought*, Albany: SUNY Press.
—— (1989) 'Existence (*wujūd*) and quiddity (*māhiyyah*) in Islamic philosophy', *IPQ* 29: 409–28.
—— (1992) 'Oral transmission and the book in Islamic education', *JIS* 3: 1–14.
—— (1996*a*) *The Islamic Intellectual Tradition in Persia*, ed. M. Aminrazavi, Richmond: Curzon Press.
—— and O. Leaman (eds) (1996*b*) *History of Islamic Philosophy*, 2 vols, London: Routledge.
—— (2006) *Islamic Philosophy from its Origins to the Present*, Albany: SUNY Press.

Nehamas, A. (1999) *Virtues of Authenticity. Studies on Plato and Socrates*, Princeton, NJ: Princeton University Press.

Netton, I. (1991) *Muslim Neoplatonists: An Introduction to the Thought of the Brethren of the Pure*, Edinburgh: Edinburgh University Press.

—— (1994) *Allah Transcendent: Studies in the Structure and Semiotics of Islamic Philosophy, Theology and Cosmology*, Exeter: Curzon Press.

Nicholson, R.A. (1921) *Studies in Islamic Mysticism*, Cambridge: Cambridge University Press.

Noth, A. (1994) *The Early Arabic Historical Tradition. A Source Critical Study*, 2nd edn, tr. M. Bonner, Princeton, NJ: Darwin Press.

Nussbaum, M. (1994) *The Therapy of Desire: Theory and Practice in Hellenistic Ethics*, Princeton, NJ: Princeton University Press.

O'Hear, A. (ed.) (1998) *Current Issues in Philosophy of the Mind*, Cambridge: Cambridge University Press.

O'Meara, D.J. (1995) *Plotinus: An Introduction to the Enneads*, Oxford: Clarendon Press.

—— (2003) *Platonopolis: Platonic Political Philosophy in Late Antiquity*, Oxford: Oxford University Press.

Oppy, G. (1995) *Ontological Arguments and Belief in God*, Cambridge: Cambridge University Press.

—— (2006) *Arguing about Gods*, Cambridge: Cambridge University Press.

Owen, G.E.L. (1986) *Logic, Science and Dialectic: Collected Papers*, ed. M. Nussbaum, London: Duckworth.

Owens, J. (1978) *The Doctrine of Being in the Aristotelian Metaphysics: A Study in the Greek Background of Mediaeval Thought*, 3rd edn, Toronto: Pontifical Institute of Mediaeval Studies.

Peters, F.E. (1968) *Arisoteles Arabus*, Leiden: Brill.

Pines, S. (1979) *The Collected Works of Shlomo Pines Volume 1: Studies in Abu l-Barakat al-Baghdadi, Physics and Metaphysics*, Jerusalem: Magnes Press.

Plantinga, A. (ed.) (1965) *The Ontological Argument*, New York: Doubleday & Co.

Putnam, H. (1981) *Reason, Truth and History*, Cambridge: Cambridge University Press.

—— (1999) *The Threefold Cord: Mind, Body, and World*, New York: Columbia University Press.

Quine, W.V.O. (1953) *From a Logical Point of View: Nine Logico-philosophical Studies*, Cambridge, MA: Harvard University Press.

—— (1960) *Word and Object*, Cambridge, MA: MIT Press.

—— (1962) 'Dream, imagination and *ʿālam al-mithāl*', in G.Von Grunebaum and R. Caillois (eds) *The Dream and Human Societies*, Berkeley, CA: University of California Press, 409–19.

—— (1966) *The Ways of Paradox and Other Essays*, New York: Random House.

Rahman, F. (1958) 'Essence and existence in Avicenna', *MS* 4: 1–16.

—— (1972) 'Mullā Ṣadrā's theory of knowledge', *Philosophical Forum* 4: 141–52.

—— (1975) *The Philosophy of Mulla Sadra*, Albany: SUNY Press.

157–80.

—— (1963) *Studies in the History of Arabic Logic*, Pittsburgh, PA: University of Pittsburgh Press.
—— (1964) *The Development of Arabic Logic*, Pittsburgh, PA: University of Pittsburgh Press.
—— (1966) *Studies in Arabic Philosophy*, Pittsburgh, PA: University of Pittsburgh Press.
—— (1987) 'Aporetic method in philosophy', *Review of Metaphysics* 41: 283–97.
—— (1991) *G.W. Leibniz's Monadology: An Edition for Students*, London: Routledge.
—— (1996) *Process Metaphysics*, Albany: SUNY Press.
Ricoeur, P. (1992) *Oneself as Another*, tr. K. Blamey, Chicago: University of Chicago Press.
Rist, J. (1967) *Plotinus: The Road to Reality*, Cambridge: Cambridge University Press.
Rizvi, S.A.A. (1986) *A Socio-intellectual History of the Ithnā ʿAsharī Shīʿīs in India*, 2 vols, Delhi: Munshiram Manoharlal.
Rizvi, S.H. (2000) 'Roots of an aporia in later Islamic philosophy: The existence-essence distinction in the metaphysics of Avicenna and Suhrawardī', *Sir.* 29: 61–108.
—— (2005*a*) 'Mysticism and philosophy: Ibn ʿArabī and Mullā Ṣadrā', in P. Adamson and R. Taylor (eds) *The Cambridge Companion to Arabic Philosophy*, Cambridge: Cambridge University Press, 224–46.
—— (2005*b*) 'Mollā Ṣadrā Šīrāzī', *Enc. Ir.* [available online at http://www.iranica.com]
—— (2007) *Mullā Ṣadrā Shīrāzī: His Life, Works and the Sources for Safavid Philosophy*, *JSS* Supplements 18, Oxford: Oxford University Press.
Roberts, J. (1986) 'The problem of being in the *Sophist*', *History of Philosophy Quarterly* 3: 229–43.
Robinson, F. (1997) 'Ottomans-Safavids-Mughals: Shared knowledge and connective systems', *JIS* 8: 151–84.
Robson, J. 'Ḥadīth', EI^2 III: 23–8.
Rorty, R. (1980) *Philosophy and the Mirror of Nature*, Oxford: Blackwell.
——, J.B. Schneewind and Q. Skinner (eds) (1984) *Philosophy in History*, New York: Cambridge University Press.
Rudavsky, T. (ed.) (1985) *Divine Omniscience and Omnipotence in Medieval Philosophy*, Dordrecht: D. Reidel Publishing Co.
Russell, B. (1905) 'On denoting', *Mind* 14: 479–93.
—— (1918–19) 'Lectures on the philosophy of logical atomism', *Monist* 28.29.
Ryle, G. (1949) *The Concept of Mind*, London: Hutchinson & Co.
Sabra, A.I. (1980) 'Avicenna on the subject matter of logic', *Journal of Philosophy* 77: 746–64.
Schmidtke, S. (2000) *Theologie, Philosophie und Mystik im zwölferschiitischen Islam des 9./15. Jahrhunderts: Die Gedankenwelten des Ibn Abī Ǧumhūr al-Aḥsāʾī (um 838/1434–35 nach 906/1501)*, Leiden: Brill.
—— and R. Pourjavady (2006) *A Jewish Philosopher of Baghdad: ʿIzz al-Dawla Ibn Kammūna (d. 683/1284) and his Writings*, Leiden: Brill.
Schubert, G. (ed.) (1995) *Annäherungen: Der mystisch-philosophische Briefwechsel*

87–108.

—— (1999) 'The ideal of godlikeness', in G. Fine (ed.) *Plato 2: Ethics, Politics, Religion*, Oxford: Oxford University Press, 309–28.
Sellars, W. (1963) *Science, Perception and Reality*, London: Routledge, Kegan & Paul.
Sells, M. (1994) *Mystical Languages of Unsaying*, Chicago: University of Chicago Press.
Sezgin, F. (1967–84) *Geschichte des arabischen Schrifttums*, 9 vols, Leiden: Brill.
Sharif, M.M. (ed.) (1966) *A History of Muslim Philosophy*, 2 vols, Wiesbaden: Otto Harrassowitz.
Shaw, G. (1995) *Theurgy and the Soul: The Neoplatonism of Iamblichus*, University Park: Pennsylvania State University Press.
Shayegan, D. (1990) *Henry Corbin: La topographie spirituelle de l'islam iranien*, Paris: Éditions de l'Herne.
Shehadi, F. (1982) *Metaphysics in Islamic Philosophy*, New York: Delmar Books.
Shields, C. (1999) *Order in Multiplicity. Homonymy in the Philosophy of Aristotle*, Oxford: Clarendon Press.
Simons, P. (1998) 'Meinong', in Craig (1998, 6: 282–6).
Siorvanes, L. (1996) *Proclus: Neo-Platonic Philosophy and Science*, Edinburgh: Edinburgh University Press.
Skinner, Q. (1969) 'Meaning and understanding in the history of ideas', *History and Theory* 8: 3–53.
—— (2002) *Visions of Politics I: Regarding Method*, Cambridge: Cambridge University Press.
Sorabji, R. (ed.) (1990) *Aristotle Transformed, The Ancient Commentators and their Influence*, London: Duckworth.
—— (2004) *The Philosophy of the Commentators, 200–600 AD: A Sourcebook*, 3 vols, London: Duckworth.
Spade, P. (1996) 'Thoughts, words and things: An introduction to late mediaeval logic and semantic theory', version 1.0, URL: http://www.pvspade.com/logic/index.html
Sprigge, T. (1998) 'Panpsychism', in Craig (1998, 7: 195–7).
Steel, C. (1978) *The Changing Self: A Study on the Soul in Later Neoplatonism: Iamblichus, Damascius and Priscianus*, Letteren en schone kunsten van België, Brussel: Koninklijke Academie.
Steinberg, B.D. and L.A. Jacobvits (eds) (1971) *Semantics. An Interdisciplinary Reader in Philosophy, Linguistics and Psychology*, Cambridge: Cambridge University Press.
Steinschneider, M. (1893) *Die arabischen Übersetzungenaus dem Griechischen*, Leipzig: Otto Harrassowitz.
Stern, S. (ed.) (1972) *Islamic Philosophy and the Classical Tradition*, Oxford: Bruno Cassirer.
Stokes, M.C. (1971) *The One and Many in Presocratic Philosophy*, Cambridge, MA: Harvard University Press.
Strawson, G. (1994) *Mental Reality*, Cambridge, MA: MIT Press.
Strawson, P.F. (1959) *Individuals: An Essay in Descriptive Metaphysics*, London: Methuen.
—— (1974) *Subject and Predicate in Logic and Grammar*, London: Methuen.
Takeshita, M. (1982) 'An analysis of Ibn ʿArabī's *Inshā' al-dawā'ir* with particular reference to the doctrine of the "third entity"', *Journal of Near Eastern Studies* 41: 243–60.
—— (1988) *The Perfect Man in the Thought of Ibn al-ʿArabī*, Tokyo: Centre for Middle East Studies.
Taylor, C. (1995) *Philosophical Arguments*, Cambridge, MA: Harvard University Press.
Taylor, R.C. (1998) 'Aquinas, the *Plotiniana Arabica* and the metaphysics of being and actuality', *Journal of the History of Ideas* 59: 217–39.

Trimingham, J. Spencer (1971) *The Sufi Orders of Islam*, Oxford: Oxford University Press.
Turner, D. (1994) *The Darkness of God*, Cambridge: Cambridge University Press.
Van Ophuijsen, J.M. (ed.) (1999) *Plato and Platonism*, Washington DC: The Catholic University of America Press.
Verbeke, G. (1977) 'Introduction doctrinale I', in S. Van Riet (ed.) *Avicenna Latinus: Liber de Philosophia Prima I–IV*, Louvain: Peeters, 1*–122*.
Versteegh, C.H.M. (1977) *Greek Elements in Arabic Linguistic Thinking*, Leiden: Brill.
Versteegh, K. (1989) 'The definition of philosophy in a tenth-century grammarian', *Jerusalem Studies in Arabic and Islam* 12: 66–92.
Vlastos, G. (1981) *Platonic Studies*, Princeton, NJ: Princeton University Press.
Vyronis, S. Jr (ed.) (1975) *Islam and Cultural Change in the Middle Ages*, Wiesbaden: Otto Harrassowitz.
Wahba, M. and M. Abousenna (eds) (1996) *Averroës and the Enlightenment*, New York: Prometheus Books.
Walbridge, J. (1992) *The Science of Mystic Lights*, Cambridge, MA: Harvard University Press.
—— (2000) *The Leaven of the Ancients: Suhrawardī and the Heritage of the Greeks*, Albany: SUNY Press.
Walker, P. (1993) *Early Philosophical Shiism. The Ismaili Neoplatonism of Abū Yaʿqūb al-Sijistānī*, Cambridge: Cambridge University Press.
Wallis, R.T. (ed.) (1992) *Neoplatonism and Gnosticism*, Albany: SUNY Press.
—— (1995) *Neoplatonism*, 2nd edn, London: Duckworth.
Wasserstrom, S.M. (1999) *Religion after Religion: Gershom Scholem, Mircea Eliade, and Henry Corbin at Eranos*, Princeton, NJ: Princeton University Press.
Wedin, M. (1997) 'The strategy of Aristotle's Categories', *Archiv für Geschichte der Philosophie* 79: 1–26.
—— (2000) *Aristotle's Theory of Substance: The* Categories *and* Metaphysics Zeta, Oxford: Clarendon Press.
Wehr, H. (1961) *Arabic-English Dictionary. A Dictionary of Modern Written Arabic*, ed. J.M. Cowan, 3rd edn, Wiesbaden: Otto Harrassowitz.
Weiss, B.G. (1992) *The Search for God's Law: Islamic Jurisprudence in the Writings of Sayf al-Dīn al-Āmidī*, Salt Lake City: University of Utah Press.
Whitehead, A.N. (1978) *Process and Reality: An Essay in Cosmology*, corrected edition by D.R. Griffin and D.W. Sherburne, New York: Free Press.
Williams, C.J.F. (1981) *What is Existence?* Oxford: Clarendon Press.
Wisnovsky, R. (2000) 'Notes on Avicenna's concept of thingness (*šay'iyya*)', *ASP* 10: 181–221.
—— (2003) *Avicenna's Metaphysics in Context*, London: Duckworth.
—— (2004) 'One aspect of the Avicennian turn in Sunni theology', *ASP* 14: 65–100.
—— (2005) 'Avicenna and the Avicennian tradition', in Adamson and Taylor (2005: 92–136).
Wittgenstein, L. (1953) *Philosophical Investigations*, tr. G.E. Anscombe, Oxford: Blackwell.
Wolfson, H.A. (1938) 'The amphibolous terms in Aristotle, Arabic philosophy and Maimonides', *Harvard Theological Review* 31: 151–73.
—— (1943) 'The terms *taṣawwur* and *taṣdīq* in Arabic philosophy', *MW* 33: 114–26.
—— (1973–7) *Studies in the History of Philosophy and Religion*, 2 vols, Cambridge, MA: Harvard University Press.
—— (1976) *The Philosophy of Kalam*, Cambridge, MA: Harvard University Press.

Wright, W. (1986–8, repr. 1995) *A Grammar of the Arabic Language*, 2 vols, 3rd edn, revised by W. Robertson Smith and M.J. de Goeje, Cambridge: Cambridge University Press.

Yarshater, E. (1978–) (gen. ed.) *Encyclopaedia Iranica*, New York: Columbia University Press.

Ziai, H. (1990) *Knowledge and Illumination: A Study of Suhrawardi's Ḥikmat al-ishrāq*, Atlanta, GA: Scholars Press.

Zimmermann, F.W. (1981) *Al-Farabi's Commentary and Short Treatise on Aristotle's* De Interpretatione, London: Oxford University Press.

Unpublished dissertations

Alaghebandi Toussi, S.K. (2008) *Ethics and Politics in the Philosophy of Mulla Sadra*, unpublished Ph.D. dissertation, University of Exeter.

Babayan, K. (1993) *The Waning of the Qizilbash: The Spiritual and the Temporal in Seventeenth Century Iran*, unpublished Ph.D. dissertation, Princeton University.

Bonmariage, C. (1998) *Le réel et les réalités: La structure de la réalité de l'être chez Mullâ Ṣadrâ Shîrâzî*, 2 parties, dissertation du grade de Docteur en Philosophie et lettres, Université Catholique de Louvain.

Esots, Janis (2007) *Mullā Ṣadrā's Teaching on Wujūd: A Synthesis of Philosophy and Mysticism*, unpublished Ph.D. dissertation, University of Tallinn.

Hamade, T. (1992) *Dieu, le monde, et l'âme chez Molla Sadra al-Shirazi*, doctorat de nouveau régime, Université de Paris I-Panthéon-Sorbonne.

Hamid, I.S. (1998) *The Philosophy and Cosmology of Process: Shaykh Aḥmad al-Ahsā'ī*, unpublished Ph.D. dissertation, SUNY at Buffalo.

Kalin, I. (2002) *Knowledge as Appropriation: Ṣadr al-Dīn al-Shīrāzī (Mullā Ṣadrā) on the Unification of the Intellect and the Intelligible*, unpublished Ph.D. dissertation, George Washington University.

Khatami, M. (1996) *The Unitary Consciousness: Towards a Solution for the Ontological Crisis in Modern Theories of the Self*, unpublished Ph.D. dissertation, Durham University.

Khorassani, S. Rajaie (1976) *Mulla Sadra's Philosophy and its Epistemological Implications*, unpublished Ph.D. dissertation, Durham University.

Moris, Z. (1994) *Revelation, Intellectual Intuition and Reason in the Philosophy of Mullā Ṣadra: An Analysis of al-Ḥikma al-ʿArshiyya*, unpublished Ph.D. dissertation, American University.

Oraibi, Ali (1992) *Shīʿī Renaissance: A Case Study of the Theosophical School of Bahrain in the 13th Century*, unpublished Ph.D. dissertation, McGill University.

Van Bladel, Kevin (2004) *Hermes Arabicus*, unpublished Ph.D. dissertation, Yale University.

Multimedia resources

Mulla Sadra Congress and the Sadra Islamic Philosophy Research Institute website: URL

Stanford Encyclopaedia of Philosophy: URL http://plato.stanford.edu

Index

Note: page numbers in bold denote glossary terms